W9-ASG-317

THE
CIVIL WAR
SOURCE BOOK

THE
CIVIL WAR SOURCE BOOK

PHILIP KATCHER

Gettysburg: Lieutenant Bayard Wilkeson holding his battery (G, 4th US Artillery) to its work in an exposed position.

Facts On File
New York • Oxford • Sydney

Facts on File, Inc.
460 Park Avenue South, New York NY 10016.

Library of Congress Cataloging in Publication Data available on request from Facts on File.

ISBN 0-8160-2823-0

Facts on File books are available at special discounts when purchased in bulk quantities for businesses, associations, institutions or sales promotions. Please call our Special Sales Department in New York at 212/683-2244 (dial 800/322-8755 except in NY, AK, or HI).

Text and jacket design by David Gibbons. Composition by Ronset Typesetters.

Manufactured by Richard Clay, Bungay. Printed in Great Britain.

10 9 8 7 6 5 4 3 2 1

This book is printed on acid-free paper.

Quality printing and binding by: Richard Clay, Bungay, England.

Jacket illustration: *Rescue the Colours* by William Trego. Prints of this and other American Civil War material are available by writing to: The Bucks County Historical Society, 84 South Pine Street, Doylestown, PA 18901, USA.

Cartography by Richard Natkiel.

CONTENTS

LIST OF MAPS

INTRODUCTION

The Civil War is the keystone of American history; it holds the fascination of millions today, either as a period deserving of serious study or at the level of *Gone With The Wind*. This book is an attempt to gather many of the basic facts of that war under one cover: a brief chronological history of the war; how each branch of service fought the war, its tactics and weapons; the organizations, Union and Confederate, that were designed for specific tasks in the war, ranging from combat arms to many support and logistical units created specifically for this war. Their uniforms and insignia are described as well as their organizations, and another section talks about what it was like to be a serving soldier or sailor, for at the end of it all, this was a low-level, fighting man's war. There are also brief biographies of the war's leading figures, with an emphasis on describing their characters as well as the hard facts about their lives. A further section discusses the basic sources used in studying the war, although the reader should also consult the specific titles in their areas of interest listed in each section. The section of miscellanea gives some basic data in chart form, while the concluding glossary defines some words of common use as well as giving some unique brigade data.

Additionally, throughout the book, there are short anecdotes that give an impression of what it was like to have lived through the war, from joining up, through combat and, perhaps, injury and capture, to eventual peace.

On a personal note, I believe that my generation is better able than any other to understand the attitudes of those who fought the Civil War. In the first place, I am an American, which means I love the country as a whole and hate those aspects of our history that have encouraged the notion that black Americans are less than worthy of sharing in everything the country has to offer. On top of that, some of my own youth was spent in California and New York, while I have presently chosen to live in Pennsylvania, not far from where Washington's troops suffered bitterly for the creation of one country. Hence, I believe in the cause of the Union, the defeat of slavery, and the victory of the Old Flag.

Yet, at the same time, I belong to the only other generation of Americans who lost their war. In the end, Vietnam, where I once served in the most minor of roles, was as lost a cause as was that of the Confederacy. And the scars of that loss burden those of us who served there as did the scars of the South's loss burdened a generation of Southerners. Both of us received much the same treatment at home. Hence, we of Vietnam are strongly drawn to those of the Confederacy; we are of a unique fraternity of Americans. Moreover, much of my youth was spent in the South, in the states of Maryland and Texas. Hence, I can weep with those who furled their bloody banners at Appomattox.

There was good enough on both sides; there was bitterness enough for both sides. With the hind-sight of well over a century and a quarter, we can now see both more clearly, but are all still relentlessly drawn to this point which in many ways marked the creation of the modern American state. Where before we Americans had said, 'these United States are', we now say, 'the United States is'.

There are many people to whom I owe great debts in the creation of this book. The first and foremost is Roderick Dymott who gave me the chance to do it. He is a mentor and friend. Other mentors, these from decades ago, who encouraged me to search for the truth, were Gerry Rolph, Bernie Mitchell, Ernie Peterkin, George Woodbridge, and the late Robert Miller – two 'rebs' and three 'yanks'.

As well, many people have contributed photographs, information, and leads that have been greatly helpful. Among them are Michael Albanese, Thomas Arliskas, Lawrence Babits, Michael F. Bremer, Jimmer T. Carden, Richard Carlile, Thomas Cartwright, Robert Cassidy, Henry Deeks, Bruce Elfast, John Ertzgaard, John ('Hooty') and Alicia Goodolf, John Jeppson, Don Johnson, Michael D. Jones, Lee Joyner, Mick Kissick, Robert L. Kotchian, John Lyle, Michael J. McAfee, Andy May, James Neel, Christopher Nelson, Sheperd Paine, Herb Peck Jnr., Russ Pritchard, Thomas G. Rodgers, Harry Roach, David Scheinmann, John Sickles, David M. Sullivan, Dr Thomas P. Sweeney, Richard Tibbals, Michael Winey, and Lee A. Wallace Jnr. A really super bunch of people.

Finally, this book is dedicated to Cathy.

Philip Katcher
Devon, Pennsylvania

I
THE CAMPAIGNS

THE CAMPAIGNS

The Causes of the Civil War

The original United States was made up of thirteen individual colonies that clung to the Atlantic Ocean seaboard of the North American continent. Their geographies were quite different, ranging from rocky soil and cold winters in New England to sandy clay and long, hot summers in the Carolinas and Georgia. Their original forms of government, although all based in English law, differed from private ownership to direct Crown rule. Even the dominant religions differed from colony to colony, from the Church of England in the South to the Society of Friends and pacifist German sects in Pennsylvania to the Puritans of New England.

Nevertheless, the colonies grew united in their anger against the mother country, England, for imposing taxes and quartering troops without their consent after the Seven Years War. In 1774 they sent delegates to a Continental Congress whose actions led to a War of Independence. In 1783, Great Britain and the new United States of America signed the Treaty of Paris ending that war and recognizing that a new nation had joined the fraternity of nations.

The new country was at first governed by the Articles of Confederation which called for a weak central government and strong state governments. States could even levy duties on products imported from other states. The Articles quickly proved unworkable and a new Constitution was adopted. This Constitution called for a stronger Federal government with powers that included regulating interstate commerce as well as foreign affairs. The first state to ratify the new Constitution was Delaware, a state in which human slavery was also allowed.

By the time the Constitution had been ratified by all the original states the question of human slavery, in this case of Africans imported specifically to serve as slaves, had become a major one. Pennsylvania, led by their Quaker minority which had come out strongly against the wrongs of slavery, had made it illegal during the War of Independence. And, abolition groups had sprung up across the country, although they were strongest in the North where slavery was already virtually non-existent.

To avoid splitting up the new country over the issue, the framers of the Constitution avoided dealing directly with it.

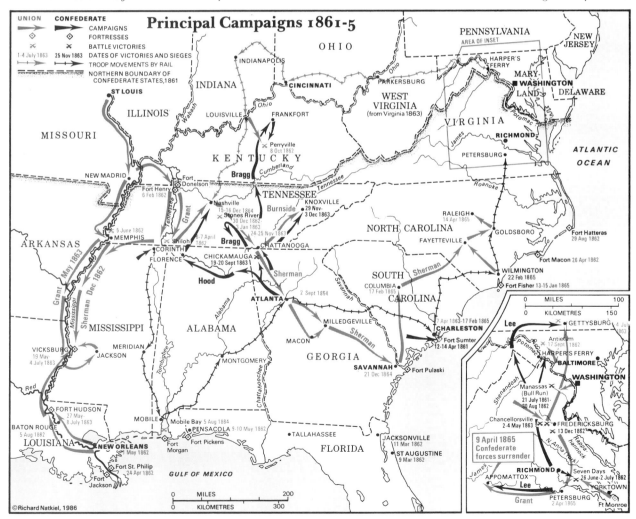

The importation of slaves would become illegal nationally, which many of the framers, such as Virginia slave-holder Thomas Jefferson, hoped would mean the system would die of its own inefficiency.

Indeed, the system was not only morally wrong but inefficient as well. 'In our opinion,' wrote North Carolinian Hilton R. Helper in 1857, 'an opinion which has been formed from data obtained by assiduous researches, and comparisons, from laborious investigation, logical reasoning, and earnest reflection, the causes which have impeded the progress and prosperity of the South, which have dwindled our commerce, and other similar pursuits, into the most contemptible insignificance; sunk a large majority of our people in galling poverty and ignorance, rendered a small minority conceited and tyrannical, and driven the rest away from their homes; entailed upon us a humiliating dependence on the Free States [most manufactured items came from the North]; disgraced us in the recesses of our own souls, and brought us under reproach in the eyes of all civilized and enlightened nations – may all be traced to one common source, and there find solution in the most hateful and horrible word, that was ever incorporated into the vocabulary of human economy – *Slavery*!'[1]

As the country grew the slavery question also grew. Would the newly added states be slave or free? In Kansas and Missouri, men took up arms and killed one another over the question. The so-called Missouri Compromise said that all states south of the line 36°30′ would be slave and above it, free. But what of slaves brought into free territories? The Supreme Court, headed by Marylander Roger B. Taney, ruled on 6 March 1857 that they had no right to sue for their freedom in a federal court. And a Fugitive Slave Act that required Northerners to return slaves to their Southern owners or pay a $1,000 fine and go to jail for six months was signed into law in 1850. Throughout the North a system of safe houses for slaves on their way to British North America, the underground railroad, came into being.

In 1858 Abraham Lincoln, once a Whig congressman from Illinois and now a member of a new political party, the Republicans, spoke at Quincy, Illinois. 'We have in this nation the element of domestic slavery,' he said. 'The Republican party think it wrong – we think it is a moral, a social, and a political wrong. We think it is a wrong not confining itself merely to the persons of the States where it exists, but that it is a wrong which in its tendency, to say the least, affects the existence of the whole nation. Because we think it wrong, we propose a course of policy that shall deal with it as a wrong. We deal with it as with any other wrong, insofar as we can prevent its growing any larger, and so deal with it that in the run of time there may be some promise of an end to it.'[2]

This kind of talk naturally both inflamed and scared the conservative Southern slaveholders, as well as the poor whites, the clear majority in the area, whose social status over blacks was one of the few things they had. But, whereas in the past, these groups had made up a major power in the country, rapid immigration into the North of Irish, Germans and other Europeans had given the North growing political and economic clout. Southern slaveholders and their fellow-travellers no longer could control the federal government.

So, in the election of 1860, when the Republicans nominated the tall Illinois railsplitter, the Democratic Party split into two factions, Southern and Northern. Indeed, a new political party also entered that election, ensuring that no nominee would win a clear majority. Under the American system that gives the office to the winner of the most states, Abraham Lincoln won the election in November.

On 20 December 1860, terrified of the social change that they thought would follow Lincoln's election, South Carolina passed an ordinance of Secession by the vote of 169 to 0. Similar ordinances were passed by Mississippi, Florida, Alabama, Georgia, and Louisiana in January, and by Texas in February. Representatives from these states quickly formed a new political organization, the Confederate States of America. On 8 February 1861 a constitution, very similar to that of the United States, was adopted and on 18 February its new president, Mississippi planter and politician, Jefferson Davis, was sworn in.

Unwilling to admit that the continuance of slavery formed the sole reason for the new Confederate States' existence, Davis voiced the standard Southern rational for secession in his inaugural address. 'It illustrates the American idea that governments rest on the consent of the governed,' he said, 'and it is the right of the people to alter or abolish them at will whenever they become destructive of the ends for which they were established.'[3]

The lame duck administration of President James Buchanan did not act against the departing states but continued to garrison various coastal forts including Fort Pickens in Florida and Fort Sumter in the harbour of Charleston, South Carolina. When Lincoln was sworn into office on 4 March 1861, an unsuccessful attempt was made to reprovision Fort Sumter. On 12 April 1861 the Confederate commander at Charleston asked for and received permission to open fire on the fort, which surrendered on 14 April. Horrified Northerners rushed to volunteer for service against those who had fired on the American flag. Lincoln called for volunteer units from all the states and, refusing to fight against fellow Southerners, Virginia, Arkansas, Tennessee, and North Carolina joined the Confederacy, while Kentucky vowed to remain neutral. War had begun in earnest.

1861: Eastern Theatre

When Virginia joined the new Confederacy, her capital city of Richmond became the new Confederate capital. The largest city in the South, Richmond boasted the South's only major iron and steel mill as well as woollen mills and other large industrial plants. Moreover, it had sufficient office space in the old US Customs House and state capital building to house the Confederate government officials.

The disadvantage of the new capital was its location, far

from the western part of the Confederacy and within several days' march of the US capital city of Washington in the District of Columbia. Indeed, the city presented a clear and reachable goal for the thousands of US volunteers. Northern newspapers called for its immediate capture.

On 15 April, after Fort Sumter had been fired on, Lincoln called for 75,000 men to serve for three months to put down the 'insurrection'. On 4 May, realizing that little could be accomplished in such a short time, Lincoln called for 42,000 volunteers to serve for three years or the war's duration, should it end sooner. On 19 April he proclaimed a blockade of the Gulf of Mexico ports.

Declaring a blockade allowed foreign powers to recognize the Confederacy as a belligerent since a country cannot, under international law, blockade its own ports. However, the British Government made it clear that if the ports were simply declared closed, it might very well recognize the Confederacy as an independent state in order to protect British-owned ships and property in Southern ports. Hence, the US government declared a blockade. On 14 May Britain recognized the Confederacy simply as a belligerent, declaring its own neutrality. Other European powers followed suit.

In actual fact, however, the US Navy, with only a handful of ships scattered around the world, was in no position to blockade all 3,000 miles of Southern coast. Davis's government made a bad decision at this time, forbidding any cotton to be shipped abroad. His purpose was to force European powers to join the war on the South's side or at least give the new state formal recognition in order to get badly needed cotton. At this point, however, cotton could have been shipped out easily through the largely paper blockade and then stored in European warehouses to be sold later, or sold immediately to raise desperately needed funds for the Confederate war effort. Later, when the South realized it needed to sell its cotton to raise funds, the US Navy had become strong enough to blockade Southern ports in fact as well as on paper.

As it turned out, there were sufficient cotton reserves in Europe to keep most mills working, although there were some mill closures in the English Midlands. Later, cotton growing spread in Egypt and India, replacing cotton that hitherto had come from the US South.

In the meantime, volunteer units were raised and began pouring into Washington. On 3 May Pennsylvania's governor offered 25 regiments 'all full and armed'; New Jersey offered '4 regiments start to-morrow, well prepared'; Massachusetts, '4 regiments (about) ready for the field; as many more at brief notice'; Vermount, '1 regiment waiting for orders'; Connecticut, '1 regiment in service'; Rhode Island, '1 regiment in field; 1 battery of light artillery'; Michigan, '1 regiment ready; 1 field battery, 4 guns, ready in four days; 2 regiments armed and nearly equipped; 3 regiments ready to be called'; Maine, '1 regiment ready, 3 nearly so'; Minnesota, '1 regiment mustered; another in two weeks'; Wisconsin, '1 regiment called and ready, another in camp; 2 more ready at day's warning'; Ohio, '22 regiments

in camp, under drill'; Iowa, '1 regiment, 1,000 strong, a week under drill, and 1 regiment now full and drilling; '3rd ready'; and New Hampshire, '1 regiment mustered; 2 others, perhaps 4, will be tendered by the State.'[4]

On 19 April, while passing through Baltimore, Maryland, on its way to Washington, the 6th Massachusetts was attacked by a pro-Southern mob. Four volunteers were killed and 39 injured; about a dozen of the mob were killed. The regiment retreated, only to return on 13 May to fortify the city's Federal Hill which overlooks Baltimore's harbour. Between those two dates, however, travel through the city was banned and Baltimore city police and militia burned railroad bridges north of the city to prevent further travel through it.

On 25 April the élite New York volunteer militia regiment, the 7th New York State Militia, flanked Baltimore, coming into Washington via Annapolis, Maryland. The nation's capital city was relieved.

Union forces swelled in Washington thereafter, as did Confederate forces into northern Virginia. Command of the Union army went to Major General Irvin McDowell and he sent troops to clear Alexandria, Virginia, just across the Potomac River from Washington on 25 May. Colonel Elmer E. Ellsworth, commanding the New York Fire Zouaves, the 11th New York, an attorney friend of Abraham Lincoln's, was killed by a hotel keeper in Alexandria after he removed a Confederate flag from the roof. Ellsworth was the first notable casualty of the war.

In western Virginia, Major General George B. McClellan led his volunteers from a victory at Philippi on to victories at Rich Mountain and Carrick's Ford.

Things were going better for the Confederates in eastern Virginia. There, in Big Bethel on 10 June, some 1,200 Confederates easily fought off a force of some 2,500 Union troops in the war's first major battle. Raw, gray-clad Union troops fired at one another in the battle's confusion, while two Union regiments in the vanguard hearing this firing assumed that the Confederates had taken them in rear and promptly fled. Union losses were eighteen killed, 53 wounded, and five missing, while the Confederates had only one man killed, with another seven missing. To many Southerners, this proved that any Southern fighting man was worth ten times as much as the typical Northern fighting man.

Bowing to public pressure, McDowell finally led his green troops towards a waiting, equally green Confederate army led by the hero of Fort Sumter, Beauregard. Farther west, J. E. Johnston's Confederates were supposed to be pinned down by Union troops led by an ageing Major General Robert Patterson. McDowell's army found Beauregard's troops around a small creek called Bull Run, not far from the village of Manassas. Both leaders planned to strike each other's left flanks and on 21 July began their moves.

McDowell took some 28,452 effectives into action, against Beauregard's 21,883. However, Patterson failed to hold Johnston, his troops reinforcing Beauregard's at a critical point and bringing total Southern strength to 32,232.

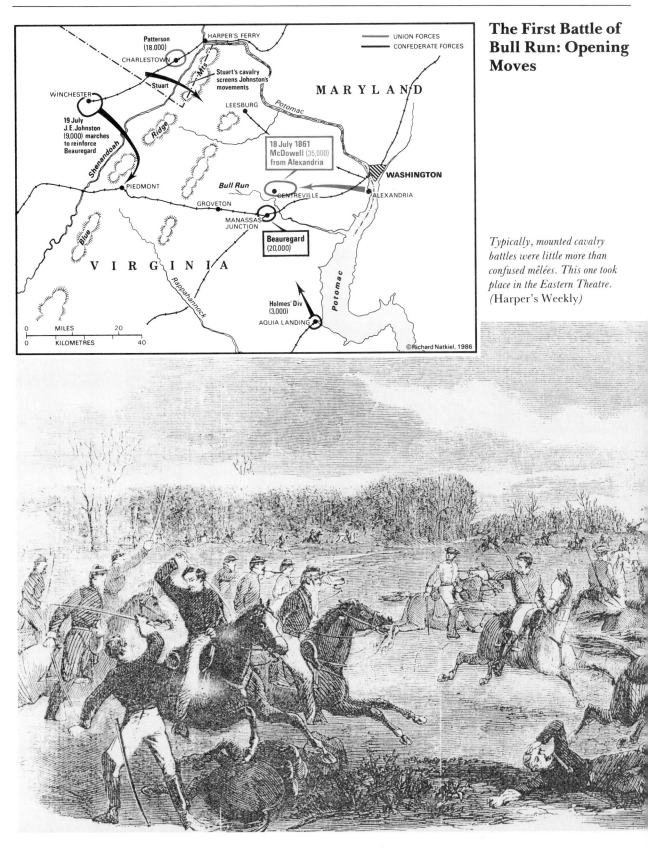

The First Battle of Bull Run: Opening Moves

UNION FORCES
CONFEDERATE FORCES

Patterson
(18,000)

HARPER'S FERRY

CHARLESTOWN

Stuart's cavalry
screens Johnston's
movements

Stuart

M A R Y L A N D

WINCHESTER

LEESBURG

Potomac

19 July
J.E.Johnston
(9,000) marches
to reinforce
Beauregard

Blue Ridge Mts

Shenandoah

18 July 1861
McDowell (35,000)
from Alexandria

WASHINGTON

PIEDMONT

Bull Run

CENTREVILLE

ALEXANDRIA

GROVETON

MANASSAS
JUNCTION

Beauregard
(20,000)

Blue

Potomac

V I R G I N I A

Rappahannock

Holmes' Div
(3,000)

AQUIA LANDING

0   MILES   20
0   KILOMETRES   40

© Richard Natkiel, 1986

*Typically, mounted cavalry
battles were little more than
confused mêlées. This one took
place in the Eastern Theatre.
(Harper's Weekly)*

The battle started well for Union hopes, but a determined stand by Stonewall Jackson's Virginia brigade stopped the Federals cold. On Henry House Hill, Jackson's 33rd Virginia, clad mostly in blue, captured two Union batteries, who had assumed they were reinforcements. Virginia cavalry led by Jeb Stuart smashed into the New York Fire Zouaves. Union troops began falling back. Civilians who came south from Washington to see the battle and have a spring picnic, fled. A wagon was disabled on a bridge over Bull Run, and a retreat turned into a full rout, not stopped until the men reached Washington. The South had won the first great battle of the war. Northern casualties totalled 1,492 with another 1,216 missing; Confederate casualties reached 1,969.

McDowell was replaced by McClellan, who began the job of building an effective fighting force. The three-months' volunteers were mustered out and went home, many to return in new units raised for three years' service. Meanwhile, Union forces began to nibble the South to death. Major General Benjamin Butler, with naval support,

captured Forts Clark and Hatteras in North Carolina. Confederate General Robert E. Lee took over the Confederate forces in West Virginia, only to fail there, the whole area ending in Union hands by November. Port Royal, South Carolina, was captured by Union soldiers and sailors on 7 November.

On 21 October another friend of Lincoln's, Colonel Edward Baker, one-time senator from Oregon, led a force across the Potomac to Ball's Bluff, Virginia. There his men were overwhelmed by Confederates and he himself was killed. The one-sided battle so shocked the nation that on 10 December Congress set up the Committee on the Conduct of the War to determine how this and other disasters had happened and how to prevent them in the future.

1861: Western Theatre

In Missouri, the governor, Claiborne F. Jackson, was pro-Confederate, while the legislature was pro-Union. Generally, the militia, which Jackson assembled, followed the

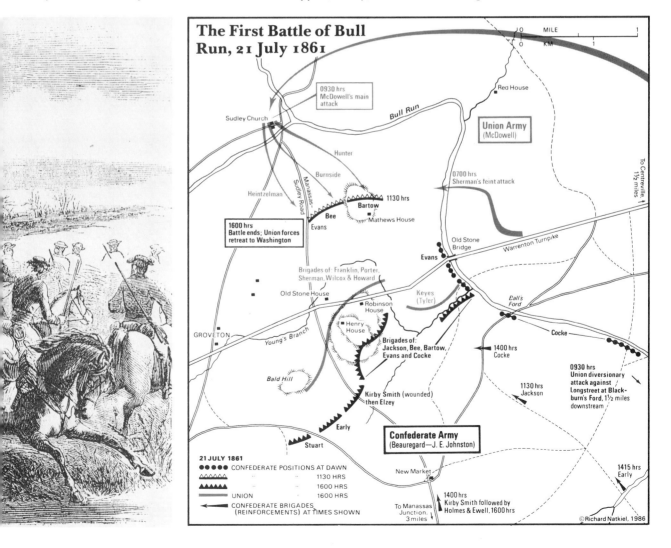

The First Battle of Bull Run, 21 July 1861

0930 hrs McDowell's main attack

Red House

Union Army (McDowell)

Sudley Church

Bull Run

0700 hrs Sherman's feint attack

Hunter

Burnside

Heintzelman

Bartow

1130 hrs

Bee

Mathews House

Evans

1600 hrs Battle ends; Union forces retreat to Washington

Old Stone Bridge

Evans

Warrenton Turnpike

Brigades of: Franklin, Porter, Sherman, Wilcox & Howard

Keyes (Tyler)

Ball's Ford

Old Stone House

Robinson House

Cocke

GROVETON

Henry House

Young's Branch

Brigades of: Jackson, Bee, Bartow, Evans and Cocke

1400 hrs Cocke

1130 hrs Jackson

0930 hrs Union diversionary attack against Longstreet at Blackburn's Ford, 1½ miles downstream

Bald Hill

Kirby Smith (wounded) then Elzey

Early

Confederate Army (Beauregard—J. E. Johnston)

Stuart

1415 hrs Early

21 JULY 1861

● ● ● ● CONFEDERATE POSITIONS AT DAWN
▵▵▵▵ "   "   1130 HRS
▲▲▲▲ "   "   1600 HRS
▬▬▬ UNION   1600 HRS
◀— CONFEDERATE BRIGADES (REINFORCEMENTS) AT TIMES SHOWN

New Market

To Manassas Junction, 3 miles

1400 hrs Kirby Smith followed by Holmes & Ewell, 1600 hrs

To Centreville, 1½ miles

© Richard Natkiel, 1986

governor's lead, although the people were divided in loyalties.

Tactically, the most important object in 1861 in Missouri was the US Army arsenal at St. Louis, where the population was generally pro-Union. There a US Army captain, Nathaniel Lyon, became suspicious that Jackson had called the state's militia out to capture the Arsenal. To prevent this, on 10 May he and his men surrounded the militia camp and forced their surrender. He paraded his militia prisoners through the streets of St. Louis, provoking a riot, but probably saving the state for the Union.

Jackson, however, then openly declared Missouri part of the Confederacy. Lyon, quickly named a brigadier general, went on the offensive against Jackson's troops, capturing his capital, Jefferson City, on 15 June. The forces clashed again at Boonville on 17 June and then again at Wilson's Creek on 10 August.

Wilson's Creek began with a surprise Union attack which initially succeeded in driving waiting Confederates from the crest of Bloody Hill. At the same time, more Union troops under Colonel Franz Sigel attacked the other side of the Confederate camp. Confederates counter-attacked on Bloody Hill, but were forced back. Sigel's men were also counter-attacked and forced back. Fighting raged on Bloody Hill, with one side and then the other attacking. Lyon was killed during this fighting, and Major Samuel D. Sturgis took command.

Finally, both sides badly bloodied and low on ammunition, Sturgis withdrew his men. The Confederates were unable to follow, instead staying in command of the field. Lyon had brought some 5,400 men into battle, losing some 944. The Confederates had some 11,600 men and losses of about 1,157.

On 30 August Major General John C. Fremont, explorer, first Republican candidate for governor, and commander of the Western Department headquartered in St. Louis, proclaimed martial law, an automatic death sentence for guerrillas, and that all slaves owned by Confederates in Missouri were free. A horrified Lincoln, fearing that this premature move would shove vacillating slave-owners in border states into Southern hands, asked Fremont to modify his order and free only slaves owned by Missourians actively working for the South. Fremont refused and was relieved from duty, to be replaced by Henry Halleck on 19 November.

Fighting continued in Missouri, with a 2,800-man Union garrison at Lexington coming under siege and surrendering to a victorious 7,000-man-strong Missouri State Guard on 20 September. Volunteers flocked to the Southern colours. Despite this victory, the Confederates were unable to equip all their volunteers and desertions began. Within a short time the Confederates could not count more than their original 7,000 officers and men to face some 38,000 Union troops. In October, a new pro-Southern legislature in Neosho voted for the state to join the Confederacy even though Union troops still controlled most of the state. Continuing the drive to clear the state, Grant attacked Belmont, Missouri on 7 November, losing his first battle of the war there.

Belmont had started out well enough, with Grant's 3,000 men landing south of the town and charging straight into the waiting Confederate lines. After a two-hour fire fight, the Confederates broke. Instead of following up on their victory, however, the Union troops began looting the Southern camp. Confederate reinforcements arrived, bringing their strength to some 5,000. Grant had the camp set ablaze, then followed his men to the boats from which they had landed. He was the last man aboard.

Although anything but a major battle, with losses on both sides of just over 600 men each, at least one Northern general seemed willing to fight. Lincoln's eye remained on Grant thereafter.

Meanwhile, the Kentucky legislature had voted that their state would remain neutral, something that would appear practically impossible since the state separated the new Confederacy from Union troops. Lincoln, however, agreed to honor the state's neutrality as long as the Confederates did so too. As in Missouri, Kentucky's governor was pro-Confederate, while the legislature was pro-Union. The state's militia divided into two organizations, one favoring one side and the other, the other.

Both Confederates and Federals sent troops to the Kentucky border, ready to pounce if the other violated the state's neutrality. There they sat, eyeball to eyeball, until the Confederates blinked first. On 3 September Southern troops occupied Columbus, Kentucky, whose bluffs commanded the River Mississippi just south of the Union camp at Cairo, Illinois. Grant, the commander at Cairo, reacted by moving into Paducah on 6 September. He faced a Confederate line of defence that reached from Columbus through Bowling Green to the Cumberland Gap. The Confederates then organized a new state government which proclaimed secession on 18 November, while the old state government, still in operation, stayed with the Union. By the war's end, some 25,000 Kentuckians had served in Confederate forces, while another 76,000 Kentuckians had served the Union.

On 8 June Tennessee, the other border state, voted to join the Confederacy. In October Union troops began their drive into East Tennessee which would eventually clear that state of Confederates.

1862: Eastern Theatre

The year in the East began as it had ended, with McClellan holding review after review but not moving. Finally, annoyed by this long wait, Lincoln ordered him to move on 22 February, Washington's birthday. The day came and went. McClellan's men drilled that day, then spent the evening as they had spent every other evening since he had assumed command of the army.

Down in North Carolina, Burnside captured Roanoke Island on 8 February, taking another bite out of the Southern coast. Then, on 14 March, Burnside took New Bern which would become a major Union post.

A typical informal battle line, in this case Union troops of Kearney's Division of the Army of the Potomac during the Peninsula Campaign. The men are free to take cover as best they can, while officers observe the fighting just behind them. The enemy is hardly visible, save as indistinct shapes and puffs of smoke in the distance. (Harper's Weekly)

Making a reconnaissance in force on 7 March, the Union forces were vastly embarrassed to discover many of the guns frowning out of the miles of Confederate fortifications were painted logs of wood, the cannoneers having long before retired farther South. As a result, on 11 March Lincoln relieved McClellan of his position as Union general-in-chief, although keeping him in command of the Army of the Potomac. On 17 March McClellan finally began his move, a bold plan that would put his men aboard ships, down to the peninsula between Virginia's James and York Rivers which led to Richmond. There he would drive east against that city and its defenders.

McClellan's army, as of 20 June, totalled 115,102 men, while the Confederates had only a handful dug in on the peninsula. Nevertheless, after landing, McClellan allowed himself to be stopped by a combination of his own inflated idea of Confederate numbers and a wily defender, Major General John B. Magruder, who used such tricks as marching the same units around time after time past Union observers, while train whistles blew in the background, to appear as if there were more defenders than there actually were. McClellan settled down for a siege of Yorktown, while the main Confederate army rushed to Richmond's defence.

On 4 May, just before the siege guns were set to fire, Union scouts found the elaborate Confederate works were empty, their forces having retired shortly before. They began a pursuit, fighting a rear-guard action at Williamsburg on 4–5 May.

While McClellan was moving his troops south, the Confederate commander in the Shenandoah Valley, an

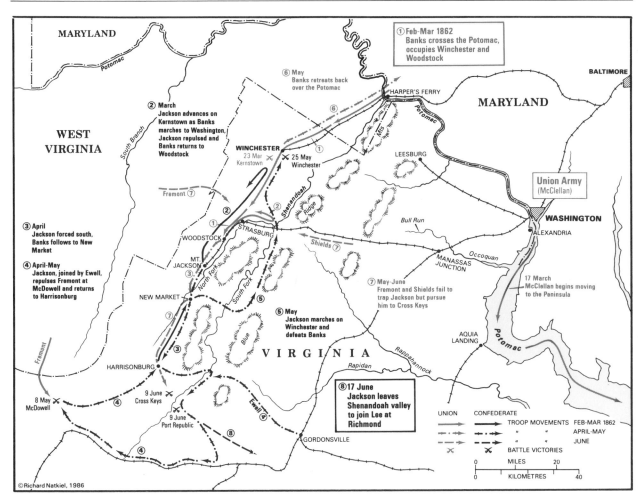

MARYLAND

WEST
VIRGINIA

① Feb-Mar 1862
Banks crosses the Potomac,
occupies Winchester and
Woodstock

BALTIMORE

HARPER'S FERRY

MARYLAND

⑥ May
Banks retreats back
over the Potomac

⑥

LEESBURG

② March
Jackson advances on
Kernstown as Banks
marches to Washington.
Jackson repulsed and
Banks returns to
Woodstock

WINCHESTER
23 Mar
Kernstown   ╳ 25 May
              Winchester

Fremont ⑦

③ April
Jackson forced south,
Banks follows to New
Market

②

①

②

WOODSTOCK

STRASBURG

Shenandoah

Ridge

Bull Run

Union Army
(McClellan)

WASHINGTON
ALEXANDRIA

④ April-May
Jackson, joined by Ewell,
repulses Fremont at
McDowell and returns
to Harrisonburg

MT.
JACKSON
③

North Fork

South Fork

Shields ⑦

MANASSAS
JUNCTION

Occoquan

17 March
McClellan begins moving
to the Peninsula

NEW MARKET

⑤

⑦

⑤ May
Jackson marches on
Winchester and
defeats Banks

⑦ May-June
Fremont and Shields fail to
trap Jackson but pursue
him to Cross Keys

AQUIA
LANDING

Potomac

Fremont

③

HARRISONBURG

Blue

V I R G I N I A

Rappahannock

Rapidan

8 May ╳
McDowell

9 June ╳
Cross Keys

④

④

9 June
Port Republic

③

⑧

Ewell

⑦

⑧ 17 June
Jackson leaves
Shenandoah valley
to join Lee at
Richmond

UNION   CONFEDERATE

TROOP MOVEMENTS   FEB-MAR 1862
      "   "   APRIL-MAY
      "   "   JUNE
╳   ╳   BATTLE VICTORIES

GORDONSVILLE

0   MILES   20
0   KILOMETRES   40

© Richard Natkiel, 1986

obscure Virginia Military Institute professor named
Thomas Jonathan Jackson, who had won laurels at First
Bull Run, started his drive to free the valley from Union
control. He struck first at Kernstown on 23 March, losing
but scaring Federal authorities into holding some troops
earmarked for McClellan's army back for Washington's
defence.

Reinforced, with a force of some 17,000 men, Jackson
used the principle of concentration and smashed Fremont's
troops at McDowell on 8 May before he could unite with
troops under Nathan P. Banks. Fremont retired to the west
and Jackson turned, with rapid marches, on Banks. On 23
May elements of the two forces met at Front Royal. Banks
was forced to retreat to the north. Jackson followed, meeting
and beating him at the First Battle of Winchester on 25
May. The Union line first held, then fell back, and Banks
again fell back.

Lincoln, seeing Jackson surrounded by Fremont, Banks
and Major General Irvin McDowell at Fredericksburg,
ordered the three to move rapidly and crush Jackson. None
of the three, however, were as quick as Jackson, who pushed
his troops to the limits of their endurance to escape the trap.
At Cross Keys, he hit Fremont's troops, forcing them back,

then turned on McDowell at Port Republic for his final
victory of the lightning campaign that freed the Shenandoah
Valley. His men had marched 350 miles, fought five battles
in which it beat three separate Union armies, removed the
threat to Virginia's food basket, and tied up thousands of
troops much needed to move against Richmond.

After very little time to rest, Jackson's command was
rushed east to join the troops fighting McClellan who was
finally moving, driving the Confederates under J. E.
Johnston to the suburbs of Richmond. Some Union troops
could actually see the city's church spires.

Johnston counter-attacked at Seven Pines and Fair Oaks
Station 31 May, with some 41,816 men against McClellan's
44,944. In the indecisive battle, Johnston was badly
wounded and Robert E. Lee took command of the force
which he then named the Army of Northern Virginia.
Joined by Jackson's troops, he began a series of punches
against McClellan. Most were unco-ordinated and failed,
but on 27 June the Confederates did break through at
Gaines' Mill where 57,018 Confederates attacked 36,790
Federals. Still believing he was greatly outnumbered,
McClellan switched his base to the James River and dug in.
On 1 July Lee struck at Malvern Hill where superior Union

◁ The Shenandoah Valley Campaign, February to May 1862

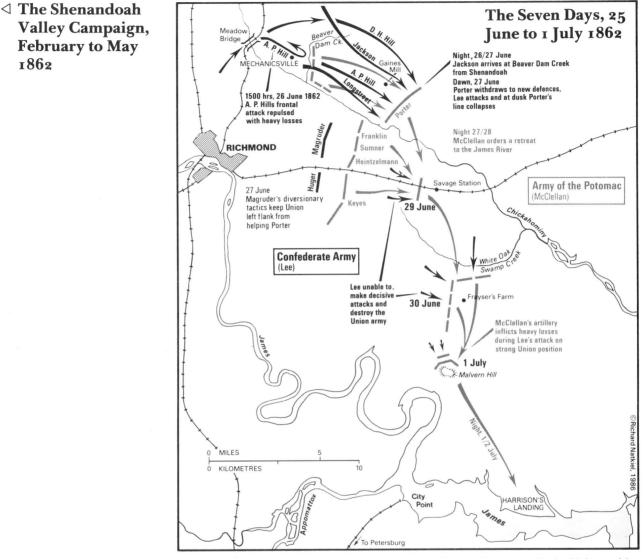

The Seven Days, 25 June to 1 July 1862

Meadow Bridge

Beaver Dam Ck.

D. H. Hill

Jackson

Gaines Mill

A. P. Hill

MECHANICSVILLE

A. P. Hill

Longstreet

Porter

Night, 26/27 June
Jackson arrives at Beaver Dam Creek from Shenandoah
Dawn, 27 June
Porter withdraws to new defences, Lee attacks and at dusk Porter's line collapses

1500 hrs, 26 June 1862
A. P. Hills frontal attack repulsed with heavy losses

Magruder

Franklin

Sumner

Heintzelmann

RICHMOND

Night 27/28
McClellan orders a retreat to the James River

Huger

Savage Station

Army of the Potomac
(McClellan)

27 June
Magruder's diversionary tactics keep Union left flank from helping Porter

Keyes

29 June

Chickahominy

Confederate Army
(Lee)

White Oak Swamp Creek

Lee unable to make decisive attacks and destroy the Union army

30 June

Frayser's Farm

McClellan's artillery inflicts heavy losses during Lee's attack on strong Union position

1 July

Malvern Hill

James

0 MILES   5
0 KILOMETRES   10

Night, 1/2 July

© Richard Natkiel, 1986

City Point

HARRISON'S LANDING

James

Appomattox

To Petersburg

---

artillery shredded his attacking forces, but the threat of McClellan's attack was gone forever.

Despairing of McClellan's doing anything, Lincoln brought in Major General John Pope, fresh from Western successes, and gave him command of an army that would take Richmond overland directly from the north. Pope began his Eastern career with a bombastic proclamation that cost him the respect of all, friend and enemy alike. Lee, seeing McClellan pinned within his earthworks, sent Jackson north to meet this threat. On 28 August Jackson hit one of Pope's divisions near Groveton so Pope concentrated his army near the old Bull Run battlefield. As fresh Union units came up he sent them one at a time against Jackson who easily beat them off.

Confederate reinforcement under James Longstreet reached Jackson. Pope, not knowing this, ordered troops under Major General Fitzjohn Porter to attack what he thought was Jackson's flank (the troops here were actually Longstreet's men). Porter refused, a refusal which cost him his career since it was widely believed that he was a McClellan supporter who had refused to attack in order to see Pope defeated and McClellan restored to overall command.

On 30 May, seeing the Confederates shorten their lines, Pope ordered his men to pursue what he thought was a retreating enemy. He was wrong, and Confederate counterattacks forced the Union troops back to Centreville and Pope to a far western command.

McClellan was restored to command, but the Peninsula Campaign was abandoned and his men were brought back to the Washington area. Spurred by his successes so far and the hope that the slave state of Maryland would provide men and supplies to his army, Lee, with Davis's permission, decided to cross the Potomac and head north. Convinced of McClellan's slowness, he divided his forces, sending Jackson to take Harpers Ferry, Virginia, while he stayed

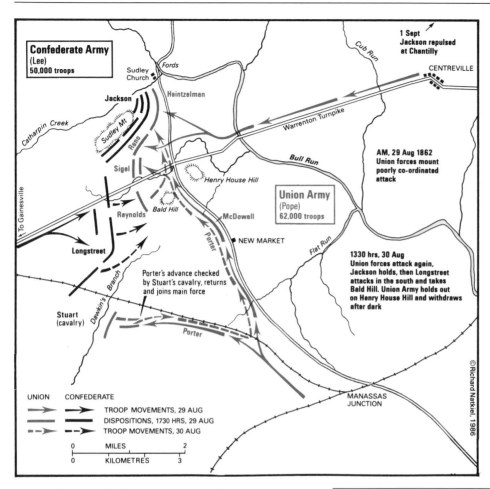

Confederate Army
(Lee)
50,000 troops

Sudley Church   Fords

1 Sept
Jackson repulsed
at Chantilly

Cub Run

CENTREVILLE

Jackson

Heintzelman

Catharpin Creek

Sudley Mt.

Reno

Warrenton Turnpike

Bull Run

AM, 29 Aug 1862
Union forces mount
poorly co-ordinated
attack

Sigel

Henry House Hill

Union Army
(Pope)
62,000 troops

Bald Hill

To Gainesville

Reynolds

McDowell

Porter

NEW MARKET

Flat Run

1330 hrs, 30 Aug
Union forces attack again,
Jackson holds, then Longstreet
attacks in the south and takes
Bald Hill. Union Army holds out
on Henry House Hill and withdraws
after dark

Longstreet

Dawkin's Branch

Porter's advance checked
by Stuart's cavalry, returns
and joins main force

Stuart
(cavalry)

Porter

MANASSAS
JUNCTION

© Richard Natkiel, 1986

UNION   CONFEDERATE

TROOP MOVEMENTS, 29 AUG
DISPOSITIONS, 1730 HRS, 29 AUG
TROOP MOVEMENTS, 30 AUG

0   MILES   2
0   KILOMETRES   3

The Second Battle
of Bull Run, 29 to
30 August 1862

some miles east of Jackson, and headed directly north.

Unfortunately, his set of orders describing this move, wrapped around three cigars, was found by a Union soldier and quickly forwarded to McClellan's headquarters. Typically waiting sixteen hours before moving, although he had quickly determined that the orders were genuine, McClellan then ordered his men to strike at Lee's troops. Within 24 hours, too, a Confederate spy had reported McClellan's good luck to Lee.

On 14 September Union troops came in contact with Confederates defending the hills that separated the two armies. At South Mountain some 28,480 Union troops forced their way past 18,714 Confederates who had, however, bought Lee time to concentrate many of his remaining forces at Sharpsburg, Maryland, near the Antietam Creek. Lee could have had more men available, but, as he wrote in his official report, 'The arduous service in which our troops had been engaged, their great privations of rest and food, and the long marches without shoes over mountain roads, had greatly reduced our ranks before the action began. These causes had compelled thousands of brave men to absent themselves, and many more had done so from unworthy motives.'[5]

Straggling and desertion in this campaign, as in every

A Confederate is captured at the Second Bull Run

'By this time I was close to the stream, and while noting the lay of the land on the opposite bank with regard to choice of a crossing place, I became aware of a man observing me from the end of the cut above. I could not distinguish the color of his uniform, but the crown of his hat tapered suspiciously, I thought, and instinctively I dropped the butt of my rifle to the ground and reached behind me for a cartridge. "Come here!" he cried; – his accent was worse than his hat. "Who are you?" I responded as I executed the movement of "tear cartridge". He laughed and then invited me to "come and see". Meanwhile I was trying to draw my rammer, but this operation was arrested by the dry click of several gunlocks, and I found myself covered by half a dozen rifles, and my friend of the steeple-crown, with less urbanity in his intonation, called out to me to "drop that". In our brief intercourse he had acquired a curious influence over me. I did so.'

(Allen C. Redwood, 55th Viriginia Regiment, 'Jackson's "Foot-Cavalry" at the Second Bull Run', *Battles & Leaders of the Civil War*, Vol. II, 1956, p. 536)

After the Battle of South Mountain

'Before the sunlight faded, I walked over the narrow field. All around lay the Confederate dead – undersized men mostly, from the coast district of North Carolina, with sallow, hatchet faces, and clad in "butternut" – a color running all the way from a deep coffee brown up to whitish brown of ordinary dust. As I looked down on the poor, pinched faces, worn with marching and scant fare, all enmity died out. There was no "secession" in those rigid forms, nor in those fixed eyes staring blankly at the sky. Clearly it was not "their war". Some of our men primed their muskets afresh with the finer powder from the cartridge-boxes of the dead. With this exception, each remained untouched as he had fallen. Darkness came on rapidly, and it grew very chilly. As very little could be done at that hour in the way of burial, we unrolled the blankets of the dead, spread them over the bodies, and then sat down in line, munching a little on our cooked rations in lieu of supper, and listening to the firing, which was kept up on the right, persistently. By 9 o'clock this ceased entirely. Drawing our blankets over us, we went to sleep, lying upon our arms in line as we had stood, living Yankee and dead Confederate side by side, and indistinguishable.

(David L. Thompson, 'In the Ranks to the Antietam', *Battles & Leaders of the Civil War*, Thomas Yoseloff, New York, Vol. II, 1956, p. 558)

These two members of the 6th Virginia Cavalry have variants of the Colt revolver. The man on the left has the Colt M1851 Navy, the other man has the earlier M1849 0.31 calibre, 5-shot Colt. The 6th was from Northern Virginia and served with the Army of Northern Virginia and in the 1864 Valley campaign. (Library of Congress collection)

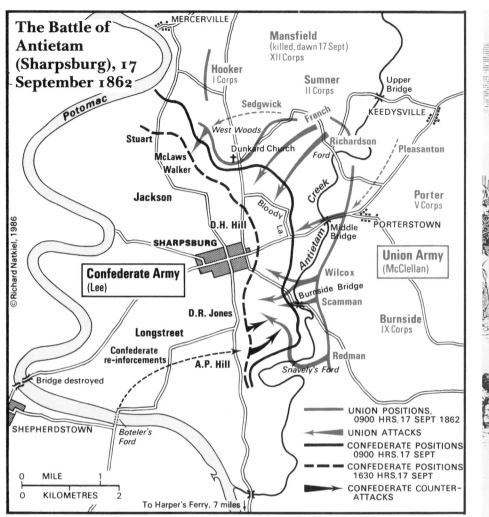

The Battle of Antietam (Sharpsburg), 17 September 1862

© Richard Natkiel, 1986

MERCERVILLE

Mansfield (killed, dawn 17 Sept) XII Corps

Hooker I Corps

Sumner II Corps

Upper Bridge

Sedgwick

French

KEEDYSVILLE

West Woods

Stuart

Dunkard Church

Richardson

Pleasanton

McLaws

Ford

Walker

Jackson

Bloody La.

Creek

Porter V Corps

D.H. Hill

PORTERSTOWN

SHARPSBURG

Middle Bridge

Antietam

Confederate Army (Lee)

Wilcox

Union Army (McClellan)

Burnside Bridge

D.R. Jones

Scamman

Longstreet

Burnside IX Corps

Confederate re-inforcements

A.P. Hill

Redman

Snavely's Ford

Bridge destroyed

SHEPHERDSTOWN

Boteler's Ford

UNION POSITIONS, 0900 HRS, 17 SEPT 1862	
UNION ATTACKS	
CONFEDERATE POSITIONS 0900 HRS, 17 SEPT	
CONFEDERATE POSITIONS 1630 HRS, 17 SEPT	
CONFEDERATE COUNTER-ATTACKS	

0 MILE 1
0 KILOMETRES 2

To Harper's Ferry, 7 miles

campaign the Confederacy fought, were as much an enemy as were the Union troops.

On 17 September McClellan hurled 75,316 Union troops against 37,330 Confederates, but, as usual, failed to take command of the battle once it had begun. Union assaults came piecemeal, first from the North under Joseph Hooker, then in the center under Joseph Mansfield and finally from across the creek under Ambrose Burnside. By quickly switching units around to meet specific attacks, Lee was able to hold his lines until A. P. Hill's reinforcements arrived in time to smash Burnside's flank and win the day.

It was the single most costly day of the war. Union losses were some 2,108 killed, 9,549 wounded and 753 missing. The Confederates, who were already running into problems filling their ranks, lost 2,700 killed, 9,024 wounded and 2,000 missing.

Lee waited the next day, willing to give battle again, but McClellan had had enough. A day later, Lee slipped back south across the Potomac.

It was no great victory, but was enough to allow Lincoln to issue his Emancipation Proclamation on 23 September giving freedom to slaves living in the Confederacy.

On 9 October Stuart led his men on a raid as far north as Chambersburg, Pennsylvania, while McClellan's army grew ever more rusty in their camps. On 7 November Lincoln replaced the unmovable McClellan with Burnside, who proposed a move against Richmond overland. He called for pontoon bridges to move ahead of his main force so that he could cross rivers before Lee. Unfortunately, the staff officer in Washington entrusted with the job of seeing to the bridges failed to understand their importance.

Therefore, when 19 November found Burnside's army on the Rappahannock River there were no bridges to cross it. Lee had time to fortify the heights overlooking Fredericksburg, Virginia. Sticking to his original plan despite the changed situation, Burnside ordered an assault when the pontoon boats finally arrived on 11–12 December. The result was a slaughter pen much like that of Malvern Hill. The Union army lost 10,884 killed and wounded, with another 1,769 missing, compared to Confederate dead and wounded rolls of 4,656 with only 653 missing.

On 15 December the army recrossed the river.

A Union soldier sees red at Antietam

'As the range grew better, the firing became more rapid, the situation desperate and exasperating to the last degree. Human nature was on the rack, and there burst forth from it the most vehement, terrible swearing I have ever heard. Certainly the joy of conflict was not ours that day. The suspense was only for a moment, however, for the order to charge came just after. Whether the regiment was thrown into disorder or not, I never knew. I only remember that as we rose and started all the fire that had been held back so long was loosed. In a second the air was full of the hiss of bullets and the hurtle of grape-shot. The mental strain was so great that I saw at that moment the singular effect mentioned, I think in the life of Goethe on a similar occasion – the whole landscape for an instant turned slightly red.'

(David L. Thompson, 'With Burnside At Antietam', *Battles & Leaders of the Civil War*, Volume II, Thomas Yoseloff, New York, 1956, pp. 661–2)

1862: Western Theatre

In Kentucky there was no winter break in the war. Confederate Brigadier General Felix K. Zollicoffer had violated Kentucky's neutrality in late November 1861, by advancing deep into the state to the town of Mill Springs. There a Union force under Major General George H. Thomas advanced to meet him, halting some ten miles away at Logan's Cross Roads. Zollicoffer decided his position was a poor one and, rather than retreat, attacked Thomas on 19 January.

Zollicoffer's men attacked in heavy rain at about daybreak, driving in Union pickets. Zollicoffer himself, however, was killed in the attack, which failed. Many Confederates were armed with flintlocks which wouldn't fire in the rain, but his rallied men made a second charge which

A. R. Waud, one of Harper's Weekly's *best sketch artists, was briefly detained by Confederates during the 1862 invasion of Maryland and produced this drawing of the 1st* *Virginia Cavalry during that campaign. Their uniforms are gray with black facings and bars across the chest.* (Harper's Weekly)

was again beaten off. The Confederate flanks were turned and the Confederates fled back to Knoxville, Tennessee. Their losses were some 533 officers and men. The Union troops lost 261. Union troops went on to occupy Bowling Green, Kentucky on 14 February.

Just below the Kentucky border the Confederates established two forts: Fort Henry on the Tennessee River and Fort Donelson on the Cumberland River. Fort Henry's 3,400 men were crowded within low-lying fortifications where water from the river actually came over the walls. U.S. Grant moved his troops towards Fort Henry while seven gunboats under Flag Officer Andrew H. Foote began bombarding the fort on 6 February. Seeing that no defence was possible, Confederate Brigadier General Lloyd Tilghman withdrew most of the garrison to nearby Fort Donel-

son, leaving gunners for two cannon to fight the gunboats. Although they did some damage in the uneven battle that followed, their guns were quickly disabled, and Fort Henry fell to the US Navy.

On 14 February Foote took his boats to bombard Donelson, but this nut proved tougher to crack. Foote himself was wounded and his flagship was knocked out of action, together with another of his boats. Grant settled down for a formal siege. On the morning of the 15th, however, the Confederates attacked the Union lines, breaking through and gaining an open road to Nashville. The attack's leader, Major General Gideon J. Pillow, however, apparently lost his nerve, withdrawing his successful men back to their own lines and allowing Grant to plug the gap in his lines.

During a council of war held that night, the Confederates decided to surrender, but cavalry commander Nathan B. Forrest refused to do so and led his men through swamps to escape. On the morning of the 16th, after Grant had announced that he would accept nothing less than unconditional surrender, the garrison stacked its arms. Once the two forts were in Union hands, it would be impossible to hold Nashville, which surrendered on 23 February, giving the Union full control of western Tennessee as well as Kentucky.

Farther west, on 10 February Union troops under Major General Samuel R. Curtis started a campaign to clean out Missouri. The Confederates, outnumbered, withdrew to north-western Arkansas, just south of Fayetteville. There, reinforced, the Confederates under Major General Earl Van Dorn marched north to attack. Curtis concentrated his forces to meet the Confederates on Pea Ridge, Arkansas.

On the morning of 7 March the Confederates attacked, charging three times and finally driving the Union troops beyond Elkhorn Tavern. A fourth charge pushed them back further, but reinforcements stabilized their line. Curtis, figuring that the Confederate ammunition supply would be low, ordered a counter-attack for the next morning. While Union artillery silenced Southern batteries, Union infantry swarmed forward to the tavern. The Confederates fell back in confusion and Van Dorn ordered a general retreat, having sustained some 800 casualties. The Union troops, who had 1,384 casualties, took some 300 prisoners and secured Missouri. Union troops went on successfully to attack Confederates at Prairie Grove, just south of Fayetteville on 7 December.

Meanwhile, after Donelson's surrender, Grant pushed south on the Tennessee River to the small town of Pittsburg Landing, some 23 miles from the Confederates at Corinth, Mississippi. General A. S. Johnston planned a sneak attack on Grant which would turn the Union left on the river and destroy Grant's forces. On the morning of 6 April Johnston's 40,335 men struck Grant's totally unprepared 41,682 men of the Army of the Tennessee. The initial attack was wholly successful, although Confederate momentum was lost as their hungry troops began looting Union camps. Moreover, pockets of stubborn resistance held along the line. One particularly stiffly held position earned the nickname of the 'hornet's nest'. There, while directing the attack, Johnston was mortally wounded at about 2.30 p.m. P. G. T. Beauregard assumed command.

The tide had turned. Reinforcements from the Army of the Ohio arrived that evening, and Grant went on the counter-attack the next morning. Although Confederate resistance was tough, the Union forces could not be stopped and Beauregard ordered a retreat to Corinth in the late afternoon. He had lost some 10,694 men to Grant's 13,047.

On 29 April Halleck assumed command of Grant's army, inching towards Corinth at the rate of a mile a day. Beauregard pulled out 29/30 May before Halleck got there, however.

On the Mississippi River, Major General John Pope's men took fortified Island Number 10 on 7 April. At the

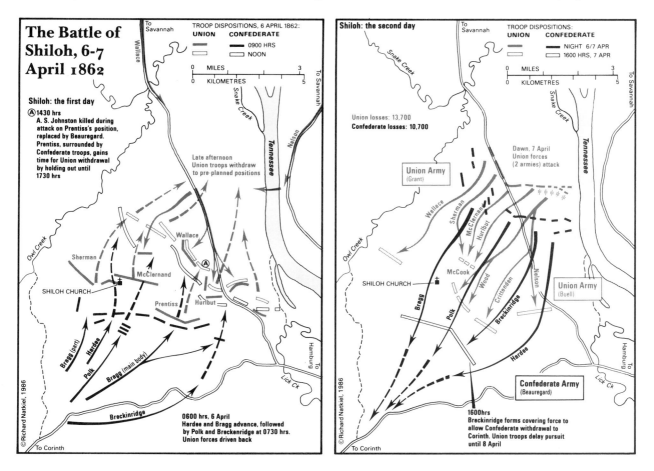

The Battle of Shiloh, 6-7 April 1862

Shiloh: the first day

(A) 1430 hrs
A. S. Johnston killed during attack on Prentiss's position, replaced by Beauregard. Prentiss, surrounded by Confederate troops, gains time for Union withdrawal by holding out until 1730 hrs

TROOP DISPOSITIONS, 6 APRIL 1862:
UNION   CONFEDERATE
0900 HRS
NOON

Late afternoon Union troops withdraw to pre-planned positions

0600 hrs, 6 April
Hardee and Bragg advance, followed by Polk and Breckenridge at 0730 hrs. Union forces driven back

Shiloh: the second day

TROOP DISPOSITIONS:
UNION   CONFEDERATE
NIGHT 6/7 APR
1600 HRS, 7 APR

Union losses: 13,700
Confederate losses: 10,700

Dawn, 7 April Union forces (2 armies) attack

1600 hrs
Breckenridge forms covering force to allow Confederate withdrawal to Corinth. Union troops delay pursuit until 8 April

river's mouth, ships under Flag Officer David G. Farragut ran the gauntlet of fire from Forts St. Philip and Jackson, and from a small Confederate fleet, and accepted surrender of New Orleans, Louisiana on 29 April. And, Union troops captured Huntsville, Alabama on 11 April.

On 4 June the Confederates abandoned Fort Pillow on the Mississippi River, and on 6 June Memphis, Tennessee, fell to the Union in a brief naval battle. Vicksburg, Mississippi, remained the major Confederate stronghold on the vital Mississippi River. On 27 June Union engineers began digging a canal that could divert the river's course and isolate Vicksburg but the project ended in swampy failure. On 27–29 December Grant tried an unsuccessful frontal assault on the city.

In July, Confederate cavalry raiders Forrest and John H. Morgan went on the offensive, Forrest taking Murfreesboro, Tennessee, on the 15th and Morgan riding through Kentucky and Tennessee. Another Confederate partisan, William Quantrill, captured Independence, Missouri, on 11 August. In Missouri, too, Van Dorn attacked Major General William S. Rosecrans at Iuka on 19 September but was beaten. He attacked again at Corinth on 3–4 October and again was beaten. Retreating, Van Dorn was attacked at the Big Hatchie River on 5 October.

In Kentucky the Confederates returned to the advance, General E. Kirby Smith reaching Covington, just across the river from Cincinnati, on 15 September, but he retired as Union troops under Don Carlos Buell reached Louisville. The Confederates, under Braxton Bragg, installed a Confederate government at Frankfort, Kentucky, on 4 October, but the government had little time to rule since Bragg's troops were attacked at Perryville, in a battle also known as Chaplin Hills, on 9 October, and badly beaten there. On 26 October they retreated back into Tennessee.

Bragg halted his retreat at Murfreesboro on Stone's River, followed closely by Rosecrans. On 31 December Bragg attacked the Union right, but Rosecrans and his subordinates Philip Sheridan and George Thomas, held on. On 2 January Bragg struck the left. Fighting was desperate but indecisive and on the evening of 3 January Bragg, having lost 9,239 killed or wounded to Rosecrans' 9,220 killed or wounded, withdrew to Tullahoma, 35 miles away. Union forces also lost 3,686 men missing, while Bragg's lost some 2,500 men missing.

1863: Eastern Theatre

On 20 January, to repair the damage to his reputation, Burnside started his army up the Rappahannock River to find a crossing and get behind Lee. Wet weather, however, turned roads into swamps so deep it was said that mules sank to their ears. By the 24th it was obvious the Army of the Potomac was going nowhere slowly and it returned to its winter quarters. On 25 January Major General Joseph Hooker replaced Burnside.

Hooker took over a very depressed army. He quickly rebuilt its morale, granting winter furloughs, getting the men enough food and clothing, and even devising a system of divisional insignia worn on cap tops and sides. He also worked out a plan by which he would move up the Rappahannock, cross it, and turn Lee's flank, forcing Lee to come out of Fredericksburg's fortifications and be beaten in the open field.

On 28 April he moved out, crossing the river and moving into an area of tangled brush known as the Wilderness. His headquarters was at Chancellorsville Court House. Troops left behind assaulted Fredericksburg. Lee, who had only 57,352 men against Hooker's 104,891, daringly split his forces. He left some 10,000 men at Fredericksburg and took the rest to meet Hooker. On 1 May Hooker paused, and Lee again, against all military maxims, split his army, sending Stonewall Jackson to flank Hooker's force. Hooker thought Jackson was retreating, but on 2 May Jackson suddenly burst on the unprepared XI Corps and put it to flight. That evening Jackson was accidentally mortally wounded, J. E. B. Stuart taking command of his corps and continuing the attack on 3 May. To the east, fighting their way through stiff opposition, Union troops managed to break through Confederate lines at Fredericksburg, but were unable to reach Hooker's main force. On 6 May a badly beaten Army of the Potomac, having lost some 11,116 killed or wounded and 5,676 missing, retreated across the river. Confederate losses totalled 12,764.

Lee then took the war north, crossing the Potomac on 15 June. Hooker followed, being replaced by Major General George G. Meade on 28 June when the Confederates were within thirteen miles of Pennsylvania's capital city, Harrisburg. Confederates, looking for shoes, reached Gettysburg, Pennsylvania, on 1 July, there to be met by Union cavalry. Both sides rushed reinforcements to the crossroads town. Confederates took the town on the first day, then halted as daylight ended. The Union line then resembled a fishhook, the right below the town ending on Culp's Hill and the left on the two Round Tops. Fighting on the 2nd centered on the two flanks, where Union forces narrowly stood off Confederate attacks. Much against Longstreet's wishes, Lee sent Longstreet's corps against the Union center, on the 3rd, in a costly failure known as Pickett's Charge after the attacking division's commander, George Pickett. At the same time, Stuart, who had been missing on a ride around the Union forces until then, was sent against the rear of the

---

Confederates wait for Pickett's Charge to start

'At Gettysburg, when the artillery fire was at its height, a brawny fellow, who seemed happy at the prospect for a hot time, broke out singing:-

"Backward, roll backward, O Time in thy flight:
Make me a child again, just for this *fight*!"

'Another fellow near him replied, "Yes; and a *gal* child at that."'

(Carlton McCarthy, *Detailed Minutiae of Soldier in the Army of Northern Virginia*, Richmond, 1882, pp. 106–7)

The Battle of Gettysburg, 1–3 July 1863

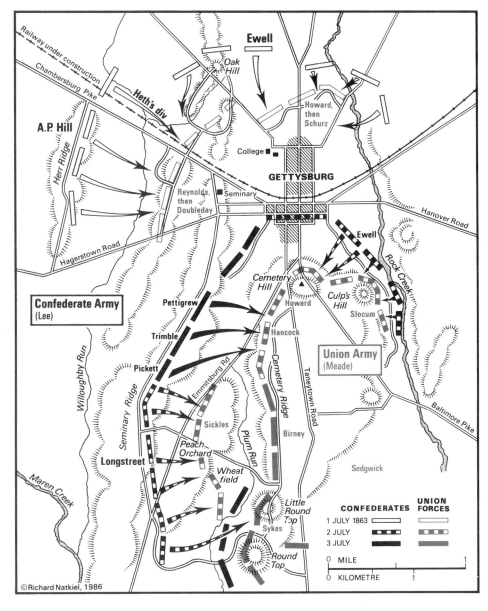

©Richard Natkiel, 1986

center. He, too, was stopped by hard-fighting Union cavalry.

On 4 July, in the rain, both sides rested, Lee starting his retreat south on the 5th. Lee had taken some 75,054 men into Gettysburg and lost 28,063. Meade had 83,289 men and lost 23,049.

By 1 August the Army of Northern Virginia was back in that state. However, news of the Northern victory was tempered by riots in New York over the new conscription law on 13–14 July in which as many as 500 people died. It took regular army troops finally to quieten the city.

Farther south, Fort Wagner, outside Charleston, South Carolina, was evacuated by the Confederates on 6 September, although Fort Sumter continued to withstand naval bombardment throughout the fall. In September, too, Lee

sent Longstreet's corps to aid Bragg in the west, and in October Lee's men fell back to lines along the Rapidan. Meade followed. Lee planned an attack on Meade's flank, heading west and north of the Rapidan on 9 October. Meade reached Centreville on 14 October, having stood off A. P. Hill's attack at Bristoe Station, while Lee's men were on the twice-visited field of Bull Run. Meade consolidated his lines and Lee, unable to find a weak spot in them, finally gave up his attack and withdrew across the Rappahannock as Meade followed.

On 7 November Meade's men crossed the Rappahannock at Kelly's Ford and Rappahannock Station, taking some 1,500 prisoners. Lee fell back, crossing the Rapidan on 10 November. On 26 November Meade began to try to turn Lee's right, but the move was slower than it should have

A Texan at Gettysburg is mortally wounded

'About five paces to my left was a large, high rock behind which several of our wounded were sheltering themselves. To the top of that, where the very air was alive with missiles of death [Private Will] Barbee [1st Texas] sprang, and standing there, erect and fearless, began firing – the wounded men below him passing up loaded guns as fast as he emptied them. But no living being could stay unhurt long in such a fire. In a few minutes, Barbee was knocked off the rock by a ball that struck him in the right leg. Climbing instantly back, he again commenced shooting. In less than two minutes, he was tumbled off the rock by a ball in the other leg. Still unsatisfied, he crawled back a second time, but was not there more than a minute before, being wounded in the body, he again fell, this time dropping on his back between the rock that had been his perch, and that which was my shelter. Too seriously wounded this time to extricate himself from the narrow passageway, he called for help, and the last time I saw him that day, he was lying there, crying and cursing because the boys would not come to his relief and help him back on to the rock.'

(J. B. Polley, *Hood's Texas Brigade*, Morningside Bookshop, Dayton, Ohio, 1976, p. 172)

been. Lee had time to dig in along the west bank of the Mine Run. Seeing Lee's strong positions, which were rather like those at Fredericksburg, Meade gave up plans for an assault and retreated to the north bank of the Rapidan and Culpeper on 1–2 December. Both armies went into winter quarters.

1863: Western Theatre

The year began with Bragg's retreat from Murfreesboro on 2 January. In Arkansas, Union Major General John A. McClernand, a political appointee, led a combined Army/Navy expedition against Fort Hindman at Arkansas Post, overlooking a bend of the Arkansas River. The post, which dominated navigation on the Mississippi, fell to McClernand on 11 January.

Grant was not pleased with having troops used to attack Ford Hindman since his main interest lay in capturing Vicksburg. Attempts to capture Fort Pemberton there between 13 March and 5 April failed, as did another attempt to pass through Steele's Bayou on 16–22 March. On 16 April ships under Rear Admiral David D. Porter passed below the city, while Grant's land forces marched overland on the river's west side. He then crossed the Mississippi at Bruinsburg below the city and turned inland. Port Gibson fell to his troops on 1 May, and Grand Gulf and its forts were therefore abandoned on 3 May. On 12 May he captured Raymond, Mississippi, and on 14 May the state capital of Jackson.

J. E. Johnston, overall Confederate commander in the state, ordered Pemberton to march east to strike Grant at Clinton. Pemberton, however, decided that such a move would be too risky and instead chose to attack Grant's reinforcements and supply train on the road between Grand Gulf and Raymond. Learning this, Grant left a corps in Jackson and took two corps to hit Pemberton. On 16 May the two armies met at Champion's Hill where Pemberton was decisively trounced, losing 27 cannon and some 3,850 men. The remainder of his 20,000 men had returned to their fortifications around Vicksburg by 18 May. Grant tried to force his way through Pemberton's lines on 19 May and again on 22 May. Both assaults failed, with the loss of 3,199 men on the 22nd alone. Grant then settled down to starve Pemberton out. The end came on 4 July when Pemberton surrendered the city. Now the western Confederacy was isolated from the eastern Confederacy and the Mississippi River was completely open to Northern commerce. In many respects, however, in terms of commerce, the opening of the river was of more symbolic than actual value since railroads running east and west had greatly reduced the use of the river for shipping purposes.

That same day, as Grant was paroling the Southerners, Johnston finally began to move a 31,000-man army to Pemberton's relief. Sherman moved to oppose him. On 5 July, reinforced by men from Grant's army, Sherman moved against Johnston who retreated towards Jackson. On 10 July Sherman began a siege of Johnston in Jackson. On 16 July Johnston retreated, this time to Morton, and Sherman took the city again. After destroying railroads and public property there, Sherman's troops rejoined the main force under Grant.

Grant next suggested taking his army against Mobile, Alabama, but his suggestion was ignored and his army was broken up into garrisons in Louisiana, Arkansas and Texas.

From 17 April until 2 May cavalry commanded by Colonel Benjamin H. Grierson rode through the south from La Grange, Tennessee, to Baton Rouge, Louisiana, meeting only token resistance and burning bridges and destroying railroads en route. The Confederacy, Grierson later said, was little more than a hollow shell.

The action then turned to Tennessee where on 23 June Rosecrans began a series of manoeuvres that forced Bragg back towards Chattanooga by 7 July with virtually no losses to the Union. On 16 August Rosecrans divided his army, sending his various corps through different passes, heading south into the mountains to try to turn Bragg's flank to the west and come into the city's rear. On 4 September Burnside occupied Knoxville and the Confederate garrison at the Cumberland Gap was captured on the 9th. Abandoning Chattanooga, Bragg again fell back to La Fayette, Georgia. Bragg's plan was to defeat each Union corps separately as it emerged from the mountains.

His first attack was on Thomas's corps on 10 September, an attack that failed due to internal high command bickering at Bragg's headquarters, as did the second attack, this time against the XXI Corps. Rosecrans, realizing his potential problems, ordered his corps to meet at Lee and Gordon's Mills. On 19 September Bragg struck at Chickamauga. A steady series of attacks and counter-attacks followed, until on the morning of the 20th Bragg's men broke through a gap in the Union lines. While Thomas's men held firm, the rest of Rosecran's army fled to Chattanooga in Bragg's greatest victory. However, Bragg's slow pursuit allowed Rosecrans to reach the city, regroup and set up firm defensive lines. Bragg followed and settled down for a long siege.

Confederate cavalry stopped supplies coming into the city. On 16 October Grant was given command of the Military Division of the Mississippi and he relieved Rosecrans and replaced him with Thomas. Reinforced by two Eastern corps under Hooker, the Union forces forced open a supply line, called the 'Cracker Line'. Further reinforcements under Sherman arrived and Grant ordered them all to assault a low line of trenches held by the Confederates on Missionary Ridge, which overlooked the city. Excited by their initial success, but fearful of the guns overlooking them on the higher lines, Thomas's troops took the rise at Orchard Knob in front of the ridge, on 23 November, and on the 24th Hooker's men dashed forward, throwing the Confederates into total confusion and sweeping over the top of Lookout Mountain. Fighting continued on the 25th, but by 26 November Bragg's army was on the road south and would not stop until it reached Dalton, Georgia.

Meanwhile, Longstreet, whose troops had been invaluable at Chickamauga, was missing from Bragg's army. The two men had not seen eye to eye, but he had persuaded Bragg to let him take his men on an attack on Knoxville while Bragg besieged Chattanooga. By 17 November Longstreet had reached the city which was defended by Burnside. On 29 November, in miserable weather, Longstreet attacked but was driven off. Before a second attack could be made, Longstreet received a telegram from Bragg announcing his retreat and ordering Longstreet to come to his support. Longstreet remained where he was until 4 December, however, in the belief that his presence there would draw Union troops away from Bragg. Longstreet finally reached Russellville where he stayed until being ordered to return east to Lee's army in March.

The result of the bad blood between Bragg and his subordinates had cost the Confederacy Tennessee and given the Union forces a jumping-off place for a campaign against the vital rail crossroads of Atlanta, Georgia. On 1 December Bragg resigned his command of the Army of Tennessee and was replaced by J. E. Johnston on 16 December.

On 12 November citizens of Arkansas met at the state capital, Little Rock, to discuss the state's returning to the Union. They wrote a pro-Union constitution and set up their own government. The result was that for the re-

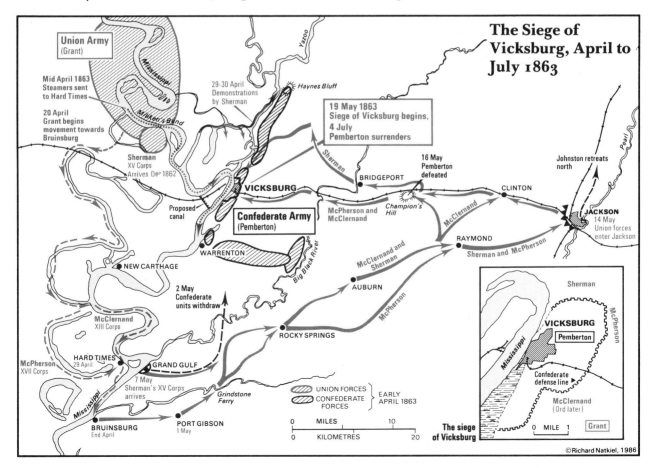

The Siege of Vicksburg, April to July 1863

©Richard Natkiel, 1986

mainder of the war Arkansas had two functioning governments.

1864: Eastern Theatre

In the deep South the new year began with a Union expedition from South Carolina into east Florida on 7 February. The morning of 20 February found Union troops near Olustee, 50 miles south-west of Jacksonville, where some 5,000 Confederates awaited them. The Union troops charged, were beaten back, and the Confederates counterattacked. Retreating Union troops reached Jacksonville on the 23rd; the Confederates failed to pursue actively, and the only major campaign in Florida came to an end.

On 28 February Union cavalry led by Brigadier General Judson Kilpatrick raided towards Richmond. Colonel Ulric Dahlgren, whose father was an admiral in the US Navy, was killed on the raid. Orders said to have been found on his body called for the murder of Jefferson Davis and other Confederate officials. Union officials declared the order counterfeit, pointing out that Dahlgren's name was misspelled in them. Foiled by bad weather as well as Confederate defenders, Kilpatrick returned to his camp on 4 March.

In March Grant, now named lieutenant general and commander of all Union armies, joined the Army of the Potomac, although Meade retained its command. Sheridan took over the Army of the Potomac's cavalry on 4 April.

On 4 May the Army of the Potomac returned to the site of its fighting only a year ago, crossing the Rapidan and moving into the Wilderness. Although Grant believed that he could get through the overgrown area before Lee reacted, Lee got his troops into the Wilderness where Union artillery and cavalry superiority would be offset by heavy underbrush. On 5 May V and VI Corps troops struggled against Hill's and Ewell's corps. On the 6th, the IX Corps for the Union and Longstreet's corps for the Confederacy joined the battle. Smouldering paper cartridges set fire to dry leaves in the dense woods; wounded men burned to death. By 7 May the inconclusive battle had ended with both sides badly battered but unbeaten. Of the 88,892 effectives Meade had brought into the Wilderness, 14,283 were casualties and 3,383 were missing. Of Lee's 61,025 effectives, some 7,750 were dead, wounded or missing.

Previous Army of the Potomac commanders would have withdrawn to rebuild their forces and recuperate, but Grant was made of sterner stuff. On 7 May he sent the Army of the Potomac around Lee's right, to try to get between Lee and Richmond. The Confederates reacted quickly, however, and with a combination of rapid marching and interior lines, reached Spotsylvania Court House and dug in before Union troops could get there. None the less, Grant hurled three corps against the Confederate lines on 10 May, but only broke through at one small point which could not be exploited. On 12 May, using the same tactics that had achieved the minor breakthrough, an entire corps managed another breakthrough, but Lee plugged the gap while building new lines on which to fall back. On 19 May Lee

moved against Grant's right, but failed to dislodge him. Union losses at Spotsylvania reached 6,820, while Lee lost about 9,000 men.

On 23 May Grant returned again to try to shift around Lee's right, and Lee again met him, this time around the North Anna River. Lee had again beaten Grant to his goal and had dug in on both sides of the river. Union troops took Lee's northern side works and actually crossed the river in several places to take works on that side, but reconnaissance showed that Lee's positions were impossible to take and Grant abandoned any idea of attacking.

Instead, on 26 May Grant again headed south, this time sending his cavalry ahead of his infantry to the village of Cold Harbor, site of Peninsula Campaign fighting in 1862. Again Lee anticipated the move, concentrating his men near Cold Harbor. Sheridan's cavalry pushed Southern troopers away from the crossroads at Cold Harbor and dug in on 31 May. Lee sent infantry to retake the position, but superior breech-loading, magazine-fed carbines used by Sheridan's troopers helped hold the infantry at bay.

Union infantry came up, in the wrong places, and made several disjointed attacks which were beaten off. Other infantry were still on the road when Lee managed to get his whole army dug in along a seven-mile front running from Pole Green Church to Grapevine Bridge. On 3 June, however, Grant ordered a general assault. 'This assault cost us heavily and probably without benefit to compensate,' Grant later admitted.[6] Union killed and wounded totalled about 12,000 in the unsuccessful fighting around Cold Harbor, compared to Southern losses of about 1,500.

Grant, however, was never a man to look back. He took his battered army south again, swinging across the James River on 15 June to take the railroad center of Petersburg, twenty miles south of Richmond. This time, Grant's move was undetected and Lee was left behind as two Army of the Potomac corps headed towards works defended by some 2,500 Confederates under Beauregard. Luckily for the South, the Union commanders moved slowly, their attacks unco-ordinated. For three more days Union bumbling allowed Beauregard to defend the city, while Lee finally realized that Grant was no longer in front of his lines. By 17 June Lee's first troops had reached Petersburg's defensive lines, the rest of the army arriving within a couple of days.

Both sides dug in for a siege, although Grant, outnumbering Lee, continued to extend his lines ever farther south and west. His men tried to cut the Weldon Railroad on 22–4 June, and had captured it by 21 August to leave Richmond only the Richmond & Danville Railroad, running across the Appomattox River west, as a lifeline.

On 30 June, following months of digging by a regiment of Pennsylvania coalminers, tons of powder was exploded under the Confederate lines. Unprepared and badly led US Colored Troops dashed into the huge crater left by the explosion, while dazed Confederates wandered about, trying to recover themselves. The Union commander, Major General James H. Ledlie, was drunk in a bunker behind the lines, the attackers failed to advance beyond the

crater, and the alert Confederate command rallied its troops and retook the position. Thousands of black soldiers were massacred by furious Southerners.

Grant attacked Lee's lines again at Peebles Farm on 29–30 September, captured Fort Harrison in the Richmond defence lines on 29 September, at Darbytown Road 7 and 13 October, and at Burgess' Miss or Hatcher's Run on 27 October. By the end of December, however, both sides held essentially the same lines as they had on 1 August.

In 1864 there was fighting elsewhere in the Eastern Theatre. On 5 May Butler's Army of the James landed at Bermuda Hundred, just fifteen miles south of Richmond and seven miles north of Petersburg. Beauregard's small garrison slowed Butler's advance to a crawl, but by 12 May Butler was only five miles from Richmond at Drewry's Bluff. There he stopped until the 16th when Beauregard attacked and scored early successes. Butler then withdrew and dug in. Beauregard followed and, for all practical purposes, Butler's men were out of the war until Butler was relieved and they were merged into the Army of the Potomac before Petersburg.

In May Major General Franz Sigel was sent to clear out the Shenandoah Valley. He was stopped by Virginia Military Institute cadets and other Confederate units at New Market on 15 May, retreated, and was replaced by Major General David Hunter. Hunter was beaten at Trevilian Station on 11 June and retreated into West Virginia. The Valley seemed to be a graveyard for Union generals' reputations.

The man who stopped Hunter was Jubal Early. Now Lee sent him north against Washington in an attempt to draw off troops from Grant's lines at Petersburg. On 6 July Early's 14,000 men crossed the Potomac and reached Frederick, Maryland. Major General Lew Wallace, better known as the author of *Ben Hur*, gathered a small force to meet Early along the Monocacy River on 9 June. Wallace lost, but bought time for the Army of the Potomac's VI Corps to reach Washington. On 11 July Early's men faced the ring of forts that surrounded Washington, manned by a handful of garrison soldiers, Veteran Reserve Corps troops, and government clerks formed into defence battalions. There was minor skirmishing that day at Fort Stevens, witnessed by Abraham Lincoln who became the only president ever to see action while serving as president. A future US Supreme Court Justice, Oliver Wendell Holmes, Jr., shouted to him there that he should get down . . . 'you damned fool'. Before Early could strike, if, indeed he ever actually intended to strike, VI Corps veterans packed the forts' walls. Early fell back, on 14 July recrossing the Potomac and returning to the Valley.

Sergeant Joseph C. LeBleu, Co K, 10th Louisiana Infantry, wears the basic infantry equipment. LeBleu served in the Peninsular Campaign, but then transferred to the 7th Louisiana Cavalry in the Western Theatre. (Michael Dan Jones collection)

Another failed Union attack came at Kernstown and Winchester on 24 July. Confederate cavalry from the Valley again raided north, partially burning Chambersburg, Pennsylvania, when town fathers could not raise $100,000 for ransom.

In early August Sheridan was given command of a 40,000-man-strong Army of the Shenandoah. Early fell back in front of Sheridan's men, digging in on Fisher's Hill. After indecisive skirmishing, the Confederates, reinforced by Lee, moved against Sheridan's left and the Northerners fell back to positions along the Opequon Creek. Finally, on 19 September Sheridan advanced and fought poorly but decisively at the Third Battle of Winchester. Early again fell back to Fisher's Hill which Sheridan attacked on the 22nd. Early was beaten, falling back to the Blue Ridge Mountains. Sheridan's men then burned and destroyed farms and anything of value in the Valley.

On 19 October the Union army was halted at Middletown, near Cedar Creek. Sheridan was on his way to Washington for consultations when Early struck at dawn. The Union troops were routed but Sheridan, learning of the attack, dashed back and on his sweat-covered horse rallied his men. Going on to the attack, by 4 p.m. he had decisively beaten Early. The Valley was at last in Union hands.

Finally, in the North itself, on 19 October some exiled Confederates rode out of Canada into St. Albans, Vermont, to rob the bank. Other Confederate agents attempted to burn down New York City, setting fire to eleven hotels and Barnum's museum. There was some damage, but most of the fires were quickly extinguished.

1864: Western Theatre

Union forces continued nibbling their way into the Confederacy in early 1864. Sherman's men left Jackson and occupied Meridian, Mississippi, on 14 February. A Union cavalry raid towards Meridian was stopped by Forrest at Okolona, Mississippi, on 22 February. And, on the Georgia-Tennessee border, sporadic fighting happened at Buzzard Roost, Rocky Face Ridge, and Tunnel Hill in February.

In March Sherman was given command of the Military Division of the Mississippi, while Major General J. B. McPherson got the Army of the Tennessee; Thomas, the Army of the Cumberland; and Major General John M. Schofield, the Army of the Ohio. On 12 March Banks was sent up the Red River to capture Shreveport, Louisiana, temporary capital of the state's Southern government, capturing Fort De Russy on 14 March.

Bank's land force was united with a naval one under Rear Admiral David D. Porter, who was concerned that falling waters on the river could trap his boats. Moving up the river, Banks was met and defeated by Confederates under General Richard Taylor at Mansfield, 40 miles south of Shreveport. Banks fell back to Pleasant Hill where he defeated a Confederate attack, and then continued his retreat. Porter's boats also retraced their wake, being fired on by Confederates lining the banks as they went. When the boats reached Alexandria, Porter was dismayed to learn

that the rapids were a good four feet too shallow for his larger boats to cross. An Army engineer, however, suggested damming the river, which was done. Eight days later the dam gave way, but the water was still high enough for Porter's boats to cross over the rapids. By the end of May the expedition had ended, a total failure.

That spring, too, Forrest's cavalry raided through Kentucky and Tennessee, capturing Fort Pillow, Tennessee. There hundreds of US Colored Troops were killed by irate slave-owners, many said deliberately after they had surrendered. True or not, it was a propaganda coup for the abolitionists.

When Grant assumed command of the whole Union army, he gave Sherman the job of destroying Johnston's Army of Tennessee, then posted near Dalton, Georgia. Sherman began his campaign south on 7 May, reaching Johnston's positions on 9 May. Keeping Johnston occupied, he sent McPherson west and south to cut the railroad in Johnston's rear. Stubborn rearguard defence, however, allowed Johnston to fall back safely. Sherman followed, meeting Johnston head on at Resaca on 14–15 May. Beaten back, he again sent troops to outflank Johnston. Again, Johnston slipped out of his grasp, reaching Calhoun and Adairsville on 17 May. Then Sherman sent troops around both of Johnston's flanks, and the Southern commander again retreated, this time to Cassville and Kingston.

There, Johnston struck out at the divided Union columns on 19 May. Hood, who was to conduct the main attack, for once failed to act aggressively enough and the Union column was not destroyed. Johnston retreated to the Altoona Pass. Sherman tried to outflank him again, and

---

The difference between the Rebel yell and Union cheer

'The peculiarity of the rebel yell is worthy of mention, but none of the old soldiers who heard it once will ever forget it. Instead of the deep-chested manly cheer of the Union men, the rebel yell was a falsetto yelp which, when heard at a distance, reminded one of a lot of school boys at play. It was a peculiar affair for a battle yell, but though we made fun of it at first, we grew to respect it before the war was over. The yell might sound effeminate, but those who uttered it were not effeminate by any means. When the Union men charged, it was heads erect, shoulders squared and thrown back, and with a firm stride, but when the Johnnies charged, it was with a jog trot in a half-bent position, and although they might be met with heavy and blighting volleys, they came on with the pertinacity of bulldogs, filling up the gaps and trotting on with their never-ceasing "ki-yi" until we found them face to face.'

(Gilbert Adams Hays, *Under the Red Patch*, Sixty-third Pennsylvania Volunteers Regimental Association, Pittsburgh, 1908, pp. 240–1)

Johnston fell back to New Hope Church. There, Thomas struck Johnston's forces on 25 May but was stopped cold. Fighting continued two days later at Pickett's mills and Mount Zion Church. On 4 June Johnston continued his retreat as Sherman tried yet another flanking move to the north-east. Johnston then dug in outside Marietta along the Brush, Lost, and Pine Mountains.

Sherman hit all Johnston's positions during a fortnight of fighting, forcing him to fall back to Kennesaw Mountain. On 27 June Sherman hit Johnston there frontally with some 14,174 men, losing 2,051 in fruitless attacks. Johnston lost only 442 men in all. So Sherman returned to the oft-tried flank movement, forcing Johnston to fall back to Marietta on 2 July. Another flank movement pushed Johnston to the Chattahoochee River, only seven miles from the South's great rail hub of Atlanta on 4 July. Sherman's troops then crossed that river past Johnston's right, and he fell back into lines around the city.

Jefferson Davis, who had been watching all this with growing unease, relieved Johnston, replacing him with the more aggressive Hood on 17 July. Almost immediately Hood went on the attack, hitting Thomas's men along Peachtree Creek on 20 July, where he was badly beaten with losses of some 2,500 compared to some 1,600 Union dead and wounded. Undaunted, he struck McPherson's troops in the Battle of Atlanta on 22 July. McPherson himself was killed in action, together with another 1,988 dead or wounded. But Hood lost some 8,000 men and lost the battle. Sherman then besieged the city and sent first his cavalry and then infantry to cut rail lines, breaking through on the Montgomery & Atlanta Railroad on 28 August. Hood tried a final sortie at Jonesborough on 31 August, but by 1 September admitted the battle, and the city, had been lost and withdrew farther south. Atlanta had fallen; a re-dedicated Northern public re-elected Lincoln two months later to see the war finished.

Sherman stayed in Atlanta ten days, rebuilding and equipping his army before starting on the next phase of his campaign. Hood tried to draw him out of the city by heading into Tennessee but Sherman refused to take the bait, instead leaving Thomas to deal with the reckless Confederate. Instead, on 15 November he began what amounted to a giant infantry raid through the heart of Georgia, cutting his supply lines and living off the land, to its coast. The handful of militia and odd Confederate units could offer little opposition. Georgia's capital, Milledgeville, was destroyed on 22–4 November, and, by 10 December, Sherman's saucy Union boys had reached the coast, outside Savannah. In their wake they left some 100 million dollars worth of damaged and destroyed property.

Savannah was garrisoned by some 10,000 troops under Lieutenant General William Hardee in a line of defences around the city. On 13 December Sherman captured Fort McCallister just south of Savannah. There he was able to get supplies from the US fleet outside the city. Other troops surrounded most of the city. Hardee, fearing being bottled up as Pemberton had been in Vicksburg, used a pontoon bridge across the Savannah River to withdraw his troops into South Carolina on 20 December. Sherman moved into the city on the 21st, offering it to Lincoln as a Christmas present.

In the meantime, Hood continued to head north into Tennessee with Thomas defending at Nashville. Hood hit the Union defenders in a totally unnecessary battle at Franklin on 30 November, after missing a chance the day before at Spring Hill. Hood sent his troops forward again and again, breaking the Union center at one point only to have it close up again. Meanwhile, the Union commander worked on getting bridges built behind him. That night, he withdrew to Thomas's works at Nashville.

Hood, apparently undismayed by the 6,352 casualties he had taken compared to the total losses of 1,326 Union losses, set siege to Nashville. For a fortnight the siege continued, Grant ordering Thomas to attack on 6 December. But Thomas slowly prepared, finally smashing out of the city on 15 December and totally destroying any organized Confederate Army of Tennessee and capturing 4,462 prisoners from the 23,207 Confederates engaged. For ten days victorious Union troops pursued Hood's fleeing men until they reached Tupelo, Mississippi, on 29 December. Hood's force was then broken up, some of his men being sent to Mobile, Alabama, others to the Mississippi, and others going east for the final fight against Sherman.

In Missouri, Confederates under Sterling Price began a raid on 29 August. By September they had reached the outskirts of St. Louis and, by 20 October, Lexington. On 23 October Union forces hit their rear, pushing them southward along the Missouri–Kansas line, in what was essentially a diversion from the main business of the war.

1865: Eastern Theatre

On 15 January Fort Fisher, North Carolina, defending the South's last port, fell to a combined Union Army/Navy force. By March Sheridan had mopped up the last few centers of resistance in the Shenandoah Valley and turned to rejoin the Army of the Potomac at Petersburg.

On 25 March Lee launched his last attack, against Fort Stedman at the extreme right of Grant's Petersburg lines to try to break them before Sheridan arrived. The attack was initially successful but the Confederates failed to exploit their success. A Union counter-attack re-took the fort that evening. Then, on 29 March, Grant sent Sheridan's forces west, through Dinwiddie Court House and north to Five Forks just south of the Southside Railroad. Almost a third of Lee's army, under Major General George Pickett, were at Five Forks. On 1 April Sheridan struck. Pickett was away at a shad bake when his forces were overwhelmed, losing some 5,200 men, four cannon, and eleven colours.

The Confederate right turned, Grant ordered a general assault on the Petersburg lines on 2 April. Lee simply didn't have enough men to hold the line. He fell back, planning to use the Richmond & Danville Railroad to travel south to join the forces of J. E. Johnston opposing Sherman in the

Carolinas, destroy Sherman with their combined forces, and then destroy Grant.

On Sunday, 2 April, when Davis was in St. Paul's Church at a morning service, he received word that Petersburg, and therefore Richmond, would be abandoned. He quickly began to oversee the loading of the trains that would take him, his family and government officials south with government documents and $500,000 in gold and silver. The burning of government supplies spread fire to much of the city, leaving little more than exposed brick walls. On 4 April Abraham Lincoln walked the streets of Richmond and sat in Jefferson Davis's chair in what had been the Confederate Executive Mansion.

The Army of Northern Virginia fled west to Amelia Court House where rations were said to be waiting. They were not, and Lee's men had to waste a day foraging while Grant's troops hurried behind them. On 6 April the Union forces caught up with the Confederate corps commanded by Richard Ewell and Richard Anderson. The Confederates fought well at first, even launching a counter-attack, but superior Union artillery tore through their ranks and infantry surrounded them. By the day's end, some 8,000 Confederates had surrendered, the largest number of prisoners ever taken at a land battle in North America.

Another delaying action was fought on 7 April at Farmville, but the Army of Northern Virginia was running out of steam. Sheridan's cavalry passed them by, cutting off their escape at Appomattox Court House. On 7 April Grant sent a message to Lee suggesting the 'hopelessness of further resistance on the part of the Army of Northern Virginia in the struggle'.[7] Lee replied that he did not think it was hopeless but asked for Grant's terms. 'Lee's army was rapidly crumbling,' Grant recalled. During the march Grant stayed at a hotel where he found ' . . . a Confederate colonel there, who reported to me and said that he was the proprietor of that house, and that he was a colonel of a regiment that had been raised in that neighbourhood. He said that when he came along past home, he found that he was the only man of the regiment remaining with Lee's army, so he just dropped out . . . '[8]

On the 8th Grant wrote to Lee, saying that he would only disqualify soldiers of the Army of Northern Virginia from taking up arms against the US again. On the morning of the 9th, Palm Sunday, when Lee's army mustered some 8,000 effectives against Grant's more than 110,000, Lee's men probed Union lines and found them too strong to break through. Lee then met Grant and surrendered his army at Appomattox Court House. On 12 April the Army of Northern Virginia stacked arms for the last time. And, on 15 April, John Wilkes Booth shot Abraham Lincoln.

1865: Western Theatre

With Sherman's men in Savannah, on the Atlantic Coast, and elements of what had been Hood's Army of Tennessee in the Carolinas, much of the so-called Western Theatre at the end of the war was actually in the east.

Sherman's plan was to march due north, destroying Southern property as he went, to join with Grant in fighting the Army of Northern Virginia. On 1 February, after foul weather in January ended, he began his march. Only a handful of Confederates under Beauregard and Hardee stood between the two giant Union armies. Moving inland, Sherman's troops cut off Charlestown, where the war had begun four years before, and took that city. Columbia, the capital of South Carolina, fell on 17 February and was virtually burned to the ground, some people saying that the damage was done by Sherman's men and others saying it was by retreating Confederates.

The Confederates, now led by a reappointed J. E. Johnston, grouped at Cheraw, then fell back to Fayetteville, North Carolina, before Sherman reached Cheraw on 3 March. Sherman occupied Fayetteville on 11 March, as the Confederates again fell back. Then, after five days spent in resting and re-equipping, Sherman headed north to meet up with troops coming west from the just-captured city of Wilmington, North Carolina.

To prevent this, Johnston struck one column at Bentonville, North Carolina, on 19 March. Although the Union left was pushed back, the Union troops still managed to dig in on the 20th and hold off Johnston's men until Sherman reached them. Sherman had taken losses of some 1,500 men, but Johnston had lost 2,600 casualties that he couldn't afford. After brief fighting on the 21st, he fell back north in the hope of uniting with Lee's army. On the way, however, he learned of Lee's surrender. On 17 April the two generals met to discuss Johnston's surrender. Originally, Sherman's terms included items covering civil policy, so Johnston's surrender under these terms were rejected by the US Government. On 26 April, therefore, the two generals met again, agreed to basically the same terms as Lee had accepted, and on 3 May the Army of Tennessee stacked its arms for the last time.

Meanwhile, on 25 March Mobile, Alabama, whose harbour was already under US Navy control, came under siege by land. Fort after fort fell to the Unionists as shells poured into the city. On 12 April the last Confederate defender surrendered and the US flag floated over the city. Learning that, and of Johnston's surrender, General Richard Taylor met with Major General E. R. S. Canby at Citronelle, Alabama, to surrender the Confederate Department of Alabama, Mississippi, and East Louisiana, some 12,000 men strong. On 4 May Taylor surrendered his command.

Other Confederate commands surrendered were those of the Department of Missouri and Arkansas, at Chalk Bluff, Arkansas on 11 May, and in Florida on 17 May.

1861–5: Far Western Theatre

In early 1861 the US Army's Major General David E. Twiggs, a native of Georgia, asked for but did not receive a decision from the War Department as to what to do about his troops in Texas should that state ask for their surrender. On 18 February, therefore, he surrendered everything

> ## A Union captain stops firing on a wounded man
>
> 'A rebel soldier was seen approaching with a limping gait, and using his musket as a support. Sergeant Dunn raised his musket, saying, "I'll drop that fellow," but before he could fire, his piece was struck down by Captain Rickards, who exclaimed, "You wouldn't shoot a wounded man!" At that instant the advancing rebel levelled his gun and shot Captain Rickards, who died a few minutes afterwards. The dastard rebel fell in his tracks, riddled with bullets.'
>
> (William P. Seville, *History of the First Regiment, Delaware Volunteers*, Wilmington, 1884, Longstreet House, Baltimore, 1986, p. 49)

owned by the Federal government within his command jurisdiction, including funds and forts, to a group of Texas volunteers led by Ben McClulloch.

For this on 1 March Twiggs was dismissed from the US Army, in which he had served since 1812 when he had been commissioned a captain. On 22 May he was commissioned a Confederate major general and given command of the District of Louisiana, but, suffering from the ailments of old age, he died in Augusta, Georgia, on 15 July 1862.

The Confederates established the Department of Texas and authorized Lieutenant Colonel John R. Baylor to raise the 2nd Texas Mounted Rifles which he then led from San Antonio into New Mexico, occupying Fort Bliss there by early July 1861. On the way, he left troops to garrison Forts Clark and Davis. From Fort Bliss Baylor headed towards Fort Fillmore, which was garrisoned by some 700 men of the 7th US Infantry Regiment. The fort's commander, Major Isaac Lynde, moved out of the fort to intercept and beat Baylor's 200-odd men at Mesilla. Lynde's attack there on 25 July was easily beaten off with Union losses of three dead and six wounded. The US troops abandoned the fort and fled, but Baylor's men caught up with and captured some of them the next day and the rest on the 27th. Union troops then evacuated Fort Buchanan.

Having cleared out all the Union troops in the area. Baylor returned to Mesilla. There on 1 August he proclaimed all the land south of the 34th Parallel to be the Confederate Territory of Arizona, with himself the new territorial governor. He then planned to assemble all the Apache Indians in his territory under the pretence of signing a treaty and then massacre them. This plan brought the wrath of the Confederate government on him and led to his dismissal. Baylor then went to Richmond as a congressman from Texas, offering another plan to invade New Mexico during the war's later years. By that time, however, the Confederacy had neither the time nor the resources for any far west diversions.

A corporal of the 106th Pennsylvania Infantry, part of the Philadelphia Brigade which held the center of the Union line at Pickett's Charge at Gettysburg. (Author's collection)

In December 1861, however, things were different. Newly commissioned Confederate Brigade General Henry H. Sibley arrived that month at Mesilla with some 3,700 Texans in his Army of New Mexico with a plan to drive west to the Pacific Ocean, capturing the gold in California, as well as adding pro-Southern recruits to the Confederate Army. In November 1861 there had even been a small skirmish between pro-Southerners and pro-Union men near Los Angeles, California. Opposing Sibley was Colonel E. R. S. Canby with 3,810 men in garrisons at Forts Craig, on the Rio Grande, and Union. Sibley left Mesilla in the first week of January 1862, reaching the abandoned Fort Thorn and heading out of there for Fort Craig on 7 February, marching along the western side of the river. Just before reaching the fort, Sibley swung his troops across the river and headed north towards Santa Fe with the idea of bypassing Canby's troops. Union troops struck Sibley's camp on the eastern side of the river on the evening of the 20th but were driven off. Canby then marched his men to Valverde to block Sibley's attempt to recross the river to the north. On 21 February the two forces met there, the Confederate charges breaking many of Canby's untrained Colorado and New Mexico volunteer units. Canby fell back to Fort Craig, while Sibley went on to Albuquerque, New Mexico, and then to Santa Fe.

Sibley had expected to capture Union supplies at Albuquerque, but they had been destroyed as other Union forces now concentrated at Fort Union. Reinforcements of newly raised Colorado and New Mexico volunteer infantry regiments from that fort attacked Sibley at Johnson's Ranch in Apache Canon, some 15 miles from Santa Fe, on both 26 and 28 March. The battle, also known as La Glorieta Pass, was indecisive, but losses, especially of his supply train which Union troops destroyed, hurt Sibley's command more than they did Union forces.

On 1 April Canby moved out of Fort Craig towards Albuquerque in an attempt to join forces from Fort Union. Sibley, low on supplies and unable to purchase any because the locals would not accept Confederate currency, evacuated Albuquerque on 12 April. Canby followed the Confederates back towards Texas, not wishing to capture them because he would be unable to feed them. Sibley's retreat through desert and thick brush and over mountains was murderous on his troops, who buried their cannon on route. In early May Sibley's command reached Fort Bliss where he learned that a column of Union troops from California was headed his way. He then began a further retreat, not stopping until his some 2,000 survivors reached San Antonio, Texas.

The California Column which Sibley feared consisted of the two California infantry regiments, one light battery, and six cavalry companies and had been authorized in July 1861 to guard the overland mail route through Utah and Nevada. It started from California in early April, reaching Fort Yuma, Arizona, on 2 May. On 20 May, Californians reached Tucson, Arizona, which had just been evacuated by Confederates. On 8 June the Column's commander, Colonel

James Carleton, proclaimed himself governor of the Union Territory of Arizona. After a month's rest, Carleton's men moved out, retaking Forts Bliss, Davis, Thorn, and Quitman by late August. On 20 September Carleton, now a brigadier general, reached Santa Fe, the headquarters for his newly created Department of New Mexico. His troops were among the last mustered out of the Union Army, not being demobilized until late 1866.

The Southwest was now completely in Union hands. Another California infantry regiment was sent, under Colonel P. Edward Conner, to garrison Salt Lake City, Utah, where the Mormon Church was headquartered. The loyalty of the Mormons was doubtful at the time, there having almost been a war between church members and the Federal government only several years before. Besides guaranteeing Mormon loyalty, Conner's major contribution to the war effort was a massacre of Shoshoni Indians at the Bear River, Idaho on 29 January 1863. Peaceful Arapaho and Cheyenne Indians were also massacred by Colorado cavalrymen under Colonel John M. Chivington at Sand Creek, Colorado, on 29 November 1864. And, in the summer of 1862, Santee Sioux Indians, under Little Crow, in Minnesota went on the war path, killing some 800 whites. Survivors fled to Fort Ridgely, where Little Crow unsuccessfully attacked on 20 and 22 August. Minnesota state militia Brigadier General Henry H. Sibley, no relation to the Confederate general, was given the job of subduing the

---

Union troops share their rations with Confederates

'The order forbidding men to pass beyond the lines [at Appomattox] did not include a prohibition to come within them, and soon the bivouac swarmed with the rebs, disposed on friendly converse, and suppliants for a stay of the famishing hunger that for days had been gnawing at their very vitals.

'The nibbling, mincing diet of the past few days had pinched the Union soldiers too. But a soldier kinship is a fellowship, liberal, self-denying, stintless in generosity, boundless in sympathy. Impressed with the same spirit of liberality as their great commander [Grant], when he ordered the issue of 25,000 rations to Lee's enhungered troops, the soldiers of Barlett's division shared their provender with their whilom foemen until every haversack was empty. The sweet aroma of real coffee staggered the Confederates, condensed milk and sugar appalled them, and they stood aghast at just a little butter which one soldier, more provident than his fellows, happened to have preserved. A Johnny looked at the bit of butter for a moment, as if trying to remember where and when he had been acquainted with its like before, and then asked in astonishment: "Do they give you rations like that?"'

(Survivor's Association, *History of the Corn Exchange Regiment*, J. L. Smith, Philadelphia, Pennsylvania, 1888, pp. 592–3)

Sioux and bringing their leaders in for hanging. He assembled some 1,400 volunteers and attacked Little Crow at the Battle of Wood Lake on 23 September 1862. The Sioux were defeated, many fleeing to the Dakotas. Of those captured, 307 were sentenced to be hanged. Lincoln pardoned most of them, but 38 were hanged and the Sioux went back on the war path a year later although not in the same numbers or as successfully as the 1862 uprising.

Colonel Christopher (Kit) Carson, 1st New Mexico Infantry, spent most of the war fighting Apaches and Navahos. In late 1862 he captured some 400 Mescalero Apaches, and in January 1864 he captured some 200 Navajos in Canyon de Chilly. November 1864 found him and his men, although outnumbered attacking a large group of Comanches at Adobe Wells, Texas, but on this occasion was forced to withdraw after a day's fighting in this, his last battle of the Civil War.

Throughout the period, too, Indians fought whites in Texas and pro-Southern Indians fought pro-Union Indians in Oklahoma, then called the Indian Territory.

Little fighting took place in Texas. On 4 October 1862 Union troops occupied Galveston, after Confederates had withdrawn. But the Confederates returned on 1 January 1863, capturing the small garrison and burning the US Revenue Cutter *Harriet Lane*. On 8 September 1863 Major General N. P. Banks began an invasion of the state with an attack on Fort Griffin, near the mouth of the Sabine River at Sabine Pass. The fort's 43 defenders held out, smashing the Union boats and taking some 400 prisoners. Finally, on 12 May 1865 a force of some 800 Union soldiers, blacks and whites, under Colonel Theodore H. Barrett, against orders, attacked some 350 Texans near the South's last town in communication with the outside world, Brownsville. The Texans, led by former Texas Ranger J. S. 'Rest In Peace' Ford, broke up the Union attack with their artillery, then dispersed them with a cavalry charge. Some 30 Union soldiers died in this last, pointless, battle of the Civil War.

On 26 May 1865 Lieutenant General Richard Taylor surrendered all the Confederate units west of the Mississippi in the name of his superior, Lieutenant General E. Kirby Smith. Smith at that time was on his way to Houston to prepare plans to rally Southerners to continue the fight. Accepting defeat, however, Smith then fled to Mexico with some 2,000 of his compatriots.

Confederate Indians in the Indian Territory, led by Brigadier General Stand Watie, surrendered to Federal authorities on 23 June 1865.

1861–5: The High Seas

The Confederacy entered the Civil War with no navy or even much of a sea-faring tradition. It faced an enemy with a well-established navy and a large reserve of sailors and shipbuilders on which to draw.

Stephen R. Mallory from Florida, who before the war had chaired the US Senate's naval affairs committee, was named the Confederate Secretary of the Navy. It was a good choice, since Mallory had a good grasp of what was needed and

what was possible, and was open to radical concepts that possibly could keep Southern ports and sea lanes open.

One part of his strategy was to destroy Northern commerce by preying on Northern ships. An immediate way of doing this was by the granting of letters of marque, permitting private ship-owners to capture Northern ships for profit. On 6 May 1861 the Confederate Congress assented, the first letter of marque being issue on 10 May. Some 24 ships, mostly based in Charleston, South Carolina, and New Orleans, Louisiana, eventually received letters of marque in early 1861.

Privateering was banned by the 1856 Declaration of Paris, of which the US was not a signatory. None the less, the US government claimed to support the Declaration, proclaiming that Southern privateers were nothing more than pirates and would be treated as such. The government's announcement came to the test when the privateer *Savannah* from Charleston was captured by the USS *Perry* on 3 June. Her crew was sent to New York to be tried for piracy. The Confederate government then set aside an equal number of Union prisoners and said they would receive the same treatment as the Southern privateers. All piracy charges were dropped when the jury failed to reach a verdict. No other Southern privateers faced these legal battles.

In the meantime, on 1 June the British government announced that its ports would henceforth be closed to prizes brought in by ships of either of the belligerents, and other European powers promptly followed with similar pronouncements. This left Southern ports as virtually the only ports where Southern privateers could dispose of their prizes for profit. With the fall of New Orleans in April 1862 and the tightening of the blockade around Charleston, Southern privateers largely quit the business.

Even so, they had been unexpectedly successful. Many Northern shipowners, fearing the loss of their vessels, quickly sold their ships to foreign neutrals. Rapidly rising maritime insurance rates put other shipowners out of business. Seeing this, Mallory decided to commission a number of deep water cruisers to seek out and destroy the Northern merchant fleet.

The first of the Southern cruisers was the CSS *Sumter* which began life as the passenger steamer *Habana*. The ship's captain, Commander Raphael Semmes, took her into the Gulf of Mexico at the end of June and had begun taking prizes by the first week of July 1861. He took six of these prizes into Cienfuengos, Cuba, where the government, after some consideration, released the prizes to their crews because of the Spanish neutrality declaration. Semmes, whose ship's coal bunkerage was adequate for only eight days' steaming, then headed for Curaçao, where his attempts to get supplies, though delayed by US State Department legal tactics, were eventually successful. Then he was off to Brazil, coaling at Surinam and Trinidad on the way.

Captain David D. Porter, commanding the USS *Powhatan*, a 3,765-ton steamer with nine guns, gave chase, having earlier intercepted one of Semmes's prizes bound for New Orleans with dispatches for Mallory. Semmes evaded Porter, capturing ships in the South Atlantic until arriving in Cadiz, Spain, on 4 January 1862. He was refused time to repair his fouled boilers there and went on to Gibraltar. Blockaded there by a small Union squadron and unable to purchase coal, he paid off his crew and returned to the South. In the course of her operations *Sumter* had captured eighteen ships.

Semmes was then given command of the most famous Confederate cruiser, the 1,050-ton CSS *Alabama*. The British-built ship was armed with six 32-pounder, one 110-pounder and one 68-pounder cannon and was commissioned on 24 August 1862. Semmes took his largely foreign crew, with Southern officers, into the North Atlantic after commissioning, where he captured and sank more than twenty ships. He then headed for the West Indies where, off Galveston, Texas, he met and successfully engaged the USS *Hatteras*, a 1,126-ton iron-hulled, three-masted steamer armed with one 20-pounder rifled gun and four 32-pounders. Semmes then made for the South Atlantic, and on to Capetown, South Africa, and then through the Indian Ocean. During her 75,000-mile passage she took some 64 prizes, most of which she burned after removing any useful cargo. Then, her bottom foul, her engines weary, Semmes put in to Cherbourg, France on 11 June 1864, where soon Union warships followed her. Semmes then challenged the USS *Kearsage*, a 1,550-ton sloop armed with two 11-inch and four 9-inch smoothbores and two 20-pounder rifled Rodman guns. On 19 June, after an engagement watched by thousands from the shoreline, *Kearsage* sank the *Alabama*.

The CSS *Florida* was commissioned on 17 August 1862 at Green Cay, Bahamas, under the command of Lieutenant J. N. Maffitt. She broke the US blockade twice, once on going into Mobile, Alabama on 4 September 1862, and on leaving that port on 16 January 1863. She spent that year in the North Atlantic, except for a period from August 1863 to February 1864 when she was laid up for repairs in Brest, France. There, because of illness, Maffitt was replaced, by Lieutenant C. M. Morris. During the ship's cruises, she captured 24 ships under Moffitt and eleven under Morris. On 4 October 1864 she entered Bahia, Brazil, where the USS *Wachusett*, commanded by Commander Napoleon Collins, was also lying. Disregarding Brazilian neutrality and against international law, Collins rammed the *Florida* and captured her during the night of 6 October, and towed her to Hampton Roads, Virginia. There the US Government acknowledged Collins's error and promised to return her to Bahia, but before that could happen, on 28 November 1864 under mysterious circumstances, she was again rammed and this time sunk by an army transport.

Other Confederate cruisers had even less success. The CSS *Georgia*, a 690-ton iron-hulled brig, was commissioned on 9 April 1863, under the command of Lieutenant W. L. Maury. Her two 100-pounder rifled gun, two 24-pounder smoothbores, and one 32-pounder smoothbore were installed at sea and she then cruised in the Atlantic, capturing

The CSS Rappahannock, *sketched in Calais, France. Although the* Rappahannock *did not see service, she was a typical Confederate commerce raider. (*Harper's Weekly*)*

nine prizes. On 28 October 1863 she put into Cherbourg with a badly fouled bottom and was thereafter decommissioned and sold. On the way to be sold, off Morocco, a shore party was attacked by Moors and the ship's guns joined in fighting them off in the Confederacy's only foreign war.

The CSS *Nashville* was a 1,221-ton brig-rigged passenger steamer armed with two 12-pounder guns. Commissioned in October 1861, she patrolled off the coast of Britain from November 1861 to February 1862, capturing two prizes. She returned to Beauford, North Carolina, only to leave again on 17 March 1862 to be sold as a blockade-runner. On 5 November 1862 she became a privateer and was sunk by the USS *Montauk* on 28 February 1863.

The CSS *Tallahassee*, previously the *Atlanta* and later the *Olustee*, was commissioned in July 1864. This 546-ton ship was armed with one 84-pounder, two 32-pounders, and two 24-pounders. She captured 40 prizes in the North Atlantic. Unable to break the blockade and return to a Southern port, she was sailed to Liverpool where she was sold in April 1865.

The CSS *Shenandoah*, commanded by Lieutenant J. L. Waddell, was a 1,160-ton composite auxiliary screw steamship, the first of its type in the world. Armed with four 8-inch and two 12-pounder smoothbores and two 32-pounder rifled guns, she was commissioned on 19 October 1864. She first cruised in the South Atlantic, then passed the tip of South America into the Pacific and arrived at Melbourne, Australia. There, far short of the full ship's complement, Waddell recruited some Australians which got him into trouble with the local authorities. Finally getting back to sea in February 1865, she captured many prizes in the Bering Straits, mainly from the whaling fleets. Learning from newspapers on one of them in August 1865 that the war had ended, Waddell then set sail for Liverpool, arriving there 6 November 1865 and striking the Confederate colours for the last time. *Shenandoah* had taken 38 prizes.

The CSS *Chickamauga*, a 585-ton former blockade-runner, armed with one 84-pounder, two 32-pounder, and two 24-pounder guns, was purchased in Wilmington, North Carolina, in late 1864 and cruised the North Atlantic for three weeks in October and November, taking seven prizes.

Losing many of the crew to desertion in Bermuda, where the ship was able to obtain only a small amount of coal, Captain James Wilkinson came back to Wilmington. She was burned to prevent her capture in Fayetteville, North Carolina on 25 February 1865.

The Confederate government also commissioned a number of cruisers that did not see action because they were seized by foreign governments for violating neutrality.

Despite the small number of ships commissioned and given letters of marque, the Confederate Navy's high seas campaign had mixed results. On the plus side, hundreds of US Navy ships that could have seen blockading duty were sent in largely fruitless searches for the Confederate cruisers. However, neither the Confederate cruisers nor the privateers did any serious damage to American exports and imports. Only some five per cent of the Northern merchant marine had been destroyed. Still, fears of being captured and rising insurance rates caused about half the North's ships to be reflagged to prevent capture. The US Merchant Marine, which had been one of the world's largest, never fully recovered its place in world shipping.

*Mobile Bay. The Confederate squadron is seen in the distance; the Union squadron is deployed along the bottom. (*Harper's Weekly*)*

1861–5: The Blockade

The US Navy, led by Secretary of the Navy Gideon Welles from Connecticut and Assistant Navy Secretary Gustavus V. Fox from Massachusetts, had one major goal – to prevent commerce from entering or leaving Southern ports. While the South had more than 3,000 miles of coast line with hundreds of inlets and small port towns, there were really only ten port cities that had deep enough harbours and rail connections leading into the interior to be commercially useful. They were New Orleans, Louisiana; Mobile, Alabama; Pensacola, Florida; Fernandina, Florida; Savannah, Georgia; Charleston, South Carolina; Wilmington, North Carolina; New Bern, North Carolina; and Norfolk, Virginia. On 19 April 1861 the US Government declared the ports from South Carolina to Texas blockaded. On 27 April the remaining Southern ports were officially blockaded.

At the war's outset, however, even these ports were more than the US Navy could effectively blockade. The Navy had some 90 ships on its list, but only three were immediately available. Others were in foreign ports, from which it would take many weeks to return home, while others were being built or repaired. Many of its ships, like the USS *Constitution*, indeed many of its officers such as the first lieutenant of the USS *Hartford* who had been in the Navy for 34 years, were obsolete, last seeing fighting service in the War of 1812. Furthermore, 322 officers resigned to join the Southern cause. There were only 207 enlisted ratings available on the Atlantic Coast.

The Navy was further hurt when, on 20 April, an unprepared Norfolk, Virginia, Navy Yard had to be burned to prevent its falling into Confederate hands. The ships lost in this débâcle included four line of battle ships, three frigates, one steam frigate, two sloops and a brig. As it turned out, the Confederates were able to salvage some 1,200 cannon, including 300 modern Dahlgren cannon, as well as the intact hull and machinery of the steam frigate USS *Merrimack*.

The Navy had some luck in that a small Army garrison at Fort Pickens, outside Pensacola, Florida, refused to surrender at the war's outset and denied the Southerners use of that port. After a failed siege, the Confederates abandoned their nearby posts on 9 May 1862, and the port became headquarters for the US Navy's West Gulf Squadron.

Welles immediately launched an aggressive programme to buy and convert merchant ships, build new warships, and recruit new volunteer officers and men. He had old, useless officers retired and replaced them with younger, energetic ones, and he sent off ships to start the blockade. Formal blockading declarations were issued by ships outside most Southern ports in May, but the blockade was not established outside Wilmington until July.

It was obvious that the best way to stop commerce at any port was not by a line of ships at sea, which could, after all, be evaded on dark nights, but actually to take the ports. This would require joint Army/Navy forces and the first of these was launched against North Carolina's Hatteras Inlet. On 27 August a squadron of two steam frigates, two sloops, a gunboat, and two transports, led by Flag Officer Silas Stringham, bombarded Forts Hatteras and Clark into surrender. Troops led by Major General Benjamin Butler then occupied the posts and closed that inlet.

On 7 November 1861 a similar force, commanded by Flag Officer Samuel F. Du Pont, using similar tactics, took Port Royal, located halfway between Charleston and Savannah, for use as a blockading fleet supply depot. Roanoke Island, North Carolina fell to Navy forces under Flag Officer Louis M. Goldsborough and Army forces under Major General Ambrose Burnside. The same pair went on to take New Bern on 14 March 1862. Fernandina, St. Augustine and Jacksonville, Florida, were taken in March and Fort Pulaski, which defended the approach to Savannah, was battered into submission on 11 April 1862. The only Southern ports left on the Atlantic coast were Charleston, Wilmington, and Norfolk.

These the Confederates vowed to defend to the end. To do so they not only built elaborate land-based forts around them, but the Confederate Navy began to build a unique class of vessel – ironclads – to smash the US Navy's wooden walls. These were angular and unattractive, but capable of being built by ordinary carpenters and mechanics rather than skilled naval craftsmen which the South lacked. The first was the CSS *Virginia*, which was built at Norfolk around the hull and faulty machinery of the USS *Merrimack*. She had sloping armored sides pierced for her ten guns and a four-foot ram built on her bow. A single funnel rose from her roof.

Hearing of this, Welles commissioned several ironclad ships for the US Navy, one of which was an odd design by a Swedish inventor, John Ericsson. The USS *Monitor*, as she was named, consisted of a revolving turret pierced for two 11-inch smoothbore guns, with a small pilot house with eye-slits near the bow, and the rest of the ship save her deck and funnels, virtually below the waterline.

The *Virginia* was commissioned in March 1862, only a few days after the *Monitor*, but was able to get among the blockading fleet at Hampton Roads on 8 March 1862 where she sank the USSS *Cumberland* and *Congress*. The next day she returned to destroy the rest of the fleet and open the port legally, only to meet the *Monitor* which had rushed from New York to meet her. The two-hour battle that followed saw the *Monitor* being hit 22 times and the *Virginia*, twenty times. Neither could do significant damage. The Confederate ship tried to ram *Monitor*, but failed, opening a gash in her own bow. Finally, the Southern crew admitted defeat and returned to port, never to fight again. But naval warfare would never be the same again, as the US Navy went on to build a fleet of Monitor-type vessels for coast-line and river duty.

The *Virginia*, with a deep draft which prevented her from being brought up the James River to Richmond, was burned on 11 May 1862 to prevent her capture by Union troops beginning the Peninsular Campaign. But her basic design was so simple, yet sound, that it was used on the CSS *Atlanta*, which was built on a blockade-runner's hull in Savannah where she served until captured by the monitors *Nahant* and *Weehawken* on 17 June 1863. It was used on the CSS *Albemarle*, which was destroyed on 28 October 1864 in a daring raid in the Roanoke River, North Carolina, and by the CSSS *Chicora*, *Columbia*, *Charleston*, and *Palmetto State* in Charleston; the *Raleigh* in Wilmington; the *Richmond*, *Fredericksburg*, and *Virginia II* in Richmond; the *Savannah* in Savannah; the *Tennessee* and *Huntsville* in Mobile; the *Arkansas* in Vicksburg; and *Manassas* and *Louisiana* in New Orleans.

The *Monitor*'s captain is wounded in action

'Soon after noon a shell from the enemy's gun, the muzzle not ten yards distant, struck the forward side of the pilot-house directly in the sight-hole, or slit, and exploded, cracking the second iron log and partly lifting the top, leaving an opening. [Lieutenant J. L.] Worden [ship's captain] was standing immediately behind this spot, and received in his face the force of the blow, which partly stunned him, and, filling his eyes with powder, utterly blinded him. The injury was known only to those in the pilot-house and its immediate vicinity. The flood of light rushing through the top of the pilot-house, now partly open, caused Worden, blind as he was, to believe that the pilot-house was seriously injured, if not destroyed; he therefore gave orders to put the helm to starboard and "sheet off". Thus the *Monitor* retired temporarily from the action, in order to ascertain the extent of the injuries she had received. At the same time Worden sent for me, and leaving [Chief Engineer A. C.] Stimers the only officer in the turret, I went forward at once, and found him standing at the foot of the ladder leading to the pilot house.

'He was a ghastly sight, with his eyes closed and the blood apparently rushing from every pore in the upper part of his face. He told me that he was seriously wounded, and directly me to take command. I assisted in leading him to a sofa in his cabin, where he was tenderly cared for by Doctor [D. C.] Logue, and then I assumed command.'

(S. Dana Greene, 'In the "Monitor" Turret', *Battles & Leaders of the Civil War*, Thomas Yoseloff, New York, 1956, Vol. I, pp. 267–72)

The *Manassas* saw action on the Mississippi River on 12 October 1861, ramming the USS *Richmond*, but damaging herself in the attempt. But her big action came against Flag Officer David G. Farragut who led a fleet of four steam sloops, an old steam frigate, three corvettes and fifteen gunboats past Forts Jackson and St. Philip and the tied-up, incomplete *Louisiana* on 24 April 1862 and accepted the surrender of the city of New Orleans on 25 April 1862.

On 31 January 1863 the Confederate fleet at Charleston attacked the blockaders, driving off two of their ships and leading the city's commander, General P. G. T. Beauregard, to announce that the blockade had been lifted. The British consul there said that he had been five miles out to sea and had seen no blockading vessels. If true, under international law, the blockade could not have been restored until new official notices had been posted, which would leave a window of opportunity for legal commerce. However, from logbooks, it is clear that the USS *Housatonic* was on the scene and had, indeed, even fired on the retiring Confederate ironclads as she came up. The blockade went on.

Even with the loss of many vital ports and the growing efficiency of an ever-larger US blockading fleet, merchandise was still reaching the South, and cotton was getting to European ports. They were being carried by a new breed of ship and sailor, blockade-runners. These were specially designed ships, built long and low and burning smokeless coal, usually with dark-gray painted steel hulls and side paddles, and holds that could carry an astonishing amount of merchandise. Most were privately owned, although the Confederate and various Southern state governments also owned their own blockade-runners. Originally, they went directly from England and France to the Confederacy and back, but later it was found more profitable for them to be based in ports such as Bermuda and Nassau, which became boomtowns, while ordinary merchant ships carried their cargoes between European and the islands. According to statistics compiled by S. C. Hawley, the US Consul in Nassau, in June 1863 the average blockade-runner made only four and a half successful trips. Of the 64-odd blockade-runners, only 40 were captured or destroyed, and it was estimated that in early 1862 two-thirds of the blockade-runners that tried to, did get into Wilmington safely. One successful trip could bring a ship's owner some £30,000 profit and two trips could pay for a ship, merchandise and crew.

For all that, the blockade played a major role in bringing down the South and winning the war for the Union.

Charleston's forts held out against attacking fleets until Sherman's troops bypassed the city and brought about her surrender on 15 February 1865. The Confederate fleet at Mobile Bay was defeated on 5 August 1864 which effectively closed that port. And the last Southern port, Wilmington, was closed with the fall of Fort Fisher on 15 January 1865.

1861–5: The River War

The Confederate Navy not only had to defend its coastline, but had to stop Union forces from driving deep into its territory through Southern rivers, especially the Mississippi. Initially, both sides' land forces were put in charge of river warfare. The Union Army authorized the building of seven ironclad ships designed by riverman James B. Eads near St. Louis, Missouri. The ships had rectangular casemates with sloped armored sides pierced for cannon, and a paddle wheel amidships near the stern. In September 1861 US Navy Captain Andrew H. Foote was given overall command of these ships, together with a staff of naval officers to command, although many of the crews came from the Union Army. The squadron of ships, which were built in three months and commissioned in January 1862, was based at Cairo, Illinois. Other locally built ironclads were added to the Mississippi River Fleet. These included the *Chillicothe*, commissioned 5 September 1862; the *Indianola*, commissioned 14 January 1863; and the *Tuscumbia*, commissioned 12 March 1863. Other riverboats were acquired and converted to warships.

Foote led his small fleet on to take Fort Henry, Tennessee, and to help in the taking of Fort Donelson, Tennessee. Foote was wounded at the latter action and was replaced by Captain Charles H. Davis, although not before capturing Island No. 10 and New Madrid. Two ships, *Tyler* and *Lexington*, bombarded Confederates and helped hold Grant's left flank at Shiloh.

The hard-pressed Confederate Navy, seeing Union successes, built their own fleet in the Western rivers. An ironclad similar in design to the *Virginia*, the CSS *Arkansas*, was started in Memphis, Tennessee, then moved to Yazoo City on the upper Mississippi River to be finished when that city fell to Federal forces. Commanded by Lieutenant Isaac N. Brown, she fought her way past a Union squadron at Yazoo City on 15 July 1862 and got to Vicksburg. Moved to Baton Rouge, she was there attacked by the USS *Essex* and, out of control, drifted to shore where she was burned on 6 August 1862. The CSS *Louisiana*, earlier mentioned in the discussion of the fall of New Orleans, served on the lower Mississippi. The CSS *Missouri*, another similar ironclad, was commissioned in the Red River, Louisiana, on 12 September 1863. She served there throughout the war until surrendering on 3 June 1865.

The lower Mississippi was also guarded by fourteen 'cottonclads', boats that had been 'armored' with compressed cotton bales, and armed with a ram. Many of these were sunk off Memphis on 6 June 1862, while several others were burned at the fall of New Orleans. A number of converted Confederate gunboats were also burned to prevent their capture when New Orleans fell.

A fascination with rams, after their use by the Confederates, led a US Army officer, Colonel Charles Ellet, Jnr., to build for the War Department a fleet of old stern- and side-wheelers converted to rams. He also organized the Mississippi Marine Brigade, with Army uniforms and Navy officers' caps with green bands. Ellet's force was ordered simply to co-operate with the Navy, rather than being placed under Naval command. These rams, followed by some gunboats, led the way in the fighting on 6 June 1862 near Memphis, which opened the Mississippi as far south as Vicksburg.

In the meantime, New Orleans had fallen and Vicksburg remained the last obstacle to free passage of the river. On 28 June 1863 ships from the southern end of the river passed Vicksburg's guns safely and both fleets were united. Now attention was turned towards helping the Army overcome Vicksburg by means of constant bombardment.

On 12 December 1862 one of these ships, the USS *Cairo*, was sunk, the first victim to a new Confederate naval weapon, the 'torpedo'. The torpedo, or 'mine' as it is known today, was an attempt to compensate the lack of Southern ship-building facilities by making and placing explosive devices in harbours and rivers and exploding them when Union ships passed over them. The Confederate Navy established its Naval Submarine Battery Service in October 1862 under the direction of Captain M. F. Maury, and torpedo stations were set up at Richmond, Wilmington, Charleston, Savannah, and Mobile. The officers and men assigned to the Service considered themselves élite because it was a dangerous duty. Several boats laying torpedoes were lost with all hands by accidental explosions. In all, from the time the *Cairo* was sunk until the last known torpedo explosion on 6 June 1864, some 40 US Navy vessels were destroyed or injured by Confederate torpedoes.

Elsewhere, Confederate sailors served on the rivers by capturing small Union vessels in cutting-out operations. On the dark night of 23 August 1862 Commander John T. Wood led such an expedition to captured the laxly guarded gunboats USSS *Satellite* and *Reliance* at the mouth of the Rappahannock. A similar expedition, also led by Wood, resulted in the capture of the USS *Underwriter* in the Neuse River, North Carolina, on 2 February 1864. Lieutenant J. P. Pelot led a force to take the USS *Water Witch* in Ossabaw Sound, Georgia on 3 June 1864, paying with his life for the prize.

At the end, however, Confederate bravery and ingenuity could not stop the US Navy and Army from going where they wanted on the South's rivers. When Vicksburg fell on 4 July 1863 the last of the major river operations were over. Thereafter, most river work simply involved routine patrolling, with the occasional sniper fire from riverbanks and the odd torpedo the main dangers to the ships and boats of the US Navy.

Why The South Lost

After the last shot had been fired, a totally defeated South lay occupied by thousands of victorious Union troops. It had taken four years and cost the Union 110,070 dead and another 249,458 injured and maimed, many for life. The

This motley collection of vessels includes a Russian frigate on a friendly visit to the USA, and a Union transport and schooner in the North River. The image forms one side of a stereoscopic card produced by E. & J. T. Anthony & Co. (Author's collection)

Confederate armies paid the price of another 329,000 killed and wounded.

Why had the South lost so totally? It comprised a huge territory, and in 1861 its inhabitants appeared to have the requisite courage and fortitude to hold at bay an even greater force than in fact they encountered. They had a military tradition and experienced leaders who had served in the US goverment and armed forces. Even if they could not defend every inch of land, they could always have used guerrilla-type tactics, striking US supply lines to the point where the Union forces, insufficiently numerous to garrison the whole of the South, would simply have had to give up.

It is quite clear, however, that at the end, the Confederacy simply blew away like a tent in the wind. Ever since then participants, and later, historians, have been arguing as to why this should have happened.

A Confederate squad learns that they've surrendered

'Lieutenant McRae, noticing a number of wagons and guns parked in a field near by, surprised at what he considered great carelessness in the immediate presence of the enemy, approached an officer on horseback and said, in his usual impressive manner, "I say there, what does this mean?" The man took his hand and quietly said, "We have surrendered." "I don't believe it, sir!" replied McRae, strutting around as mad as a hornet. "You mustn't talk so, sir! You will demoralize my men!" He was soon convinced, however, by seeing Yankee cavalrymen walking their horses around as composedly as though the Army of Northern Virginia had never existed. To say that McRae was surprised, disgusted, indignant, and incredulous, is a mild way of expressing his state of mind as he turned to his squad and said, "Well, boys, it must be so, *but it's very strange behavior.* Let's move on and see about it." As though dreaming, the squad and the disgusted officer moved on.'

(Carlton McCarthy, *Detailed Minutiae of Soldier Life in the Army of Northern Virginia*, Carlton McCarthy and Co., Richmond, Virginia, 1882, p. 152)

The first, and obvious, answer was quickly put forward by members of the losing side – they were simply out-manned, out-gunned, out-produced, and out-lasted. Jefferson Davis, in his apology for the war, written years later, pointed to the ' . . . Southern people, in their unequal struggle . . . '[9] Raw numbers certainly bear this out. The Union Army was able to put 2,898,304 men into the field. The South appears to have had some 1,228,000 men in its armies.[10]

This discrepancy disappears, however, at any given engagement when both sides generally brought roughly the same numbers on to the field, this despite the fact that the Confederate government insisted on garrisoning every point

---

The Union v. The Confederacy

A comparison of economic factors of the states making up the Union and Confederacy before the Civil War. The Union here includes two slave states, Maryland and Delaware, of which Maryland supplied some support to the South; the Confederacy includes border states such as Missouri, Kentucky, and Tennessee that were split by the war and supported both sides.

	Union	Confederacy
Population, 1860	19,798,866	7,215,525
Militia, 1852	1,437,936	736,783
Exports, tonnage 1855	4,506,606	601,526
Square Miles	670,000	780,000
Railroad miles, 1857	18,572	6,142
Patents issued, 1856	1,986	211

---

that could be attacked by Union forces, often in response to local demands, and the disarming habit of Southerners to straggle or to desert to help out at home. Despite these facts, they still fought equally in every major battle.

Nor do standard economic indicators such as iron and steel production, miles of railroad line, exports, or agricultural production account for the defeat. Although the North's economic indicators were in every way superior to those of the South, basically the South was able to survive and, indeed, by the end of the war, was producing more in both industrial and agricultural terms than ever it had before the war. In 1862 and 1863 Southerners developed an iron ore industry in Alabama where there had been none before. Copper for percussion caps was found at Cleveland, Tennessee. There was even a fishery set upon the Cape Fear River in North Carolina to make fish oil for waterproofing ground sheets, the workers eating the fish used in the process. What couldn't be made in the Confederacy, especially consumer luxury goods, was imported, often at great cost, by blockade-runners. Southern ingenuity had triumphed and the South remained economically viable virtually until the end.

But what the South also took with it into its new Confederacy were the seeds of its own defeat.

Much as Southerners boasted of being an entirely different breed from the hated Yankees and the foreigners settling in Northern cities, the fact was that they were not. People from both sides had grown up on the same stories of the American Revolution, a Revolution that saw a Rhode Island Quaker commanding Americans in the South, while a Virginia planter commanded Yankees outside Boston. George Washington, a Virginian to be sure, was the first father of all the United States. The very symbols of nationhood, the flag, the seal, the patriotic songs, were the same North and South, and Southerners never really gave them up. So a basic feeling of being a different nation was actually missing among Southerners as a people.

So, wrote Jefferson Davis, the South's purpose was ' . . . to prove . . . that each of the States, as sovereign parties to the compact of Union, had the reserved power to secede from it whenever it should be found not to answer the ends for which it was established'.[11] While this meant to Davis that the rebelling states should simply transfer their allegiance to the new Confederate government, it meant something quite different to many Southern political leaders. Georgia's Governor, Joseph Brown, for example, saw his state as more of an ally of the other Southern states and the central government, able to ignore any legislation or actions that he felt were counter to Georgia's interests. Brown stopped many Georgians from being conscripted into the Confederate Army, creating his own Georgia State Line in 1862 instead. Nor was he the only governor to act in this way. North Carolina's governor did much the same things as did Brown, while governors across the Mississippi River, after the fall of Vicksburg, were virtually free to run their own states as they pleased. The very legalistic issue of states' rights, which many Southerners felt that they had left the Union to defend, was eating away from within to destroy the Confederacy's chances.

Not that the idea of states' rights was one that could inflame the Southern populace, even if it were workable. Most Southerners simply went off to war because their friends and neighbours did and because they felt their lands were threatened by people they didn't know. They were a deeply religious people, through all walks of life. As long as the Confederate Army was blessed by God with victories, they supported their government. But, after defeats in the

West, cresting at Gettysburg and Vicksburg, it became clear to many of them that God had turned against them. Religious revivals swept the Southern armies, but defeats continued and when Southerners asked why, all they could point to was human slavery which virtually all the rest of the world said was wrong. It was clearly the thing that kept England and France from recognizing their cause and their country. It must be that God, too, thought slavery was wrong and hence their cause and country were doomed. So at the end, Southerners accepted their defeat with remarkable calm, and without resorting to partisan warfare that could have gone on for years more.

Notes

1. Hilton R. Helper. *The Impending Crisis of the South.* Collier Books, New York, 1963, p. 35
2. Roy E. Appleman. *Abraham Lincoln From His Own Words and Contemporary Accounts.* National Park Service, Washington, DC, 1946, p. 19
3. James D. Richardson (ed.). *A Compilation of the Messages and Papers of the Confederacy.* United States Publishing Co., Nashville, Tennessee, vol. I, p. 32
4. War Department. *The War of the Rebellion: A Compilation of the Official Records of the Union and Confederate Armies.* Washington, 1899, Series III, vol. I, pp. 148–9
5. Clifford Dowdey and Louis H. Manarin, eds., *The Wartime Papers of R. E. Lee.* Bramhall House, New York, 1961, p. 322
6. U.S. Grant. *Personal Memoirs of U.S. Grant.* World Publishing Co., Cleveland, Ohio, 1952, p. 442
7. Ibid.
8. Ibid., p. 551
9. Jefferson Davis. *The Rise and Fall of the Confederate Government,* D. Appleton & Co, New York, 1881, vol. 2, p. 764
10. Thomas L. Livermore. *Numbers and Losses in the Civil War.* Morningside Bookshop, Dayton, Ohio, 1986, p. 39
11. Davis, op. cit.

BATTLES OF THE CIVIL WAR

Date	Action	Victor	Defeated
1861			
Eastern Theatre			
12–14 April	Ft Sumter, SC	CS (Beauregard)	US (Anderson)
1 June	Fairfax Courthouse, VA	US (Thompkins)	CS (Ewell)
3 June	Philippi, WV	US (Rosecrans)	CS (Lee)
10 June	Big Bethal, VA	CS (Magruder)	US (Butler)
11 July	Rich Mountain, WV	US (Rosecrans)	CS (Pegram)
13 July	Carrick's Ford, WV	US (McClellan)	CS (Garnett)
21 July	First Bull Run, VA	CS (Beauregard)	US (McDowell)
10 September	Carnifex Ferry, WV	CS (Floyd)	US (Rosecrans)
10–15 September	Cheat Mountain, WV	US (Reynolds)	CS (Lee)
8–9 October	Santa Rose Island, FL	US (Brown)	CS (Anderson)
21 October	Balls Bluff, VA	CS (Evans)	US (Baker)
Western Theatre			
10 May	Camp Jackson, MO	US (Lyon)	CS (Frost)
10 August	Wilson's Creek, MO	CS (McCulloch)	US (Lyon)
20 September	Lexington, KY	CS (Price)	US (Mulligan)
7 November	Belmont, MO	CS (Polk)	US (Grant)
Far Western Theatre			
26 July	Fort Fillmore, NM	CS (Baylor)	US (Lynde)

Date	*Action*	*Victor*	*Defeated*
1862			
Eastern Theatre			
8 February	Ronaoke Island, NC	US (Burnside)	CS (Wise)
14 March	New Bern, NC	US (Burnside)	CS (Branch)
23 March	Kernstown, VA	US (Banks)	CS (Jackson)
5 April–4 May	Yorktown, VA	US (McClellan)	CS (Magruder)
4–5 May	Williamsburg, VA	US (McClellan)	CS (Magruder)
8 May	McDowell, VA	CS (Jackson)	US (Banks)
16–17 May	Princeton, WV	CS (Marshall)	US (Cox)
23 May	Front Royal, VA	CS (Jackson)	US (Banks)
24 May	Newton, VA	CS (Jackson)	US (Banks)
25 May	Winchester, VA	CS (Jackson)	US (Banks)
27 May	Hanover Court House, VA	US (Porter)	CS (Johnston)
30 May	Front Royal, VA	US (Kimball)	CS (Connor)
31 May–1 June	Fair Oaks/Seven Pines, VA	US (McClellan)	CS (Johnston)
8 June	Cross Keys, VA	CS (Jackson)	US (Shields)
16 June	Secessionville, SC	CS (Lamar)	US (Benham)
25 June	Oak Grove, VA	US (McClellan)	CS (Lee)
26 June	Mechanicsville, VA	US (McClellan)	CS (Lee)
27–28 June	Cold Harbor, VA	CS (Lee)	US (McClellan)
29 June	Savage's Station & Allen's Farm, VA	US (McClellan)	CS (Lee)
30 June	White Oak Swamp, VA	CS (Lee)	US (McClellan)
30 June	Turkey Bridge, VA	US (Sykes)	CS (Lee)
1 July	Malvern Hill, VA	US (McClellan)	CS (Lee)
9 August	Cedar Mountain, VA	CS (Jackson)	US (Pope)
23 August	Catlett's Station, VA	CS (Stuart)	US (Pope)
28–29 August	Groveton, VA	CS (Lee)	US (Pope)
30 August	Second Bull Run, VA	CS (Lee)	US (Pope)
1 September	Chantilly, VA	CS (Lee)	US (Pope)
12–15 September	Harpers Ferry, VA	CS (Jackson)	US (Miles)
14 September	South Mountain, VA	US (McClellan)	CS (Lee)
17 September	Antietam, MD	US (McClellan)	CS (Lee)
19 September	Blackford's Ford, VA	CS (Lee)	US (McClellan)
12 October	Monocacy, MD	CS (Stuart)	US (Pleasonton)
13 December	Fredericksburg, VA	CS (Lee)	US (Burnside)
Western Theatre			
10 January	Middle Creek, KY	CS (Marshall)	US (Garfield)
19 January	Mill Springs, KY	US (Thomas)	CS (Zillicoffer)
6 February	Ft Henry, TN	US (Grant)	CS (Tilghman)
14–16 February	Ft Donelson, TN	US (Grant)	CS (Pillow)
5–8 March	Pea Ridge, AR	US (Curtis)	CS (Price)
13–14 March	New Madrid, TN	US (Pope)	CS (McCowan)
6–7 April	Shiloh, TN	US (Grant)	CS (Johnston)
30 April–30 May	Corinth, MS	US (Halleck)	CS (Beauregard)
14 May	Jackson, MS	US (Grant)	CS (Johnston)
1 July	Booneville, MS	US (Sheridan)	CS (Chalmers)
5 August	Baton Rouge, LA	US (Williams)	CS (Breckenridge)
29–30 August	Richmond, KY	CS (Kirby Smith)	US (Nelson)
14–17 September	Munfordville, KY	CS (Bragg)	US (Wilder)
19–20 September	Iuka, MO	US (Rosecrans)	CS (Van Dorn)
3–4 October	Corinth, MO	US (Rosecrans)	CS (Van Dorn)
5 October	Big Hatchie River	US (Ord)	CS (Van Dorn)
8 October	Perryville, KY	US (Buell)	CS (Bragg)
22 October	Old Fort Wayne, AR	US (Blunt)	CS (Cooper)

Date	Action	Victor	Defeated
13 November	Holly Springs, MS	US (Grant)	CS (Pemberton)
28 November	Cane Hill, AR	CS (Marmaduke)	US (Blunt)
7 December	Prairie Grove, AR	US (Blunt)	CS (Hindman)
18 December	Lexington, TN	CS (Forrest)	US (Ingersoll)
19 December	Jackson, TN	US (Sullivan)	CS (Forrest)
20 December	Holly Springs, MS	CS (Van Dorn)	US (Grant)
27–29 December	Chickasaw Bluffs, MS	CS (Smith)	US (Sherman)
30 December–3 January	Murfreesboro, TN	US (Rosecrans)	CS (Bragg)
31 December	Parker Cross Roads, TN	US (Dunham)	CS (Forrest)
Far Western Theatre			
21 February	Valverde, NM	CS (Sibley)	US (Canby)
28 March	La Glorieta Pass, NM	US (Chivington)	CS (Sibley)
20–22 August	Fort Ridgely, MN	US (Sibley)	Sioux Indians
23 September	Wood Lake, MN	US (Sibley)	Sioux Indians

1863

Eastern Theatre

Date	Action	Victor	Defeated
6–7 February	Barnett's Ford, VA	CS (Lomax)	US (Merritt)
17 March	Kelly's Ford, VA	CS (Stuart)	US (Averell)
11 April–4 May	Suffolk, VA	US (Peck)	CS (Longstreet)
1–4 May	Chancellorsville, VA	CS (Lee)	US (Hooker)
3–4 May	Salem Church, VA	US (Sedgwick)	CS (Lee)
9 June	Brandy Station, VA	US (Pleasonton)	CS (Stuart)
13 June	Berryville, VA	CS (Rhodes)	US (McReynolds)
13–15 June	Winchester, VA	CS (Ewell)	US (Milroy)
14 June	Martinsburg, WV	CS (Jenkins)	US (Tyler)
17 June	Aldie, VA	CS (Munford)	US (Pleasonton)
17 June	Middleburg, VA	CS (Stuart)	US (Duffie)
19 June	Middleburg, VA	US (Gregg)	CS (Stuart)
20 June	Greencastle, PA	CS (Ewell)	US (Pierce)
27 June	Fairfax Court House, VA	CS (Hampton)	US (Remington)
29 June	Westminster, MD	CS (Stuart)	US (Knight)
30 June	Hanover, PA	US (Kilpatrick)	CS (Stuart)
30 June	Sporting Hill, PA	US (Ewen)	CS (Lee)
1–3 July	Gettysburg, PA	US (Meade)	CS (Lee)
10, 18 July	Fort Wagner, SC	CS (Taliaferro)	US (Gillmore)
24 July	Battle Mountain, VA	CS (Hill)	US (Custer)
1–3 August	Rappahannock Station, VA	CS (Stuart)	US (Buford)
14 October	Bristoe Station, VA	CS (Lee)	US (Meade)
14 October	Catlett's Station VA	US (Owen)	CS (Stuart)
19 October	Buckland Mills, VA	CS (Stuart)	US (Kilpatrick)
7 November	Rappahannock Bridge & Kelly's Ford, VA	US (Meade)	CS (Lee)

Western Theatre

Date	Action	Victor	Defeated
11 January	Ft Hindman	US (McClernand)	CS (Churchill)
4 March	Spring Hill, TN	CS (Van Dorn)	US (Coburn)
12–14 April	Irish Bend & Fort Bisland, LA	CS (Taylor)	US (Banks)
17 April–2 May	Grierson's Raid	US (Grierson)	CS (Johnston)
1 May	Port Gibson, MS	US (Grant)	CS (Pemberton)
12 May	Raymond, MS	CS (Gregg)	US (McPherson)
14 May	Jackson, MS	US (Grant)	CS (Johnston)
16 May	Champion's Hill, MS	US (Grant)	CS (Pemberton)
27 May–9 July	Port Hudson, LA	US (Banks)	CS (Gardner)
4 July	Vicksburg, MS	US (Grant)	CS (Pemberton)

Date	*Action*	*Victor*	*Defeated*
4 Jul,	Helena, AK	US (Prentiss)	CS (Price)
5 July	Bardstown, KY	CS (Morgan)	US (Sullivan)
19 July	Buffington Island, OH	US (Hobson)	CS (Morgan)
19–20 September	Chickamauga, TN	CS (Bragg)	US (Rosecrans)
6 October	Baxter Springs, KN	CS (Quantrill)	US (Blunt)
10 October	Blue Springs, TN	US (Burnside)	CS (Williams)
28 October	Wauhatchie, TN	US (Grant)	CS (Bragg)
16 November	Campbell's Station, TN	US (Hantraft)	CS (McLaws)
23–25 November	Chattanooga, TN	US (Grant)	CS (Bragg)
29 November	Fort Sanders, TN	US (Benjamin)	CS (Longstreet)

Far Western Theatre

29 January	Bear River, ID	US (Conner)	Shoshoni Indians
8 September	Sabine Pass, TX	CS (Downling)	US (Franklin)
27–29 November	Fort Esperanza, TX	US (Banks)	CS (Kirby Smith)

1864

Eastern Theatre

20 February	Olustee, FL	CS (Finegan)	US (Seymour)
28 February–4 March	Richmond, VA	CS (Lee)	US (Kilpatrick)
17–20 April	Plymouth, NC	CS (Hoke)	US (Wessells)
4–16 May	Drewry's Bluff, VA	CS (Beauregard)	US (Butler)
5–7 May	Wilderness, VA	CS (Lee)	US (Grant)
5–9 May	Todd's Tavern, VA	CS (Stuart)	US (Sheridan)
9 May	Ware Bottom Church, VA	CS (Beauregard)	US (Butler)
11 May	Yellow Tavern, VA	US (Sheridan)	CS (Stuart)
15 May	New Market, VA	CS (Breckinridge)	US (Sigel)
20 May	Ware Bottom Church, VA	US (Butler)	CS (Beauregard)
23–27 May	North Anna River, VA	CS (Lee)	US (Grant)
28–31 May	Totopotomy Creek, VA	CS (Lee)	US (Grant)
28 May	Haw's Shop, VA	US (Gregg)	CS (Lee)
31 May–12 June	Cold Harbor, VA	CS (Lee)	US (Grant)
5 June	Piedmont, VA	US (Hunter)	CS (Jones)
9 June	Petersburg, VA	CS (Wise)	US (Butler)
11–12 June	Trevilian Station, VA	CS (Hampton)	US (Sheridan)
15–18 June	Petersburg, VA	CS (Beauregard)	US (Butler)
17–18 June	Lynchburg, VA	CS (Early)	US (Hunter)
22–23 June	Weldon Railroad, VA	CS (Lee)	US (Grant)
9 July	Monocacy, MD	CS (Early)	US (Wallace)
12 July	Fort Stevens, MD	US (Wright)	CS (Early)
14 July	Falling Waters, VA	CS (Heath)	US (Meade)
20 July	Stephenson's Depot, VA	US (Averell)	CS (Ramseur)
23–24 July	Kernstown, VA	CS (Early)	US (Crook)
27–29 July	Deep Bottom Run, VA	CS (Lee)	US (Grant)
7 August	Moorefield, WV	US (Averell)	CS (McCausland)
13–20 August	Deep Bottom Run, VA	CS (Lee)	US (Grant)
18–21 August	Globe Tavern, VA	US (Grant)	CS (Lee)
25 August	Reams' Station, VA	CS (Lee)	US (Grant)
31 August	Martinsburg, WV	CS (Rhodes)	US (Averell)
16 September	Coggin's Point, VA	CS (Hampton)	US (Grant)
19 September	Winchester, VA	US (Sheridan)	CS (Early)
22 September	Fishers Hill, VA	US (Sheridan)	CS (Early)
28–30 September	New Market Heights, VA	CS (Lee)	US (Grant)
30 September–2 October	Poplar Springs Church, VA	US (Grant)	CS (Lee)
7 October	Darbytown and New Market Roads, VA	US (Kautz)	CS (Lee)

Date	Action	Victor	Defeated
9 October	Tom's Brook, VA	US (Torbert)	CS (Rosser, Lomax)
13 October	Darbytown Road, VA	CS (Lee)	US (Kautz)
19 October	Cedar Creek, VA	US (Sheridan)	CS (Early)
27 October	Hatcher's Run, VA	CS (Hill)	US (Hancock)
27–28 October	Fair Oaks, VA	CS (Lee)	US (Butler)
7–11 December	Weldon Railroad, VA	US (Warren)	CS (Hill)
7–27 December	Fort Fisher, NC	CS (Lamb)	US (Butler)

Western Theatre

Date	Action	Victor	Defeated
20–21 February	West Point, MS	CS (Forrest)	US (WS Smith)
22–27 February	Dalton, GA	CS (Johnston)	US (Sherman)
8 April	Sabine Cross Roads, LA	CS (Taylor)	US (Banks)
9 April	Pleasant Hill, LA	US (Banks)	CS (Taylor)
9–13 April	Prairie D'Ane, AR	US (Steele)	CS (Kirby Smith)
12 April	Fort Pillow, TN	CS (Forrest)	US (Booth)
25 April	Mark's Mill, AR	CS (Fagan)	US (McLean)
30 April	Jenkins' Ferry, AR	CS (Smith)	US (Steele)
1–8 May	Alexandria, LA	US (Banks)	CS (Taylor)
5–11 May	Rocky Face Ridge, GA	US (Sherman)	CS (Johnston)
13–16 May	Resaca, GA	US (Sherman)	CS (Johnston)
14–16 May	Avoyelles Prairie, LA	US (Banks)	CS (Taylor)
18 May	Bayou De Glaize, LA	CS (Taylor)	US (Banks)
10 June	Brice's Cross Roads, MS	CS (Forrest)	US (Sturgis)
11 June	Cynthiana, KY	CS (Morgan)	US (Hobson)
27 June	Kenesaw Mountain, GA	CS (Johnston)	US (Sherman)
5–17 July	Chattahooche River, GA	US (Sherman)	CS (Johnston)
13–15 July	Tupelo, MS	US (A. J. Smith)	CS (S.D. Lee)
20 July	Peachtree Creek, VA	US (Sherman)	CS (Hood)
22 July	Atlanta, GA	US (McPherson)	CS (Hood)
28 July	Ezra Church, GA	US (Sherman)	CS (Hood)
3–23 August	Forts Gaines, Morgan, Powell, AL	US (Granger)	CS (Maury)
5–6 August	Utoy Creek, GA	CS (Hood)	US (Sherman)
14–16 August	Dalton, GA	US (Laiboldt)	CS (Wheeler)
19 August	Jonesboro, GA	CS (Jackson)	US (Kilpatrick)
2–6 September	Lovejoy, GA	CS (Hood)	US (Sherman)
5 October	Altoona, GA	US (Tourtelotte)	CS (French)
23 October	Westport, MO	US (Curtis)	CS (Price)
4–5 November	Johnsonville, TN	CS (Forrest)	US (Thompson)
16 November	Lovejoy, GA	US (Kilpatrick)	CS (Wheeler)
21–22 November	Griswoldville, GA	US (Walcutt)	CS (Wheeler)
23–25 November	Ball's Ferry, GA	US (Howard)	CS (Hartridge)
26 November	Sandersville, GA	US (Sherman)	CS (Wheeler)
29 November	Waynesboro, GA	US (Kilpatrick)	CS (Wheeler)
29 November	Spring Hill, TN	US (Schofield)	CS (Hood)
30 November	Honey Hill, SC	CS (Smith)	US (Hatch)
30 November	Franklin, TN	US (Schofield)	CS (Hood)
7, 15 December	Murfreesboro, TN	CS (Forrest)	US (Rousseau)
13 December	Fort McAllister, GA	US (Hazen)	CS (Anderson)
15–16 December	Nashville, TN	US (Thomas)	CS (Hood)

Far Western Theatre

Date	Action	Victor	Defeated
6 January	Cañon de Chelly, NM	US (Carson)	Navajo Indians
25 August	Sacramento Mountain, NM	US (Carson)	Navajo Indians
25 November	Abobe Walls, TX	Comanche Indians	US (Carson)
9 December	Sand Creek, CO	US (Chivington)	Cheyenne, Arapahoe Indians

Date	Action	Victor	Defeated
1865			
Eastern Theatre			
6–15 January	Fort Fisher, NC	US (Terry)	CS (Lamb)
5–7 February	Hatcher's Run, VA	CS (Mahone)	US (Warren)
2 March	Waynesboro, VA	US (Custer)	CS (Early)
25 March	Fort Stedman, VA	US (Hartranfat)	CS (Gordon)
29 March	Quaker Road, VA	US (Grant)	CS (Lee)
30 March–1 April	Five Forks, VA	US (Grant)	CS (Lee)
3 April	Namozine Church, Willicomack Creek, VA	US (Custer)	CS (Lee)
5 April	Amelia Springs, VA	US (Davies)	CS (Gary)
6 April	High Bridge, VA	CS (Rosser)	US (Read)
6 April	Saylor's Creek, VA	US (Meade)	CS (Lee)
7 April	Farmville/High Bridge, VA	US (Meade)	CS (Lee)
9 April	Appomattox CH, VA	US (Grant)	CS (Lee)
10 May	Florida's Surrender	US (Wilson)	CS (Jones)
Western Theatre			
16 March	Averasboro, NC	US (Slocum)	CS (Hood)
19–21 March	Bentonville, NC	US (Sherman)	CS (Johnston)
1–9 April	Blakely, AL	US (Canby)	CS (Maury)
26 April	Johnston's Surrender	US (Sherman)	CS (Johnston)
Far Western Theatre			
13 May	Palmito Ranch, TX	CS (Ford)	US (Barrett)
26 May	Trans-Mississippi Surrender	US (Canby)	CS (Taylor)

THE NAVAL WAR

1861			
12 October	*Manassas/Richmond*	CS (Stevenson)	US (Pope)
7 November	Port Royal Sound, SC	US (DuPont)	CS (Drayton)
1862			
8 March	*Virginia/Cumberland*	CS (Buchanan)	US (Morris)
8 March	*Virginia/Congress*	CS (Buchanan)	US (Prendergast)
9 March	*Monitor/Virginia*	US (Worden)	CS (Jones)
24 April	*Governor Moore/Varuna*	CS (Kennon)	US (Boggs)
24 April	*Pensacola/Governor Moore*	US (Morris)	CS (Kennon)
25 April	New Orleans, LA	US (Farragut)	CS (Lovell)
6 August	*Essex/Arkansas*	US (Porter)	CS (Stevens)
1863			
11 January	*Alabama/Hatteras*	CS (Semmes)	US (Blake)
31 January	*Palmetto State/Mercedita*	CS (Ingraham)	US (Stellwagen)
31 January	*Chicora/Keystone State*	CS (Tucker)	US (Le Roy)
17 June	*Weehawken/Atlanta*	US (Rogers)	CS (Webb)
27 June	*Archer/Caleb Cushing*	CS (Savvy)	US (Davenport)
8 September	Fort Sumter, SC	CS (Beauregard)	US (Dahlgren)
1864			
16 February	*Hunley/Housatonic*	CS (Dixon)	US (Pickering)
19 April	*Albemarle/Miami, Southfield*	CS (Cooke)	US (Flusser)
19 June	*Kearsage/Alabama*	US (Winslow)	CS (Semmes)
5 August	Mobile Bay, AL	US (Farragut)	CS (Buchanan)
4 October	*Wachusset/Florida*	US (Collins)	CS (Maffitt)
27 October	CSS *Albemarle*	US (Cushing)	CS (Cooke)

II
WEAPONS AND THE PRACTICE OF WAR

WEAPONS AND THE PRACTICE OF WAR

WEAPONRY

Infantry Weapons

The basic infantry weapon for both sides was the rifle-musket, generally called a 'musket'.

The Confederate army's main supplier of infantry weapons – and indeed of all military goods – was the US Army. In the year ending 30 September 1864, for example, the Confederates reported the capture of some 45,000 US-issued small arms. Captures in battle, as well as what was taken from US stores inside states' borders after the Confederacy had been formed, meant that much of what can be said about the US Army in terms of weaponry is equally true of the Confederate army.

Essentially, the basic American-made rifle-musket, whether produced by the Confederate Richmond Armory or the US Springfield (Massachusetts) Armory, was patterned on the Model 1855 rifle-musket. Known as the 'Springfield', it had a 40-inch brightly polished barrel, a walnut stock, was 74 inches long from butt plate to muzzle, weighed almost ten pounds, and was 0.58in in calibre. It was a single-shot, muzzle-loading weapon. The separate bayonet was a three-sided, steel-tipped iron spike whose 18-inch blade was mounted on a 3-inch socket which fitted around the muzzle, a ring holding it fast to the front sight.

The M1855's pure lead bullet, known as the 'Minié ball' after its French inventor, was conical, and had a hollow base. When it was fired, the base expanded to fit tightly into the musket's rifling for improved accuracy. The bullet had parallel rings around it that were designed to catch fouling and help keep the musket barrel clean during firing.

To load and fire the weapon, the soldier stepped slightly back with his right foot, keeping his left foot on line, and dropped the musket butt to the ground near the right foot so that the muzzle pointed away from him, towards the sky over his target. He then took a cartridge from his cartridge box. The cartridge was self-contained, the measure of powder and the bullet being wrapped in paper. He bit the end of the paper off and poured the powder down the barrel, shoving the paper-wrapped bullet after it. He then withdrew the ramrod from its groove under the barrel, spun it around and placed the head into the barrel. He then quickly tamped the bullet snugly down to the breech. He then replaced the ramrod; in a fixed position such as a trench he might stick it into the ground for faster use. Then he brought his left hand to the balance of the piece, around its middle, and brought the musket butt up to about waist level until the muzzle was pointing towards his target. He half-cocked the hammer and flipped off the old copper percussion cap (keeping the fired cap on the nipple prevented air from getting into the barrel and a premature discharge when the powder was being poured into the barrel). He pulled out a new percussion cap, which was filled with fulminate of mercury, and fitted it snugly on the nipple. His weapon was now loaded and ready. To fire, he fully cocked the weapon by pulling the hammer back as far as it would go, put the musket butt into his shoulder, aimed, and pulled the trigger.

The M1855 rifle-musket had a highly adjustable ladder-style sight graduated by 100-yard increments to 900 yards. It also had a patented Maynard primer which replaced the separate percussion cap by a roll of paper caps, rather like a modern child's cap pistol, with charges pressed between two pieces of paper that had been water-proofed with varnish. When the weapon was half cocked, a short arm pushed the paper forward, the next firing charge centering over the nipple, or cone as it was known.

With these two items the M1855 was fairly expensive and time-consuming to manufacture and in wet weather the Maynard caps were not as dependable as the copper percussion cap. When the war broke out, therefore, the

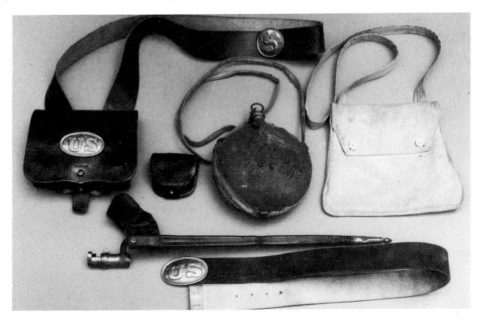

The foot soldier's equipment, in this case Union although Confederate equipment was roughly similar. Top row, from left: leather cartridge box which contained 60 rounds in two tin containers; leather percussion-cap pouch; tin canteen covered with grey wool; Massachusetts-issue duck haversack. Below them, an M1855 Springfield bayonet in its leather scabbard with a brass tip, and a buff leather waist-belt with brass keeps at one end and an oval brass, lead-backed belt-plate at the other. (Author's collection)

Muzzle-loading muskets, rifle-muskets and rifles. From top: a Committee of Safety copy of the British Short Land Model *musket dating from 1775; an M1795 musket; an M1803 rifle; an M1817 rifle; an M1808 musket; an M1841* *('Mississippi') rifle; an M1861 rifle-musket; a P1858 British-made rifle-musket; an M1863 rifle-musket; a Whitneyville* *rifle made under US Navy contract. (Bannerman's Catalog of Military Goods for 1927)*

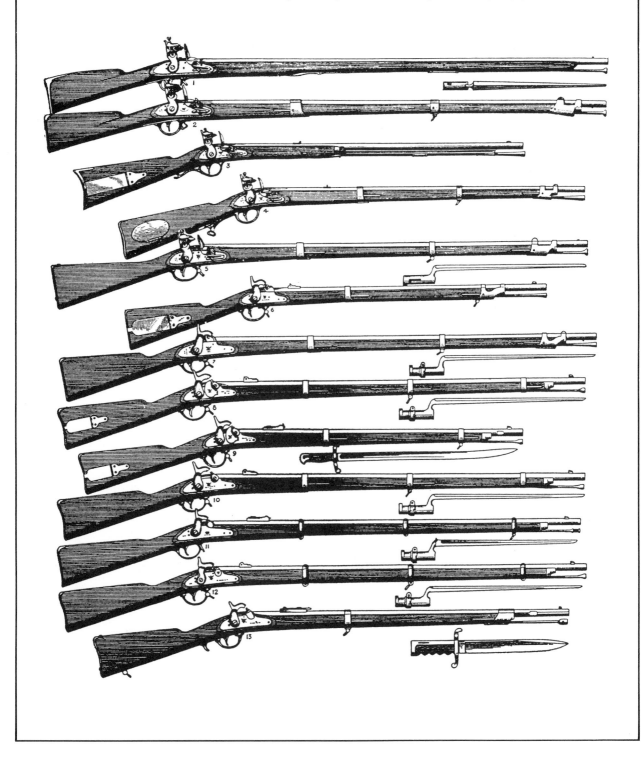

Union Army adopted the M1861 which simply replaced the old sight by a simple leaf sight set for 100, 300 and 500 yards, and dispensed with the Maynard primer.

The Confederate adaptation of the M1855 was made from machinery captured at the US Army's Harpers Ferry, Virginia, Armory, and set up in Richmond. It, too, was produced without the elaborate sight, although old parts were used up so some did have these sights, or the Maynard primer. Unlike the M1861 Springfield, however, the Richmond rifle-musket lockplate retained the distinctive 'hump' that marked the Maynard primer lockplate. Production of these weapons from October 1861 to 30 November 1863 was 23,381.

In 1863 a final variation of the M1855 was adopted by the US Army. This had a different, stronger hammer to replace the old one which had been designed to fit over the Maynard primer hump, and did away with the clean-out screw that was located directly under the cone in the M1855 and M1861. M1861 and M1863 rifle-muskets were made not only in the government's Springfield Armory, but by some 22 private contractors as well, but they were all made to exact government specifications, with interchangeable parts. From 1 January 1861 to 30 June 1866 the US Army acquired 670,617 Springfield rifle-muskets.

The use of private contractors was not new, but both sides were extremely hard-pressed to supply sufficient infantry long arms from their stocks or to manufacture rapidly sufficient quantities for the thousands of volunteers in 1861, so they turned to Europe.

Variations of the British Army's P1853 rifled musket were imported in such quantities that they became the standard Confederate infantry long arm and the second most issued Union infantry long arm. The P1853, known as the 'Enfield', although few weapons in American use actually were produced in Enfield, was very similar to the M1855. It differed in that it was 0.577in in calibre, was 55 inches long, and had a 39-inch browned barrel. Its nosecap, butt plate, and trigger guard were brass, unlike the all-iron M1855. Its ladder-type sight was quite similar to that of the M1855 and was graduated to 1,000 yards. The bayonet was also similar to the US-designed bayonet, with blade and socket of the same size. The US Army acquired 428,292 Enfields during the war.

Both the British and American long arms also came in rifle form although rifles saw considerably less use than rifle-muskets. The only difference between the M1855 rifle-musket and the M1855 rifle was that the rifle had only a 33-inch-long barrel and, therefore, only two bands to secure the barrel to the stock. There was no M1861 or M1863 rifle. Confederates, however, made copies of the M1855 rifle at the Fayetteville, North Carolina, Armory. The British version was the P1856 short rifle which also had a 33-inch barrel and two barrel bands. The US Army purchased 8,034 P1856 rifles. Rifles came with sword rather than spike bayonets, but on 14 January 1864 with a view to saving metals, manufacture of sword bayonets at Fayetteville was abandoned in favour of the spike bayonet.

There were also dozens of other types of infantry long arms imported or brought out of storage to help solve the armament problem. The Confederate *Field Manual for the Use of the Officers on Ordnance Duty*, printed in Richmond in 1862, stated that Southern troops were armed with, besides Enfields and M1855s and copies thereof, M1822 and M1840 US smoothbore, 0.69in calibre muskets; obsolete British-made 0.75in calibre smoothbore muskets; US Army 0.69in calibre musketoons, which were essentially short smoothbore muskets used by cavalry and artillery; 0.7in calibre Belgian rifles; and 0.70in calibre Brunswick rifles.

What Confederate ordnance officers called the M1822, and was more properly designated either the M1835 or M1816, was a smoothbore, 0.60in calibre, flintlock musket. The flintlock pre-dated the percussion cap. It looked generally similar, but the hammer held a piece of knapped flint in its jaws. The soldier poured loose powder into a small pan where the nipple of the percussion cap musket was located. He then snapped an 'L'-shaped battery over it, cocked the hammer, aimed and pulled the trigger. The flint

A completely equipped Union private with his P1853 Enfield rifle-musket; black waterproofed haversack; and M1853 knapsack which had straps designed to be used with the M1855 rifle belt but were more commonly worn across the chest. (Kean E Wilcox collection)

A water-logged musket ruins an inspection

'On one occasion, on a bleak, cold night, intensely dark, William T. Godwin, of Company F [118th Pennsylvania Infantry], on his way with the relief to a picket outpost, slipped from a log that spanned a a narrow creek on the route to his destination and fell headlong into the stream. He was the last man in the detail and his splash bringing the advance to a halt, they returned and by the light of a torch fished him out. His musket, which was loaded, filled with water that immediately froze hard, and, as he would be useless at the front, he was sent back to the reserve. This happened on a Friday night. Saturday the pickets were relieved and through the day, the weather continuing freezing cold, he worked manfully with his piece, but to no avail; there was the load and there was the ice nearly to the muzzle. The next day, Sunday, an inspection was announced by Colonel Herring. In the vain hope to divert attention from the inside of his gun, Godwin devoted special attention to the outside, until the barrel shone with unusual brightness. In the morning the temperature rose materially . . . The sad effects of a thaw inside his piece had not dawned on Godwin. The colonel was especially complimentary. The rammers had not been sprung [done before an inspection to ensure that the weapons were unloaded], when, unfortunately, the colonel raised the hammer. A long, black stream spouting from the nipple disfigured his clothing and entirely changed the color of his clean white gloves.'

(Survivor's Association, *History of the Corn Exchange Regiment*, J. L. Smith, Publisher, Philadelphia, Pennsylvania, 1888, pp. 384–5)

in the hammer struck the battery, the force shoving it up and opening the pan. Sparks flew downward as the flint struck the steel battery, landing in the powder in the pan. This powder ignited, flames passing through a small hole in the barrel and setting off the main charge. High winds or wet weather could render the weapon useless.

The US Army Ordnance Corps also listed all these weapons as being in its inventories. They also purchased, from 1 January 1861 to 30 June 1866, 226,294 Austrian, 57,467 Belgian, 59,918 Prussian, 14,250 French and even 5,995 Italian rifles, in addition to other weapons. European powers took advantage of the American buying spree to clean out their arsenals of unwanted, often obsolete, infantry weapons.

Generally, all these weapons were issued as they became available but not always in any set pattern, so that frequently the men of an infantry regiment were equipped with a wide variety of weapons.

For example, during the fourth quarter of 1862, one Illinois infantry regiment was armed with 96 0.58in calibre M1855 or M1861 rifle-muskets, four 0.577in calibre P1853 rifle-muskets, 143 M1842 0.69in calibre muskets which had been rifled, 72 Belgian 0.69in calibre rifle-muskets, 22 0.58in

Austrian rifles and eleven Austrian 0.54in calibre 'Lorenz' rifles. Ammunition resupply must have been the regimental quartermaster officer's nightmare.

Generally, units early in the war and western units were less well armed than eastern and late-war units. However, the quarterly ordnance return for Co. B, 72nd Pennsylvania Volunteers, an élite zouave unit in the Army of the Potomac's Philadelphia Brigade, for 31 March 1863 shows that the company had twenty Springfields, seventeen Enfields, four Belgian rifles, and one 0.58in calibre Austrian rifle.

Some infantrymen were issued with, or even purchased weapons that were considerably superior to the single-shot

Private John T. Davis from Alabama wore his cartridge box on his waist-belt instead of on a shoulder-belt. This was common among Confederate troops as well as Union Zouaves. His weapon is the P1858 Enfield rifle-musket. (US Army Military History Institute collection)

muzzle-loader. There were two main types of magazine-fed, breech-loading weapons in use. The Spencer had a 30-inch barrel. Seven 0.56in brass-case cartridges were loaded into a tube that was inserted into the rifle's butt. Every time the hammer was cocked and the trigger guard advanced the old cartridge was ejected and a new one came into the firing position. Some 12,471 Spencer rifles were purchased by the US Army Ordnance Corps.

The other magazine-fed breech-loader was the Henry. Its magazine, holding fifteen 0.44in calibre cartridges, ran underneath the barrel. A lever on the trigger guard enabled a spent cartridge to be ejected and a new cartridge chambered. Only 1,731 Henry rifles were issued, but thousands more were purchased widely by soldiers who liked the security of being able to fire without having to stand and reload every shot, and of having so many shots in reserve. Most of these weapons, even when captured, were of limited value to the Confederates who were largely unable to manufacture the requisite brass cartridge cases.

The infantry long arm's conical bullet could do a great deal of damage. Its muzzle velocity was only 960 feet per second, compared to the US Army's Second World War M1 rifle which had a muzzle velocity of 2,800 feet per second. The large, soft bullet, travelling so slowly, caused terrible wounds since it did not pass quickly though a body but tumbled about, smashing bones and tearing organs apart. And, at 200 yards the bullet would penetrate pine boards to a thickness of eleven inches; at 600 yards, six and one-third inches; and at 1,000 yards, three and one-quarter inches. Modern tests, using original weapons on the carcases of horses, showed that penetration of just over an inch would cause 'very dangerous' wounds. So, the rifle-musket had an effective killing range of more than a thousand yards. This fact would radically affect infantry tactics during the four years of war.

At times infantry units were supported by various types of multiple-firing guns, early versions of machine-guns. The US Army had a weapon called the Ager or Coffee Mill gun which fired 120 0.58 in calibre rounds per minute and had a range of some 1,000 yards. The M1862 Gatling Gun used multiple barrels, unlike the single-barrelled Ager. It saw limited use at the Siege of Petersburg. The Requa Battery had 25 barrels which all fired simultaneously. A three-man crew could fire seven volleys, or 175 shots, a minute. They saw use against Fort Sumter, South Carolina, in August 1863. The US Ordnance Department, however, discouraged the use of these early machine-guns as wasteful of ammunition and very few saw action.

The Confederates' entry in the machine-gun race was the Williams rapid-fire gun. It had a 4-foot barrel and a 2-inch bore and was mounted on a small cannon carriage. The

---

A Confederate fires seven rounds at once

'A curious little Irishman in our company, nicknamed "Dublin Tricks", who was extremely awkward, and scarcely knew one end of his gun from the other, furnished the occasion of another outburst of laughter, just when the bullets were flying like hail around us. In his haste or ignorance, he did what is so often done in the excitement of rapid firing by older soldiers; he rammed down his first cartridge without biting off the end, hence the gun did not go off. He went through the motions, putting in another load and snapping his lock, with the same result, and so on for several minutes. Finally he thought of a remedy, and sitting down, he patiently picked some priming into the tube. This time the gun and Dublin both went off. He picked himself up slowly, and called out in a serio-comic tone of voice, committing the old Irish bull, "Hould, asy with your laffin' boys; there is sivin more loads in her yit."'

(William G. Stevenson, *Thirteen Months in the Rebel Army*, A. S. Barnes and Co., New York, 1959, pp. 53–4)

---

range was 2,000 yards. The operator turned a crank which moved the breech-block back to allow a paper-wrapped cartridge to fall from a hopper into the open breech. The breech-block then ran forward and shoved the cartridge into the barrel. A hammer fired a percussion cap automatically to discharge the piece. At the Battle of Seven Pines on 31 May 1862, it appeared to be so successful that six more were ordered from their Southern maker, but it turned out that when fired rapidly the brass breech expanded and eventually cracked, so the weapons were discarded.

Non-commissioned officers were authorized to wear swords, although these were rarely carried in battle. The US Army's M1840 non-commissioned officer's sword had a straight blade, 31.75-inches long, with an all-brass hilt. Musicians carried similar swords, but these had shorter blades and lacked the counterguards of the non-commissioned officers' swords. Officers also carried light sabers. Captains and below carried the M1850 foot officers' sword, which had a slightly curved, heavily engraved 32-inch blade, brass hilt, and grips wrapped in fishskin with twisted brass wire around them. Staff officers and those of higher rank than captain carried the M1850 staff and field officers' sword which was similar to the foot officers' sword but included the cast letters 'US' in the hilt. Officers also carried revolving pistols, either 0.44in 'army' calibre or 0.36in 'navy' calibre.

The Confederate Army actually manufactured and issued non-commissioned officers' swords, despite the fact that they were clearly a waste of precious materials. Confederate officers' swords were copies of the US Army swords, although they tended to be cruder, with unstopped blades and grips with untwisted brass wire. Their Southern-made handguns were copies of the Colt revolvers that US officers

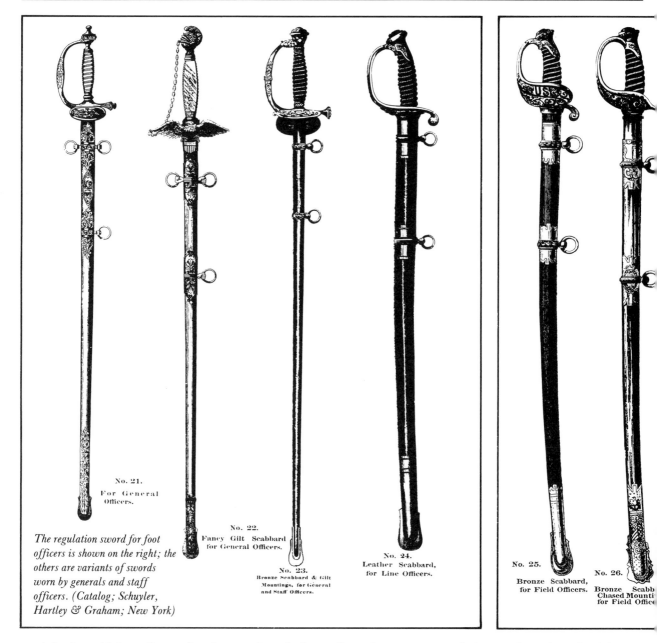

No. 21.
For General
Officers.

The regulation sword for foot officers is shown on the right; the others are variants of swords worn by generals and staff officers. (Catalog; Schuyler, Hartley & Graham; New York)

No. 22.
Fancy Gilt Scabbard
for General Officers.

No. 23.
Bronze Scabbard & Gilt
Mountings, for General
and Staff Officers.

No. 24.
Leather Scabbard,
for Line Officers.

No. 25.
Bronze Scabbard,
for Field Officers.

No. 26.
Bronze Scabb
Chased Mounti
for Field Office

carried, often with brass frames since iron was in such short supply.

Finally, Union infantrymen also used grenades to some extent. The most widely used was the Ketchum which had an iron case filled with powder, a plunger at the front and a wooden tail with four paper fins. When thrown, the plunger was driven back smashing a percussion cap which set off the powder. The US Army purchased 25,556 1-pound, 42,799 3-pound and 24,845 5-pound versions. They also issued 5,000 Adams grenades. This grenade had an iron case containing a cannon friction primer attached to a strap that was hooked to a leather wrist-strap. When thrown, the strap would pull out the friction primer and explode the grenade.

Grenades saw use mostly in trench warfare. Confederates occasionally used grenades, too, although they were mostly improvised in glass bottles.

Cavalry Weapons

The cavalry was the most expensive branch of the service in terms of equipping individuals; not only horses but sabres, carbines and pistols were required.

The sabre was the traditional cavalryman's weapon. In 1860 a new light cavalry sabre had been introduced for the US cavalry, but there were still enough stocks of the older M1840 heavy cavalry (dragoon) saber to ensure that it saw a great deal of service throughout the war. From 1 January

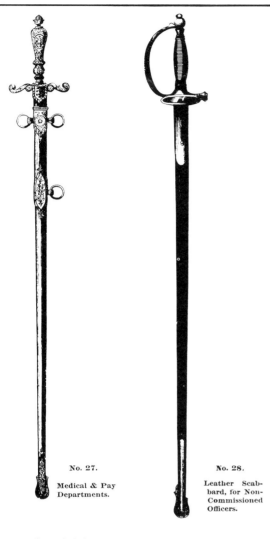

No. 27.
Medical & Pay
Departments.

No. 28.
Leather Scab-
bard, for Non-
Commissioned
Officers.

The two swords on the left are for field-grade officers and have the letters 'U.S.' on their guards; sword number 27 is the type used by medical and pay

department officers; and sword number 28 is the M1840 non-commissioned officers' sword. (Catalog; Schuyler, Hartley & Graham; New York)

Lieutenant Horace Dunn, 22nd Ohio Infantry, holds his foot officer's sword. He is wearing dress epaulettes and a crimson sash. The 22nd served in the

Army of the Tennessee from 1862 until ordered to the Department of Arkansas in 1863. (Author's collection)

1861 to 30 June 1866 the US Army acquired 203,285 light cavalry and 189,114 heavy cavalry sabers. It also acquired 1,279 cavalry officers' sabers, which were virtually the same as the M1860 light saber but with the addition of engraving on the hilt and blade.

All three types of saber were very similar, being designed after the French light cavalry model of 1822. They had brass hilts with three branches topped with a Phrygian helmet pommel. The grips were of wood wrapped with black leather with twisted strands of brass wire wound around it. The M1840 had a curved blade 3.75 inches long; the M1860's blade was 34⅝ inches long. The M1840 blade was 1.25 inches wide, the light blade was a quarter of an inch

narrower. Scabbards were of iron.

The Confederate cavalry saber was a copy of the US Army type. Generally, however, it was a cruder weapon than the US saber, often using oilcloth around the grip, with untwisted copper wire, and the hilts were much redder since more copper was used in the brass. Scabbards often had brass mounts and, indeed, many scabbards were made wholly of brass.

While the saber was considered to be the cavalryman's primary offensive arm, the carbine was his defensive weapon. Generally, US cavalrymen had breech-loading carbines while Confederate cavalrymen were forced to take muzzle-loading carbines because of the inability of Southern

*This unknown Union company-
grade cavalry officer wears the
issue belt with the regulation
officer's cavalry sabre. Note it is
worn with the hilt to the rear*

*which was the standard
procedure. (Author's collection)*

*First Lieutenant J. H. Wells,
7th Kentucky Cavalry, is armed
with both regulation sabre and
pistol. The 7th was organized in
September 1862 and fought with*

*J. H. Morgan, most of its
members being captured in July
1863 after which the regiment
was never re-organized. (John
Sickles collection)*

industry to manufacture breech-loaders in any great
number.

There were two main types of US-issued carbine: those
that use combustible, usually linen, cartridges and those
that used some form of cartridge that had to be extracted
after each shot. Unlike rifle-muskets, neither was manufactured by the government, but were produced by various

private companies under contract. The M1859 Sharps
carbine was the first leading carbine of the US Army, with
80,512 of these weapons that used disposable cartridges
being acquired. The 0.52in calibre Sharps was loaded by
moving the triggerguard, which was also the loading lever,
out. This dropped the block to expose the bore. A cartridge
was inserted into the bore, the lever returned to shove the

Single-shot carbines. From top: an experimental version made by Jenks; the Symmes; the Gibbs; the Schroeder; the Greene; the Joslyn; the Cosmopolitan; the Starr; the Smith; the Warner; the Maynard; the Palmer; the Gallager; the Wesson; the Burnside; the Perry Navy carbine; the Merrill, Latrobe, and Thomas. (Bannerman's Catalogue of Military Goods, *1927)*

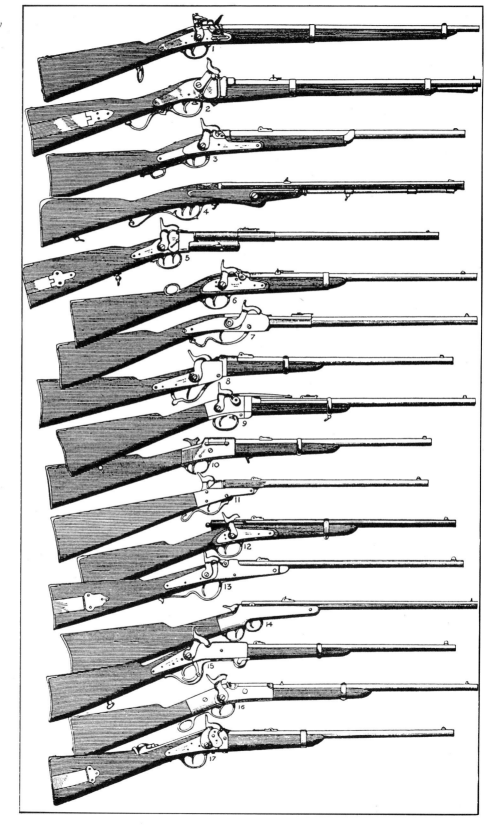

block up, the hammer half cocked, and a percussion cap placed on the nipple. When fully cocked it was ready to fire.

Similar carbines include the Starr, of which 25,603 were acquired, and the Gwyn & Campbell, of which 9,342 were purchased. Carbines that broke at the breech like shotguns to accept a disposable cartridge included the Gallager, of which 22,728 were acquired; the Gibbs, 1,052; the Lindner, 892; the Maynard, 20,002; and the Smith, of which 30,062 were acquired. The Smith differed in that it took a special rubber cartridge. Other breech opening systems were used by the 14,495 Merrills and the 11,261 Joslyns purchased.

Other carbines used metallic cartridges. The US Army's 55,567 Burnside carbines, which came in 0.54in calibre, used brass cartridges which were inserted into the breech after the user had lowered the trigger-guard which also served as a loading lever. The Ballard, of which, 1,509 were acquired, could use either rimfire or combustible cartridges. It used the trigger-guard to lower the breech mechanism.

Finally, magazine-fed carbines that used metallic cartridges became the cavalry standard. The 0.50in calibre Ball, of which 1,002 were acquired, fired seven cartridges that were held in a tubular magazine beneath the barrel. But the most popular carbine of the period in the US Army was the Spencer, of which 94,196 were purchased by the Ordnance Department, none reaching the troops before 1863. The Spencer carbine was of the same design as the Spencer rifle and had a tubular magazine which was inserted through the butt. The Spencer's real advantage was in its reloading rate. Modern firing tests show that, using pre-loaded magazines, it can be reloaded in ten to 12 seconds.

Confederate-issued carbines were less technologically advanced. There were some breech-loading carbines that had not been captured from the Union army, but were Southern-made. Leading these was a copy of the Sharps 0.52in calibre carbine made in Richmond, initially by a private concern but later by the government after it took over the factory. The 'Richmond Sharps' earned a bad reputation when a number of its first models burst on trial. There were apparently some quality control problems in its manufacture, but generally the Southern-made 'Sharps' appears to have been a serviceable weapon. About 5,200 of them were produced.

Other breech-loading carbines were produced, but only in small numbers. They included the Tarpley, a 0.52in calibre carbine made in Greensboro, North Carolina; the Perry or Maynard apparently made by N. T. Read in Danville, Virginia; and the 'rising block carbine', of whose maker nothing is known today. In Greenville, South Carolina George Morse even made about one thousand single-shot 0.50in calibre carbines which used brass cartridges. One other breech-loader should be mentioned if only because Confederate cavalry commander J. E. B. Stuart owned one. This was the British-made Calisher & Terry carbine, a 0.56in calibre weapon which looked rather like the muzzle-loading P1853 artillery carbine, but had a mechanism that pulled back and out to expose the breech. Only a very limited number saw Confederate service.

Indeed, most Confederate carbines were muzzle-loading short copies of the rifle-musket. The Richmond Armory made some 2,800 carbines that looked like short versions of their M1855 rifle-musket. The bulk of muzzle-loading carbines were imported copies of the British-made 0.577in calibre P1856, 'East India Pattern' cavalry carbine. It was 37 inches long and looked rather like a P1853 rifle-musket. The ramrod, however, had a swivel attachment to prevent it being dropped while the user was on horseback, as well as a sling bar on the left side. This was hooked to a broad strap the user wore from his left shoulder to his right side. The use of the same calibre ammunition for both infantry and cavalry long arms simplified supply measures, while US quartermaster officers had to have a variety of ammunition for the different branches of service. On 31 October 1863 the British-type carbine was accepted as the standard issue Confederate cavalry carbine. Copies of it were made by Cook & Brother in Athens, Georgia and, in March 1865, in a new Confederate armory set up in Tallassee, Alabama. The first 500 of the new carbine were ready for shipment on 3 April 1865 – a bit too late to be of much use.

Although carbines such as the Merrill, the Maynard and the Gallager were sighted to 500 yards, the smaller cartridge and shorter barrel than used in the rifle-musket meant that they had a considerably shorter effective range. The US Ordnance Corps reported that the effective range of the Sharps, whose sight could be set for 800 yards, was 500 yards. Battle range was considered to be 300 yards. Modern firing tests with original weapons resting on sandbags, however, show that at the close, but typical fighting range of 100 yards, most are quite accurate. Shots fired from a Merrill were grouped within five inches, as were shots fired from a Smith and a Sharps. Shots fired from a Gallagher landed within a six-inch circle. The Spencer was less accurate. Sighted for 1,000 yards, it was supposed to have an effective range of 400 yards with a battle range from 200 to 300 yards, and be able to place a six-inch group at 100 yards. In the modern test, at 100 yards all the Spencer shots landed within nine inches of the bulls-eye. Besides loss of accuracy, the lighter carbine ball, at least in Union carbines, was less damaging, although it was heavy enough to inflict serious injury.

The final weapon the cavalryman could use was the pistol. In 1861 the leading pistol maker in America was Samuel Colt whose products were in use around the world. Colt's revolvers had a revolving cylinder holding six combustible cartridges, a nipple with a small percussion cap mounted behind each one. Basically, two types of Colt revolver saw service: the M1851 0.36in calibre 'navy' revolver and the M1860 0.44in calibre 'army' revolver. An M1861 'navy' revolver, which looked like a smaller army revolver, was also made, although in only small numbers due to its lack of popularity. The US Army purchased 129,730 Colt 'army' and 17,010 Colt 'navy' revolvers from 1861 to 1866.

The M1851 Colt 'navy' was widely copied by Southern manufacturers for Confederate issue because it was the CS

Two soldiers of Co D, 11th Michigan Cavalry, play about with their weapons for the photographer. The revolver is a Remington. The soldier holding the sabre is probably Private Ephraim P. Warner. The 11th was mustered in late 1863, served in Kentucky and Tennessee and was merged with the 8th Michigan Cavalry on 20 July 1865. (John Sickles collection)

This cavalryman holds a pre-war Virginia Manufactory sabre and has a Colt-style revolver stuck in his belt, which also has a Virginia state belt-plate. (Herb Peck Jr. collection)

Ordnance Department's standard. Makers included Griswold & Gunnison, with some 3,600; Leech & Rigdon, with 350; Rigdon & Ansley, with 2,330; the Columbus Fire Arms Manufacturing Co., with 7,500; and Schneider & Glassick, with a record total of fourteen pistols manufactured. Most Confederate copies differed from Colt originals in that they had round barrels. Many, such as the Griswold & Gunnison, had brass frames due to iron shortages.

The second most popular US Army pistol was made by Remington in Ilion, New York. It came in both 0.36in and 0.45in calibre and looked rather like the Colt save that it had a bar over the top of the cylinder, which added greatly to the weapon's strength. The US Army bought 125,314 Remington army revolvers and 1,901 navy revolvers.

The Whitney 0.36in calibre revolver also used a strap over the cylinder. The US bought 11,214 Whitney revolvers. In all, some 1,400 Southern-made copies with a brass frame were made by Spiller & Burr for the Confederate army. Just before the war copies of the Whitney, using brass frames, were made by Shawk & McLanahan in St. Louis, Missouri, and the small number made probably saw duty on both sides.

Other revolvers purchased by the US Army were the Starr, 47,952; the Savage, 11,284; the Roger & Spencer, 5,000; the Pettengill, 2,001; the Joslyn, of which, 1,100 were purchased. Both sides also imported large quantities of Adams, Deane, Kerr, and Tranter army revolvers from Great Britain, and Lefaucheux 0.45in calibre revolvers from France. Indeed, the US Army purchased 12,374 of the French weapons which were unusual in that they were pinfire rather than percussion.

One final French-made pistol that should be mentioned, if only because J. E. B. Stuart carried one, was the LeMat.

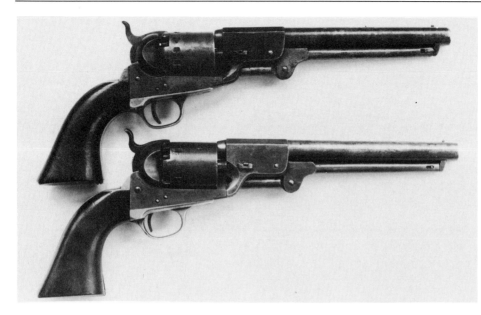

Two Southern-made copies of the Colt Navy revolver. The one on top is a Rigdon-Ansley, made after the firm was founded in January 1864. Below this is a Leech & Rigdon revolver made some time before December 1863. (Russ Pritchard collection)

This unique revolver was designed by a Dr. LeMat from New Orleans but manufactured by him in France after New Orleans fell. The LeMat had a cylinder for ordinary cartridges built around a smoothbore barrel in its centre. This came in both 16- and 18-gauge and fired buckshot. The cylinder held nine rounds, some models in 0.35in and some in 0.40in calibre. LeMat revolvers used in the Confederate cavalry had spur triggerguards, those used in the Confederate Navy had round trigger guards. The idea of having an extra shotgun load in a cavalry mêlée certainly would appeal, but the LeMats were generally were of poor quality and saw little use.

Artillery Weapons

Initially the M1841 smoothbore 6-pounder gun was the most widely used, especially by the Confederates. It was designed to fire solid shot against troops at ranges from 600 to 2,000 yards; spherical case shot against troops from 500 to 1,500 yards, and canister (tins of balls) against charging troops, from closer than 500 yards. Shells were used ideally at some 1,500 yards to destroy buildings, scatter troops in woods, or in pursuit. They were also used when a moral, rather than physical, effect was needed.

Artillerymen, however, wanted a gun that would be as light as the 6-pounder but have a larger bore, and later the most common gun on both sides was the M1857 Napoleon. At the war's outset, the US Army had only five Napoleons in service, but they acquired 1,127 of them as the war progressed. The Confederate Army either made or acquired from private Southern makers 481 documented Napoleons, starting in December 1861. There could have been as many as 100 more cast, and, of course, they added to their arsenal through captures.

The Napoleon fired a 12-pound ball from a smoothbore 1,200-pound bronze tube. Carriages were of wood painted olive-green with black-painted iron hardware. Because of material shortages, some Confederate Napoleons were made with iron tubes with reinforced breeches, which seemed to work well enough. Some Confederate Napoleons had 1,320-pound tubes, apparently made heavier to compensate the poor quality material used in their construction.

The Napoleon's minimum range with shot or shell was 300 yards. It could fire a solid shot against masses of troops some 600 to 2,000 yards' distant. Spherical case shot was used against masses of troops at ranges from 500 to 1,500 yards. A 12-pound shell could be fired at any range from 300 to 1,500 yards, but it was most effective at the greatest distance. Canister could be fired effectively at short ranges and certainly at less than 500 yards.

The US Army experimentally rifled the bore of at least six Napoleons, but this practice never became standard. US Army General Charles T. James devised a method of rifling bronze smoothbore tubes, but they wore out quickly and presented some danger of premature explosions from smouldering cartridge bag remains in their deep grooves.

Instead, rifled artillery tubes were generally of iron and came in two designs: the 3-inch Ordnance Rifle and the 10-pounder Parrott gun. During the war the US Army acquired 587 10-pound, 2.9-inch bore Parrott guns. These generally resembled the Napoleon save for their black tubes with tell-tale heavy iron reinforcing bands around the breech. Despite this reinforcement, they developed the reputation among cannoneers for bursting just ahead of the breech-band after lengthy use. They had a range of as much as 2,000 yards which made them useful for such work as counter-battery firing. And, despite the rifling, the Parrott could be used to fire canister against charging troops, although less effectively than the Napoleon. The US Army also acquired 338 20-pounder, 392 30-pounder, 237 100-pounder, 90 200-pounder and 40 300-pounder Parrotts. The heavier guns, of course, were fired from fixed positions.

The 3-inch Ordnance Rifle, made of heavy wrought iron,

A 10-pounder Parrott gun on the Gettysburg battlefield. (Author's collection)

was rather more dependable, yet had the same firing characteristics as the 10-pounder Parrott. The US Army acquired 925 of them.

The US Army also acquired 388 M1841 12-pounder mountain howitzers. These short-barrelled bronze tubes were designed for use at shorter ranges than the Napoleon or the rifled gun, with a maximum range of some 1,072 yards. The carriage, tube, ammunition chest and wheels could all be disassembled in the field and carried on three pack mules. Given this ease of transport over rough terrain, they saw the most service in the far west where, moreover, their short ranges presented no problems from counter-battery fire. Field howitzers, 12-, 24- and 32-pounders, were also available.

There were some breech-holding cannon available during the war, but relatively few of them saw use. The Army of Northernern Virginia had a battery of British-made 12-pounder Whitworths which had a range of 4,059 yards and were, according to one British test, spot on at 2,300 yards. However, a lack of indirect fire control and target acquisition equipment meant that the weapons' accuracy at such ranges was by and large wasted.

Essentially, loading and firing all field artillery cannon involved the same drill. Each crewman was numbered, numbers one and two standing on each side of the muzzle, three and four on each side of the breech, and five, six, and seven back by the limber chest, which was located six yards behind the gun. Number one, to the left of the muzzle, swabbed out the bore with water as number three, to the left of the breech, covered the vent with his leather-wrapped thumb to prevent sparks from igniting. Number six passed a round, for example a round ball strapped to a wooden sabot with a flannel powder bag containing a charge, to number five. He put it in a leather haversack and brought it to number two who then placed it in the muzzle. Number one rammed it home. Then number four pierced the powder bag

with an iron vent pick and stuck a friction primer in the vent. He then stuck a hook on one end of a lanyard into the friction primer and stepped back. All the other crew members also stepped back, but made a point of always watching the muzzle to be sure that their gun rather than a neighbouring one had gone off before resuming the drill. On the gunner's command, 'fire!' number four pulled the lanyard which set off the primer which discharged the piece. The drill was then repeated. A well-trained gun crew could get off about two aimed rounds a minute, although Union artillery doctrine called for a standard rate of fire of one round every two minutes.

Siege artillery was simply field artillery made bigger. In addition to the various weights of Parrott guns previously mentioned, the Union Army used 8-inch, 10-inch, 13-inch, 15-inch and 20-inch Rodman guns. Coastal guns came in 24-pounder and 42-pounder models. Confederate siege artillery included 8-, 10-, and 15-inch columbiads; 32- and 42-pound sea coast guns; 8- and 10-inch sea coast howitzers; and 18- and 24-pounder siege and garrison guns. The seven men needed to serve a 15-inch columbiad could load and fire the weapon in one minute and ten seconds.

One last artillery type should be mentioned. The mortar was a stubby tube attached to a wooden base and was designed to throw shells in a high arc at a target. The bronze 24-pounder coehorn could move with the army, but remained in a fixed position during a battle or siege. The US Army acquired 298 of these. Other iron mortars came in 8-, 10- and 13-inch calibres and were used for siege warfare, some being mounted in small boats or on railroad flatcars. The US Army acquired 199 8-inch and 188 10-inch siege howitzers, and 90 13-inch sea-coast howitzers during the war. The three- to five-man mortar crew, the number depending on the mortar's size, could fire twelve shots an hour under normal conditions, although in an emergency they could get off 20 rounds in an hour.

Union mortar crews in 1862. The cannoneer standing just ahead of the cannon-ball has an artilleryman's issue leather haversack. (US Army Military History Institute collection)

An unknown Union light artillery sergeant holds the M1840 light artillery sabre. His headgear is the regulation dress shako; the plume hides the eagle and crossed cannon cap badge. (Michael F. Bremer collection)

Personal Weapons

Officially, swords were the only personal weapons issued to individual artillerymen. The Union light, or field artilleryman was supposed to carry the M1840 light artillery saber. It had a deeply curved blade, 32 inches long by 1.25-inches at the hilt. The grips were of wood wrapped in black leather with twisted brass wire around them. The single guard was brass ending in a Phrygian helmet pattern pommel. The scabbard was of iron. The US Army obtained 20,757 light artillery sabers from 1 January 1861 to 30 June 1866. However, artillerymen often carried the light cavalry saber instead of the M1840 on active service. The officers' version was the same, but engraved on the guard, pommel, and blade. The Confederate army issued similar (some Southern-made) versions of this weapon which were, typically, cruder in manufacture and materials, and were actually rarely carried.

The US Army also obtained 2,152 foot artillery swords. These were designed to be carried by artillerymen who manned the large pieces usually used in fortifications. The M1832 foot artillery sword was probably the greatest waste of material and money of any weapon issued by either army – and both issued versions of this sword. It was designed after a French version of the Roman short sword, with a 19-inch blade, 1⅜ inches wide at the hilt. It had an all-brass hilt with grips moulded to look like eagle feathers, and a pommel stamped with an eagle and shield. The scabbard was of black leather with brass mountings.

Both types of sword were designed to serve as personal defence weapons in case of the battery or fort being overrun. In fact, the revolver would be a superior weapon in that event, and revolvers were widely carried by cannoneers on both sides. Sheath knives worn from the belt were also useful, not only as personal defence weapons but for camp duties as well.

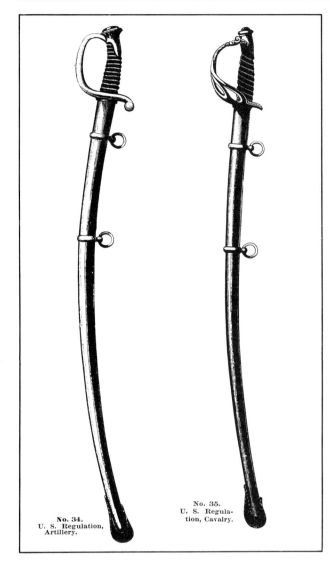

Sword number 35 is the regulation cavalry sabre; sword 34 is the light artillery sabre.

This unknown private of the First Company, New Hampshire Volunteer Heavy Artillery Regiment, wears the standard foot soldier's equipment as was common for foot artillerymen. His weapon is a variant of the M1861 rifle-musket. He has a brass shoulder-scale on each shoulder. (Author's collection)

NAVAL WEAPONRY

The Ships

At the war's outset, the mainstay of the US Navy were its unarmoured ships, the largest of which were the ship-of-the-line sailing vessels, all of which had been laid down before 1822. Most of these were being used as store or receiving ships. The Navy's frigates, two of which had been laid down in 1796, were available in both steam and sailing versions and saw use largely as blockading and high sea vessels, and the Navy had a variety of smaller vessels, both steam and sail, such as sloops, gunboats, and brigs.

The Confederate Navy started with nothing and had to build a fleet from scratch, with little money, material, or shipbuilding expertise. For river and harbour defence they came up with the idea of building ironclad ships which would have sloping armor walls pierced for guns, with a ram mounted on the bow, the bow and stern being virtually under water. The first one of these was the CSS *Virginia*, built on the salvaged hull and machinery of the USS *Merrimack*, which was commissioned in March 1862. The concept proved so successful that the Confederate Navy made 27 more of these, varying, however, in details such as number of guns and dimensions.

The CSS Alabama *anchored off Capetown, South Africa on 6 August 1863. (Cape Archives, South Africa, collection)*

The receiving ship USS North Carolina, *once a proud ship-of-the-line. Laid down in 1816, she was commissioned in 1825 and ended her days as a receiving ship in New York. (Author's collection)*

Confederate naval and marine officers on the CSS Chicora *in Charleston's harbor, while Confederate sailors, with light-colored broad shirt collars and darker colored shirts, row a longboat. The* Chicora *was similar in design and appearance to all Confederate ironclads. (Old Court House Museum, Vicksburg collection)*

The Confederate War Department also purchased four-teen vessels at New Orleans which they covered with compressed cotton bales for protection and armed with an oak and iron ram and a couple of guns each. These 'cottonclads' saw service at the Fall of New Orleans and later at the Battle of Memphis on 6 June 1862.

For the high seas duty of preying on Northern commerce, the Confederate Navy had a number of cruisers built in Britain, and converted passenger ships for the purpose. A number of smaller sailing vessels were purchased and turned into gunboats.

The Confederate Navy also built fourteen spar torpedo and three submarine torpedo boats. These were designed to sit low in the water, or beneath the surface in the case of submarines, and attack a Union ship either by ramming or attaching a torpedo (virtually a mine). These submarines were small, steam-powered boats known as 'Davids' (the Confederates were up against a large fleet and saw themselves as giant-killers) and although they trimmed right down until only funnel and conning tower showed, they could not submerge completely and cannot really be classed as submarines. The best known of these was the *H. L. Hunley*, a submarine which attacked the USS *Housatonic* near Charleston, South Carolina, on 17 February 1864. The spar torpedo she attached to the Union ship's hull exploded and sank the ship, but the Confederate submarine appar-ently foundered while returning to port and was lost with all hands.

The Confederates also used a variety of types of torpedo in fixed locations or as free-floating mines in rivers and harbours to destroy Union ships. Some used percussion caps that were set off by the victim actually hitting the torpedo or its trigger. An electric torpedo was connected to an electric battery on the shore by gutta-percha-covered wires. An operator fired it when a target passed over it. Drift torpedoes were set loose to float some feet below the surface beneath an enemy ship. It was hoped that the ship's propellers would foul the trigger lines attached to pieces of wood floating on the surface and set the torpedo off. Other torpedoes, some with clockwork timers and others with percussion-cap triggers, were placed on rafts and floated among enemy shipping. A so-called 'coal torpedo' was simply a tube of cast iron filled with powder and painted black. It would be tossed into any US Navy coal yard by a Confederate agent in the hope that it would end up in a ship's boiler. One of these caused a great deal of damage at City Point, Virginia, in 1864.

The US Navy met the Confederate Navy's ironclad challenge with an ingenious ship of its own, the USS *Monitor*, designed by a Swede, John Ericsson. This was nothing more than a turret pierced for two 11-inch smoothbore guns mounted on a deck whose freeboard was so low that only the pilot house and funnels showed above the water. Although the original ship was not fit for deep sea action and indeed foundered and sank off Cape Hatteras, North Carolina during a storm, the idea was so successful that the Navy commissioned 51 more such vessels. These

came in different configurations. Most were like the original ship, but the *Roanoke* had three turrets, while others were built with two turrets and were ocean-going craft. Another improvement to the original design was the mounting of the pilot house on top of the turrets to give the guns a clear firing arc over the bows. Some of these ships had an extremely shallow draft which made them ideal for river warfare; they were unusual in that they had curved, turtle-like decks. Other river monitors were built with one or two turrets and a casement aft.

Several ships that looked like traditional sailing ships, but with iron-plated sides, were also launched, but they were found to be less successful than the Ericsson-designed craft. After experimenting with six tugs armed with torpedoes, the Navy commissioned a spar torpedo boat, the *Stomboli*. It even launched a hand-propelled submarine, the *Alligator*, in 1862 but she was lost after having been cut adrift from the ship towing her during a storm off the North Carolina coast on 2 April 1863.

A blockade-runner escapes US Navy blockaders

'As we neared Beaufort [North Carolina] every light was carefully covered at night, even the binacle lamps being masked . . . No one slept much that night, and as soon as the fog lifted in the morning every eye was on the alert. Beaufort harbour was plainly visible some miles distant, and we saw, besides, what we did not care to see. "Sail astern!" shouted the lookout; and then came the cry: "Sail on the starboard bow!" and then again: "Sail on the port bow!" Things looked rather blue . . . The "Stars and Stripes" were run up at the mainmast head, and then a small private signal of Messrs. Spofford & Tileston, the former agents of the vessel, was run up at the foremast. Our course was then changed so that we headed for the nearer of the two United States vessels . . . On we went . . . until Beaufort harbor was not more than five or six miles distant on our starboard bow. We could see the officers on the quarter-deck of the blockader, and the men at the guns. The engines were slowed down, and we blew off steam. The blockader nearest us to us thought that we had something to communicate, and lowered a boat. As this was done, we hove round, the "Stars and Sripes" came fluttering to the deck, and the Confederate flag was run up at the foremast, the mainmast and the peak. With all the steam we could carry, we dashed on toward Beaufort. The Yankee now saw the trick, and fired a broadside at us. No harm was done. She followed rapidly, firing occasionally from the bow guns; but without injury we crossed the bar under the protection of the guns of Fort Macon . . . '

(Francis W. Dawson, *Reminiscences of Confederate Service*, Louisiana State University Press, Baton Rouge, Louis-iana, 1980, pp. 27–9)

A number of purchased vessels were also used by the US Navy, including nineteen ferry boats from New York waters. These had their decks strengthened to take the heavy guns placed at each end. The advantage of these boats was that they could go about without having to describe a large half-circle to do so. This enabled them to get away quickly from a riverbank ambush, and they were very manoeuvrable on narrow rivers. Another type of river craft used by the US Navy was the mortar schooner. This was little more than a sailing boat armed with a 13-inch mortar and a couple of other guns. Mortar boats, which were simply rafts with a 13-inch mortar hidden behind seven-foot high ironclad walls, were also used in river engagements. Ironclads, built like the Confederate ironclads with sloping walls pierced for guns, were built in Missouri for river use. The *Cairo* class of seven of these ironclads were armed with fourteen guns. Other classes had more or fewer guns, but all were effective riverine warships. These ironclads used paddlewheels hidden within the armored walls, unlike the Confederate ironclads which had screw propellers. Partially armored Union sidewheelers were known as 'tinclads'. They looked like the famous Mississippi riverboats, but had the lower deck armored, its sides pierced for a number of guns. Finally, the Army Quartermaster Department had seven river steamers converted to rams with reinforced bows but few or no guns. They saw use at the Battle of Memphis.

Naval ordnance was essentially the same as army siege guns, although the US Navy's standard broadside gun was the 9-inch Dahlgren which had been designed by one of its admirals, John Dahlgren. The army friction primer, which sent slivers flying when the gun fired, could not be used at close quarters because many of the gun crew fought in bare feet, so a lock like a giant musket lock was used on naval guns instead.

Personal Weapons

Ratings could be armed with rifles. In the US Navy the standard rifle was the M1861 0.69in calibre Whitney Navy Rifle. This came with two different bayonets, a saber bayonet with a 22-inch blade, and a knife bayonet with a blade 11⅞ inches long and 1⅝ inches wide, which looked more like a Bowie knife than a bayonet. The Navy also issued 6,000 Sharps & Hankins breech-loading cartridge carbines, which were unique in that their barrels were covered with leather for protection against the salt air, and 500 Sharps & Hankins breech-loading cartridge rifles. M1851 Colt navy revolvers were standard, although Colt, Whitney, Remington and Starr Army and Navy revolvers were also issued. Ratings also used M1841 and M1860 cutlasses. The M1841 had an all-brass hilt, the grip being designed to look like eagle's feathers, and a 21-inch-long straight blade. The M1861 had leather-wrapped grips and a large brass half-basket guard for hand protection. Its slightly curved blade was 24⅞ inches long. Officers carried a similar cutlass with the letters 'US' or 'USN' cut into the guard. Otherwise they carried the M1852 officer's sword which was similar to the Army's foot officer's sword but used white fishskin for the grips and was engraved with nautical motifs.

Confederate sailors were armed with a variety of long arms according to where they were stationed. However, the Confederate Navy acquired British-made P1858 naval rifles, which were similar to Enfield rifles, and copies of Royal Navy cutlasses. The LeMat pistol, with its nine bullets and one shotgun charge, was an official CSN pistol as well as a cavalry one, and Southern-made copies of Northern pistols and British-made pistols were also widely used. The regulation officer's sword was also British-made and featured a gold-plated sea monster on its backstrap and

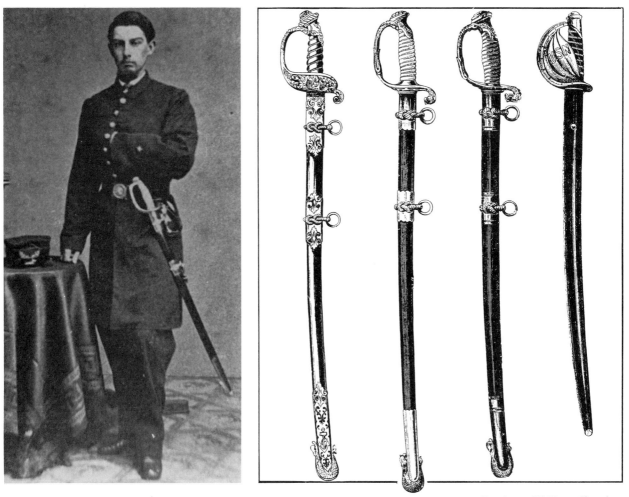

This unknown US Navy master's mate, his rank indicated by the star on the cuff and plain *wreath cap badge, wears the regulation officer's sword and belt. (Author's collection)*

Regulation US Navy officers' swords. (Catalog; Schuyler, Harley, & Graham, New York)

pommel, with white sharkskin grips wrapped with twisted brass wire. Scabbards were of black leather with gold-plated brass mountings. Southern makers also produced several other types of navy officers' swords.

References

William A. Albaugh III and Edward N Simmons, *Confederate Arms*, The Stackpole Co, Harrisburg, Pennsylvania, 1957

William A. Albaugh III, *Confederate Edged Weapons*, Harper & Bros, New York, 1960

Jack Coggins, *Arms and Equipment of the Civil War*, Doubleday & Co, Garden City, New York, 1962

William B. Edwards, *Civil War Guns*, The Stackpole Co, Harrisburg, Pennsylvania, 1962

Berkeley R. Lewis, *Small Arms and Ammunition in the United States Service, 1776–1865*, Smithsonian Institution, Washington, DC, 1956

Francis A. Lord, *Civil War Collectors Encyclopedia*, The Stackpole Co, Harrisburg, Pennsylvania, 1963

H. Michael Madaus, *The Warner Collector's Guide to American Longarms*, Warner Books, New York, 1981

Official, *The Field Manual for the use of the Officers on Ordnance Duty*, Richmond, 1862, reprinted, 1984

Official, *The Ordnance Manual for the use of the Officers of the United States Army*, J.B. Lippincott, Philadelphia, 1861

Harold L. Peterson, *American Knives*, Charles Scribner's Sons, New York, 1958

Harold L. Peterson, *The American Sword, 1775–1945*, Ray Riling Co, Philadelphia, 1983

Harold L. Peterson, *Round Shot and Rammers*, Bonanza Books, New York, 1969

Joseph W. Shields, Jr., *From Flintlock to M1*, Coward-McCann, New York, 1954

Paul H. Silverstone, *Warships of the Civil War*, Naval Institute Press, Annapolis, Maryland, 1989

Frederick P. Todd, *American Military Equippage 1851–1872*, The Company of Military Historians, vol. II, Providence, Rhode Island, 1977; vol. III, Westbrook, Connecticut, 1978

Donald B. Webster, Jr., *American Socket Bayonets 1717–1873*, Museum Restoration Service, Ottawa, Ontario, 1964

THE ART OF WAR ON LAND

Weapons that were improved technologically altered radically the way men fought, but the mentality of the tactics system writers and the generals rarely caught up with them. Generals continued to send their men into combat as if they were fighting Monmouth Court House, Lundy's Lane, or Buena Vista. But the men themselves, both small-unit commanders and privates on the line, learned new ways to fight and survive on the battlefield.

Infantry Tactics

Basic infantry tactics were simple in concept, virtually the same in 1861 as they had been in 1775, 1812 and 1846. Moreover, since the leaders of both Northern and Southern armies came from the same military academy and had studied the same books, their tactical systems were the same.

The infantry company, the basic building block of the battle, marched in column to the battlefield where it was deployed in a line two deep. Volleys were fired on command until the enemy was so weakened that a quick bayonet charge would rout him.

That was the theory. In reality, wrote Union General David H. Strother in late 1862, 'I have observed in this war that the fire of infantry is our main dependence in battle. There has been no bayonet charge from either side that amounted to anything. The opposing forces have never crossed bayonet to my knowledge.'[1] There were certainly bayonet charges, although bayonets *per se* were rarely fixed, muskets being used like clubs in the rare hand-to-hand combat. More often, however, either the charging side would be broken up by fire before it reached the enemy lines, or the enemy would run before the chargers reached them. Which was, after all, one of the purposes of the bayonet charge – to intimidate the enemy.

There were several tactical systems, or drill systems as they are known today. The one most commonly used by both sides was written by William Hardee, who became a Confederate general. Under his system, the men would line up in two ranks, usually assembled with the tallest men in the rear rank. They would then number off by twos from left to right. On the command 'Right face!' they would turn to the right, 'twos' then stepping forward and to the right so as to make a column of four men across. On the command 'Left face!' the 'twos' would step back to form a line two deep once more. Columns could also be turned into a line facing in the direction the column was heading by the commander ordering, 'Company into line, march!' Or, a column could turn into a line facing right by the officer commanding, 'Right by file into line, march!' One advantage of this over previous drill systems was that the change from column into line could be performed on the march; moving columns could turn instantly into moving lines, facing in any direction.

Once in line, the company could wheel to face any direction; it could march straight ahead or to the left or right

Colonel Thomas Cass, 9th Massachusetts Infantry, wears a comfortable field uniform consisting of a pull-over smock and white canvas and brown leather 'sporting shoes'. His foot officer's sword is in a metal scabbard. Cass was killed on 27 June 1862 during the Peninsula Campaign. (Author's collection)

oblique. It could fire by volley, in a rolling fire from right to left, or at will.

The regiment was drawn up with all its companies in line, regimental colours in the centre, drums and officers and staff non-commissioned officers at appointed positions to the rear to control their men. Higher commands simply continued this, putting regiments in a continuous line, although some were generally held in reserve.

Generally speaking, a mid-war company would have numbered some 50 officers and men. They would be formed into two ranks thirteen inches apart, captain and corporals in the front rank and other officers and non-commissioned officers behind as file closers. According to figures in *U.S. Infantry Tactics*, published by J. B. Lippincott, Philadelphia, in 1862 under authority of the Secretary of War, they would occupy a front of some 16.5 yards. A regiment of ten companies, again the norm, would take up a 165-yard front. However, the usual practice was to deploy two companies or 10 per cent of the men from each company some 100–175 yards in advance of the regiment as a skirmish line. This would reduce the regimental front to 132 yards. Regiments were generally posted twenty yards apart, brigades were separated by 25 yards and divisions by 50 yards. Therefore, a brigade of typically five regiments, with a skirmish line, would have a front of 740 yards; a division of three brigades, 2,270 yards, and a corps of three divisions, 6,910 yards – almost four miles. Such an impressive spectacle was seen at the Battle of Winchester in 1864 when two corps were drawn up in full line of battle with virtually no intervals between them. A column would take about half the distance of a line, since the men would be doubled up.

Battle lines were usually drawn up from 500 to 200 yards from each other. 'The fire of infantry then has been the main reliance, and its fire has been terribly destructive,' Strother wrote. 'At a short range (say two hundred yards) no troops can stand it more than a few minutes.'[2] Many engagements

took place at less than 200 yards, however, especially in heavily wooded terrain such as the Wilderness. Fighting time was limited by the amount of ammunition that could be carried. Each soldier carried 40 rounds in his cartridge box and, when fully equipped, another 60 in his haversack. Firing at the absolute maximum efficiency of some ten rounds a minute, his ammunition would have been expended in only ten minutes. Even the average five rounds a minute would exhaust his ammunition in twenty minutes. At this rate, of course, his weapon would be too hot to handle. Moreover, the black powder used in the rifle-musket caused the weapon to foul after a dozen or so shots, making it slower and more difficult to load. Generally, a regiment's ammunition would last up to two hours, but there were times when troops ran out of ammunition after a fire fight, such as when Starke's Louisiana Brigade at Second Bull Run had to resort to hurling rocks to stand off charging Union troops.

According to Hardee's manual, a soldier advancing at the double quick step, i.e., the charge, would cover 33 inches of ground a step and take 165 steps per minute. This would mean he could go just over 150 yards in a minute, given a relatively flat terrain with no brush or fences in his way. If he started his charge within a short range of 200 yards to the

Captain DeWitt Clinton Lewis, Co F, 97th Pennsylvania Infantry, holds his foot officer's sword. Lewis, who later was breveted major and lieutenant colonel, received the Medal of Honor for saving one of his men at the Battle of Secessionville, South Carolina. The numeral '97' is clearly visible within the loop of his cap-badge horn. (Author's collection)

Colonel James Kemper, 7th Virginia Infantry, was photographed before his promotion on 3 June 1862. His field-type uniform is quite plain. (Library of Congress collection)

The regulation Confederate uniform of a first lieutenant is worn by this man photographed   *in New Orleans. (John Wernick collection)*

A picket bayonets an enemy

'That night I stood picket on the Potomac with a detail of the Third Arkansas Regiment . . . Before nightfall, I took in every object and commenced my weary vigils. I had to stand all night. I could hear the rumblings of the Federal artillery and wagons, and hear the low shuffling sound made by troops on the march. The snow came pelting down as large as goose eggs. About midnight the snow ceased to fall, and became quiet. Now and then the snow would fall off the bushes and make a terrible noise. While I was peering through the darkness, my eyes suddenly fell upon the outlines of a man. The more I looked the more I was convinced that it was a Yankee picket. I could see his hat and coat – yes, see his gun. I was sure that it was a Yankee picket. What was I to do? The relief was several hundred yards in the rear. The more I looked the more sure I was. At last a cold sweat broke out all over my body. Turkey bumps rose. I summoned all the nerves and bravery I could command, and said: "Halt! Who goes there?" There being no response, I became resolute. I did not wish to fire and arouse the camp, but I marched right up to it and stuck my bayonet through and through it. It was a stump.'

(Sam R. Watkins, *"Co. Aytch"*, Collier Books, New York, 1962, pp. 34–5)

enemy, it would take just over a minute and three-quarters to cover the distance. During that time, each enemy soldier firing an average of five rounds a minute could fire about eight shots with his rifle-musket. That estimate may well have been optimistic in favour of the attacker. For one thing, few troops could actually run very far at the double quick step without becoming exhausted. The 1862 Confederate ordnance manual gives a more reasonable rate, saying that a man will cover 109 yards in a minute at the double quick, which would give a defender time for yet a couple more shots.

Losses among charging troops could be staggering. At Fredericksburg, the 81st Pennsylvania Infantry took 261 officers and men into battle and lost fifteen killed, 141 wounded and twenty missing for a casualty rate of 67.4 per cent. The 5th New Hampshire Infantry at the same battle lost 63.6 per cent of its officers and men. The Confederate 2nd Maryland Infantry Battalion charged up Culp's Hill on the second day at Gettysburg with 400 officers and men and had 52 of them killed and 140 wounded.

This is not to say that all charges were failures, broken up with disastrous losses. Indeed, shock effect could and did work, but it depended on the defenders losing their nerve. At Gaines Mill during the Peninsula Campaign the 4th

Texas Infantry was ordered to fix bayonets and charge Union troops behind a line of entrenchments. The men came on with such determination that the defenders only fired scattered shots before fleeing. Their panic infected Union troops behind them and the next two defensive lines also fled. In this particular instance, the brigade commander, John Hood, yelled at his men to continue pressing their charge, fearing that if they paused to return fire, a static fire fight would develop and a little would be gained.

Generals, seeing this type of success, tended to depend on the charge to win their victories, although such successes were rare indeed. Pickett's Charge at Gettysburg or the assault at Fredericksburg were more typical of the result of a massed infantry charge. It has been suggested that Confederate generals in particular were more prone to place their hopes on a massed infantry assault, but it is apparent that Union generals were quite as taken with the idea as being the major way to victory.

In passing, one unique Confederate weapon that boosted the charge should be mentioned – the 'rebel yell'. This was a high, piercing scream, a series of yips, constantly changing in volume and pitch, which both scared Union defenders and reassured Confederate attackers. Union troops had nothing like this, although they were apt to give 'manly' cheers on achieving their particular goals.

Even with morale-building yells, however, odds were on the side of the defender and most battles turned into static fire fights. The rifle-musket, accurate to 500 yards and deadly in its effect, made the old-style Napoleonic warfare,

The honor guard for the burial of Brigadier General William H. Lytle, on 21 October 1863, was drawn from combat veterans of the largely Irish 10th Ohio Infantry. Although their uniforms and equipment have *been cleaned for the occasion, they wear fatigue, rather than dress, uniforms as they would in the field. The enlisted men are armed with Enfield rifle-muskets. (James F. Neel collection)*

with its strict battle lines, obsolete. This did not mean that the average distances of engagement changed very much from Napoleonic warfare, but that the fighting was managed rather differently. Confederate infantryman Berry Benson recalled that at the war's outset he believed that soldiers really did line up perfectly, shoot on command, and charge as if in a picture. Later, however, he wrote that infantrymen entered the battle in good order, ' . . . but at the first "pop! pop!" of the rifles there comes a sudden loosening of the ranks, a freeing of selves from the impediment of contact, and every man goes to fighting on his own hook; firing as, and when he likes, and reloading as fast as he does. He takes shelter whenever he can find it, so he does not get too far away from his Co., and his officers will call attention to this should he move too far. He may stand up, he may kneel down, it is all right, tho' mostly the

men keep standing, except silent under fire – then they lie down.'[3]

Skirmishers became more important. The initial purpose of skirmishes was to press the enemy line, to harass and disrupt any preparations for attack. In early 1862 Major General George B. McClellan, then commanding the Army of the Potomac, authorized the commander of the 42nd Pennsylvania Infantry to test new skirmishing tactics the colonel had devised that would use the whole regiment as a skirmish line. While the colonel's tactics were not accepted to replace earlier tactical systems, as time went on the number of men sent out as skirmishers grew until by 1864 entire regiments fought as skirmishers rather than in Napoleonic line of battle.

Skirmishing duty was tough, calling for the soldier on the line often to be out of sight of his comrades, away from the banter that steadies the soldier under fire. 'Going into action as skirmishers five paces apart (oftener ten), and frequently in brushy places or thickets out of sight of the comrade right and left, often far ahead of the regular battle line, each man looking out for himself,' wrote a US Sharpshooter, made each skirmisher as alert as possible.[4]

Skirmish drill called for two lines of soldiers, each individual some yards from his fellows. One line would

Private Oliver S. Daugherty, Co E, 11th Indiana Infantry, was photographed on the field of Shiloh on 28 April 1862. He wears his regiment's second zouave-style uniform and is armed with an M1855 Harpers

Ferry rifle, sword bayonet and small pistol with ivory grips. Daugherty eventually became an officer of US Colored Troops, resigning his commission in June 1864. (Kean Wilcox collection)

This unidentified corporal in a state-issued jacket, holds an Enfield rifle-musket with a

brass tompion in its muzzle to keep out dirt and moisture. (Richard F. Carlile collection)

cover the other. If they were advancing, the line in the rear would load while the first fired, then rush by them, kneel some yards ahead and fire while the second loaded. The second line would then rush forward. If retreating, the first line would fire, then fall back past the second which had loaded and now fired. Then the second would fall back past the first which would lay down covering fire. If in a static position, the first and second would simply run back and forth, loading when in the rear and firing when in the front.

In fact, skirmishing was much less orderly than the tactics system would indicate. 'The skirmishers', wrote 105th Illinois Infantry Private Robert H Strong, 'being ahead of our line, would have to stand the first brunt of a charge. Rebel sharpshooters would pay us plenty of attention while their lines were re-forming to charge. But as we could hide behind trees and protect ourselves, and had no hard work to do such as the boys in the line were doing, it was not such a bad place to be in after all. In case the Rebs charged us and we skirmishers could not check or stop them we would fall back on to the line.'[5]

In addition to an increase in the number of skirmishers deployed and the looseness of the actual line of battle as the war progressed, soldiers also learned to dig in whenever they got the chance. This was a basic tactical innovation which the men in the front lines devised for themselves. No generals issued orders requiring this to be done; none probably thought of doing it. No entrenching tools of any type were issued to the men, who had to use bayonets, tin cups and plates to dig in. Moreover, each regiment had only a handful of pioneers so each man would have to participate. Private Rice Bull, of the 123rd New York Infantry, later wrote, 'We had no tools at first, but we had become adept at trenching and could use anything in reach to quickly dig and throw dirt ahead of us. We worked in pairs at each pit, first loosening up the ground with our bayonets and then using anything we could find to push the dirt to the front. Our hands and the dish we had in our haversacks would do this work when we had no picks and shovels. It was really wonderful how fast one could pile up material sufficient to stop bullets when they were singing about him.'[6]

Cavalry Tactics

America's leading military philosopher before the war, D. H. Mahan, wrote in a handbook widely used by officers on both sides, 'The arm of cavalry by itself can effect but little; and in many circumstances, does not suffice even for its own safety. The smallest obstacles are sufficient to render it powerless; it can neither attack nor hold a post without the aid of infantry, and at night is alarmed, and justly so, at every phantom.'[7]

With such negative thinking, it is not surprising to find that cavalry was not considered a major force on the battlefield, and not much was expected of it. The Confederates, at least initially, made the best use of cavalry under such dynamic leaders as Nathan B. Forrest and J. E. B. Stuart. Largely, however, they used cavalry for large raids, which produced few strategic results, and for reconnaissance. Union leaders tended to split up their cavalry in penny packets, wasting its force on courier duties and as headquarters guards.

At the outset of the war the Poinsett, or 1841, system of cavalry tactics was in use. This called for two ranks to be deployed so that wounded men in the first rank during a charge could be replaced on the run. Also, two ranks would ensure a more solid shock value, which was one of the cavalry's main ways of overcoming an enemy formation. The Army of the Potomac's cavalry commander – the term is misleading since he really functioned more as a staff officer, the men being under others' commands – changed this system. He ordered a one-rank system which was easier to learn and use. Under Cooke's tactical system, each cavalry line would be made up of ten squadrons of six companies each. The two squadrons at each end of the line would be automatically deployed as flankers. The problem was that the standard US Army cavalry regiment contained only three squadrons. The system produced a formation that was more difficult for a commander to control; a brigade of some 2,400 men made a line a mile and a half long in column, allowing for normal intervals between battalions and companies. None the less, the single-rank system remained in use throughout the war, particularly in the less conservative western theatre.

In theory, the shock value of a saber-waving cavalry charge could break up any formation. Charges were to be made in single line, columns of fours, or double columns of fours. A column of four would occupy a great deal of space, since each horse occupies about three yards and a yard would be left between ranks. A 96-man company in a column of four would then take up 95 yards. Sheridan's three divisions and six batteries during the Richmond Raid extended over thirteen miles.

Cavalry could advance at 100 yards a minute at the walk, 200 yards at the trot and 400 yards at the gallop. A charge could combine all three, saving the gallop for the last 450 or so yards. Therefore, a cavalry unit 1,500 yards from a typical mid-war infantry company with 40 firing muskets on line would take three minutes and 24 seconds to reach the men, using the typical combination of walk, trot and final gallop. The final gallop would start at a point 400 yards from the defenders. During that time infantry could fire a total of 644 rounds of bone-breaking conical bullets into the charging mass. A charged artillery battery could get off seven rounds, ending with double canister.

During fighting in the Valley Campaign, a group of Union cavalrymen charged a Confederate infantry position. 'Just as these hundred men had reached the fence', a Confederate observer later wrote, 'the cavalry came thundering by, but a deadly volley stopped their wild career. Some in front, unhurt, galloped off, on their way, but just behind them horses and riders went down in a tangled heap. The rear, unable to check themselves, plunged on, in, over, upon the bleeding pile, a roaring, shrieking, struggling mass of men and horses, crushed, wounded and dying. It was a sickening sight, the worst I had ever seen then, and for a moment I felt a twinge of regret that I had ordered that little line to that bloody work.'[8]

There were successful cavalry charges. These were against other bodies of cavalry or disorganized infantry or artillery units. For example, at First Bull Run, J. E. B. Stuart's 1st Virginia Cavalry routed the green 11th New York (Fire Zouaves), which was posted on a hill in support of an artillery battery. In this instance, however, the 11th broke and ran at the very sight of the charging cavalry, giving the horsemen only a scattering fire as they passed by the running infantrymen. Well-organized and disciplined infantry or supported artillery were virtually impossible to

---

Confederates form square against Union cavalry

'Halloo! here comes a cavalry charge from the Yankee line. Now for it; we will see how Yankee cavalry fight . . . They thunder down upon us. Their flat-footed dragoons shake and jar the earth. They are all around us – we are surrounded. "Form square! Platoons, right and left wheel! Kneel and fire!" There we were in a hollow square . . . They charged right upon us. Colonel Field, sitting on his gray mare, right in the center of the hollow square, gives the command, "Front rank, kneel and present bayonet against cavalry." The front rank knelt down, placing the butts of their guns against their knees. "Rear rank, fire at will; commence firing." Now all this happened in less time than it has taken me to write it. They charged upon us, no doubt expecting to ride right over us, and trample us to death with the hoofs of their horses. They tried to spur and whip their horses over us, but the horses had more sense than that. We were pouring a deadly fire right into their faces, and soon men and horses were writhing in their death agonies; officers were yelling at the top of their voices, "Surrender! Surrender!" but we were having too good a thing of it. We were killing them by scores, and they could not fire at us; if they did they either overshot or missed their aim. Their ranks began to break and get confused, and finally they were routed . . .'

(Sam R. Watkins, "Co. Aytch", Collier Books, New York, 1962, pp. 147–8)

Private Joseph H. Lawrence, Co D, 1st Maine Cavalry, holds his Colt Army revolver. The 1st served in the Army of the Potomac from March 1862 until being mustered out on 1 August 1854, having seen action in most of that army's battles. (John Sickles collection)

Private James O. Sheppard was a member of the Cadet Company of the 6th South Carolina Cavalry. He is wearing a US Army mounted man's belt-plate. Sheppard was killed in action at Trevilian Station on 12 June 1864. (Brigadier General James Daniels/US Army Military History Institute collection)

overrun with a mounted cavalry saber charge. A mounted cavalry saber charge had a better chance against other mounted cavalry which would usually advance to meet the charge with a counter-charge, the shock value working for one side or the other. Indeed, in cavalry versus cavalry fights, the saber remained an important weapon, some Confederate cavalry commanders complaining late in the war that their troops were useless in fights with Union cavalry since they lacked sabers. Their men were lucky in that strictly cavalry fights were, on the whole, rare during the war.

None the less, most cavalry commanders saw that the day of the saber charge was over and devised informal tactics the better to use the mounted arm. 'I believe I was the first cavalry commander who discarded the saber as useless and consigned it to museums for the preservation of antiquities. My men were as little impressed by a body of cavalry charging them with sabers as though they had been armed with cornstalks,' wrote Confederate partisan Colonel John S. Mosby. 'I think that my command reached the highest point of efficiency as cavalry because they were well armed with two six-shooters and their charges combined the effect of fire and shock.'[9]

In the west, Nathan B. Forrest preferred the shock value of shotguns fired from horseback at close range as the perfect cavalry weapon. The trouble with shotguns is that they lacked range in fighting against troops armed with rifle-muskets or carbines. Moreover, their pellets did not distinguish between friends and foes in a mêlée.

Watching a cavalry battle

'Observing that our [Union] cavalry seemed to be coming back at rather a livelier pace than usual, I noticed what appeared to be either a large regiment or a small brigade of Confederate cavalry emerge from the woods to the south of the plain. They formed their lines and moved to the attack.

'Our men, also, were soon in motion. As they approached each other the two bodies increased their pace, until both seemed to be moving at full speed. They met with a jar, and for some moments it was impossible to distinguish friend from foe. There could only be distinctly seen the flashing of sabers in the sunlight as blows were struck and parried, and the puffs of smoke from revolvers and carbines. For ten minutes or more the stirring fight went on without any apparent advantage to either side. But now another regiment of our cavalry, which had been out of sight up the river at the beginning of the fight, came down upon the Confederates at a hard gallop. It was but a minute before the latter were retreating back to the timber, perhaps hurried a little by a few shells from our shore batteries.'

(Julian W. Hinkley, *A Narrative of Service with the Third Wisconsin Infantry*, Wisconsin Historical Commission, 1912, pp. 39–40)

Confederate staff officers rout Union cavalry

'On the march, by the way, there was an exciting incident. General [R. H.] Anderson, with the staff and couriers, was far ahead of the infantry column, and we had a squadron of cavalry as our escort and advance guard. A couple of shots were suddenly fired, and in an instant our cavalry broke and came clattering to the rear. The indignation of General Anderson was painful to see. He cried out to our cavalry: "What manner of men do you call yourselves?" and putting his hand involuntarily to his side, said: "Oh, if I had my saber!" Turning to his staff and couriers, he said: "Charge those people in front," pointing to the blue-coated cavalry, who were as much astonished at coming upon us as we were at meeting with them. It was a mutual surprise. The staff with the couriers dashed at the handful of cavalry who had driven in our advance guard, and we had a glorious race down the turnpike to the suburbs of Winchester [Virginia]. I think we captured four or five Yankees, without any loss to our side, and my share in the plunder was a very good McClellan saddle and a small sum in greenbacks.'

(Francis Dawson, *Reminiscences of Confederate Service*, Louisiana State University Press, Baton Rouge, 1980, pp. 121–2)

Generally, therefore, cavalry became essentially mounted infantry, riding to a point to attack or defend, dismounting, and fighting on foot with carbines. One man in four would remain behind the firing line, holding all four horses, as the other three advanced in a loose skirmishing line. This sort of thing appalled the traditionalist. 'Cavalry skirmishing went on until quite dark, a determined attack having been made by the enemy, who did his best to prevent the trains from crossing the Potomac at Williamsport,' wrote Coldstream Guards Colonel A. J. L. Fremantle, an observer with the Confederate Army in 1863. 'It resulted in the success of the Confederates; but every impartial man confesses that these cavalry fights are miserable affairs. Neither party has any idea of serious charging with the sabre. They approach one another with considerable boldness, until they get to within about forty yards, and then, at the very moment when a dash is necessary, and the sword alone should be used, they hesitate, halt, and commence a desultory fire with carbines and revolvers.'[10]

The cavalry had become essentially a skirmishing force whose horses let them move from point to point on the

Private John P. Sellman, Co K, 1st Virginia Cavalry, wears the plain gray jacket and trousers typical of Confederate cavalry in the second half of the war. His belt-plate is the regulation US Army mounted man's model. Charles T. Jacobs/US Army Military History Institute collection)

It was a common practice in the Army of the Tennessee to mount infantry. Regimental Quartermaster Sergeant Robert G. Huston, 118th Illinois Mounted Infantry, was photographed in Baton Rouge in a typically western informal slouch hat and custom-made blouse. The image was taken some time between his appointment on 26 January 1864 and 5 August 1865 when he quit the job. (Richard K. Tibbals collection)

impossible to provide. A captain commanded the battery. Two guns made up a section under a lieutenant, and a single gun (called a piece) was commanded by a sergeant.

Each piece took up an area five yards deep with about two yards of front. Some fourteen yards were to be left between pieces. Hence, a six-gun battery would offer a front of 82 yards. The limber chest, in which ammunition was stored, was placed six yards behind the piece. It was taken off its limber for ease of use, but the limber and the six horses used in pulling the limber and attached gun remained nearby. Some eleven yards behind them, spare caissons with extra ammunition chests, as well as the battery wagon and forge, were posted. The distance from the back of the spare caisson to the face of the piece was some 47 yards. In the Union artillery, the ammunition supply in these chests was 400 rounds per gun but, this had been reduced to 250 rounds per gun by mid-1863, because in 1862 batteries had been firing as many as 300 to 400 rounds even in small skirmishes and the Army of the Potomac artillery commander thought that this was far too much.

As a combat support arm, each battery was generally assigned to a division and the captain commanding reported directly to the divisional commander or chief of artillery. This command structure meant that rarely could artillery be massed for its best effect. The particular army chief of artillery did not actually command all the artillery in that army. As with all other field armies, the Army of the Potomac established an artillery reserve which was, in this case, commanded by a brigadier general. At Gettysburg, where massed artillery played an important part of Pickett's Charge, this artillery reserve consisted of eighteen batteries divided into five brigades mostly commanded by captains, three with four batteries and one with two batteries. At Antietam where it saw great use, the Army of Northern Virginia's reserve artillery, also commanded by a brigadier general, consisted of four battalions commanded by field grade officers with five batteries in three battalions and four batteries in one of them. It also had five independent batteries.

According to Mahan, artillery was to be posted where it could silence the enemy's artillery so that the infantry could attack. Cannon would accompany the assaulting infantry, some posted on its flanks and a section about a hundred paces ahead of the attacking infantry column. During the war, however, the rifle-musket made this too dangerous to be practicable. If it was intended that the column be deployed into line before opening fire, the artillery would

battlefield with more speed than the infantry. Indeed, in the western theatre, a number of regular infantry regiments were mounted in such organizations as Wilder's Lightning Brigade to take advantage of this speed.

Artillery Tactics

The duties of field artillery, wrote America's leading military philospher during the years just prior to the Civil war ' . . . are to support and cover the other arms; to keep the enemy from approaching too near; hold him in check when he advances; and prevent him from *debouching* at particular points.'[11]

The artillery on both sides was initially organized into batteries of six guns each, although the Army of Northern Virginia was forced to reduce its batteries to four guns in 1864 as provisions for enough horses for six guns became

A section of Battery F, 3rd South Carolina Artillery Battalion, the 'Palmetto Light Artillery', which served for four years in the lines around Charleston. The officer standing with his arms folded has an M1833 dragoon sabre. The men apparently have a red band on the forage cap, while number 1, who is ramming a shot, is wearing an M1839 US Army forage cap. (Library of Congress collection)

Officers of the 1st Connecticut Heavy Artillery Regiment gather before a Revolutionary War British bomb-shelter near Yorktown, Virginia during the Peninsula Campaign. (Library of Congress collection)

move to the flanks and fire case shot in support of the infantry. If the infantry attacked with the bayonet, the artillery would fall back, preparing to cover the infantry should the attack fail and a retreat be necessary.

Union artillery, which had more rifled guns, carried out more of the counter-battery work proposed by Mahan than did the Confederates who had more smoothbores with shorter ranges. The Confederates tended to hold their fire, awaiting targets of opportunity such as massed infantry within 500 yards. Orders issued to the Confederate attackers at Shiloh called for guns to be massed in groups of twelve, but during the battle this did not come about; most batteries were posted individually. The only Confederate artillery concentration was accidental when some 24 guns happened to be together on a crest near Shiloh Bridge just west of the Pittsburg–Corinth Road to fire into Union camps and, later, at Battery B, 1st Illinois Light Artillery.

The Confederate orders for the attack also called for rifled cannon to aim mainly at reserves and the enemy's second line. Counter-battery fire was actually discouraged.

The Confederates did use artillery as Mahan suggested on the third day of Gettysburg to soften up the enemy for Pickett's Charge. There they massed 138 cannon against 80 Union guns. The counter-battery work went on for some time until the Union artillery reserve commander ordered his guns to cease firing to save their ammunition for the infantry attack that was sure to follow. Seeing that, and knowing that Confederate ammunition supply was getting low, the infantry advanced. Once the Confederate infantry went forward, their artillery ceased fire, but Union artillery again opened fire, this time at the advancing infantry.

A Confederate cannoneer described a counter-battery fight during Shiloh in his diary: 'We were ordered to silence a battery of nine pieces that had our range, just in our front.

Confederate cannoneers fire on the USS Escort *near Washington, North Carolina. (*Harper's Weekly*)*

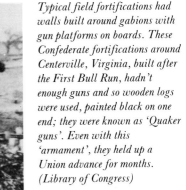

Typical field fortifications had walls built around gabions with gun platforms on boards. These Confederate fortifications around Centerville, Virginia, built after the First Bull Run, hadn't enough guns and so wooden logs were used, painted black on one end; they were known as 'Quaker guns'. Even with this 'armament', they held up a Union advance for months. (Library of Congress)

Before we could fire a gun a shell blew up one of our ammunition chests; another cut off the spinter bar of the third detachment; another almost cut our wheel rider (Bowen) in two. He was killed instantly. Wm. Jones had his right arm shot off. Oh, how I wished that I were a dwarf instead of a six-footer. My hair, good heavens, is standing on end like the quills of a porcupine. Silence that battery is the command from Cheatham, and we did silence it; for we opened with our six guns and an awful artillery duel was kept up for some minutes (seemed like an hour to me). Finally, we succeded in silencing the battery. Our infantry support made a charge about this time and the battery was taken. With our well-directed fire we disabled every piece save one.'[12]

It was generally assumed that the artillery was extremely vulnerable to infantry fire, given the vastly improved range of the rifle-musket over the smoothbore musket. For example, at Shiloh a gun from Polk's Tennessee Battery was ordered close to Union lines, to blow open a gap for an infantry attack. Before it was able to fire, however, Union infantry fire disabled all the horses and killed or wounded several crewmen. The survivors fled, leaving the gun behind. Indeed, when Polk's infantry support fell back, leaving his entire battery exposed to infantry and artillery fire, he lost two guns, six caissons, 24 out of 102 men, and 30 out of 81 horses. Polk himself, with a broken leg, was captured.

However, there were several notable occasions when artillery batteries stood off enemy infantry after their own infantry supports had retreated. Captain Hubert Dilger, who had been an officer in the German Army before the war, used one gun from his Battery I, 1st Ohio Light Artillery, to slow down Stonewall Jackson's attack at Chancellorsville, getting the gun safely off the field after most of the rest of the XI Corps had fled. The 9th Massachusetts Battery withdrew virtually alone from the Peach Orchard during the second day's fighting at Gettysburg, firing and dragging their guns off slowly with ropes called prolonges when the III Corps was battered there. On the rare occasion when a battery was overrun, as were Rickett's and Griffin's regular US Army Batteries at First Bull Run, it was apt to be because they were no longer firing. In the case of the two Union batteries, they thought an advancing unit was a new Union infantry unit coming to their support – it was actually the 33rd Virginia Infantry.

Signals

Communications in battle had become better than ever thanks to a number of technological advances just prior to the war. In the US Army a surgeon, A. J. Myer, during campaigns against the Navajos, experimented with a system of sending messages by waving flags during the day and torches at night. Both sides knew of these experiments and set up their own signalling systems almost immediately.

The Confederates set up their Signal Corps first. It was divided into squads of from three to five mounted men, each squad being commanded by a lieutenant or a sergeant and assigned to an infantry division or cavalry brigade. A Signal Corps officer was also carried aboard every blockade-runner to communicate with the forts defending the harbours. Confederate Signal Corpsmen used flags that were four feet by two and a half feet. The flags were white for use against a dark background, dark-blue for use against sky, and scarlet for use in snow. Each flag had a square of a contrasting colour in its centre. Torches and flares were used at night.

The US Signal Corps began with the organization of a permanent signal party at Fortress Monroe, Virginia, on 10 June 1861. Later, acting signal officers were assigned to duty with the Army of the Potomac where they performed yeoman service. On 2 March 1863 the US Army was authorized its own Signal Corps with Myer as its first commander. Their signal flags were white with a red square in the center and red with a white square in the center. If the signaller had served bravely under fire he was entitled to have a star in his flag's center with the name of the battle in it instead of a square, as per general orders dated 19 March 1862. In February 1863 the battle names were ordered to be removed.

In battle signalmen, on both sides, as well as serving at important headquarters, were sent to occupy all the high posts in the area. Their lines of communications, from post to post, often stretched as far as 30 miles. In the absence of a convenient hill, they built platforms in trees or constructed wooden towers from which to observe and signal. If nothing else were available, they even put signal stations on the tops of artillery limbers. The Army of the Potomac's chief signal officer was able to report after Gettysburg that by 11 a.m. on 2 July, ' . . . every desirable point of observation was occupied by a signal officer, and communication opened from General Meade's headquarters to those of every corps commander.

'A station was established upon Round Top Mountain, on the left of our line, and from this point the greater part of the enemy's forces could be seen and their movements reported. From this position, at 3.30 p.m., the signal officer discovered the enemy massing upon General Sickles' left, and reported the fact to General Sickles and to the general commanding.'[13] The signal station on Little Round Top was constantly under fire from Confederate snipers across

the way at the Devil's Den.

Union Signal Corpsmen were also responsible for maintaining signal telegraph trains and wire between telegraph locations during battle. Special wagons were fitted out with electric batteries and telegraphic equipment so as to be able to move as quickly as the army. Once in position, Signal Corpsmen stretched insulated copper wire between the wagons, unrolling the wire from light carts or, in difficult terrain, from portable reels.

The telegrams themselves, however, were operated by civilians who belonged to a quasi-military organization, the US Military Telegraph Corps. Myer tried desperately to get them assigned to the Signal Corps, which certainly would have made sense, but private telegraph companies successfully fought any such move. In March 1864 any involvement of the US Signal Corps with telegraph ended when they surrendered their field-trains to civilian control. Confederate telegraphs were limited by the very small quantity of wire that Southern makers could produce. Generally they were only to be found in fixed positions and major headquarters.

On both sides Signal Corpsmen were also used as scouts, which was highly dangerous work. In fact, the chief acting signals officer of the Army of the Potomac, Captain B. F. Fisher, was captured while on a reconnaissance near Aldie, Virginia on 17 June 1863. Confederate Signal Corpsmen also had reconnaissance and spying duties.

*A signal party at the headquarters of the Army of the James signals at night by use of torches across the James River. A signal flag, to be used during daylight hours, hangs from the signalman's stage. The officer reads incoming signals through his telescope. William Waud produced the sketch. (*Harper's Weekly)

*As the woods caught fire in the Wilderness, everyone, not just Ambulance Corps members, helped to get the wounded to safety. (*Harper's Weekly*)*

*Specially designed railroad cars were used to transport wounded from field hospitals to general hospitals in Northern cities. A hospital steward, standing right, keeps an eye on his patients. (*Harper's Weekly*)*

Medical Services

Soldiers fight better when they know they will be well cared for if wounded. They must first be evacuated, often under fire, to a place of safety where they can be examined and proper care can be taken of them.

Both sides included in their regimental rosters a surgeon and an assistant surgeon, although many actually had only one medical officer and his enlisted assistant, a hospital steward. When the surgeon learned that the regiment was going into battle, he would select a building, such as a farmhouse, which would be out of the line of fire, for his hospital. This would be marked by a yellow flag six by four feet in size with a green capital letter 'H', 24 inches high, in its centre. The assistant surgeon, accompanied by members of the regimental band, usually wearing yellow or white armbands, would follow directly behind the regiment as it went into battle. The hospital steward or an orderly, carrying a specially designed knapsack filled with medical instruments, ligatures, sponges, dressings and stimulants, accompanied the assistant surgeon.

When a man was wounded, the assistant surgeon would give first aid, controlling bleeding with ligatures, tourniquets or bandages and compresses; fixing broken limbs, and administering water or stimulants, usually whisky, or anodynes. Typically, he would be treating a bullet wound; according to US Army medical records, 94 per cent of all wounds were caused by bullets; 5.5 per cent by artillery, torpedoes or grenades, and 0.4 per cent by edged weapons. Union Army records indicate that 13.6 per cent of all gunshot wounds resulted in death. Wounds to the limbs predominated – 71 per cent; torso wounds (usually fatal) 18 per cent, face or head wounds 11 per cent. Chest wounds were almost three times as frequent as abdominal wounds.

After first aid had been given the bandsmen on infirmary duty would carry the wounded off the field to the regimental hospital. According to US Medical Department regulations, the route to field hospitals was to be marked by yellow bunting, 14 by 28 inches, with an inch-wide strip of green on each side.

At the field hospital, the surgeon would check each patient to determine what should be done about him. If the wound were not immediately life threatening he would be laid aside. If the ball were still in the wound bullet-forceps were used to bring it out. Many of the wounds were deep, with bones shattered. In these cases the usual treatment was amputation, performed as quickly as possible before the patient went into deep shock. In all cases, the surgeon preferred to amputate after the patient had been given general anesthesia, usually chloroform. In the Confederate service, due to severe shortages, it was sometimes necessary to amputate without anesthesia. At times red garden poppy opium was used as an anesthetic, among other herbal medicines substituted for chemicals.

Operations were performed under very insanitary conditions; that bacteria could cause sepsis was as yet unrealized. A rubber groundcloth was thrown over a table or board, perhaps a door, to serve as the operating table. It may or may not have been sponged clean between operations depending on the time available. The surgeon did not sterilize his instruments but simply dipped them in a pan of bloody water and sponged them off with a dirty sponge. The wounds themselves often included pieces of dirty woollen uniform cloth. Gangrene, pyemia, or erysipelas resulted from 20 per cent of all operations; 97 per cent of those who developed pyemia (pus in the blood) died.

When the patient was thought well enough to be moved

he was taken to a general hospital by ambulance, specially designed railroad car, or even by hospital boat, and would stay there until well enough to return to duty, or discharged as medically unfit, or die. In Union general hospitals most patients survived their injuries; the death rate was eight per cent. The Confederate Army had some 72,713 men wounded in 1861–2. In that period they reported 1,623 deaths in field hospitals, but 2,618 deaths in general hospitals.

Indeed, getting the men from the field to the hospital was the major problem. As it turned out, bandsmen made poor medical corpsmen. They were not motivated or trained and in fact, in July 1862, to save money all Union Army regiment bandsmen were ordered to be discharged. Some regiments then used their pioneers for the infirmary detail, but with no better results. The problem was solved in the Army of Northern Virginia by appointing several permanent Infirmary Corp privates to each regiment. Distinguished by red cap badges, and carrying wounded soldiers, they were the only personnel who were allowed to leave the battlefield.

In the US Army it took longer to resolve the problem. The 1861 regulations for the Medical Department held that it was the responsibility of the divisional quartermaster to set up an ambulance system, with centrally located ambulance depots marked by red flags. The depot was essentially a field hospital where the wounded would get immediate attention before being transported to a general hospital. This system simply didn't work as the quartermasters failed to devote sufficient attention to their ambulances and depots. Moreover, they didn't have command of the men necessary to do the job. Various Army of the Potomac medical officers therefore campaigned for the setting up of

an ambulance corps under medical department supervision, but they were all ignored until a civilian doctor, whose wounded son had failed to receive attention on the field, started his own campaign for such a corps.

In the meantime, on 30 October 1862 the medical director of the Army of the Potomac, Dr Jonathan Letterman, set up a new system based on the divisional, rather than the regimental, field hospital. Under it, the assistant surgeon maintained a field aid station, while the rest of the surgeons in the division were concentrated at a central hospital to perform specialized tasks. Not all operated; some kept records, some dressed wounds and some handled administrative responsibilities. One assistant surgeon was given the task of erecting hospital tents as soon as a battle was likely. He was then to have bedding and hot coffee and food ready for the wounded. There were four operating teams, each consisting of a head surgeon and three assistant surgeons, known as 'operating surgeons'. Each divisional hospital had sufficient equipment to deal with up to 8,000 men.

The Army's medical director also set up a system of regularly assigned regimental stretcher-bearers who were commanded by a sergeant and in battle reported to the regimental assistant surgeon. The result of both the stretchers and the divisional hospital systems were that medical care in the Army of the Potomac was much better than in any other Union army. The Surgeon General tried to get them all to adopt the divisional hospital system. It was adopted in the Army of the Tennessee on 8 April 1863.

On 11 March 1864 Congress set up the US Army Ambulance Corps with assigned enlisted men under Medical Department control. Quartermasters were still in charge of ambulances and horses, but the ambulances were not allowed to be used by any but medical personnel. Only Ambulance Corps personnel were allowed to accompany wounded men off the field. On the march, the divisional ambulances travelled together, accompanied by a surgeon, an assistant surgeon, a hospital steward, a cook and three or more nurses. The new corps in the Army of the Potomac had 600 ambulances in service at the Wilderness.

In mid-1864 the system in the Army of the Potomac was changed: an 'ambulance hospital' with four tents and a detail of medical personnel was set up at the end of each day's march to care for those who had fallen sick or been slightly injured that day. Patients needing more care than they could get in the ambulance hospital were sent back to base hospitals.

In static positions such as at Petersburg, Virginia, corps hospitals were set up. These were elaborate affairs complete with dispensaries, male nurses from the Sanitary Commission's Auxiliary Relief Corps, general and special diet kitchens, dining-rooms for convalescents and a Sanitary Commission station. In 1864 the Army of the Cumberland also had a 'travelling general hospital' in which all wounded and sick were kept until discharged or returned to duty. It was housed in some 100 tents and could hold 1,000 patients at a time.

Brigadier General George Sykes (sitting centre) and staff. Sykes commanded a division of V Corps, containing mostly Regular troops, during the Peninsula Campaign, being promoted to major general on 29 November 1862. The staff officer on the right still wears infantry officer's insignia, while the one on the left has replaced his shoulder-straps with the plain devices of his rank. (Library of Congress collection)

Higher Formations

When he went to war, the typical soldier, North or South, joined a local company which went to a central receiving or training camp where it was assigned with other companies to a regiment. Light artillery batteries were unique in that they generally served independently. Each regiment was then assigned a designation which indicated its state of origin and its ranking within the list of regiments enrolled from that state, e.g., 7th New Hampshire Volunteer Infantry Regiment. Some also bore nicknames, such as 'Baxter's Fire Zouaves', which was actually the 72nd Pennsylvania.

Regiments were then assigned to brigades, each brigade under command of a brigadier general. In practice, a colonel could, and often did, command in the absence of a brigadier general. Confederate brigades generally were made up of regiments of the same state, although in some cases regiments from various states might also be brigaded together. Hood's Texas Brigade included, at various times, a Georgia and an Arkansas regiment.

As few as two regiments might make up a brigade. Towards the end of the war, as the Confederate Army lost men, as many as fifteen regiments went into one brigade. Generally, however, between four and six regiments formed one brigade. The brigade was the single largest organization of a single branch of service, usually infantry. Above that, various branches were combined.

At times brigades became important organizations and had proud battle records. In the Union Army, for example, the Iron Brigade, made up of mid-westerners, became one of the most famous fighting organizations in the Army of the Potomac, while Wilder's Lightning Brigade served with distinction in western campaigns. The Philadelphia Brigade was made up of troops drawn from that city. Among Confederates, the all-Virginia Stonewall Brigade, originally commanded by Stonewall Jackson, was among the best in the Army of Northern Virginia.

Early in the war another formation, the legion, was favoured, but generally was later abandoned. The legion was a small, self-contained combat team combining artil-lery, infantry and cavalry in one regiment- or brigade-sized unit. A colonel usually commanded a legion. For example, the 56th New York Volunteer Infantry was also known as the Tenth Legion and had infantry, cavalry, rifle and artillery companies in its organization, each soldier distinguished by the unit's unique branch-of-service coloured shield, under the roman numeral 'X', on the breast of his uniform. But the legion was more popular in the South. Hampton's South Carolina Legion contained a 'voltigeur battalion', which later became an infantry regiment; a cavalry battalion, which was later transferred to the 2nd South Carolina Cavalry; and an artillery battalion, which became independent in 1862 when the rest of the legion was broken up.

Brigades, as well as artillery batteries or battalions, and sometimes cavalry as provost guards, were assigned to divisions. Generally Union divisions contained three brigades, but this could vary depending on circumstances. Each brigade was simply numbered, i.e., 1st Brigade, 3rd Division, in the army's table of organization. Confederate divisions generally had four brigades. However, A.P. Hill's Division at Chancellorsville had six brigades. Confederate brigades and divisions drew their name from their commanders' name, i.e., Heath's Brigade, Hill's Division. A division was to be commanded by a major general, but in default, a brigadier general might actually hold that post.

Divisions were assigned to corps, a term taken from the French, *corps d'armée*. The corps as a command under a major general was established in the Union Army in March 1862. Thereafter, the corps remained the largest formation under the army with the brief exception of the several months in late 1862 when the Army of the Potomac was organized as three 'Grand Divisions', the Right, Centre, and Left Grand Division, each under a major general. Each Union corps was usually made up of three divisions and reserve artillery and cavalry, although as many as five divisions could and did serve in some corps at various times.

The Union Army eventually fielded 25 corps, each designated with a roman numeral, i.e., IX Corps. On 21 March 1863 each member of a corps in the Army of the

Colonel William R. Lee originally commanded the 20th Massachusetts Infantry, being captured at Balls Bluff and exchanged in time to be wounded at the White Oak Swamp. He served as the provost marshal for the Department of North Carolina in August 1863. (Author's collection)

US Army Corps Badges, 1863–5

Corps	Badge	Adopted	Notes
I	Sphere	21 March 1863	
II	Trefoil	21 March 1863	
III	Lozenge	21 March 1863	
IV	Equilateral triangle	26 March 1864	
V	Maltese cross	21 March 1863	
VI	Greek cross	21 March 1863	Light Div, green
VII	Crescent encircling a star	6 Jan 1865	
VIII	Star with six rays	never officially adopted	
IX	Shield with figure '9' in centre crossed with a fouled anchor & cannon	4 Oct 1864	
X	4-bastioned fort	22 May 1864	
XI	Crescent	21 March 1863	
XII	Star	21 March 1863	
XIII	None adopted		
XIV	Acorn	26 April 1864	
XV	Transverse square, cartridge box with motto '40 rounds'	14 Feb 1865	
XVI	Circle with 4 Minié balls, points to centre cut out of it	never officially adopted	
XVII	Arrow	25 March 1865	
XVIII	Cross with foliate sides	June 1864	
XIX*	4-pointed star	18 Feb 1863	
XIX**	Fan-leaved cross with octagonal centre	17 Nov 1864	
XX	Star	26 April 1864	4th Div, green
XXI	None adopted		
XXII	Quinquefoliate shape		Not official
XXIII	Shield	25 Sept 1864	
XXIV	Heart	18 March 1865	
XXV	Square	20 Feb 1865	

*Gulf.   **Middle Military Div.

Potomac was assigned a unique insignia to wear on his cap front or side or left breast so that he could be identified easily on the battlefield. The practice spread until by the end of the war most Union corps had some unique insignia. These cloth or metal badges were generally red for the first division, white for the second division and blue for the third division. Corps with added divisions used green for the fourth and orange for the fifth divisions.

The Confederate Army set up its corps, each under command of a lieutenant general, in November 1862. Before that, higher formations that included divisions were set up for unique needs and were generally called 'wings'. Longstreet's Wing of the Army of Northern Virginia at Antietam contained five divisions. The Army of Northern Virginia thereafter had three corps, each designated with a spelt out number, and a Fourth Corps which was largely administrative. At Chancellorsville, the First Corps had two divisions, the Second Corps four divisions and the Cavalry Corps had four brigades and a horse artillery battalion. The Third Corps was added after the army was reorganized following Jackson's death at Chancellorsville. The Army of Tennessee also had three infantry corps, as well as Forrest's and Wheeler's Cavalry Corps.

Corps served under field armies, which were the largest, active field commands created. There were eventually sixteen Union armies, each named after the department in which it served, such as the Army of the District of North Carolina, which was formed in August 1863. In most cases, the departments, and hence the field armies, bore the names of rivers such as Army of the Tennessee. A major general commanded each field army. The Confederates had 23 field armies, in theory each commanded by a general, and each bearing the departmental name, generally a state name.

Each field army served within a department. These departments varied tremendously in size and importance and in fact were constantly being re-defined as needs changed. For example, until 12 January 1863, the Union Army had a Department of New England which was mainly

These officers of the 2nd Delaware Infantry display some of the varieties of corps badge styles, in this case the badge of II Corps. First Lieutenant Thomas M. Wenie, far left, wears his on top of his forage cap, while the others wear them on their slouch hat sides. (Author's collection)

manned by garrison troops, prisoner-of-war camp, supply depot and training camp personnel. Thereafter it was merged into the Department of the East. The Department of the Potomac covered all of Delaware, Maryland, and north-eastern Virginia, and saw some of the war's hardest fighting. Departments contained districts, as well as field armies in some of them. The Department of Pennsylvania included the Juniata District, Lehigh District, District of the Monongahela and District of Philadelphia.

At first Confederate Departments were numbered, but later state names were used for their designations. Department No. 2, for example, covered eastern Arkansas, north-eastern Louisiana, western Mississippi, and West Tennessee. It folded on 25 July 1863 and most of its territory was taken into a new Department of Tennessee.

The Union army had one higher formation, the Military Division. These included the Military Division of the Atlantic, the Military Division of the James, the Middle Military Division and the Military Division of the Potomac.

Commanders of Divisions, Departments and field armies reported to their Secretary of War, the civilian head of the War Department. He was aided by civilian assistant secretaries, military staff officers and civilian clerks who administered the various war efforts. In 1863 the US War Department had the Secretary of War, Assistant Secretary of War, Solicitor of the War Department, a chief clerk, 26 clerks, a messenger, three assistant messengers and a labourer, in addition to hundreds more clerks and messengers assigned to departments such as the Quartermaster General's Office.

Neither side had a general staff or, until late in the war, a general who commanded all the forces in the field. Eventually, Grant was given command of all Union forces and Lee, all Confederate forces, but before that the generals commanding the army were little more than advisers to the President and Secretary of War. The constitutions of both sides made the President the actual commander-in-chief of the armed forces. Both Presidents took their duties seriously, going as far as actually issuing orders to their field generals.

THE ART OF WAR AT SEA

The naval Civil War was generally fought with many ships in a confined area, such as a harbour or river, or as single-ship actions in open waters.

When the CSS *Alabama* engaged the USS *Kearsage* it was in open waters, several miles from the French coast. The battle was fought in large circling movements as both ships pounded each other with the heavy guns. The Confederate cruiser tried to close with the Union ship to board her, but the faster Union ship kept her distance. She had been prepared for the fight by the laying of anchor chains to serve as armour plate and this did prevent some damage. Moreover, faulty Southern ammunition, which had been in storage too long, failed to explode. Finally, when some 400 yards apart, the *Alabama* began to sink, stern first.

This type of long-range pounding was typical of ship-to-ship open water engagement. In areas where there was less room to manoeuvre, artillery pounding still counted, but both sides also began to rely on the ram. This iron- or steel-tipped projection, mounted on the strengthened bows of a ship, was intended to pierce the side of an opposing ship. In fact rams worked, as the Confederates found out when the CSS *Virginia*, an iron-clad which had been fitted with a ram, attacked and sank the USS *Cumberland* with a combination of gunfire and ram. Rams also saw much use on the Western rivers.

However, it was usually not too difficult to avoid the ram or at least manoeuvre so that the ram simply glanced off the side. During the Battle of Mobile Bay on 5 August 1864, the

*Union ironclads unsuccessfully bombard Fort Sumter on 7 April 1863. (*Harper's Weekly*)*

iron-clad CSS *Tennessee* supported by three other smaller armed boats, attempted to ram an attacking Union squadron but they nimbly avoided her. The Confederate ship's poor machinery forced her to steam slower than the Union ships she was attacking. She did damage six ships by gunfire before retiring for the night to the safety of Fort Morgan. The next day, however, a Union ship rammed the slower *Tennessee* and then, as she was stalled in the water, other Union ships surrounded her and pounded her with artillery until, her commander wounded and her armour cracking, the Confederate ship surrendered.

A variation of the ram was the spar torpedo. This was an explosive device mounted on the end of a long pole which was placed in the bows of an attacking boat. The boat would charge into its enemy and detonate the torpedo when it hit the enemy's side, either electrically or by percussion caps mounted at the head of the torpedo. A small steam launch with a spar torpedo attacked and sank the CSS *Albemarle* in her dock on the Roanoke River, North Carolina on 28 October 1864.

Confederates also planted torpedoes in rivers and harbours to sink Union ships. Union devices for finding and removing torpedoes included rafts fitted to the bows of Monitor-type ships that dragged chains which would explode the torpedoes under the rafts, away from the ship's hull. Also, light sweeps made of wooden poles and chains which could be raised or lowered from any ship's bow were used.

Confederate blockade-runners had to evade Union blockading ships. Typically they would wait until dark before trying to slip past. Moonless nights were favoured. Late in the war, some Union blockaders had locomotive headlights mounted in their bows. Usually, the blockade-runner would fly misleading flags, sometimes US and sometimes foreign, and fire off flares that made no sense. At times a runner would make straight for a US ship, in an endeavour to make the captain think that the Confederate ship was a US Navy supply ship. Then, at the last minute, he would lower his US flag and raise a Confederate one and change course for his destination. A Confederate signals officer on board

The dangers of riverine warfare. The USS Barrataria *is snagged on the Amite River, in Louisiana, while Confederate infantrymen keep her closed up with their small-arms fire. (*Harper's Weekly*)*

would signal Confederate forts guarding the harbour approaches with coloured flares that this was indeed a blockade-runner. The forts would offer covering fire as the blockade-runner drew closer.

To prevent this, much of the Union Navy had to spend its efforts against land-based Confederate fortifications. Typically, the ships would gather in line and direct their fire on the fort in an attempt to knock out its guns and flatten its walls. For example, a squadron of seven Monitor-type ships and two other iron-clads attacked Fort Sumter, at the mouth of the Charleston, South Carolina, harbour on 7 April 1863. What they discovered is that ships can't sink forts.

'The action lasted two hours and twenty-five minutes, but the chief damage is reported by the enemy to have been done in thirty minutes. The *Keokuk* did not come nearer than nine hundred yards of Fort Sumter; she was destroyed,' the Confederate commander, P. G. T. Beauregard, reported. 'The *New Ironsides* could not stand the fire at the range of a mile; four of her consorts (monitors) were disabled at the distance of not less than thirteen hundred yards. They had only reached the gorge of the harbor – never within it – and were battled and driven back before reaching our lines of torpedoes and obstructions which had been constructed as an ultimate defensive resort as far as they could be provided.'[14]

Had the fort's guns been silenced, Marines would have been landed to capture it. A typical rehearsal for such an amphibious operation in 1861 was described by Samuel Mercer, captain of the USS *Powhatan*. 'The Marines of the Squadron and the small arm men took up their positions in the Boats from their respective Ships immediately in the rear of their respective Howitzer Boats.' These howitzer boats had 12-pound smoothbore howitzers with bronze tubes mounted in their bows. These guns came with carriages so that the tubes could be dismounted from the boats and put on carriages to allow the artillery to be used on land. Mercer continued: 'After they were all arranged in the order here presented, at a preconcerted Signal from me, the Boats having the Howitzers mounted upon them discharged their pieces twice – whereupon the Boats with the Marines and small arm men dashed in and landed, formed in line immediately and delivered two discharges of musketry – when the Howitzer Boats pulled in and landed their Howitzers as fast as possible, formed in line and fired each piece with a blank cartridge twice.'[15]

The Navy 'small arms men', or landing parties, at the capture of Fort Fisher, North Carolina, were armed with cutlasses and revolvers. They were, in fact, beaten back by Confederate artillery and infantrymen armed with rifle-muskets.

Notes

1. Cecil D. Eby, Jr., *A Virginia Yankee In The Civil War*, University of North Carolina Press, Chapel Hill, North Carolina, 1961, p. 119
2. Ibid., pp. 119–20
3. Susan W. Benson, ed., *Berry Benson's Civil War Book*, University of Georgia Press, Athens, Georgia, 1962, p. 22
4. C. A. Stevens, *Berdan's Sharpshooters in the Army of the Potomac*, Morningside Bookshop, Dayton, Ohio, 1972, p. 271
5. Robert H. Strong, *A Yankee Private's Civil War*, Henry Regnery Co., Chicago, Illinois, 1961, p. 192
6. K. Jack Bauer, ed., *Soldiering*, Berkley Books, New York, 1988, p. 158
7. D. H. Mahan, *An Elementary Treatise on Advanced-Guard, Out-Post and Detachment Service of Troops*, John Wiley, New York, 1861, p. 39
8. Henry K. Douglas, *I Rode With Stonewall*, Fawcett Publications, Greenwich, Connecticut, 1961, pp. 61–2
9. John S. Mosby, *The Memoirs of Colonel John S Mosby*, Indiana University Press, Bloomington, Indiana, 1959, pp. 284–5
10. Walter Lord, ed., *The Fremantle Diary*, Capricorn Books, New York, p. 227
11. Mahan, op cit, p. 39
12. Mike Spradlin, 'The Diary of George W. Jones', *Camp Chase Gazette*, April, 1981, p. 7
13. *The War of the Rebellion, A Compilation of the Official Records* (hereinafter OR), Government Printing Office, Washington, DC, 1889, Series I, vol. XXVII, p. 202
14. P. G. T. Beauregard, 'The Defense of Charleston', *Battles and Leaders of the Civil War*, Thomas Yoseloff, New York, 1956, vol. IV, p. 12
15. 'Amphibious Exercise 1861', *Fortitude*, Quantico, Virginia, vol. III, No 4, p. 14

References

George W. Adams, *Doctors In Blue: The Medical History of the Union Army in the Civil War*, Collier Books, New York, 1952
Silas Casey, *Infantry Tactics*, D Van Nostrand Co, New York, 1862
Jack Coggins, *Arms and Equipment of the Civil War*, Doubleday & Co, Garden City, New York, 1962
Philip St. George Cooke, *Cavalry Tactics*, J.B. Lippincott, Philadelphia, Pennsylvania, 1862
Horace H. Cunningham, *Doctors in Gray: The Confederate Medical Service*, Louisiana State University Press, Baton Rouge, Louisiana, 1958
Larry J. Daniel, *Cannoneers in Gray*, The University of Alabama Press, University, Alabama, 1984
Fairfax Downey, *The Guns at Gettysburg*, Collier Books, New York, 1962
John Gibbon, *The Artillerist's Manual*, Van Nostrand, New York, 1860
Mary C. Gillet, *The Army Medical Department 1818–1865*, US Army, Washington, DC, 1987
Paddy Griffith, *Battle Tactics of the Civil War*, Yale University Press, New Haven, Connecticut, 1987
William J. Hardee, *Rifle and Light Infantry Tactics*, J.B. Lippincott Co, Philadelphia, Pennsylvania, 1863
Francis A. Lord, *They Fought For The Union*, Stackpole Co., Harrisburg, Pennsylvania, 1960
Grady McWhiney and Perry D. Jamison, *Attack and Die*, The University of Alabama Press, University, Alabama, 1982
L. Van Loan Naisawald, *Grape and Canister*, Oxford University Press, New York, 1960
Official, *Medical and Surgical History of the War of the Rebellion (1861–1865)*, Government Printing Office, Washington, DC, 1875–88
Foxhall A. Parker, *Squadron Tactics Under Steam*, Von Nostrand, New York, 1864
Stanley S. Phillips, *Civil War Corps Badges and Other Related Awards, Badges, Medals of the Period*, Walsworth Publishing, Marceline, Missouri, 1982
Stephen Z. Starr, *The Union Cavalry in the Civil War*, Louisiana State University Press, Baton Rouge, Louisiana, 1979
Frank J. Welcher, *The Union Army 1861–1865*, Indiana University Press, Bloomington, Indiana, 1989
Jennings C. Wise, *The Long Arm of Lee*, J. P. Bell Co., Lynchburg, Virginia, 1915

III
MILITARY LIFE

MILITARY LIFE

Joining Up

The initial excitement of declarations of secession, the firing on Fort Sumter and speeches by impassioned civic leaders on both sides created a situation where young men literally thronged to join units leaving for the front. Volunteer militia companies offered their services to their state governors and were called up into regiments organized for three months' or a year's service. Individual volunteers often enlisted to prove their masculinity to their peers rather than from any deep-seated belief in the cause. They then elected their own officers and passed a very rudimentary medical test. Finally they stood in line proudly as some local politician spoke of honor and courage and a local woman presented a flag which their new commanders promised never to dip in defeat or have stained with shame. The flags represented home, community, to the men who proudly received them. Then the men piled into railway cars or tramped off down the road, leaving weeping relatives behind them. They were off to 'see the elephant', the period slang for seeing some major event such as the elephant in P. T. Barnum's New York museum and sideshow.

Not all were as keen to be cannon-fodder as the initial volunteers. Period newspapers suggested that women should refuse the attentions of these stay-at-homes. Boston's best-known poet of the period, Oliver Wendell Holmes, even wrote a widely published 15-verse poem, *The Sweet Little Man*, which was 'Dedicated to the Stay-at-Home Rangers'. A sample verse:

'Bring him the buttonless garment of a woman!
Cover his face lest it freckle and tan;
  Muster the Apron-string Guards on the Common,
That is the corps for the sweet little man.'

Soon, however, not even such pointed sarcasm could bring in new recruits. At the same time, the units that had joined for three months in the North and those for one year in the South were coming to the end of their terms of enlistment.

In the North, the three-month units were discharged so soon after the major defeat at Bull Run that enough men, many of them veterans of the short-term units, could be found to join new units for three years or the war's duration, whichever came first. Again, there was no problem in getting enough volunteers to meet the call for 700,680 men issued on 6 August 1861.

In the South, however, most men's one-year enlistment came up in early 1862 after the Confederacy had been successful in most of its battles, when spring planting was due, and when it seemed that the North was not going to invade soon, at least to the men in the field. Confederate leaders feared the loss of the greater part of their army in the field. On 11 December 1861 the Confederate Congress offered its soldiers a 60-day furlough and a $50 bounty if they would enlist for two more years or the duration of the war. Most of the 1st Maryland Infantry accepted the offer. However, most men were due to be discharged in the spring. Quickly the Confederate Congress passed a conscription act on 16 April 1862. Men already under arms were offered a choice of a bounty and a chance to elect new officers in their present units, or a chance to enlist in a unit of their choice, or the strong possibility of being conscripted and assigned to a unit at the army's pleasure. Those who were under 18 or more than 35 years of age were free to go home.

The hope was that enough voluntary re-enlistments to keep the army manned would result. 'The majority soon re-enlisted but often in new commands; some did not re-enlist at all; others did much later,' a Confederate officer later noted. 'Many of the regiments reorganized with new officers. The general effect was to break up very much the

At the beginning, many of both sides' troops were drawn from the ranks of pre-war volunteer militia companies which varied in quality from being well trained and equipped to being little more than social clubs. This independent company is the Iredell Blues, which was mustered into the 52nd Regiment, *North Carolina Volunteer Militia on 20 April 1861. It was later reorganized as Co A, 4th Regiment, North Carolina State Troops. The company was photographed in front of Stockton Hall, built in 1859, in Statesville, North Carolina. (North Carolina Division of Archives and History collection)*

Copies of the uniforms worn by George Washington's men in the Revolution were popular among volunteer militia outfits from Louisiana to Connecticut. This man wears the uniform of Connecticut's Putnam Phalanx with a red over black feather on his black hat; a blue coat with buff facings; a buff waistcoat; and black breeches and stockings. The unit was founded in 1858 and never was a part of Connecticut's National Guard. (Author's collection)

Both Private Thomas Duval (left) and Lieutenant William Duval served in the 3rd Missouri Infantry, CSA, mustering in 10 December 1862. Here they wear 'battle shirts'. William, the eldest of three brothers in the unit, was killed at Corinth on 4 October 1862, while Thomas was killed in the Battle of Champion's Hill on 16 May 1863. The third brother, Henderson, was also killed at Champion's Hill. (Dr Thomas P. Sweeney collection)

organization of the army.' [1] Old, strict disciplinarians who were also good officers were out; friendlier types, often less fit than the original officers, replaced them. Infantrymen joined the cavalry to avoid those long foot marches. Also, volunteers who would have re-enlisted resented being forced into service; morale was damaged. For some time afterwards, the Confederate army was in a chaotic state.

Even with the threat of conscription and with Union forces closing in on the South, enough volunteers never came forth to fill the Confederacy's ranks. A revised Act that raised the upper age of liable men to 45 was passed on 27 September 1862 and the eligible ages were changed to 17 to 50 in February 1864.

At first, instead of instituting mass conscription, the United States issued quotas to the states, stipulating that permanent militias could be called up by the federal government if there not enough volunteers to meet quotas. Beyond patriotism, the United States and the Northern states depended on fiscal inducements to get men into the ranks. Bounties were paid by the US government, the state government and many local governments. The result could be a lump payment many times the $156 annual pay an infantry private received in 1862.

For example, the 7th Indiana Cavalry, raised in the fall of 1863 for three years' service, advertised that $400 in bounty would be paid to men who had had nine months' prior military experience in the US Army. Men with no experience at all could get a $100 bounty. To keep men from

The Waukesha Home Guard, seen here in a pre-war parade, became Co F, 5th Wisconsin Infantry. The frock-coats are gray apparently trimmed with black or dark-blue; the trousers are dark-blue. (Milwaukee Public Museum collection)

The Mobile Cadets, from Alabama, wore the traditional volunteer militia uniform, with a shako and a swallow-tail coatee with worsted epaulettes and a standing collar trimmed with false buttonholes. In most of these units, trousers were the same color as the coat in winter and white in summer. Gray was the traditional US volunteer uniform color; the Regular Army wore blue. (Herb Peck Jnr collection)

deserting the minute they got their bounty money, the 7th paid $25 with a month's pay in advance, the rest on discharge. Men joining the 23rd Michigan Infantry received a $300 US government bounty, a $100 state bounty and a $100 town bounty.

Bounties did attract recruits, although not necessarily the best-motivated recruits. A Wisconsin man joined a cavalry regiment in 1864, later freely admitting: 'I enlisted for the bounty. I thought the war was nearly over, and that the probabilities were that the regiment I had enlisted in would be ordered home before I could get to it. In fact the recruiting officer told me as much, and he said I would get my bounty and a few months' pay, and it would be just like finding money.'[2]

The bounty system had several negative resuls. To the Army, it brought in a calibre of soldier considerably below that of the original volunteer and created tension between the groups of volunteers and bounty men, thus lowering morale. Many of the bounty men deserted at the first chance, sometimes re-enlisting in a new unit to get additional bounty. For the Navy, it made recruiting extremely difficult since state and local bounties were paid only to Army recruits, there being no state quota for the Navy or Marine Corps. Indeed, volunteers for the Navy were not allowed the same bounty as Army volunteers until 1 July 1864.

With the failure of the bounty system, the US Congress passed its Conscription Act on 3 March 1863. Both sides' conscription acts allowed for a number of exemptions for physical disabilities or vital occupations. Also both sides allowed conscripts to pay a commutation tax to avoid service, $500 in the Confederacy and $300 in the Union. This practice led to charges of its being a 'rich man's war and a poor man's fight'. Finally, both sides initially allowed

John Booker wearing the first uniform of the Cumberland Grays, which served as Co D, 21st Virginia Infantry. Typically, volunteers brought extra arms and equipment, such as this revolver and Bowie knife, into the field, and sent it home after the first long march. (Richard Carlile collection)

The 63rd Pennsylvania Goes To War

'When we arrived at the train we speedily embarked and then occurred a most touching scene. Fathers, mothers, wives, children, brothers, sisters and other friends were lined up on each side to bid the last farwell to their loved ones. Here an aged father stretched a trembling hand to grasp that of a dear son, while he supported the weeping mother with the other arm, or a wife, with tears streaming down her pale face, held up a laughing, unconscious baby to give the departing father one more farewell kiss. Sisters, with tear-dimmed eyes, were bidding a fond adieu to loved brothers, while brothers, with husky voices, were bidding good-bye to brothers, and here and there blushing maidens were saying farewell to lovers, striving hard, but unavailingly, to keep back their tears. It was a scene no one cares to look upon a second time. As the train pulled out we all turned to take one last look at the familiar scenes, and as we gazed at the surroundings, bathed in the mellow light of the setting sun, many realized they would not behold the same again. Many a hearty cheer, and many a God speed were wafted to the boys, and the sad and weeping friends moved off to their homes, feeling that there was a vacant chair at the fireside that perhaps would never again be filled by the absent one.'

(Gilbert Adam Hays, *Under the Red Patch*, Sixty-third Pennsylvania Volunteers Regimental Association, Pittsburgh, Pennsylvania, 1908, pp. 16–17)

conscripts to hire a substitute. A bitterly resented feature of the law, substitution was declared illegal in the South in 1863, while in the North there sprang up a whole breed of professional substitute brokers who found substitutes, often deserters, runaways and drugged or unfit men, for conscripts at a fee. Although not liable for the draft, President Abraham Lincoln hired a substitute to serve in his name, while young and able banker J. Pierpont Morgan paid his commutation tax in 1863. Indeed, only some six per cent of the 249,259 men whose names were drawn for conscription actually served in the Army.

Initially, conscription did not help the navies of either side. In early 1862 the Confederate Navy offered a $50 bounty for every recruit, except boys, who enlisted for three years or the war. But, both navies needed to draw on the manpower pool allotted to the armies. Technically, it was possible for skilled sailors to transfer from the army to the navy on both sides, but on both sides army officers were not keen on letting good men get away. It was not until March 1864 that the Confederate Adjutant and Inspector General ordered a mass release of sailors to the Confederate Navy, while in February of that same year the US Congress changed its conscription laws to allow local draft quotas credit for recruits who went into the US Navy.

Except for Wisconsin, most Northern states raised new units every time a new state quota was issued by the federal government; this allowed the governor to issue new commissions which was good politics. In Wisconsin and Southern states, new men went into old, already established units, as did conscripts on both sides. This allowed a mixing of green troops and veterans, which was important since there was no training camps for individual recruits or conscripts in either side's armies. Veteran regiments often sent recruiting parties home to gain replacements; indeed, many volunteers preferred to go into a blooded unit, often with slightly older friends. There was, however, no army-wide standard operating procedure for these recruiting parties.

Army Life

The army recruit of 1861 went with his new unit to a camp or permanent fort where he received his initial training. Most camps at first housed officers and men in tents, although barracks were later built in many permanent camps.

The standard enlisted man's tent of 1861 was the Sibley Tent, a patented tent copied from the Plains Indian's teepee and put into use before the war. It was a conical tent, some eighteen feet in diameter, and had an iron stove in the centre, the stove-pipe passing out through the 12-foot high roof. It could house twenty men and their equipment, although not comfortably. They had to sleep 'spoon fashion,' i.e., on their sides with their legs slightly bent and nestling between the man on each side.

Officers used wall or hospital tents, so called since field hospitals used the same tent. They had side walls 4.5 feet high with a roof eleven feet high in the center. Rectangular in shape, the most common wall tent was 14 feet by 14.5 feet. A fly, 21.5 feet by 14 feet, was usually placed on poles in front of the tent. Most captains and above had a cot, a trunk, a table and field desk, and a chair in their tent. Lower-grade officers usually shared a tent.

In permanent posts, barracks were little more than large rooms with a fireplace at one end for cooking and heating. Double bunks of rough wood planks lined both walls, tables and benches in the centre of the room were used for eating and recreation. Most barracks in Eastern forts were two storeys high, made of brick, with covered porches the length of the barrack in front of each barrack.

In the field, the Sibley tent was rarely seen after the first year of the war. In fact, in the Confederate Army few tents at all were seen, most men spending the night rolled-up in blankets, waterproofs or carpet fragments under a tree or near a fire. Even company-grade officers rarely used tents among the Confederates after 1861.

The 8th New York State Militia, in camp at Alexandria, Virginia in July 1861, are just getting used to camp life. They still wear their regiment's gray fatigue uniform and have large tents which will later be used only by officers and as hospitals. (Michael McAfee collection)

Even troops from relatively rural areas such as Arkansas came well equipped with camping gear in 1861. These are troops from Co D, 19th Arkansas Infantry in Northern Virginia. (Harper's Weekly)

Union troops break camp; notice the tents in the foreground. Several, standing near the musket stacks, are ready to move off, their shelter halves worn bandolier-style around their chests. Others are still in shirt sleeves. (Kean E. Wilcox collection)

A Virginia town sees its boys off to war

'The next morning, early, the [55th Virginia Infantry] regiment and the cavalry troop came into Tappahannock and broke ranks for a few moments to say good-bye. I shall never forget that scene. You may be sure everybody was there. There were good-byes and cheery words – no tears. Then the drums beat for formation. There was a moment of stir; then silence; then the order "Forward march!"

'I can never forget that silence, nor the scrape of feet as the column moved down the silent street. The women on the sidewalks waved and smiled encouragement though there were tears running down their cheeks. Not even a child made a sound. Tom Gordon was marching with an extra pair of shoes hanging down his back over his knapsack. The Regiment was gone! It left a sad little town behind it.'

(Evelyn D. Ward, *The Children of Bladensfield*, The Viking Press, New York, 1978, pp. 48–9)

There were times when Union soldiers, too, declined to set up tents. Then soldiers slept in pairs, putting one's waterproof, rubber side down, on the ground first and then his blanket on top of that. Lying on that, the two covered themselves with the other soldier's blanket and waterproof, rubber side up. This kept them fairly warm and dry from morning dew.

In early 1862, however, Union soldiers received shelter-halves, called 'dog tents', for field use. These were made of thin cotton drilling or duck, 5 feet two inches long by 4 feet 8 inches wide (in 1864 the size was changed to 5 feet 6 inches by 5 feet 5 inches), with 23 buttonholes on the upper edge and side, and nine zinc or tin buttons on the top edge and seven on the end. Three loops were attached to each end. A six-strand, manila rope, 6 feet 10 inches long, came with each shelter-half. Two shelter-halves could be buttoned together, a musket stuck bayonet down into the ground each end and the rope run from trigger guard to trigger guard to provide a small tent for two men. At times six men buttoned theirs together to make a tent that provided more protection from the elements.

Camps required large amounts of supplies, ranging from food to new equipment, brought in by both railroad and wagon. Two Sibley tents are pitched just to the rear and left to the left-hand box car. (David Scheinmann collection)

A Union soldier finds it hard to adjust to furniture

'I remember two things in particular after I got home for good. It was hard for me to sit in a chair or sleep in a bed. In the army, only captains and up had chairs. I hadn't sat in a chair in three years or about that. As for beds, they were too soft to sleep in. For a long time, I preferred to sleep and to sit on the floor.'

(Robert H. Strong, *A Yankee Private's Civil War*, Henry Regnery Co., Chicago, Illinois, 1961, p. 218)

During winter in the field, the men were free to make pretty much any type of cabin and four to ten men, each making up a 'mess', usually built a small log cabin with a stone-lined fireplace and a chimney made of wooden barrels lined with mud. Walls were usually about eight feet high, packed with mud between the logs. The floor was usually hard packed mud. Tents were buttoned together over the roof for further waterproofing.

The day began with the sounding of 'reveille' by drums in foot units or bugles in mounted ones at 5 a.m. in summer and 6 a.m. in winter. The men then had fifteen minutes to wash and dress before 'assembly' was sounded and they formed up by sections while each sergeant called his section's roll. The sergeants then reported 'all present or accounted for' or mentioned anybody missing to the first sergeant who then read off any special orders for the day and dismissed the men. Mounted men went off to tend their horses while foot soldiers had breakfast. After breakfast came the call 'infirmary', whereupon any sick men went to the surgeon's tent. Fatigue call summoned specified details to clean up the camp, chop firewood, and perform other necessary chores.

At eight in the morning guard mount was called. The first sergeant inspected his company's guards for the next 24 hours. He then marched them to the regimental parade ground for inspection and assignment by the regimental adjutant and sergeant major. Each man stood two hours of sentry-duty out of six hours.

Company and perhaps regimental and even brigade drill for everyone but men on detail followed until noon when 'roast beef', the call for dinner, was sounded. The men had some free time after dinner, followed by more drill. At about 4.30 p.m. the men were released to prepare for the formal retreat ceremony held every evening. With their polished weapons and buckles, blackened leather equipment, and brushed uniforms, they fell in on the sounding of 'attention' at 5.45 followed by 'retreat' with a final roll-call, inspection and dress parade. Official orders and communications and the results of courts-martial were read at this formation.

After the troops had been dismissed, they formed up for supper. At 8.30 the musicians sounded 'attention', and then 'assembly'. At this formation, called 'tattoo', the day's last roll-call was taken and the men were ordered to their quarters. At 9, 'taps' was sounded and all lights were to be extinguished.

The only day the routine varied was Sunday when a formal regimental inspection was held in the morning following several hours of intensive preparation. During the inspection each man's knapsack, unslung and lying in front of him, was examined for minute particles of dirt. This inspection, called 'knapsack drill' by the men, was not limited to the troops, but quarters, grounds, kitchens and

A Union officer of the day, his duties marked by the sash he wears from right shoulder to left hip instead of around the waist, writes a dispatch for a waiting rider. The rider wears a havelock, a cap cover that hung down over the back of the neck, supposedly to prevent sunstroke. These items were common in the first months of the war but quickly disappeared, having been used as coffee-strainers and gun patches. (John R. Sickles collection)

hospitals were also inspected. Sunday afternoons were free time, although church attendance was mandatory in some units. Otherwise, the men spent their time writing letters home, singing popular songs in groups, playing cards, gambling in dice games such as craps and chuck a-luck, and seeing the local sights. Literacy was high, especially among Northern men who had generally attended free public schools. The men read everything from newspapers and magazines to classic literature, popular novels, and paperback comics and 'dime novels'. Some Union units published their own newspapers, usually printed in nearby printed shops or with small portable presses they carried with them. Snowball fights, involving as many men as a brigade, were especially popular among Confederates. Officers, and sometimes the men, often organized theatrical companies, especially in winter camps.

Many Union, and some Confederate, troops played baseball, a fairly new game which had become quite popular in large cities such as New York, New Orleans and Philadelphia. Many Union regiments had their own teams which played other regimental teams. Baseball's rules were slightly different from today's game. The square field had three bases and home plate, each one 42 yards apart from the neighboring bases. Each hitter hit the ball with a wooden bat and then ran around the field, touching all bases before coming back to home to score a point. He could stop at any given base safely and advance on the next hit. He also could take three misses or 'strikes' at the ball. The ball was thrown underhand; the final strike had to be caught or it was a fair ball. The hitter was out if the ball was caught on the fly or he was tagged with the ball by a fielder before he touched a base. Three outs retired the side; an inning was completed when both sides had three outs. The game was played until one side got 21 points, although both sides played an equal number of innings. Balls were often made from walnuts wrapped with yarn while bats were carved

Union company-grade infantry officers rest after a long day. The captain is just pulling the cork out of what appears to be a wine bottle. Although all are infantry officers, they carry light cavalry officers' sabres. (Kean E. Wilcox collection)

from tree branches or boards. Evidence of how the war spread the game can be seen in the fact that the 1861 meeting of the National Association of Base Ball Players drew delegates from 34 clubs, while the 1865 meeting had delegates from 91 clubs and the 1867 meeting had delegates from 237 clubs.

Mornings on the march began like other mornings with company formations, roll-calls, and breakfast. Musicians sounded the 'general' an hour before the march was begun to allow the men time to douse fires, strike their tents, if any, and pack their belongings. If the men had been in camp for some time, many personal belongings had to be either tossed out or sent home to lighten the man's load. Most Union troops had a choice of taking their dress or fatigue coat while the other would be boxed up. Confederates rarely had that problem.

Then the troops fell in and began marching as directed. The column was frequently halted to rest and reform the troops, and an hour's break for supper as well as rest was usually taken at noon. Men on the march were not allowed to fall out to forage or get water, but in practice frequently did. Men also fell out from exhaustion or foot problems; Confederates were especially noted for their straggling on the march.

Marches varied in distance according to the terrain and if it were important to make speed. For example, the Third Brigade, Second Division, XII Corps, during the Gettysburg campaign, marched eleven miles on 28 June; 21 miles on 29 June; twelve miles on 30 June; thirteen miles on 1 July; thirteen miles on 5 July; 29 miles on 7 July; fifteen miles on 8 July; eleven miles on 9 July; seven miles on 10 July; six miles on 11 July.

The end of the column was brought up by wagons, often musicians, a provost guard to prevent straggling, and hospital wagons carrying the sick. At the march's end, the soldiers were dismissed to set up their tents, if any, and make supper. This was followed by the usual formations and roll-calls at retreat and tattoo, as well as taps.

Rations

According to army regulations, Union soldiers were supposed to receive a ration consisting of 22 ounces of bread or flour or a pound of hard bread, three-quarters of a pound of pork or bacon or one and a quarter pound of fresh or salt beef; and, for every hundred rations or twice a week, eight quarts of beans or 150 ounces of desiccated potatoes and 100 ounces of mixed vegetables; ten pounds of coffee or one and a half pounds of tea; 15 pounds of sugar; and four quarts of vinegar. A pound of potatoes was to be issued per man at least three times a week.

The regulation Confederate ration differed only in that each man was to receive either a pound of beef or a half-pound of bacon or pork and no more than a pound and a half of flour or meal. For every hundred rations, eight quarts of peas or beans or ten pounds of rice, with six pounds of coffee, twelve pounds of sugar, and four quarts of vinegar were to be issued. However, this generous ration was more

---

A Confederate tries to adjust on furlough

'Two years having elapsed since any furloughs had been given, except to the sick and wounded. The granting of them was now revived, and those who had been longest from home were, of course, to be served first. My turn came in March. I shall never forget the impression made on me as I sat at the supper-table at home, on the evening of my arrival. My father, mother, sisters, and little niece were present; and, after the noise, loud talking, etc., in camp, the quiet was painful. It was just as it had always been, except the vacant places of the boys at the front; still, I felt that something was wrong. Equally as impressive was the mild diet of cold bread, milk, and weak-looking tea. The effect was the same as that produced by a sudden transition from a low to a high altitude, or vice versa, requiring time for adaptation, as I soon experienced.'

(Edward A. Moore, *The Story of a Cannoneer Under Stonewall Jackson*, Neale Publishing, New York, 1907, p. 217)

---

than the Confederate commissary could actually issue. The meat ration was ordered to be reduced in January 1863. The bacon ration in the west was ordered to be reduced to a third of a pound in late 1863, while the flour or meal ration was cut to a pound in 1864.

The usual meat issued by Union commissaries was salt pork. Union rations were supplemented by issues of dried peaches, dried apples, split peas and onions to prevent scurvy. These issues, however, were generally made in camp. On the march, Union soldiers generally received a pound of hardtack, three-quarters of a pound of salt pork, sugar, coffee and salt. Hardtack was a hard flour and water cracker measuring three and an eighth by two and seven-eights inches, about half an inch thick. Nine or ten hardtack crackers made up a pound. Often they were moldy from being left in wooden boxes exposed to the weather; at times they were riddled with weevils or maggots.

Each man was responsible for preparing his own food. Hardtack, of course, could be simply eaten as issued which made it handy while on the march. However, when given the chance, most men modified hardtack, often by breaking each cracker up in a tin cup of coffee suspended over an open fire. In this way, dead weevils could be skimmed off before drinking. Hardtack could also be crumbled into soup as thickening or stuck on the end of a stick or ramrod and toasted over an open fire. Crumbled hardtack in water could be fried in animal, usually pork, fat; this dish was known as skillygalee. Hardtack was often turned into milk toast with the addition of condensed milk which was then available in tin cans and sold by most Union army sutlers.

In the Union Army coffee, the soldier's favourite beverage, was issued as beans. Soldiers usually kept these beans in a small bag in their haversack. The beans were beaten into grounds with a musket butt on a flat rock. Then they added sugar to the bag's contents. In 1862 the Union commissary began issuing a mixture of coffee, milk and sugar called essence of coffee. One teaspoon would make a cup of coffee. This experiment at instant coffee was unpopular, however, and it was quickly discontinued. Whenever the column halted men were sure to build fires and begin brewing up coffee in the tin cups they all carried in their haversack.

The men cooked their meat in one of several ways. Salt pork generally had to be soaked for hours to remove the brine; tying it to a tree and throwing it into a running brook was a common method of doing this. The easiest way of cooking the prepared meat was to stick it on the end of a ramrod or sharp stick and hold it over a fire until prepared. It could also be placed on the coals, then the ashes brushed off, salt and pepper added, and eaten. Many men carried small frying-pans, but veterans preferred broiled meat as it was thought to be a healthier method of preparation. Frying-pans were often made from a Union Army canteen half, the canteen having first been heated so that the solder holding the two sides melted.

Union soldiers had to prepare the desiccated vegetables which their army issued to prevent scurvy. The dessicated vegetable ration was a two or three inch cube of green dried vegetable matter about an ounce in weight. When soaked in water it became a pulpy soup with clearly visible turnips,

A Southern Mennonite becomes an army cook

'In the month of June, 1861, I was drafted for service in the war; but I refused to go for two reasons; First I was conscientiously opposed to war; second, I claimed exemptions on the ground of bad health. So I remained at home until I was forced to go. When I arrived at camp, I refused to bear arms, again claimed exemption, was examined, and placed on the sick list by order of the doctor of the regiment; but I was compelled to remain in camp. Within three weeks, I took the measles, and through the influence of the captain of the company, I got a furlough to come home for ten days. The captain told me to go home and stay there until he sent for me. So I came home and remained till December of the same year, when I was forced to go back to the army, contrary to the captain's orders. After reaching camp again, I was taken before a court of inquiry and court-martialled, and sentenced to be drilled alone two hours a day for a certain number of days. I again refused to drill or learn the art of war. For this I was threatened to be punished severely; but I still refused to bear arms. Finally, I was asked if I would assist in cooking for the company. To this I consented, and I was not punished.'

(Edward N. Wright, *Conscientious Objectors in the Civil War*, A. S. Barnes & Co., New York, 1961, p. 170)

A Union soldier is arrested for not killing a chicken

'On one of the long marches when rations were scarce, a man in Company A [1st US Sharpshooters] stole a chicken, notwithstanding the general orders against foraging, and not knowing when he would have a chance to cook it carried it alive in his haversack. The chicken kept peeping, and as he marched at the head of the regiment, Col. [Hiram] Berdan could not well pretend that he didn't hear it, as the night was still and the chicken had a good voice – a stalwart peeper. So he ordered the man under arrest, and when he came before the colonel's drum-head court-martial with others the next day, the colonel asked him for what he was under arrest. The man replied: "For stealing a chicken." "Are you sure?" asked the colonel. "Yes," said the man, meekly. "Keep him under guard at the rear of the regiment," ordered the colonel. In a day or two he was questioned in the same way, giving the same answer. The third time he was asked why he was arrested, becoming more out-spoken with his long humiliation, he replied: "For not having cut the chicken's head off." "Go to your company!" at once said the colonel. There were no more chickens carried alive in haversacks.'

(Captain C. A. Stevens, *Berdan's United State Sharpshooters in the Army of the Potomac 1861–1865*, Morningside Book-shop, Dayton, Ohio, 1972, p. 240)

One man prepares supper, pouring water into a frying-pan from his canteen, while his messmates wait. (James T Carden collection)

parsnips, carrots, cabbage leaves and a small amount of onion. Desiccated potatoes were also issued and these were usually used in soups or as a flour to make small cakes.

Confederate rations were both less varied and less certain. Transportation difficulties meant that sometimes, perhaps for several days on end, no rations were issued. Each man's daily ration in the Army of Northern Virginia just before Chancellorsville was four ounces of bacon and eighteen ounces of flour, with small amounts of rice, molasses and sugar. Even when rations were issued, there were often shortages; coffee might be issued but perhaps no sugar to go with it.

Confederates cooked their food in the same manner as did Union cooks. One different treat was coosh or slosh. To make this form of hash, when available, flour or corn meal was mixed with diced beef and animal fat and fried. Corn meal was also used to make corn biscuits or bread much more frequently than in the Union Army. Bread made from ground field peas and meal was issued during the siege of Vicksburg. Coffee was highly prized but not issued in anything like the quantities issued in the Union army because it had to be imported. Coffee substitutes were made from dried apples, parched peanuts, peas, potatoes, rye and corn. Corn was also issued on the cob when available as were peanuts, called goober peas. Indeed, a standard Southern joke was that CSA stood for 'corn, salt and apples', the basic issue ration.

To make up for the soldiers' monotonous diet, both sides foraged liberally. Union soldiers could buy food, notably fruit pies, at sutlers but few Confederate regiments had sutlers. Confederates were often able to improve their rations with captured Union food; they even found items such as canned lobsters when they captured supply trains during the Second Manassas campaign. Civilians often sold food to the soldiers. The folks back home often sent food to their men at the front. Otherwise, soldiers stole farmers' chickens and pigs in great numbers or hunted for wild game in the woods. In the Union army, the Sanitary Commission also provided some delicacies such as fresh fruit and vegetables in an endeavor to prevent scurvy.

Most men in both armies formed messes, small groups of four to eight members, to prepare their food. Usually one man was a more skilled cook and did most of the actual cooking; in some companies regular cooks, who were exempt from drilling, were appointed. They used large pots in which to boil the salt pork, and were allowed to stow these in the company wagons. Company cooks often boiled peas or beans with salt pork. When ovens were available soft bread was produced which was preferred to hardtack.

Discipline

Life in the army was very different from anything the recruit had known before. The most marked difference was the total control men with chevrons or gold rank insignia had over the men in the ranks. Officers or non-commissioned officers told them when to get up, what to eat, what to wear, what to do during the day, and when and where to sleep. This was

---

A Wisconsin man becomes a cook

'We drew flour while at Corinth [Mississippi]. We had a sheet-iron over on two wheels to bake bread for the regiment [14th Wisconsin Infantry]. A number of the boys had tried making bread, but some would find fault if the cook had poor luck, and the cook would quit. The oven had to be watched or it would burn the bread, or not bake fast enough, So, as no one else would do it, I took the job. I knew Bill Bradley of another company always had nice-looking bread. So I went over where he was kneading out his bread, and he told me how he made it, and I never had poor bread, and I made bread about two months.

'The darky, Old Abe, did the other cooking and all I had to do was to cut the bread and see that the meals were on time, as we had to have them at a certain hour when the call was given on the drum or bugle. We had a table and benches to sit on, and a canvas over it to keep the sun and rain off. The cook was excused from guard duty, but when the regiment was called out on those raids, I had to go with them.'

(Bryon R. Abernethy, ed., *Private Elisha Stockwell, Jr. Sees the Civil War*, University of Oklahoma Press, Norman, Oklahoma, 1958, pp. 42–3)

---

something for which the average, rural American of the 1860s was completely unprepared.

This control sprang from the unique set of laws, the 101 Articles of War, which governed both armies, and indeed were the same for both armies. In theory, every violation of an Article of War could lead to a formal court-martial, but in fact most violations were drunkenness, insubordination, theft from fellow soldiers and civilians, disrespect to superiors, sitting while on guard, leaving a post without authority, and being absent from camp without a pass. The company's first sergeant usually kept a list of petty offenders and their names were sure to be mentioned whenever an especially unpleasant task came up. They might have to dig or fill up latrines, bury dead horses, or help company cooks.

If the offense were sufficiently serious the culprit might be tried by a special court-martial. This was convened by a regimental or garrison commander, or commander of similar rank, and consisted of three officers. Chaplains, surgeons, assistant surgeons, and paymasters were not allowed to serve on the board. The special court-martial's jurisdiction was limited to non-capital cases. Officers could not be tried before a special court-martial. If found guilty, the defendant could not be sentenced to lose more than a month's pay or serve more than a month in prison or at hard labor. Non-commissioned officers could be demoted to the ranks.

In fact, these courts-martial often imposed shorter, but harsher sentences than specified in the Article of War. A

Union soldier buys a turkey with a counterfeit bill

'While moving towards the hills, a soldier was seen approaching from the direction where the enemy were supposed to be located. This man proved to belong to a New England regiment, and had been "skirmishing" on his own account far outside our lines, and was carrying on his shoulders a large turkey. Our field officer questioned him as to where he had been, and how he came in possession of the prize. Pointing to a farm-house in the distance, he replied, "I bought it of those people." After taking his name and the number of his regiment, he was allowed to go on his way to camp. When the picket-line was properly established, the officer stopped at the house for something to eat, and, while sitting on the porch, the owner produced the note with which the enterprising Yankee purchased the turkey. It was a new ten-dollar Confederate bill, bearing, like the genuine article, the words, "Ten years after a treaty of peace" but, unfortunately for the seller, it had been printed and issued by a publisher in Philadelphia as an advertising dodge. The farmer in his ignorance had parted with his fowl and given seven dollars of real Confederate money in change for this piece of paper. It is needless to say that Yankee soldiers were unpopular in this vicinity ever after.'

(Charles H. Banes, *History of the Philadelphia Brigade*, J. B. Lippincott & Co., Philadelphia, Pennsylvania, 1876, pp. 128–9)

Confederates issue horsemeat for rations

'No soldier will forget his first horse-meat breakfast.

'It was comical to see the facial expression as they viewed the platters of hot steak fried in its own grease or the "chunk" of boiled mule as it floated in a bucket of "stew". However, there seemed to be perfect good humor as they one after the other "tackled the job", and numerous jokes and badinage were indulged in by the partakers of the viands. Occasionally would some stalwart fellow throw back his head and utter a long and loud "Ye-ha, ye-ha, ye-haw!" in imitation of a jackass or mule, while another would step aside and kick at any one near by and trot off, moving his head from one side to the other in imitation of a trotting mule. All this was pure jollity, and such fun soon grew contagious and could be heard all along the battle front or breastworks.'

(Arthur W. Bergeron, Jr., and Lawrence L. Hewitt, *Boone's Louisiana Battery, A History & Roster*, Elliott's Bookshop Press, Baton Rouge, Louisiana, 1986, pp. 17–18)

man could be bucked and gagged, that is be made to sit with a gag in his mouth, his knees raised and arms outstretched. A thin log would be passed under his knees and over his elbows and his hands and ankles would be tied so that he could not move. He might be kept in that position for six to twelve hours. At the end of that time, the prisoner would usually be carried to his quarters, unable to walk, often sobbing uncontrollably.

A prisoner might be made to wear a cannon-ball, some six to 32 pounds in weight, shackled to one leg by a two to six foot long chain for a similar period. A man could be made to stand on a barrel for hours on end, perhaps wearing a sign indicating his offense, or holding a log on his shoulders, or he could be made to march around the camp wearing a barrel whose top and bottom had been knocked out. An artilleryman could be lashed to the spare wheel at the rear of the caisson, the caisson perhaps being driven over rough roads to add to the prisoner's discomfort. A cavalryman could be made to 'ride' a wooden horse or parade around the camp carrying his saddle. An infantryman might be made to march around the camp wearing a knapsack full of rocks.

At the beginning of the war flogging was a legal punishment, but it was banned in the US Army in August 1861 and in the Confederate Army in August 1862.

Thereafter officers did occasionally have their men flogged, but this usually ended up with the officer facing a court-martial. Branding, however, remained legal throughout the war. Deserters were branded, usually on the forehead, cheek, hand, or hip, with the first letter of their crime: 'D' for deserter, 'C' for cowardice, 'T' for thief, or 'W' for worthlessness. Not all branding was done with hot irons; indelible ink was often used instead.

In serious cases, including capital offenses, any soldier, regardless of rank, would be tried by a general court-martial. This was convened by army or department commanders, and in the US Army after 24 December 1861 by division and detached brigade commanders. The board consisted of from five to thirteen officers, all higher in rank than the accused. The senior officer was the President of the court and he both conducted the court and ruled on questions of law. A judge-advocate was also present to certify that the court was correctly conducted, as well as to summon witnesses and try the case. He was also to serve as the counsel to the defendant until a plea had been entered. The defendant could also seek an outside counsel, although this counsel was not allowed to address the court but was present only as a 'friend of the prisoner'.

Although not strictly legal, both sides resorted to 'drumhead courts-martial' in emergency situations. These were quickly convened by a commanding officer to punish extremely bad behaviour, and just as quickly adjourned, the defendant having been found guilty and punished. At least one Union soldier was hanged as the result of a drumhead court-martial.

Since it had to rule so much territory without civilian governments, as the war progressed the US set up military commissions to try cases involving local civilians and soldiers.

Privates William McKee and William Groover, 46th Pennsylvania Infantry, and Christopher Drumbar, 13th New Jersey Infantry, deserters from XII Corps, are shot at Leesburg, Virginia on 19 June 1863. (Harper's Weekly)

Soldiers convicted of serious crimes were usually imprisoned in a federal jail. Deserters and cowards were often drummed out of the service. Their sentences were read out at the retreat parade or a special parade, their buttons and rank insignia were ripped from their uniforms, their heads usually shaved, and, wearing a sign proclaiming their guilt, they were marched out of the camp surrounded by soldiers carrying their arms reversed. Drummers beat 'The Rogues' March', or, in the Confederate Army, 'Yankee Doodle'.

In extreme cases such as murder, mutiny, treason, rape, desertion or sometimes even theft or pillage, the sentence was death. In all, 287 Union soldiers were executed for these crimes, most having been found guilty of desertion.

Most military executions involved firing-squads. In some cases, such as black soldiers being found guilty of raping white women, hanging was used. During the early days of the war, crimes against civilians such as rape or murder were usually punished by hanging, while military crimes were punished by firing-squad. Later, the firing-squad was the usual method of execution, although prisoners were occasionally hanged throughout the war. In both types of execution, all nearby units were made to witness the execution to bring home the seriousness of such crimes.

When a soldier was executed by firing-squad a fairly set ritual was followed. Witnessing units were formed on three sides of a square, facing in. The prisoner, after praying with a clergyman of his choice, was dressed in civilian clothing, usually a white shirt and dark trousers, so as not to disgrace the uniform, and was placed in a wagon with his coffin to go to the place of execution. Led by a corporal, a funeral squad of eight men, marching with arms reversed, accompanied the wagon, with drummers beating a funeral march.

A firing-squad of a dozen men waited at the site. The prisoner, having arrived, was helped off the wagon and in turn often helped carry his own coffin to the grave which had already been dug. He then sat on the coffin while his sentence was read aloud. Another prayer from the clergy-

A Confederate is forced to witness an execution

'One afternoon the whole division was ordered out to witness the execution of three Confederate soldiers from another division. They were to be shot for some violation of the laws of the army. The division formed three sides of a hollow square, the fourth being open. Three stakes were fixed in the ground about the center of this open side. Soon after our formation, an officer and a guard appeared with the prisoners. The condemned were made to kneel with their backs to the stakes, to which they were securely tied. Cloths were fastened over their eyes. Twelve men then picked up the twelve guns lying on the ground in front of the prisoners. The guns had already been loaded. It is said that six had balls and six did not – so no man would know whether he killed one of the prisoners. The twelve men took their places about thirty feet in front of the three prisoners. The order to fire was given and, at the report of the guns, two men were killed – the balls going through each. The third man, while shot, was not killed. One of the detail was ordered to place another gun against the man's breast and to fire. This shot killed him instantly. This was the only execution I witnessed; if I live a thousand years, I will never be willing to see another.'

(John H. Worsham, *One of Jackson's Foot Cavalry*, McCowat-Mercer Press, Jackson, Tennessee, 1964, p. 120)

A Union officer and an enlisted man are cowards

'A lieutenant, belonging to the Twenty-first New Jersey regiment, had been tried by a court-martial, and convicted of cowardice at the battle of May 3d. The whole brigade was brought out at the hour for evening parade, and formed in a hollow square. To the center of the inclosure the culprit was brought. His sentence was then read to him, which was that he be dismissed [from] the service in disgrace. The adjutant general of the brigade then preceeded to execute the details of the sentence. The sword of the cowardly officer was taken from him and broken over his head; his shoulder-straps and buttons were then cut off, and his pistol broken and thrown away. The sentence, and the manner of its execution, were ordered to be published in the newspapers of the county where the regiment was raised. A similar sentence was executed in the Seventy-seventh regiment on the same evening. Lewis Burke, of Company F [an enlisted man] was convicted of cowardice at the same battle. He was brought before the regiment, which stood in line; his sentence read, his buttons and the blue cord on his coat cut off, and placard marked "COWARD" hung on his back. A guard, with fixed bayonets pointing at his back, then marched him off, the band playing "The Rogues' March". Burke went to serve out his time at the Dry Tortugas (Florida) at hard labor, without pay or allowance.'

(George T. Stevens, *Three Years in the Sixth Corps*, S. R. Gray Publishers, Albany, New York, 1866, p. 221)

man followed and he was then given a chance to say his last words. Some men showed bravado, one even drinking stagnant water from his own grave. Some wept or shook with fear. The condemned man was then blindfolded and his hands were tied behind him. He then knelt either before the grave or on the coffin; the provost marshal gave the command, and the firing-squad fired the volley. It is said that the weapon of one man in the firing-squad was loaded with a blank cartridge, the idea being that each man might take comfort from the thought that he might not have fired the fatal shot. The fact, of course, is that there is very little recoil when firing a blank cartridge.

A surgeon then proclaimed the man dead. If, as often happened, the prisoner survived the volley, the provost marshal advanced and administered the *coup de grâce*.

In virtually all executions, witnesses were horrified by what they saw, and often felt anger at their own officers; they often felt that the condemned man was more victim than transgressor.

Indeed, often they were, for the law was applied on both sides with a very uneven hand. In late 1862 six deserters from the Army of Tennessee got off with some 'fatherly advice' from their commanding general, while other Confederates were noted as having deserted as many as six times, caught, but simply returned to the ranks without punishment. On the other hand, Private Samuel Mapp, a black soldier from Virginia, was convicted of mutiny, disobedience of orders, and threatening the life of a superior officer for joining a protest against the inequality of pay scales between black and white soldiers. He was shot at City Point, Virginia, on 20 April 1865.

Combat

The ultimate reason for being in the army, and the ultimate test of everyone who was in it, was combat, that terrifying maelstrom which changed everyone who experienced it. Yet, on both sides, most men believed that only battle would end the war.

Generally, the men get increasingly nervous as they approach the front. Smoke covers the front lines in the distance. The crackle of small arms and the booming of cannon grow louder. Worse, as they pass field hospitals, they see severed arms and legs piled nearby and hear the cries of the wounded and dying. Rows of dead, usually uncovered, lie near the hospitals.

For minor infractions of regulations, cavalrymen often were made to ride horses such as this one named 'Molly'. The first two words on her hindquarters are 'For Millersville'. (Robert L. Kotchian collection)

A coward is drummed out of the service from the Army of the Potomac. Note how the front rank hold their weapons at 'reverse arms'. (Harper's Weekly)

A Union colonel teaches recruits discipline

'Colonel [Edward D.] Baker [71st Pennsylvania Infantry] personally exercised the officers in the manual of arms as well as in the school of the battalion, in both of which he displayed considerable knowledge and proficiency. A trifling incident occurring during one of the drills which served to illustrate an important trait in his military character – promptness in obeying an order without stopping to consider either its necessity or the means for its accomplishment. At the time referred to, the officers were formed in line, drilling in the manual, and at the position of "arms at order", when Colonel Baker gave the command, "support arms", omitting the intermediate position of arms at a shoulder. Some obeyed the order by going regularly through the drill, from one position to another; others kept their pieces resting on the ground, and looked at their commander, with a smile at his error. Baker stood erect, looking the picture of determination, and said, with an emphasis not to be mistaken, "I want the officers to understand that when an order is given it must be obeyed."'

(Charles H. Banes, *History of the Philadelphia Brigade*, J. B. Lippincott & Co., Philadelphia, 1876, pp. 24–5)

A Confederate colonel teaches recruits discipline

'Colonel [George H.] Steuart [1st Maryland Infantry] was in the habit of testing his men on guard in some lonely spot by rushing upon them on foot or on horseback, taking them by surprise if possible. One night a sentinel had been posted near the colonel's tent, and part of his duty was to protect a lot of tent-flies piled up close by. In the small hours of the night, Colonel Steuart crept out of the rear of his tent, and stealthily approaching, while the sentinel was learning on his musket, gazing at the stars and probably thinking of his sweetheart or his mother, took up one of the tent-flies, shouldered it, and was walking off with it when the sentinel, turning, rushed upon him, and pretending not to recognize him, seized him by the shoulders and gave him such a shaking that the colonel could hardly get breath to cry, "I'm your colonel – I'm your colonel!" Then when the sentry let go his hold and apologized, the colonel slapped him on the back and said, "Good soldier! Good soldier! I'll remember this."'

(Randolph H. McKim, *A Soldier's Recollections*, Zengler Publishing Co., Washington, DC, 1983, pp. 41–2)

Waiting, tense and apprehensive, men react in various ways. Some throw away playing cards, dice or pornographic pictures, fearful that these may end up being sent home with their personal effects. Some men, nervously over-loud, make jokes about everything. 'There's somebody's darling,' was a common joke among Confederates whenever a particular horrible-looking corpse was to be seen. 'Somebody's darling' referred to a popular but morosely sentimental song that went, in part, 'Into the ward of the clean whitewashed halls, where the dead slept and the dying lay, wounded by bayonets, sabres, and balls, somebody's darling was borne one day.' The jokers tend to be men going under fire for the first time; veterans are more solemn. Some veterans of many actions, however, have become so blasé that they are capable of taking a short nap before getting into formation for battle. Others, also usually veterans, become unusually quiet, filling their minds with thoughts of home and wives or God to steel themselves for what is to come. Many pray; in some units chaplains offer brief services before the men go into action. Many regimental colonels make short speeches which they hope will prove inspirational.

Now it is time. As they advance in column or line, mounted officers seek to calm their nerves by constantly calling them to 'close up' and 'dress'. Drums beat a steady pace, and the flapping regimental colour gives a focal point to the advance. Bands are often stationed just behind the lines, playing patriotic and popular airs. Indeed, Confederate bands behind Pickett's men at Gettysburg played polkas.

Nevertheless, some men try to drop out, to hide in a ditch or behind a fence or tree. Most are spotted by file closers, who prod them with musket butt or sword. They usually jump up and run back into the ranks, serving well for the

A Confederate wins a hand-to-hand battle

'A captain, I think of a New York regiment, ran up to me and grabbing the flagstaff called out to me, "You damned little rebel, surrender." I held on and jerked him to me, striking at him at the same time with my sword, which was hung to my wrist by a sword knot. He at once jumped back and fired at me with his pistol, cursing me all the time and tugging at the flagstaff. I kept jerking it back and striking at him with my sword, while at the same time struggling to get from under my dead horse, which was lying on my legs.

'One ball from the pistol stuck the star of my collar and burned my neck like fire, while another struck my little finger, breaking it and smashing a seal ring which I wore. Another just grazed my leg, but that one felt like a double-heated, hot iron, and made me struggle so that I found myself free from my horse and on my feet.

'Our troops by this time were pouring in and the Yankees running, my opponent among them. But he was a little too late, and I caught up with him. I cut down on him with both hands, expecting to split him, as we used to read of in novels, but my sword bounced off him, knocking him to his knees. He rose and turned, facing me with his pistol in his hands. I never doubted but that he was about to shoot again and ran him through. He lived only a few minutes, trying to say something. I told him that I would send his effects to his people, which was apparently what he was trying to ask.'

(John Haskell, *The Haskell Memoirs*, G. P. Putnam's Sons, New York, 1960, pp. 33–4)

A Confederate officer loses his dinner

'We were going through some pine woods when a wild turkey was started up near me. These fowls do not take wing readily on level ground and this one went off running at a rapid gait. Animated by the hope of game for supper, I put spurs to my horse and chased it for a couple of hundred yards or more. It doubled several times but finally came to an old worm [wood rails in zigzags] fence through which it stuck its head and foolishly tried to force its body between the rails. I started to dismount when the fluttering of the wings made my horse rear a little and I had to retain my seat. Just then a wretched soldier from the ranks ran by my horse's head and grabbed the prize. My memory is a photographic one, and I recall and see in my mind this chase, from start to finish, like a modern moving picture. Rations were scarce and uncertain at this time and my disappointment, for myself and the staff, was great.'

(McHenry Howard, *Recollections of a Maryland Confederate Soldier and Staff Officer under Johnston, Jackson and Lee*, Morningside Bookshop, Dayton, Ohio, 1975, p. 228)

Colonel H. S. Roberts, 1st Michigan, waits under fire

'We formed in double column at half distance, and laid down, and for about four hours we took solid shot, shell and canister, in awful profusion; the roar of the cannon was tremendous, our batteries were playing magnificently on them in the woods, the gunboats were hurling their shell over our heads into the enemy, and the enemy were doing the best they could, opening battery after battery in new positions. The noise was infernal, and our losses began to be respectable. I do not believe that troops have often lain so long under as hot a fire as my fellows did. It is the most trying position a soldier has to endure, to stand these horrid missiles, crouched low, seeing them strike all about him, hearing them burst all around him, and yet unable to move or do a thing but wait in that awful suspense. Now a pause, and your heart beats quicker, for you know they are getting a new range. Zim! and now it comes, and they have got a cross fire on you – grin and bear it – shut your teeth and swear and beg for a chance to move on them – anything but this. But no faltering, not a bit of it; occasionally, yes, frequently, some young fellow picks up his leg or his arm, and hobbles off to the rear; then some fellow, less fortunate has to be picked up. Finally, a stop to their shell . . .'

(Captain C. A. Stevens, *Berdan's Sharpshooters in the Army of the Potomac*, Morningside Bookshop, Dayton, Ohio, 1972, p. 153)

These men, probably from Jenkin's South Carolina Brigade, were killed in a cornfield near Sherrick's House at the Battle of Antietam.

Another Alexander Gardner photograph which gave people back home some idea of the bleakness and horror of war. (Library of Congress collection)

A Union officer sleeps with the dead

'At the moment [during the Second Battle of Bull Run] Major McGee with his squadron of the Third Virginia [US], rode up and informed us he had been ordered to the point in question. I advised the major, in case this post was attacked, to throw his men into the houses and defend it to the last extremity. He promised to do so. Having attended to my duties I left John to watch the horses grazing in the Court House yard, and went myself into the vestibule of the building to sleep. Seeing a long pine box there I stretched myself upon it. A sentinel stepped up and informed me that the box contained the body of a Colonel. Looking through an opening I saw the ghastly features of the dead officer. I felt no loathing, but rather a sentiment of friendly respect – a glow of pride in our brotherhood; so I told the sentinel we would not disturb each other, and returned to my sleep.'

('A Virginian,' 'Personal Recollections of the War', *Harper's New Monthly Magazine*, November 1867, p. 722)

Confederates strip Union dead

'There was a great deal of pilfering performed on the dead bodies of the Yankees by our men. Some of them were left as naked as they were born, everything in the world they had being taken from them. I ordered my men to take their fine guns and canteens if they wished, but nothing else ... The only thing I took was a fine canteen which I cut off a dead Yankee who was lying on his face in our path as we marched along. Just the sight of the battlefield after the fight was in itself horrible. For 7 or 8 days after the battle every man I saw asleep appeared to me like a dead man.'

(Lieutenant J. B. Mitchell, 34th Alabama Inf., 'As naked as they were born ...', *Civil War Times Illustrated*, November 1977, p. 41)

rest of the battle. A few refuse to move, and these are usually court-martialled for cowardice after the battle.

Finally, they are in action. The true horror of a Civil War battlefield affected almost all the senses simultaneously. The weather was rarely good; it was freezing cold at Fredericksburg and Stone's River and terribly hot at Gettysburg and Vicksburg. Men are deafened for hours afterwards by the overwhelming explosions of artillery and the constant rattle of rifle-muskets and pistols; the constant yelling of officers and non-commissioned officers, the cries of the wounded, the cheering and swearing, bugles and drums raise the noise level. The air, particularly in small dales and valleys, becomes almost unbreathable because of the heavy sulphur smoke given off by black powder. As each cartridge is bitten off to expose the powder and ball, particles of black powder cling to the lips, giving a foul, sharp, pepper-like taste that fills the mouth. After a while, the musket barrel becomes almost too hot to touch. No matter where the soldier looks he sees smoke, fire and terribly mutilated bodies.

Strangely enough, however, the very act of going into battle and finally being able to control some part of one's life by loading and firing, seems to effect a change in the attitudes of most soldiers. Some report that their sense of fear is replaced by a sense of extreme rage at the enemy. Yet others, however, say that they become remarkably calm under fire. Indeed, the men of the Confederate 1st Maryland Infantry at the First Manassas were so relaxed that they stopped in the middle of a charge to pick blackberries. Most men in action, however, usually pay more attention to what they are about. They load and fire their weapons not precisely as if on the parade ground but coolly enough.

A Union soldier is captured in the Wilderness

'I walked back a few steps and listened, when I discovered that a rebel skirmish line was moving through the woods. Taking my gun at a trail arms, I started to run across the clearing, and had almost reached the other side, when the word "Halt!" from a skirmisher at the edge of the wood brought me to a sudden stop. Thinking, however, that I had reached the Union lines, I stopped but an instant, when I advanced, gun in hand, exclaiming, "Do not fire – I am a Union soldier!" The reply was, "Drop that gun and march in here or I will put a ball through you." I again stopped, but did not drop the gun. The rebel repeated the order, when I threw down my gun and surrendered.'

(John W. Urban, *My Experiences mid Shot and Shell and in Rebel Den*, Lancaster, Pennsylvania, 1882, p. 409)

Men fell in heaps where fighting was heaviest. These dead were from Starke's Louisiana Brigade and lay where they died along the Hagerstown Pike, 500 yards north of the Dunker Church, at the Battle of Antietam. The photograph was taken by Alexander Gardner. (Library of Congress collection)

In the noise and turmoil, however, many men are unable to tell whether their own weapon has fired or not. They actually load cartridge on top of cartridge without firing a shot. One rifle-musket found at Gettysburg after the battle had 23 rounds in it; some 6,000 weapons were found to have between three and ten loaded rounds. Twice that number had two cartridges in the barrel, indicating that the user had realized his mistake and picked up a wounded soldier's weapon rather quickly after loading his second round. Some weapons that had been fired repeatedly grew so hot that

---

Private John Meehan, Co. A, 118th Pennsylvania, faces fire

'As this was my first time actually under enemy fire, I was greatly excited. My feelings are hard to describe. When walking across the open field, with the artillery firing overhead and the rebels firing at us, I felt afraid. My heart beat tumultuously. I thought I might be killed, and had no wish to die. I longed to live, and thought myself a fool for voluntarily placing myself in the army. Yet I had no idea at all of turning back. My feelings were, that if ordered to go on, I would go, but gladly would I have welcomed the order, "About face". By the time the river was reached I was much calmer, the dread was working off me, and while not eager, as I had been to start, I felt that if we crossed the river and charged the rebels I could do what the rest could.'

(Survivor's Association, *History of the Corn Exchange Regiment*, J. L. Smith, Philadelphia, 1888, pp. 80–1)

A Confederate goes under fire for the first time

'I recall distinctly the sad, solemn feeling produced by seeing the ambulances brought up to the front; it was entirely too suggestive. Soon we reached the woods and were ascending the hill along a little ravine, for a position, when a solid shot broke the trunnions of one of the guns, thus disabling it; then another, nearly spent struck a tree about half-way up and fell nearby. Just after we got to the top of the hill, and were within fifty or one hundred yards of the position we were to take, a shell struck the off-wheel horse of my gun and burst. The horse was torn to pieces, and the pieces thrown in every direction. The saddle-horse was also horribly mangled, the driver's leg was cut off, as was also the foot of a man who was walking alongside. Both men died that night. A white horse working in the lead looked more like a bay after the catastrophe. To one who had been in the army but five days, and but five minutes under fire, this seemed an awful introduction.'

(Edward A. Moore, *The Story of a Cannoneer Under Stonewall Jackson*, Neale Publishing, New York, 1907, pp. 30–1)

---

they discharged immediately when the powder was poured down the barrel. And, some soldiers found themselves so calm that they were able to disassemble and repair their weapons even under fire.

Few men ran for the rear when they came under fire although this might be seen to be a rational move. More than a century before the Civil War, an Englishman, Dr Samuel Johnson, wondered why, and in 1759 came up with an answer that has been verified in 20th-century studies on why American soldiers fight. Johnson wrote that each English soldier, although not terribly well trained or endowed with property to defend or even affected by theoretical ideas of liberty, believed himself responsible for himself and that no man was his superior. Hence, he fought bravely to earn the esteem of his peers, for the sake of his reputation among his brother soldiers, rather than for theoretical ideas such as Union or states' rights or abolition.[3]

Some, a rare few, found that they loved battle, that it created a natural high that could never be found in any civilian occupations. The very threat of extreme danger, the seriousness of the business, made it something extremely enjoyable for these men.

After a few hours in battle the men are transformed in appearance. Their hands are black from powder fouling on their ramrods and as they wipe their faces, their faces also became black. A black ring is left around each mouth by powder spilling from the bitten cartridge end.

Fighting is a thirsty business. Canteens are soon emptied and several men from each company are given all their comrades' canteens to get water from nearby ponds or streams, even in the midst of battle. A wait to get water at Gettysburg delayed the attacking Alabama troops long enough at the Little Big Top on 2 July to allow the Union troops to get well settled in before the Confederate attack.

After the battle comes a great letdown. The men are exhausted both physically and mentally. Men who have been fighting for some hours even keel over and fall asleep in the midst of the fighting as happened at Antietam and the Wilderness. Not even close shell explosions can wake them. Those who remain awake search for wounded and dead comrades. A sense of depression, of 'survivor's guilt', often sets in among these survivors. Some only learn of the loss of a friend or relative during the evening roll-call. Some men search the battlefield for relics such as enemy officers' insignia and personal weapons or items from enemy soldiers' haversacks. Then most write home to let loved ones know of their survival, and give news of other men from the same area in their unit.

Generally, the more action a soldier has seen, the less personally affected by its aftermath he appears to be. Veterans develop a vital ability to block out much. Many veterans would argue their generals' strategies, while others would tell 'war stories' of what they had seen and done. Enlisted men liked to tell stories of the cowardice of high-ranking officers or others whom they believe to live well while they themselves live poorly.

Union prisoners hang outlaws in Andersonville

'About twenty men [Confederates] came in this morning to put up the scaffold . . .

'It had become known that we were going to hang some of our own men [prisoners who had been robbing and killing weaker prisoners]. When the appointed time arrived a large crowd of citizens – men, women and children, gathered on the high ground between the principal forts and the prison to witness the hanging . . .

'The six raiders were hanged this afternoon; it was an awful sight; the judge, jury, etc., were all prisoners, no rebels participating at all. At about half-past four, Captain [Henry] Wirz [camp commandant] rode into camp at the head of the guards who had the condemned men in charge to the scaffold, and delivered the sentenced men to our police, who stood around with clubs. One of the condemned men escaped through the crowd to the swamp but was soon brought back . . .

'The six men were hanged together; after hanging about twenty minutes, they were taken down and carried out to the dead house. I was one of the six who carried Mosby [nicknamed after the Confederate partisan], the leader, out, and was glad to breathe fresh air for a few minutes.'

(Michael Dougherty, *Diary of a Civil War Hero*, Pyramid Books, New York, 1960, pp. 102–3)

Confederate prisoners escape from Point Lookout

'The prisoners were allowed to go outside of the enclosure on the beach to bathe. And if an empty barrel or box happened to be floating on the water, a prisoner in bathing would watch his opportunity, slip his head under the barrel or box, and then as the tide drifted up the river, would follow it, keeping as near the shore as necessary until he got beyond the reach of the guard, and then take to the woods.'

Luther W. Hopkins, *From Bull Run To Appomattox*, Fleet-McGinley, Baltimore, Maryland, 1908, pp. 171–2)

impossible to give exact figures, it appears that some 194,743 Union soldiers and 642,634 Confederate soldiers became prisoners of war at some time during the war. The Confederate number is so much larger because it includes entire garrisons, such as the one at Vicksburg. Most of these garrisons were parolled, rather than interned, with some 247,769 Confederate and 16,668 Union soldiers being parolled in the field. Parolled soldiers were released after signing a form that indicated that they would not take up arms again until officially exchanged for a captured enemy soldier. Most Confederates simply went home to await

Life in the Prison Camps

For some, the end of battle was simply the beginning of a new hardship, life as a prisoner of war. While it is

Although the wooden barracks look neat enough, they were drafty and poorly heated. Camp Douglas, near Chicago, had one of the worst death rates of any Union prisoner-of-war camp. (Harper's Weekly)

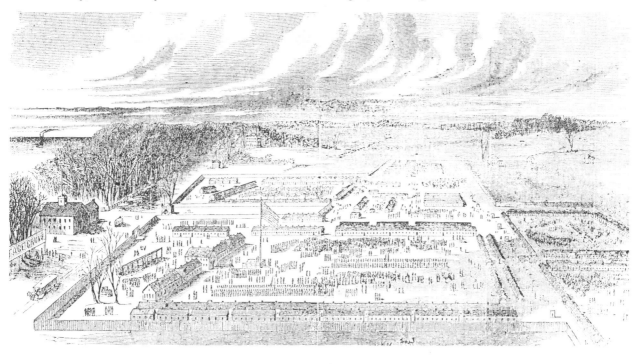

A guard at Andersonville shoots a soldier for getting water

'My attention was drawn to the nearest guard who, with rifle in his hand, was watching the men getting water. His countenance displayed as much eagerness as that of the hunter when he discovers his game and expects to have a good shot. I was watching the demon and wondering whether it was really possible that he would fire at the men who had gathered there for no other purpose than to get water when I was horrified to see him deliberately raise his gun and fire into the crowd. I turned in the direction of the gathering but too late as the ball had sped on its deadly mission and the soul of one more unfortunate had left its earthly abode . . . One of the prisoners in his eagerness to get pure water had dipped under the dead line [line which prisoners were forbidden to cross] and the guard who had been watching and waiting for just such a chance . . . fired at him. The ball missed the mark it was intended for but unfortunately hit one of the others who was in the act of stooping for water at the rear of the one shot at. The ball passed through his head and the soldier fell dead along the side of the stream.'

(Milton E. Fowler, ed, *Dear Folks At Home*, Cumberland County Historical Society, Carlisle, Pennsylvania, 1963, pp. 134–5)

Northern civilians tour prisoner-of-war camps

'I was at this time in the first room [of Fort Delaware] – nearest the head of the steps and whose window looked straight across the middle of the fort enclosure, but happened to be one morning in the next room, occupied by the Morgans [Colonel Richard C. and Charlton H.] and others when a gray-haired old man . . . with a bevy of young girls unceremoniously came inside the door and coolly looked us over. When they left, passing on to the next room I was expressing my indignation when Captain [George] Ahl [Pittsburgh Heavy Artillery] appeared at the door and looked at me inquiringly. I said, "Captain Ahl, we are glad at any time to give any Northern people information about friends in the South or any other proper information, but we protest against being exhibited like wild animals." His face flushed but he withdrew without making any reply. "Dick," Morgan said to me, "You have made an enemy of Ahl and will have cause to worry for it." I refused to be sorry but experienced his mean enmity soon afterwards.'

(McHenry Howard, *Recollections of a Maryland Confederate Soldier and Staff Officer under Johnston, Jackson and Lee*, Morningside Bookshop, Dayton, Ohio, 1975, p. 310)

Union enlisted prisoners lived in tents on Belle Isle, in the James River near Richmond. Nice in the summer, they suffered terribly from the cold in winter.
(Harper's Weekly)

Exchanged Confederate take any medicine available

'We were put on a steamer and carried to a point below Richmond, on the James river, where we met a like number of Federal prisoners that came down from Richmond, and there the exchange was made. The vessel that carried us up the river was a small one, and the sick were packed on the deck and in the hold of the vessel as thick as they could lay. They were all sick, but had to lie on the hard decks with no attention, except that a doctor now and then went through the vessel handing out pills to any who wanted them. He carried them loose in his pocket, and as he stepped between and over the men as they lay on the hard beds, he would say, "Who wants a pill?" And all around him the bony, emaciated arms would be stretched up to receive the medicine. What the pills contained no one knew, but the suffering men swallowed them and asked no questions. They were sick, and needed medicine, and this was medicine. What more did a sick soldier need?'

(Luther W. Hopkins, *From Bull Run To Appomattox*, Fleet-McGiney, Baltimore, Maryland, 1980, pp. 179–80)

An ex-prisoner finds a shirt while washing

'While at this camp an old member of an adjoining regiment returned from the southern prisons in a very shabby condition. Being furnished with a new outfit of clean clothes, he was requested to go with the boys to the river and take a good wash. So they went down, and got the old fellow in up to his neck, when the boys scrubbed away, after first lathering him with Rappahannock mud, and finally began to get some of the prison dirt off. But [they] were for awhile nonplussed at the curious color of his body, when to their surprise they developed an old shirt stuck close to his skin, which he said he thought he had lost long before – had missed it among his scanty wardrobe, and it didn't know it was there. He laughed at their taunts, saying he was so much ahead. Yet they didn't allow him to preserve it as a memento, but cast it afar off into the current, and as the owner eyed it floating away, he sighed and walked away as if he had lost an old friend, as the shirt must have been, for it had certainly stuck to him very close.'

(Captain C. A. Stevens, *Berdan's United States Sharpshooters in the Army of the Potomac*, Morningside Bookshop, Dayton, Ohio, 1972,, p. 237)

notification that they had been exchanged; Union soldiers, much to their displeasure, were sent to camps such as Camp Parole, Maryland, to await official exchange.

At the moment of capture during battle, the prisoner was usually confused, cut off from his friends, tired and sometimes wounded. Badly wounded prisoners were treated at field hospitals, usually not until their captors' soldiers had been treated. At times their own surgeons, also finding themselves behind enemy lines, treated them. They were then transferred to hospitals in the rear, usually associated with prison camps, that had been designated to receive and treat prisoners of war. Once recovered to the point where they could move about, they were transferred to regular prison camps. Unwounded prisoners were sent to the rear immediately where they were gathered into groups and forwarded to prison camps in the rear.

Civil War soldiers received no training as to what to do on being captured, or how to escape. It was not until 7 April 1864 that a circular issued by the Army of Northern Virginia warned its members when captured to 'preserve entire silence with regard to everything connected with the army, the positions, movements, organizations or probable strength of any portion of it'. Prisoners were allowed to give only their name, company and regimental designations.[4]

No suggestions on how best to escape were published. The best chance lay in slipping away as soon and as near to

Although the iron bars on the window confirm that this is indeed a prison, these Morgan's Confederate Raiders seem to be getting enough to eat. They are, from left: Captain William Curry, 8th Kentucky Cavalry; unidentified; Adjutant Leeland Hathaway, 14th Kentucky Cavalry; Second Lieutenant H. D. Brown, 7th Kentucky Cavalry; First Lieutenant Will Hays, 2nd Kentucky Cavalry. (John Sickles collection)

North and South, aides de camp. *Left, First Lieutenant James B. Washington, aide to Confederate General J. E. Johnston, was photographed with West Point friend Union Second Lieutenant George A. Custer, a member of the staff of Union General George B. McClellan for only a couple of* *days, on the day Washington was captured, 31 May 1862, while on an important mission during the Seven Pines. Washington's jacket is apparently trimmed in yellow, which has photographed black, and he wears Union shoulder-straps. Custer wears a regulation uniform. (US Army Military History Institute)*

A Union prisoner in Andersonville finds 25 cents for food

'One morning, upon examining the pockets of an infantryman . . . who had just died, I had the wonderful luck to find a silver quarter. I hurried off to tell Andrews of our unexpected good fortune. By an effort he succeeded in calming himself . . . and we went into committee upon the state of our stomachs to consider how the money could be spent . . .

'At the south side of the stockade, on the outside of the timbers, was a sutler's shop kept by a rebel, and communicating with the prison by a hole two or three feet square cut through the logs . . . The articles for sale were corn meal and bread, flour and wheat bread, meat, beans, molasses, honey, and sweet potatoes. I went down to the place, carefully inspected the stock, priced everything there and studied the relative food value of each. I came back, reported my observations and conclusions to Andrew, and then stayed at the tent while he went on a similar errand. The consideration of the matter was continued during the day and night, and the next morning we determined upon investing our twenty-five cents in sweet potatoes, as we could get nearly a half-bushel of them, which was "more fillin' at the price", to use the words of Dickens' fat boy, than anything else offered us. We bought the potatoes, carried them home in our blanket, buried them in the bottom of our tent to keep them from being stolen, and restricted ourselves to two per day until we had eaten them all.'

(John McElroy, *This Was Andersonville*, Bonanza Books, New York, 1957, pp. 252–3)

A Confederate prisoner's rations at Fort Delaware

'No exercise of any kind was permitted to us, and we only left the room to march down to the mess-hall. For breakfast we had a cup of poor coffee without milk or sugar, and two small pieces of bad bread. For dinner we had a cup of greasy water misnamed soup, a piece of beef two inches square and a half inch thick, and two slices of bread. At supper the fare was the same as at breakfast. This was exceedingly light diet. Some of the officers behaved disagreeably; and eight or ten of us, principally Virginians, associated ourselves together for mutual protection, and formed a mess of our own. We contrived to make some additions to our diet by purchases at the Sutler's store. When we had no money the Sutler would take watches or other valuables in pledge, and let us have the provisions.'

(Francis W. Dawson, *Reminiscences of Confederate Service*, Louisiana State Press, Baton Rouge, Louisiana, 1980, p. 73)

the front as possible, while there was still a great deal of confusion. Neither side had a specially trained military body to handle prisoners so sending them back to the rear was an informal business.

Treatment at the hands of front-line troops varied; sometimes, prisoners were best treated during the period when they were being taken to the rear since combat troops tended to treat their enemy brothers better than did troops who had nothing to do but guard prisoners. Indeed, one group of Confederate prisoners was being escorted to the rear by veterans after Spotsylvania when a non-veteran regimental band began playing the 'Rogues' March.' The Union veterans grew so angry at this insult to the fighting Confederates that they threatened to smash the musical instruments; the music stopped. Other prisoners reported their captors as being so overwrought that they feared for their lives until they reached the rear. Union prisoners were often forced to surrender items of clothing, especially shoes, to the more poorly equipped Confederates during this stage.

Prisoners, often directed by their own officers or non-commissioned officers, were herded into clearings behind

Many Confederate prisoners, such as this one photographed in Philadelphia, received northern-made Confederate uniforms which had wooden rather than brass buttons. (Michael D. Jones collection)

A Union prisoner enters Andersonville prison camp

'As we marched through the gate I could hardly believe it to be possible that this horrible place was to contain us even for a few days, and my blood froze with horror as I looked around and saw men who but a short time before enjoyed health and strength, worn down by suffering and disease, until they hardly looked like human beings. Some of them were almost naked, and all were covered with dirt and vermin, presenting an appearance that made our hearts sink within us as we looked upon them; and the terrible thought would continually force itself into my mind, How can I ever expect to live in this horrible place?'

(John W. Urban, *My Experiences mid Shot and Shell*, Lancaster, Pennsylvania, 1882, pp. 460–1)

the lines. At Spotsylvania Union troops set up poles with Confederate regimental designations and in-coming prisoners were told to report to their respective regiments. Officers were often taken away to be questioned by Signal Corps or Provost Marshal personnel. Sometimes rations were issued, but most prisoners reported that they received no food until they reached a prisoner-of-war camp, which could be several days later.

When as large a number of prisoners as was feasible had been collected, and as much information as possible extracted from them, they were moved in groups to railroads or boats to be shipped back to central prisoner-of-war camps. Civilians often lined the way to see them pass, usually taunting them but occasionally giving them food.

On reaching prisoner-of-war camps, soldiers were searched and most valuables were stolen. Prisoners tried to hide at least their money. Hollow buttons were pried apart and paper money was stuffed into them. Union mounted troops hid money, even coins, in the belt support pillars on the backs of their jackets.

Prisoner-of-war camps varied tremendously in type and size. The Confederates improvised more than the Union authorities in converting civilian sites to prison camps. Their first major prison camp was an old tobacco warehouse in Richmond owned by a firm named Libby which left its name on the outside and hence gained it its name. It was a three-storey brick building, lit by gas, and furnished with pine mess tables, cots, and benches. It soon became an officer's prison camp. Enlisted men in Richmond were sent to Belle Island, in the James River where as many as 7,000 enlisted men lived in tents, sleeping on damp ground, even in the sub-freezing weather.

Tobacco warehouses were also used as prison camps throughout Richmond, in Danville, Virginia and Salisbury, North Carolina. A cotton shed was used in Cahaba, Alabama, and barracks in Petersburg, Virginia. The worst Southern prisoners were simply wooden log stockades built around an open field in which Union prisoners of war were dumped without shelter or adequate sanitation facilities. Camp Sumter at Andersonville, Georgia, was the best known of these. It was opened to prisoners in February 1864, and was holding some 32,000 Union enlisted men by July. Of these, 12,912 were buried in its graveyard, although total deaths were probably higher and certainly were if later deaths caused by poor treatment in the camp are included in the total.

Originally, civilian prisons were used to house Confederate prisoners of war. As the numbers grew, however, most were transferred to new camps and such places as Elmira, New York; Camp Chase, Ohio; Camp Douglas,

Illinois; and Camp Morton, Indiana. Fort Delaware, on Pea Patch Island in the Delaware River, housed officers within its stone walls and enlisted men in wooden barracks built on the island. Confederate Navy prisoners ended up at Fort Warren, in the harbour near Boston.

While Confederate prisoners of war were housed in barracks with a stove at each end of them, they still complained bitterly of the cold, being unused to Northern winters and inadequately clothed to face them; the wooden walls were usually only one-board thick. The US government did issue overcoats to prisoners, and the Confederate government was allowed to have Confederate uniforms made by Northern manufacturers for its prisoners of war.

Rations were the main problem for both Union and Confederate prisoners of war. Neither side issued enough food of good enough quality to prevent periodic epidemics of diarrhea, scurvy and other such diseases. In some cases, local civilians helped out by providing fresh vegetables; at least one such party was turned away from the gates of Camp Sumter. Confederates were often better supplied with food from Southern sympathizers and even relatives in the North, especially near cities like Baltimore. In other cases, soldiers were able to buy food from sutlers who were allowed to operate small shops within prison walls. When such money as they had been able to conceal had run out, prisoners sold their remaining bits and pieces to the guards. Union prisoners were able to sell their buttons, brass buttons being in short supply among the Confederates. Others carved items such as chess sets from bone and wood to sell.

Boredom was the second great enemy after hunger. As much to kill time as to get out, prisoners constantly plotted escapes. They dug tunnels under prison walls and a great number actually managed to escape that way. Confederates on island prison camps tried to swim to freedom. In all, 2,098 Confederate and 2,696 Union prisoners managed to escape.

Reading material was in short supply and much prized. Letters rarely crossed the front lines. Religious meetings were a common feature of all prisons, as were debating societies, and theatrical productions.

All prisoners spent a great deal of time discussing the question of when they would get home. Most expected to be exchanged or parolled. On 22 July 1862 the two sides set up an agreement for exchanging prisoners according to rank. Selected prisoners were thereafter delivered to a neutral site for exchange, but problems soon arose. Confederate officials refused to recognize white officers of US Colored Troops as eligible for exchange and, as a result, the Union government suspended the exchange of commissioned officers on 28 December 1862. Moreover, Union prisoners were coming back in poor health, unable to serve again, while Confederate prisoners were returning straight to the ranks. Rather than continue this, the Union government suspended all exchanges on 25 May 1863. Thereafter, prisoners on both sides simply had to suffer until they escaped or died or the war ended.

By the war's end, some 25,976 Confederate and 30,218 Union soldiers had died in captivity, representing totals of 12 per cent Confederate and 15.5 per cent Union troops. Officers, usually better educated and more highly motivated, survived in greater numbers than did enlisted men.

Medicine

The greatest danger the Civil War soldier faced was not bullets but disease. Soldiers from rural areas had not been exposed to many common diseases such as chicken pox, measles or mumps, and entire regiments were swept with such illnesses. Most men were not accustomed to spending so much time wet and cold outdoors. Soap was often in short supply and personal hygiene was often neglected. Lice, especially on men in the field, were almost universal. Physical examinations were rudimentary; indeed, it was not until the fall of 1862 that the Confederates even implemented mandatory recruit physical examinations. Union medical authorities reported that while 41,238 US soldiers were killed in battle and another 49,205 died of wounds, a total of 186,216 died of disease.

The sick soldier, if unable to rest and cure himself, as many preferred, reported to the surgeon on the morning 'sick call'. Sick call, due to the fact that medical training was the same on both sides, was conducted in the same way in both armies. The men lined up before the surgeon's tent as the surgeon stood in front of the tent accompanied by his hospital steward and, in the Confederate army, often a hospital clerk, who noted the surgeon's prescription on a regulation form. The typical medicines prescribed were opium, quinine, 'blue mass' or 'blue powder', (a mixture of mercury and chalk used for intestinal complaints) and whiskey, sometimes replaced by brandy or wine. One Confederate doctor later recalled asking one basic question of every soldier, 'How are your bowels?' If open, he prescribed opium, if closed, blue mass. Usually, surgeons prescribed a mixture of the medicines, according to the specific complaint. The hospital steward, who supposedly had pharmaceutical training, made up and issued the medicines.

According to Union medical records, the leading killer of diseases was chronic diarrhea, of which 30,836 died. Acute diarrhea accounted for another 4,291 deaths. Among Confederates, 226,828 soldiers out of 848,555 in hospitals east of the Mississippi prior to 1863 had diarrhea or dysentery. Soldiers called diarrhea 'quickstep', usually after the local state name, i.e., 'the Virginia quickstep', or 'the Tennessee quickstep'.

The second biggest killer was typhoid fever, from which 29,336 Union men died. Chronic dysentery killed 3,855 Union soldiers, while acute dysentery accounted for another 5,576 Union deaths. All these diseases were caused by contaminated food and water and could have been prevented by modern sanitation methods. Soldiers often drank from streams occupied by dead bodies or human waste or ate uncooked, spoiled meat. Although the US Sanitary Commission tried to make conditions more sanitary, at least for Union soldiers, rarely were soldiers trained to avoid these pitfalls. It was obvious to many, however, that maintaining clean camps helped cut down on these types of disease. US Regulars who were strictly disciplined had fewer cases of intestinal disease than did Eastern volunteers who, in turn, had fewer cases than the poorly disciplined Western volunteers. And uneducated Confederates fared the worst of all.

Most surgeons, however, had no idea of the causes of these diseases. Many felt that diet played a major role, either in how the food was prepared or what foods were or were not available. Other surgeons, seeing that most cases were reported in summer months during active campaigning, blamed the weather. They suggested that soldiers could prevent them by wearing a flannel band, a 'belly band', around the waist under the shirt. Other suggested causes included the fumes, or 'effluvia', of decaying corpses, too much coffee, and nerves. Indeed, 'miasmas', breezes carrying disease, were often thought to be a major cause of many diseases, and ample ventilation for barracks was urged as a general preventive.

The common treatment for intestinal diseases was a laxative prescription given in the morning alternated with opium in the evening. Castor oil and epsom salts were the generally prescribed laxatives. Some surgeons also prescribed quinine and calomel, although calomel was forbidden to Union surgeons in May 1863 on the grounds of over-use. At times Confederate surgeons had to resort to substitute medicines, due to the blockade and, more commonly, a decaying transportation system, although it was not until late in the war that medicines became truly scarce. They used vegetable compounds as laxatives, with derivatives of blackberry, willow and sweetgum as astringents. Strong purgatives and whiskey were also prescribed for diarrhea in an effort to get rid of the irritant. Opium was often used in cases of dysentery, and strychnine used for chronic dysentery.

The childhood disease of measles accounted for 5,177 Union deaths, while 8,000 men in the Confederate Army of the Potomac contracted the disease in July–September 1861. Smallpox and varioloid killed another 7,058 Union soldiers, with 1,020 Confederates in Virginia dying of it between 1 October 1862 and 31 October 1864. Whiskey was commonly prescribed in these cases, obviously without good effect. Medical authorities on both sides relied on vaccinations for the prevention of smallpox; indeed, many soldiers vaccinated themselves using lancets and scabs from the arms of fellow soldiers. The results of these often overgenerous vaccinations were less than perfect. An infectious disease associated with swine, erysipelas, killed 2,107 Union soldiers. Tuberculosis, then called 'consumption', cost the Union army 6,497 lives during the war, although many more cases were discharged and the victims died later. Richmond's Chimborazo hospital treated 189 cases, with 52 deaths. Tuberculosis could only be treated by prolonged, totally quiet bed rest, although dry air in places like the Western frontier was thought to help weak lungs.

> **A wounded Union soldier meets a wounded Confederate**
>
> 'In a barn [after the battle of Slaughter Mountain] were lying two badly wounded soldiers, one in blue, the other in gray.
>
> '"Johnny, where are you shot?" asked the one in blue.
>
> '"Lost my leg – where are you?"
>
> '"Ah, you're in a devil of a fix for dancing. I've only lost my arm," said the blue one.
>
> '"I'm sorry for you, Yank. You'll never be able to put your arm around your sweetheart again." And then after a moment he asked, "What did you come down here for anyway, fighting us?"
>
> '"For the old flag," was the proud response.
>
> '"Well, take your darned old flag and go home with it. We don't want it," was "Johnny's" last shot.'
>
> (Henry Kyd Douglas, *I Rode With Stonewall*, Fawcett Publications, Greenwich, Connecticut, 1961, p. 131)

Various fevers, mostly malaria, accounted for the deaths of 14,379 Union soldiers. Indeed, 41,539 cases of malaria were reported in the Confederate Department of South Carolina, Georgia, and Florida from January 1862 until July 1863 when the Department's average strength was only 25,723 men. The cause of malaria was then unknown. Some soldiers in barracks along the Southern seacoasts did put mosquito netting around their beds, but they did so to avoid bites rather than prevent malaria. Again, miasmas were often blamed for the disease.

Fevers were treated with quinine, often mixed with whiskey in an ill-tasting concoction that soldiers still demanded in order to receive a free alcoholic drink. Doses of between three to five grains of quinine were given every two hours for six hours before the patient had one of the fits typical of the disease. Confederate surgeons who had no quinine made substitutions. One popular substitute was made up of a mixture of whiskey and the bark of dogwood, poplar and willow. In September 1863 the Confederate Surgeon general ordered turpentine to be used externally instead of quinine for cases of malaria. Other preparations used in fighting malaria included ammonia, blue mass, cod-liver oil, cream of tartar, cinnamon, sweet spirits of niter, soda, morphine, syrup of wild cherry, sulfuric acid and potassium. Fevers were treated by frequent cold water-soaked towels being wrapped around the head and cold water being sprayed on the body. Opium was given to quiet the patient.

Exposure to cold and damp often caused pneumonia. Mustard plasters were often applied in an attempt to cure pneumonia, as well as various medicines. In fact, in that period, time alone cured or killed with pneumonia, as, indeed, was the case with most diseases. Rheumatism was caused by exposure, and 59,772 Confederates east of the

Mississippi River were suffering from the disease by 1863. Electricity was sometimes prescribed for its cure.

Venereal diseases were common. Indeed, the Union Army opened a hospital in Nashville and the Confederate Army opened one in Kingston, Georgia in early 1864 solely for venereal cases. Mercury was the most commonly prescribed cure. One Confederate surgeon prescribed pine rosin and blue vitriol pills combined with silk-weed tonic for gonorrhea, apparently, according to him, with some success.

On the whole, medical thinking of the period depended greatly on pharmaceuticals to cure diseased patients, but most of these pharmaceuticals were of little or no value, and surgeons did not know how to prescribe correctly those that were of value. It is no surprise, then, that most of the soldiers nicknamed their surgeons 'opium pills', 'quinine', or 'saw bones', and preferred to take their chances with their friends rather than submit to the surgeon's tender mercies. Often they relied on patent medicines sent from home.

Modern experts say that roughly a quarter of all combat soldiers suffer from 'battle' or 'combat' fatigue at some time during their service. Combat fatigue is caused by extreme stress which reduces the chemicals in the brain needed for rational action. Its symptoms can include muteness, deafness and an inability to respond to commands or even to move one's limbs. A Union staff officer wrote about the Confederate bombardment at Gettysburg prior to Pickett's Charge: 'Near us was a man crouching behind a small disintegrated stone, which was about the size of a common water bucket. He was bent up, with his face to the ground, in the attitude of a Pagan worshipper before his idol. It looked so absurd to see him thus, that I went and said to him, "Do not lie there like a toad. Why not go to your regiment and be a man?" He turned up his face with a stupid, terrified look upon me, and then without a word turned his nose again to the ground. An orderly that was with me at the time, told me a few moments later, that a shot struck the stone, smashing it in a thousand fragments, but did not touch the man, though his head was not six inches from the stone.'[5] Temporary mental disorders of this nature were so common in the Confederate army that they were a major subject of discussion between Generals Lee and John B. Gordon on 3 March 1865.

Modern experts hold that the best treatment for combat fatigue includes sleep, hot meals, a chance to clean up and talking out one's feelings to one's friends all as quickly as possible, as close to one's own unit as possible. As after most Civil War battles the soldiers went into camp and did just that, most cases of combat fatigue were automatically cured. In some cases, especially during the war's later stages when fighting was continuous, soldiers were more permanently affected. These soldiers were often discharged by the regimental or hospital surgeon and put on a train home without supervision, often with only a name and home town pinned to the soldier's jacket. They were largely diagnosed as suffering from 'nostalgia', 'mania', or 'dementia'.

After a public outcry about the number of these men wandering about on Northern city streets, the Union army dedicated the Turner Lane General Hospital in Philadelphia, with 275 beds, to cases involving the nervous system. Physical nervous system injuries there were treated with electric shocks, administered together with morphine and atropine to calm the patient. Patients who had not been cured were sent to insane asylums after the war. Confederate medical authorities requested such a hospital as early as June 1864, but it was not until 27 March 1865 that the Louisiana Hospital in Richmond was given over to mental cases. A Western hospital was also sought, but not found before the war's end. Prior to that, Confederate soldiers with mental problems were officially to be taken before justices of the peace to be sent to asylums.

Dentistry was only slightly ahead of psychology in terms of medical acceptance. Neither side had a dental corps, although the Confederates discussed the idea as early as March 1863. Instead, they conscripted dentists, giving them the grade of hospital steward. They not only filled and extracted teeth and removed tartar, but also treated facial wounds including setting broken bones. Indeed, one hospital in Atlanta was set aside for maxillary bone treatment.

A Union soldier gets his arm amputated without chloroform

'About noon July 1st Surgeon White came to me and said: "Young man, are you going to have your arm taken off or are you going to lie here and let the maggots eat you up?" I asked if he had any chloroform or quinine or whisky, to which he replied "No, and I have no time to dilly-dally with you." I said it was hard, but to go ahead and take it off. He got hold of my arm, pulled the bandage off, pushed his thumb through the wound and told me to "come on", and helping me up we walked to the amputation table . . . They put me on the table, cut off blouse and shirt sleeves filled with maggots, and after a lot of preliminary . . . poking and careless feeling around my arm and shoulder – it appeared rough to me – they made me sit up in a chair, and wanted to hold my legs, but I said "No, I won't kick you, but steady my shoulders," then set my teeth together and clinched my hand into my hair, and told them to go on. After cutting the top part of my arm and taking out the bone, they wanted me to rest an hour or so; to which I refused; as they had mangled my arm I wanted but one job to it, for I was as ready, I said, to kick the bucket then as in another hour. To this they replied; "He's pretty spunky, let's make a good job of it." Then they finished it, while I gasped for breath and the lower jaw dropped in spite of my firm clinch. I was then led away a short distance and left to lie on the hot sand . . . '

(James Winchell, "Wounded and a prisoner", C. A. Stevens, *Berdan's United States Sharpshooters in the Army of the Potomac*, Morningside Bookshop, Dayton, Ohio, 1972, pp. 520–1)

It was impossible for soldiers not to have relations with civilians. Here soldiers, apparently New Yorkers in the state-issued jacket, check passes on the Virginia side of the Potomac River across from Georgetown, DC. (Library of Congress collection)

Relations with Outsiders

The soldier lives in a very isolated world, away from familiar faces and ideas, and the Civil War soldier was no exception. At the beginning, of course, the recruits were more civilian than soldier. Their image of war was that of the civilian who prized manly courage in battle above all. 'Death before dishonor' was the common motto, even engraved on knives and embroidered on battle flags. A man was to be distinguished by his courage in battle, his ability to stand exposed to the worst an enemy could hurl at him. Courage alone would carry any battlefield. That was the ideal of the soldier and what soldiers and civilians alike expected the Civil War to embody.

In fact, soldiers soon learned that war was something very different. 'The glories of war were lost in its sickening sights,' wrote a Massachusetts officer after fighting in the Wilderness. 'The gay parade, with the old-time flag gracefully floating in the evening breeze, the nodding plumes, gaudy uniforms with brightly polished buttons, which were the admiration of the fair sex, the inspiring notes of the military band and all the pomp and glamor of war that shone so beautifully as the regiment marched out from their home camp for embarkation, had lost their charms for him, although his aching heart still clung tenderly to the pathetic notes of "The girl I left behind me." Now it had become a life of real danger, hardships, deprivation and suffering. He looked for the bright side which he knew could only come with returning peace. He tried in vain to understand why all this misery and human suffering should be.'[6]

Civilians, however, clung to the idea of the heroic charge and the brilliant victory, even while the soldiers were learning that it was better to hide behind a tree, ducking from enemy fire. The soldiers grew hard and uncaring about the local civilian populace or anyone outside their own unit.

A Southerner expected to lose everything from 1861

'We halted one day in front of a large house [in Alabama]. The man was leaning on the fence talking with the boys when a long-legged rooster came between the house and road with two soldiers after him. If ever a rooster ran, that one was doing it. The man seemed to enjoy the race as well as the rest of us. They were soon out of sight in the shrubbery.

'I said to the man, "It is tough to have men chase your chicks in your dooryard."

'He said, "I expected that when the war broke out. You fellows have got to have something to eat. That rooster is the last living thing on this place, and if they can catch him they are welcome to it." But the Rebs got the most of them. He didn't claim to be Union or Reb, but I believe he was Union. He was at least a sensible, pleasant man.'

(Bryon R. Abnerethy, *Private Elisha Stockwell, Jr. Sees the Civil War*, University of Oklahoma Press, Norman, Oklahoma, 1958, p. 72)

Shelling disrupts a ball in Petersburg, Virginia

'In Petersburg, people were very kind and though in daily peril entertained as if no war was going on. I remember one night attending a ball at the house of Mr. W. R. Johnson. This ball was attended, not only by the ladies of Petersburg, but by numbers of others who had come over from Richmond. While it was going on, two twelve-inch shells fell in the little front yard, bursting and throwing dirt over guests who were in the garden, but only stopping the dance for perhaps five minutes. People paid scarcely any attention to the shelling, though several non-combatants were killed by it.'

(John Cheeves Haskell, *The Haskell Memoirs*, G. P. Putnam's Sons, New York, 1960, p. 80)

Southern women shame their men into winning

'I think it was in the winter of 1864 that our regiment, the 1st Maryland Cavalry, C.S.A., was . . . ordered to saddle up and go as quickly as possible to the relief of General [William C.] Wickham's brigade, which was driven back by a superior force of the enemy. When we arrived . . . he had been driven back immediately in front of his own house, and his mother, with her two beautiful granddaughters, was standing on the front porch, and we, being between the enemy and his house, the balls were spattering uncomfortably thickly around those three ladies. Colonel Dorsey, of our regiment, asked me to ride over to General Wickham and ask him to send us a regiment, as we badly needed support. General Wickham told me that we would have to do the best we could as he didn't have men enough for himself, but "ride down to the house and tell my mother and the young ladies that I commanded them to go into the house". Mrs. Wickham drew herself up as only a Virginia woman of those days could, and said to me: "Go and tell General Wickham that he may command the men of the South, but he does not command the women of the South, and we will stand here and die with you until you whip those Yankees. Go and do it." I wheeled my horse and, without going to General Wickham, rode down to my own regiment, and said: "Boys, Mrs. Wickham says that she and the girls will stand there and die unless we whip those Yankees. Let's do it."

'The regiment charged and Wickham's brigade also charged with us, and I think we ran those Yankees for five miles.'

(Hobart Aisquith, 'A Confederate Mother', *Confederate Veteran*, Nashville, Tennessee, February, 1928, p. 75)

They were increasingly unable to describe their true feelings to the folks back home, finding themselves seeking the company of fellow soldiers even when on long-desired furloughs. There was a very real gap between civilians and soldiers. Moreover, soldiers came increasingly to resent civilians, especially those who failed to support the war effort fully or who did well in civilian occupations while soldiers were enduring such hardships for their cause. At the same time many civilians regarded soldiers, especially enlisted men, as second-class citizens, usually drunkards and positively as men who should be kept away from their daughters. Soldiers believed that, as a class, they were barred from using some towns' sidewalks because of civilian dislike. The result was a bitterness that did not die for years after the war.

These feelings took time to develop, however. At the outset there was a bitterness against another type of civilians, those who opposed the cause. In many Northern states, especially southern Ohio, Indiana and Illinois, the Knights of the Golden Circle supported the Confederates'

war aims. 'Tell the traitors all around you', ran one verse of a popular song, *Just Before The Battle, Mother*, 'that their cruel words, we know, in every battle kill our soldiers, by the help they give the foe.' But opposition to the Confederacy was more widespread in many areas of the South. For example, the Peace and Constitutional Society started in Arkansas in 1861 and had some 1,700 members when Confederate authorities tried to break the organization up. The Heroes of America flourished in Alabama, North Carolina, south-west Virginia and Tennessee. Indeed, most of the 22nd Virginia were Heroes and deserted when they got a chance. There they joined pro-Union civilians in large areas of western Virginia, western North and South Carolina, northern Alabama, eastern Tennessee, western Florida, northern and southern Mississippi, central Louisiana, north-western Arkansas and parts of Texas. While Union soldiers simply grew angry at the pro-Confederate civilians back home, many Confederates took advantage and looked to pro-Union citizens to protect them when they deserted. And, of course, blacks throughout the South actively supported Union war aims.

At the beginning of the war, most blacks were civilians. Southerners from all walks of life were used to blacks and most of them considered blacks to be lazy and stupid, an

Women and children escape the battle

'The First Ohio [Cavalry] was formed on the left of the road and just as we moved "front into line" a battery – perhaps the Chicago Board of Trade – came down the road on the gallop and went crashing through the brush and over the logs on the right of the road. Immediately in front of their line and but a few yards distant was a little pine log cabin with a few acres cleared around it. Hearing a piercing cry as if coming from the cabin, and looking in that direction, we saw a woman running from the door and through the yard with a child in her arms and two or three other small children clinging to her dress. The mother and children were all screaming most pitifully. In front of them was the rebel line, in the rear was our line. Halting for a moment at the rail fence around the yard, she looked imploringly around, and after lifting the children over the fence, and with the babe in her arms and another little one clinging to her hand, she started through the little cornfield parallel to our line, while the balls from the skirmish lines of the enemy were cutting the corn blades on every side. But she seemed to have a charmed life and soon disappeared in the woods on the right, and a fervent "thank God" went up from the long line of blue, and not one of those old veterans, that could stand unmoved amid the carnage of battle, but would have risked his life between those two skirmish lines to save that mother and her little ones.'

(W. L. Curry, *Four Years in the Saddle*, Freedom Hill Press, Jonesboro, Georgia, 1984, p. 112)

image widely encouraged by blacks so as to avoid having to deal with whites. At the same time, a constant threat of a slave insurrection, and there had been several before the war, led to a real fear of blacks, especially in groups. However, many white Southerners had a positive affection for blacks. Often they had grown up together and shared many similar experiences. Most slave-owners thought of themselves as being kind masters, and thought that their slaves appreciated, indeed loved, them. In large part the whites' feelings were totally wrong, since years of slavery had taught blacks never fully to trust any whites, and certainly never to let them know what they really felt. So while Southern whites thought they knew blacks well, they were usually deluding themselves. Therefore, they felt betrayed by blacks who joined the Union army to fight them, and reserved a special hatred for this group. Few Confederates would willingly take black prisoners.

Union soldiers, on the other hand, usually knew next to nothing about blacks; indeed, many of them wrote home describing blacks since they were so unknown in their rural Northern home-towns. They were especially interested in their habits such as holding large outdoor dances and religious services which were also described in letters home, sometimes positively, sometimes with scorn.

Some Union men were already abolitionists, but most saw themselves simply as fighting for their country. Indeed, many Union men felt that blacks were, as indeed in a way they innocently were, responsible for the war and treated them brutally. Most, however, on seeing how the blacks were forced to live under slavery came to hate the system and became, if not outspoken, at least practical abolitionists. Others rapidly appreciated the advantage local blacks gave them as intelligence sources. Moreover, when blacks became fellow soldiers and proved themselves in combat, many more Union soldiers came to respect the black man as worthy of the highest accolade, that of 'fellow soldier'.

Soldiers on both sides went into war with a blanket hatred of the enemy. To many Confederates the Union soldier was

Politicians and soldiers often had the most thorny relations of all. President Lincoln and General McClellan had more than their fair share of problems. Here they meet after the Battle of Antietam to discuss McClellan's failure to move after that battle. An aide, a Captain George A. Custer, leans against the tent flap on the right. (Author's collection)

a cowardly, often foreign-born, invader of Southern soil and despoiler of Southern women. 'Yanks' were money-hungry thieves. For many Union troops, the Confederate soldier was a base, ungrateful traitor to the greatest nation on earth. 'Rebs' were merciless, unfair killers.

After a rather short spell of combat, however, views on both sides changed. The enemy, whether he wore blue or gray, displayed those signs of manly courage so lauded by one and all. Moreover, both sides belonged to that fraternity of soldiers that was exclusive to them; they had more in common with their enemies than with the civilians back home. Indeed, many Union troops resented the treatment many Southern civilians gave their returning troops in 1865, feeling that the civilians weren't grateful enough for Confederate sacrifices.

Northern women plead for their hogs in 1863

'During supper [in Pennsylvania, just after Gettysburg], women came rushing in at intervals, saying – "Oh, good heavens, now they're killing our fat hogs. Which is the General? Which is the Great Officer? Our milch cows are now going." To all which expressions [Lieutenant General James] Longstreet replied, shaking his head in a melancholy manner – "Yes, madam, it's very sad – very sad; and this sort of thing has been going on in Virginia more than two years – very sad."'

(Walter Lord, ed., *The Fremantle Diary*, Capricorn Books, New York, 1960, p. 224)

A Maryland woman salutes Confederates with a US flag

'As Floweree's band, playing "Dixie" was passing a vine-bowered home, a young girl rushed out on the porch and waved a United States flag. Then, either fearing that it might be taken from her or finding it too large and and unwieldy, she fastened it around her as an apron, and taking hold of it on each side and waving it in defiance, called out with all the strength of her girlish voice and all the courage of her brave young heart:

'"Traitors – traitors – traitors, come and take this flag, the man of you who dares!"

'Knowing that many of my men were from a section of the country which had been within the enemy's lines, and fearing lest some might forget their manhood, I took off my hat and bowed to her, saluted her flag, and turned, facing the men who felt and saw my unspoken order. And don't you know that they were all Virginians and didn't forget it, and that almost every man lifted his cap and cheered the little maiden who, though she kept on waving her flag, ceased calling us traitors, till letting it drop in front of her she cried out:

'"O, I wish – I wish I had a rebel flag; I'd wave that, too."'

(George Pickett, *The Heart of a Soldier*, Seth Moyle, New York, 1913, pp. 82–3)

This fraternal feeling was admittedly more widely felt among Union troops than among Confederates because in the long run the Confederates did not threaten the lives of loved ones back North as did Union troops down South. Union troops did more damage to Southern homes than Confederates did to Northern homes. Moreover, Union troops were better educated, which generally creates a more liberal frame of mind, and less religious, which tends to make one more comfortable with people of different beliefs, than their Confederate counterparts.

Yet on both sides the men had too much in common to be able to avoid coming together from time to time. They shared a common language, religious background and history. Many belonged to the same organizations, such as the Masonic Order. Therefore, when given the chance, enlisted men on picket posts and in trenches often called for informal truces. Bands often played near front lines, alternating friendly with enemy tunes. Usually it was noted that *Home Sweet Home* was the last piece during these concerts. Officers generally disapproved of and tried to stop these truces whenever possible, but were rarely successful for any length of time.

Soldiers on both sides held their fire during the truces, and the truces often became social events. Confederates traded tobacco and Southern newspapers (with important war news often censored) to Union troops for coffee and Northern newspapers (also without military information). At times, small groups would meet between the lines to discuss the war, curse out officers, and play friendly games of cards. Indeed, a group of Union and Confederate Irish patriots met in the winter of 1862–3 near Falmouth, Virginia, to discuss strategy against England after the war by a joint Union/Confederate Fenian Army.[7]

Navy Life

Navy enlistments varied between the duration of a ship's cruise, to six months, to three years or the war's end. Neither side had enough skilled seamen for its navy. Landsmen, some from the armies, were recruited. The US Navy began drawing on blacks as early as July 1861. Studies indicate that some eight per cent of the Union Navy were black, although only five per cent of a ship's complement were to be black, according to regulations. Blacks were not segregated into separate crews, as they were in the Army, but they could not hold any rating higher than that of petty officer. The Confederate Navy also had a number of blacks; three free blacks, probably skilled seamen, served as regularly enlisted seamen in the CSS *Chicora*. Men of foreign birth, and even citizenship, were common in ships of both navies, especially in Confederate high seas cruisers. The crew of the CSS *Alabama* included seamen from England, Ireland, Holland, France, Italy and Spain.

Except for recruits for Confederate cruisers, which put straight to sea, recruits on both sides first went to a receiving ship. These were usually old sailing ships that had been stripped of guns and some of their masts. Here the recruits were issued with their first uniforms and taught basic seamanship, gun and cutlass drill, and living skills such as sleeping in hammocks and caring for their personal effects. The period aboard receiving ships varied from a couple of days to several weeks until a crew for a new ship was put together or replacements for an old ship were called for.

Once aboard the seaman's regular ship, life took on a very regular, even boring, aspect. Reveille was sounded by a Marine bugler in large ships or a boatswain's mate in smaller vessels at 5 a.m. in the Confederate Navy and 5.45 in the US Navy.* Men who had been on the midnight to 4 a.m. watch, the midwatch, berthed separately and were allowed to sleep in until 7.30. Seamen then stowed their hammocks and reported for duty, scrubbing down the berth and gun decks with salt water. The spar deck was holystoned with blocks of sandstone. Brass fixtures were polished and sails were secured. This work done, the crew was free to clean themselves up using salt water and a special soap made from cocoa-nut or palm-wood oil which cleaned but did not foam; most men did not bother to shave.

At 8 a.m. the crew was piped to breakfast. At 9.30 a Marine drummer beat 'to quarters', at which time every crewman reported to his battle station. Different drills followed; these included gun drill, practising fire-fighting,

---

* Clocks and watches in the Army of Northern Virginia, and perhaps the eastern South, were set about 20 minutes ahead of those in the Army of the Potomac and, perhaps, the eastern North, according to evidence from after-action reports.

landing-party and small-arms drill, and boarding-party drills. Crewmen in ironclads were sometimes trained to abandon their ship quickly, since there were so few escape hatches. Dinner was at noon, followed by more drill in the afternoon. At 4 p.m. 'knock off ship's work' was piped and crewmen not on watch were free to eat supper and then amuse themselves as best they could. Hammocks were piped down at 8 p.m. at which time sailors not on watch could sleep.

Food was of prime interest to the average sailor, eating being one of the bright spots of each day. Each sailor was part of a mess, generally groups of 10–12 men, who worked together, gun-crews, coal-heavers or firemen. An orderly, either a permanent position or one that rotated within the mess, fetched the day's food in a kid from the ship's cooks and distributed it to the mess. If the mess acquired some food unofficially, he was responsible for seeing that the ship's cooks prepared it. In their mess, petty officers ate the same food as the ship's company, but had their own steward. Also, petty officers supplemented their diet with food bought ashore, and often drank 'warrant officers' champagne', a grog mixed with ginger ale. Food for the officers' wardroom was prepared in a separate galley.

Confederate seamen generally ate better than did Confederate soldiers since they were often near farmlands that were little touched by war. A Confederate sailor whose ship was in North Carolina waters in January 1865 reported obtaining a bag of potatoes, two geese and a chicken from a local civilian for his mess. Hard bread, fresh pork or beef, and green peas, often dried and boiled in a cloth and called a 'dog's body', were the common, regulation, issue. In May 1864 seamen in the CSS *Virginia II* complained that they were down to three biscuits a day. Confederate cruisers largely relied on captured supplies, and food in them was, therefore, always of uneven quality and quantity.

The regulation US Navy ration included a pound of salt pork or beef, a half-pint of beans or peas, a quarter-pound of dried fruit, two ounces of butter, two ounces of cheese, fourteen ounces of biscuit and a quarter-ounce of tea or coffee. Every week the sailor received a half-pound of pickles or cranberries, half a pint of molasses, and half a pint of vinegar. Fresh food was common in the US Navy on the rivers, where landing-parties could forage for vegetables and eggs. After several weeks, most meals consisted of the regulation issue. Biscuits and cheese were often infested with insects and were of poor quality. The same desiccated potatoes, thought to cure scurvy by the US Army, were issued in the US Navy. Both sides also supplemented their diet with fresh-caught fish.

Every man aboard ship was assigned to port or starboard watch which was divided into sub-divisions. The daily watch schedule began with the midwatch from midnight to 4 a.m.; the morning watch to 8 a.m.; the forenoon watch until noon; the afternoon watch to 4 p.m.; the first dogwatch to 6 p.m.; the second dogwatch to 8 p.m.; and the night watch to midnight. Watches were maintained both at sea and while in port.

Saturdays and Sundays had slightly different routines. Saturdays were traditionally 'make and mend' days when seamen's clothing was inspected and either condemned, in which case it was often thrown overboard, or ordered repaired. The seaman then had time to mend his worn clothing. Also the paymaster opened his stores of new clothing, called 'slops', to be supplied as needed. Washing was also done then, many ships presenting a most un-military appearance as wet clothing was hung from every railing and line. Usually one or more of the crew served as a barber (paid by each individual), who cut the men's hair and shaved them on Saturdays as well.

Sundays were marked by a captain's inspection of the entire ship and ship's company at 10 a.m., followed by the captain's reading of the Articles of War and a religious service. If available, a chaplain would conduct the service, otherwise the captain or an appointed officer would read from the *Bible* or *Book of Common Prayer*. On Sundays, too, the captain would often hold 'captain's mast', when men accused of petty offences were brought before the captain for punishment which usually involved cancelling liberty, extra duty, less than seven days in confinement or put in irons for ten or fewer days. Flogging had been earlier outlawed, although a Confederate sailor recorded in his diary on 16 February 1865, 'In the afternoon Tom King was put under guard for refusing to whip a boy. The boy refused to black one of the officer's shoes and he ordered him to be whipped, but as Tom refused to whip him he was put under arrest also.'[8] More serious crimes were punished by summary or general courts-martial.

Each evening each sailor was allowed his grog ration, one gill of spirits or a half-pint of wine, at the discretion of the captain. It was issued on his command, 'splice the main brace'. This custom was ordered to be abolished in the US Navy on 14 July 1862, to date from 1 September 1862, although officers were still allowed to maintain a wine mess in their wardroom. Each US seaman received five cents a day in extra pay in lieu. Thereafter shore liberty was especially prized since it enabled the seamen to get a drink, which was one of his favourite activities, and to smuggle some back aboard. Sailors aboard blockading vessels were sometimes given a chance to go ashore when the ship put in for coal or repairs at one of the ports along the Southern coast. Because most of these places were far from home, the US Navy desertion rate during the war was only six per cent, or 4,649 men.

Confederate sailors also smuggled liquor aboard when they came back from liberty even though they were allowed a spirit ration throughout the war. Since many Confederate Navy vessels spent most of their time in port, while US Navy vessels were blockading or cruising, Confederate sailors had more opportunity for liberty than did US sailors. But as the war drew to a close and defeat appeared certain, and families were threatened by starvation or Union troops, many of them deserted. Whole boats' crews sometimes deserted, while cruisers often lost men in foreign ports where they could not be easily recovered.

Other common recreational activities for sailors in both navies included theatricals, reading, writing home, fishing from the vessel's side, and music. Most vessels had some sort of band or singing group, while many put on plays. Minstrel shows that portrayed blacks in a bad light were even put on in US ships from time to time, although they naturally caused some friction between black and white shipmates. Many vessels had boat crews that raced against one another in regattas.

The damp, often hot, weather, as well as poor food and local insects, caused many of the same diseases as soldiers suffered from, and sailors were treated in the same manner. From 1 January to 1 October 1863, 6,122 sick Confederate sailors were treated, 59 of them dying. The US Navy treated 145,000 cases of disease, of whom 2,784 died. Each large vessel had its own sick-bay where mild cases were treated. More serious diseases and injuries were treated at the central hospitals which both navies maintained.

After the War

When the end came, the Confederacy fell apart extremely quickly. Perhaps amazingly, there was no overall retribution by the US government for the crime of rebellion; no mass hangings or prison terms for any but a handful of Confederate leaders. Heinrich Wirz, commandant of Camp Sumter, was hanged for personally mistreating and killing prisoners after the world's first war crimes trial. Jefferson Davis spent two years in Fort Monroe, Virginia, without ever being brought to trial. He was finally released and allowed to resume civilian life. On the whole, however, the North was sick of bloodshed. The Confederate armies were simply disbanded; Robert E. Lee and the other important Southern military leaders were left alone in their homes. Many ex-Confederate civilian and military leaders even eventually returned to positions of authority in the US government; Confederate Major General Joseph Wheeler is said to have rallied his troops as a US Major General of volunteers in Cuba in 1898 with the cry, 'Come on, boys, we've got the damnyankees on the run.'

However, the Confederates at the moment of surrender were left without any money, with only a little food, and far from home. Moreover, much of the South's transportation system had been destroyed, so that most ex-Confederates had to walk home.

Most Union units participated in the Grand Review of the Army of the Potomac on 23 May and the Army of the Tennessee on 24 May, down Pennsylvania Avenue from the capital building, around the Treasury Building, and past the White House; the reviewing stand there was occupied at different times by President Andrew Johnson, General Grant and other top brass. Then they boarded ships and trains to return to the towns they had left such a long time before. There they went into a final camp, turned in their equipment, although many purchased their rifle-musket for $6, Spencer carbine for $10 or sword for $3, and cleared their final accounts. After receiving their pay, including any bounty money due, they attended their last parade at which

> ### Civilians live well or poorly in Richmond, Virginia
>
> 'A portion of the people look like vagabonds. We see men and women and children in the streets in dingy and dilapidated clothes; and some seem gaunt and pale with hunger – the speculators, and thieving quartermasters and commissaries only, looking sleek and comfortable . . .
>
> 'In these times of privation and destitution, I see many men, who were never prominent secessionists, enjoying comfortable positions, and seeking investments for their surplus funds.'
>
> (Earl S. Miers, ed., *A Rebel War Clerk's Diary*, Sagamore Press, New York, 1958, pp. 126 and 152)

they were addressed by their officers, broke ranks, shook hands and dispersed, hoping to forget the war.

One Illinois lieutenant whose regiment had stayed behind in the occupation of the South didn't get home until late 1865. 'When I returned home', he later wrote, 'I found that the farm work my father was then engaged in was cutting and shocking corn. So, the morning after my arrival, September 29th, I doffed my uniform of first lieutenant, put on some of father's old clothes, armed myself with a corn knife, and proceeded to wage war on the standing corn. It almost seemed sometimes as if I had been away only a day or two, and had just taken up the farm work where I left off.'[9]

Not everyone found forgetting easy. Confederate soldiers returned home to often hostile civilians. Many, especially civilians in the deep South, had been unaware of how badly the war was going for them and treated the returning veterans as cowards for giving up. Most returning Confederates had to beg food or steal on their way home, and were resented for that; many civilians shut their doors to them as they passed on the roads, although others gave generously. When they finally got home, they often found their property in ruins, the fields untended, fences and buildings down and taxes not paid. Small things that had worn out or been broken or lost, things like pins and pocket knives, were impossible to replace.

Most tried to rebuild. Many moved to cities to get jobs clearing streets and rebuilding. Some men who had numbered among the social élite before the war, such as large plantation owners, often ended up in some menial position for the US Army such as clerk or mechanic. Some, like the James Brothers and James Younger, who had served with Quantrill's raiders, went West and became gun-fighters and desperados. Others went West to find silver in Nevada or Colorado or gold in California. For years after the war there were more cows than people in Vermont, in large part due to the loss of so many soldiers from that state. Many Confederates moved even farther away; some went to Brazil, others formed a colony near Cordova, Mexico, a move welcomed by besieged Mexican Emperor Maximillian. Indeed, Maximillian even named ex-Confederate Navy officer Matthew F. Maury 'Imperial Minister for Colonization'. Many other professional ex-officers found employment in the Egyptian Army.

Union soldiers, on the other hand, were relatively well off when released. The average private soldier's final reckoning came to $250, while officers naturally took away even more. Many lost the money gambling on the way home or to thieves, but even more invested it in bonds or business schemes or sent it home. And Union soldiers came home victorious, to an appreciative civilian population.

Yet, Union soldiers, too, had a difficult time dealing with civilians who could not understand them and what they'd gone through. Many also found that they missed the excitement of combat and the close relationships with others that Victorian society tended to discourage. On Memorial Day, 1884, the Supreme Court Justice Oliver Wendell Holmes, years before a junior officer in the 20th Massachusetts, told a crowd, 'Through our great good fortune, in our youth our hearts were touched with fire.'[10] And ex-soldiers from both sides reacted in different ways to these feelings.

One way was to maintain close relationships with people who had seen similar sights and had had similar feelings. As early as 1866 many veterans formed regimental associations that met as a form of support group to help out those in need. Since most regiments were formed of neighbors who had known each other before the war, during the war and after the war, they were natural support groups. National associations such as the Soldiers' and Sailors' National Union League and the United Service Society began formation as early as 1865. Union officers, pledged to aid the government in case of another insurrection, formed the Military Order of the Loyal Legion of the United States, which in April 1865 became simply a social organization. The largest national Union veterans' organization, the Grand Army of the Republic (GAR), was formed in April 1866 and had posts in every major American city by mid-1867. Many of these posts had not only meeting-rooms and libraries but museums of war-time relics.

Yet, throughout the 1870s only two per cent of eligible Union veterans joined the GAR, for the memory of war was just too painful. In the Centennial year of 1876 the GAR numbered only 26,889, and did not reach its peak membership of 427,981 until 1890 by which time memories of war's terrors had healed.

As members of a defeated army, few Southerners wanted to join any organization that would remind them of that defeat. While the 57th Massachusetts Infantry's regimental association was formed in 1866, the 30th Georgia's regimental association was not formed until 1884, by which time its veterans had prospered enough and their memories of the war's hardships and defeat had faded. The Southern Historical Society, although not a true veteran organization, was founded in New Orleans in 1869 with the unexpressed, but real, purpose of making defeat more palatable through the creation of what became modern Confederate myths

---

A Southern woman allows a Union soldier to fill his canteen

'The next day . . . one member of the [63rd Pennsylvania] regiment was going down the main street, he saw a well in the back yard of a handsome house. His canteen being empty at the time, he went in at a gate and around the house to the well. As he reached it, he saw standing on the back porch a most pleasant looking old lady, and asked her if he could fill his canteen with water.

'"Oh, yes," she replied quickly. "You uns are masters here now, but it's only for a short time."

'He said nothing, and after filling his canteen, started to go out of the yard, but the dear old soul had a few more shots to fire at him.

'"See here, young man," she said. "Don't imagine that because you have taken this town you'll be allowed to keep it. No indeed. You Northern people can never conquer the South; we have the brains, the understanding and the real blood, and our men are much braver than any of the Northern nigger worshippers –"

'And this she went on for nearly half an hour, extolling the South and denouncing the North. He made no reply as she was an old lady, and it seemed to do her so much good to vent her anger on some Northern soldier. His passive manner appeared to put her in a better humour, but as she passed out she fired this parting shot at him:

'"Young man, when you uns are taking the back track through here with our boys at your heels, you can stop here for some more water."'

(Gilbert A. Hays, *Under the Red Patch*, Sixty-third Pennsylvania Volunteers Regimental Association, Pittsburgh, Pennsylvania, 1908, pp. 89–90)

---

such as Lee the invincible warrior, the ragged Confederate soldiers being overwhelmed by Northern resources and manpower, and the loss of Gettysburg because of Longstreet's bumbling. Even with this boost to Confederate veteran morale, it was not until June 1889 that the United Confederate Veterans (UCV) was formed, but at its peak in 1904 it numbered only 160,000 veterans.

Eventually, the bitterness of war abated to the point where the GAR and UCV began holding occasional joint encampments. In 1913, for the 50th anniversary of Gettysburg, 54,000 veterans from both sides gathered. The high point of the event was when 180 veterans of the Philadelphia Brigade, which had defended the centre of the Union line, met 120 survivors of Pickett's Division who had formed up 100 feet from the stone wall defending line and marched under their original colours towards the wall. When they got there, the two sides clasped hands across the wall while spectators cheered.

These, however, were veterans who had overcome the depression many experienced at the war's end. Indeed, depression was a common trait among many veterans on both sides. They came home withdrawn, often not responding to civilians. Their tempers flared up unpredictably and often violently. Many of them just wanted to be alone, and moved ever farther West, living in huts they built in the wilderness. Many turned to drink.

One Georgia soldier, John S. Watson, who had been twice wounded during the war, displayed typical, if extreme, symptoms. When he got home, his first act was to try to build a fancy, pillared mansion near his pre-war log cabin. He went broke in 1868 and then moved to Atlanta where he ran a boarding-house and bar. That, too, failed, and he moved his small family to a small tract of poor, rural land. There he spent weeks on end unable to get out of bed, his face turned to the wall in total silence. These fits grew more and more frequent until his death.

Today, these are recognized as symptoms of Post Traumatic Stress Disorder (PTSD), something that affected thousands of veterans although they didn't have a name for the problem. PTSD is the re-living of a terrible experience, such as combat, through dreams or waking memory and handling that experience by becoming psychologically numb. It was a common post-Civil War veteran ailment.

Other soldiers suffered physical injuries that made returning to their pre-war jobs impossible. After 16 July 1862 the US Government, paid for artificial limbs for its veterans. Some Southern state governments also paid for their veterans' artificial limbs, as did various Southern aid societies. The US government paid its veterans who were unable to work a pension of $8 a month for the loss of a limb, $20 for the loss of both feet, or $25 for the loss of both hands or both eyes. They supplemented these pensions by selling cheap publications and photographs of themselves on street corners. Pensions for veterans and their dependents were increased at various intervals in later years. Also they could live, when space became available, in the Soldiers' Home in Washington or one of three regional Homes for Disabled Volunteer Soldiers set up in 1866. Naturally, there was no pension for disabled Confederate veterans from the US government, but as soon as the new Southern state governments were set up and became fiscally able, they granted their veterans pensions and set up old soldiers' homes for them, too.

Silent tears on seeing the old flag destroyed

'As spring advanced, a great number of strangers came to Tappahannock [Virginia]. Very often they were [US] army and navy officers who had resigned to come South . . .

'There was a Captain Baldwin who had resigned from the United States Navy. Everyone liked him. He was a pleasant, dignified man. While he was at our house, our grown sisters and some other Tappahannock girls were making a flag for the Fifty-fifth Virignia out of a United States flag. [The] Captain sat by as, laughing and chatting, the girls ripped the old flag to pieces. Captain Baldwin was silent. Looking up, the girls saw tears running down his cheeks. He rose up, and without a word went out of the room.'

(Evelyn D. Ward, *The Children of Bladensfield*, The Viking Press, New York, 1978, pp. 40–2)

Notes

1. John Haskell, *The Haskell Memoirs*, G. P. Putnam's Sons, New York, 1960, p. 28
2. George W. Peck, *How Private George W Peck Put Down The Rebellion*, Belford Clarke, Chicago, 1887, p. 13
3. Samuel Johnson, 'The Bravery of the English Common Soldiers', *The Brigade Dispatch*, Brigade of the American Revolution, New Windsor, New York, October 1970, p. 2
4. Clifford Dowdey and Louis H Manarin, eds., *The Wartime Papers of R. E. Lee*, Branhall House, New York, 1961, p. 693
5. Frank A. Haskell, *The Battle of Gettysburg*, Wisconsin History Commission, Madison, 1910, pp. 101–2
6. Warren Wilkinson, *Mother, May You Never See the Sights I Have Seen*, Harper & Row, New York, 1990, p. 87
7. Thomas F. Galwey, *The Valiant Hours*, Stackpole, Harrisburg, Pennsylvania, 1961, pp. 244–5
8. Robert Watson, 'Yankees were landing below us', *Civil War Times Illustrated*, April 1976, p. 17
9. Dixon Wecter, *When Johnny Comes Marching Home*, The Riverside Press, Cambridge, Massachusetts, 1944, p. 160
10. Mark D. Howe, ed., *Touched With Fire*, Harvard University Press, Cambridge, Massachusetts, 1946, frontispiece

References

Robert I. Alotta, *Civil War Justice*, White Mane Press, Columbia, Maryland, 1989
Carleton Beals, *War Within A War*, Chilton Books, Philadelphia, 1965
John D. Billings, *Hardtack and Coffee*, Benchmark Publishing, Glendale, New York, 1970
Arch F. Blakey, *General John H. Winder C.S.A.*, University of Florida Press, Gainesville, 1990
William O. Bryant, *Cahaba Prison and the Sultana Disaster*, The University of Alabama Press, Tuscaloosca, 1990
Dudley T. Cornish, *The Sable Arm*, University of Kansas Press, 1987
William C. Davis, *The Fighting Men of the Civil War*, Gallery Books, New York, 1989
Rod Gragg, *The Illustrated Confederate Reader*, Harper & Row, New York, 1989
Jim D. Hill, *The Civil War Sketchbook of Charles Ellery Stedman, Surgeon, United States Navy*, Presidio Press, San Rafael, California, 1976
Gerald F. Linderman, *Embattled Courage, The Experience of Combat in the American Civil War*, The Free Press, New York, 1987
Carlton McCarthy, *Detailed Minutiae of Soldier Life*, Carlton McCarthy, Richmond, Virginia, 1882
Reid Mitchell, *Civil War Soldiers*, Viking Press, New York, 1988
James I. Robertson, Jr., *Soldiers Blue and Gray*, University of South Carolina Press, Columbia, 1988
William Still, 'The Common Sailor', *Civil War Times Illustrated*, Harrisburg, Pennsylvania, February–March 1985, pp. 12–39
John W. Urban, *My Experiences mid Shot and Shell and In Rebel Den*, Lancaster, Pennsylvania, 1882
Bell I. Wiley, *The Life of Johnny Reb*, Bobbs-Merrill Co, Indianapolis, Indiana, 1943
— *The Life of Billy Yank*, Bobbs-Merrill Co, 1951
— *The Common Soldier of the Civil War*, Civil War Times Illustrated, Harrisburg, Pennsylvania, 1973
Bell I. Wiley and Hirst D. Milhollen, *They Who Fought Here*, Macmillian Co., New York, 1959

IV
THE FORCES OF
THE UNITED STATES

THE FORCES OF THE UNITED STATES

General Officers and Staff Departments

There were two grades of general officer, brigadier general and major general, until 9 March 1864 when Congress appointed Grant to yet a higher grade, that of lieutenant general. A brigadier general commanded a brigade; all higher formations were commanded by major generals. The Union Army had one lieutenant general, 132 major generals and 450 brigadier generals of full rank, plus 1,367 generals by brevet, a temporary rank. These general officers were assisted by staff officers in a number of departments.

Adjutant General's Department This was responsible for military orders, correspondence, regulations, personnel records, manuals, printed forms, recruiting for the Regular Army, mustering volunteer units in and out of service, and pension claims. By a general order issued on 10 August 1861, it included the Adjutant General (brigadier general); an Assistant Adjutant General (colonel); two Assistant Adjutant Generals (majors); and twelve Assistant Adjutant Generals (captains). An additional colonel, two lieutenant colonels and nine majors were added to the department a year later, at which time it was ordered that only majors and above were to serve in the Department. In 1863 the Department's headquarters in Washington employed 70 civilian clerks and three messengers. In addition, an assistant adjutant general was assigned to each brigade and higher formation headquarters.

Bureau of Military Justice

The Judge-Advocate General was the army's lawyer, responsible for overseeing all courts-martial. The position, with the equivalent rank of a cavalry colonel, was created in 1862, the first man to hold it being appointed on 3 September. Also, a judge-advocate, equal to a cavalry major, was appointed to each field army. In 1864 Congress set up the Bureau of Military Justice and the judges-advocate transferred to it. In all, 33 judges-advocate served during the war in various departments and field armies.

Inspector General's Department This monitored all military organizations and their affairs to ensure that they were being conducted according to regulations. In 1861 there were only two colonels in the department. In August 1861 an additional five inspector generals, ranking as cavalry majors, were appointed. Still not enough men for the job, on 29 July 1862 an assistant inspector general (lieutenant colonel) was appointed to the staff of every corps and higher formation. Brigade and division staffs also received a line officer as an assistant inspector general. In 1863, the Department in Washington included four inspector generals and five assistant inspector generals.

Quartermaster Department This was responsible for providing quarters and transportation for troops, and storage and transportation of all army supplies, uniforms, camp and garrison equippage, horses, fuel, forage, straw, bedding material and stationery. In January 1863 the Regular Army Department consisted of the Quartermaster General (brigadier general); three Assistant Quartermaster Generals (colonels); three Deputy Quartermaster Generals (lieutenant colonels); eleven Quartermasters (majors); 48 Assistant Quartermasters (captains) (five of whom were actually serving in higher ranks with volunteer units); and twelve Military Storekeepers. In addition, 488 volunteer captains acted as Assistant Quartermasters. Each regiment also assigned a lieutenant to the staff position of Regimental Quartermaster. An Assistant Quartermaster served at brigade; a Quartermaster at division; a Deputy Quartermaster General at corps; and an Assistant Quartermaster General at field army. The Department also employed master wagoners, paid as cavalry sergeants, and wagoners, paid as cavalry corporals, who were civilians.

Subsistence Department This department, which supplied the Army's food, was headed by the Commissary General of Subsistence (brigadier general). There were only twelve officers in the Department in 1861, but by January 1863 the Commissary General was aided by two Assistant Commissary Generals of Subsistence ranked as colonels, two more ranked as lieutenant colonels, eight Commissaries of Subsistence ranked as majors, and sixteen ranked as

Major General Daniel Sickles, who was commissioned because he was a Democrat who endorsed the Union cause rather than for any military abilities, placed his III Corps in an exposed position at Gettysburg. He lost his right leg there which put an end to his fighting career. He wears a version of the fatigue blouse with gold stars of his rank on each end of a plain piece of black cloth. (David Scheinmann collection)

captains. Each regiment had its own commissary officer (a lieutenant), and regimental commissary sergeant. The Army of the Potomac had its own Chief Commissary, first appointed on 1 August 1861.

Pay Department This was responsible for handling Army funds. In January 1863 the Regular Army Pay Department consisted of the Paymaster General (colonel); two Deputy Paymaster Generals (lieutenant colonels); 24 Paymasters (majors); and 313 Paymaster's Clerks stationed across the country. However, the law also provided for one paymaster for every two new regiments, so that in 1865 there were 447 paymasters in service.

Ordnance Department This was in charge of all the army's arsenals and armouries and furnished all ordnance and ordnance service. Its officers were also responsible for the inspection of all ordnance to ensure that it was of proper quality. In 1861 the Department's establishment consisted of a colonel, a lieutenant colonel, four majors, twelve captains, twelve first lieutenants and six second lieutenants.

By 1863 this had increased to a brigadier general (Chief of Ordnance), a lieutenant colonel, three majors, twelve captains, fourteen first lieutenants and thirteen second lieutenants. At its armouries, arsenals and depots the Department hired civilians as master carriage-makers, master blacksmiths, and master armorers. Enlisted men in the Department were called laborers. Non-commissioned officers were Ordnance Sergeants, who had to have served eight years prior to their appointment. Each post was to have one Ordnance Sergeant assigned to take care of the post's arms and munitions.

Provost Marshal Department This was formed on 17 March 1863 as the Army's policemen and to organize conscription. It was headed by the Provost Marshal General (a brigadier general), in Washington. All the district provost marshals reported to him. He was assigned troops, usually from the Veteran Reserve Corps, as needed. In addition, an acting assistant provost marshal general was named for each state to retrieve deserters and draft-dodgers and serve as volunteer recruiting service superintendent. Each field army also named a provost marshal and assigned him troops, usually but not always, cavalry, to police itself.

All officers wore a dark-blue frock-coat with standing collar, three buttons on each cuff, and with gold epaulettes for dress and gold-edged shoulder-straps on a black velvet ground for all other duty. Generals had a black collar and cuffs and two rows of buttons down the front. A lieutenant general wore eight buttons in sets of four, and three silver stars on his shoulder insignia. A major general wore nine buttons in threes and two silver stars; a brigadier general wore eight buttons in pairs and one silver star. Their trousers were plain dark-blue, as were Ordnance Department officers' trousers. Dress head gear consisted of a black felt hat, 6.25 inches high with a 3.25-inch brim. The hat cord was gold with acorn-shaped ends; the hat brim was hooked up on the right side with a gold-embroidered eagle. Three black ostrich feathers were worn on the left. In front, on a black velvet background, was a gold-embroidered eagle and the letters 'U.S.' in Old English letters embroidered in silver. The same cap badge was worn on the front of the dark-blue cloth forage cap which was shaped like a French kepi and worn for occasions other than dress.

According to the 1861 army dress regulations, each officer of the general staff and staff corps could also wear a 'light French chapeau, either stiff crown or flat . . . officers below the rank of field officers to wear but two feathers'. Physical examples indicate that the chapeau was 17.5 inches long with a black cockade under a gold loop of lace and a spread eagle, with gold-fringes at each end. These hats were little worn.

Generals had a black sword-belt with three rows of parallel gold embroidery around it. A buff silk sash with silk bullion fringe ends was worn around the waist under the sword belt, the ends hanging over the left hip. The sword was to be the M1860 staff and field officers' sword, although the M1850 staff and field officers' sword was also widely worn. The M1860 was a frail weapon with a straight blade,

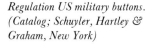

Regulation US military buttons. (Catalog; Schuyler, Hartley & Graham, New York)

GENERALS & STAFF. — No. 169.
No. 170.

INFANTRY. — No. 171.
No. 172.

ARTILLERY. — No. 173.
No. 174.

CAVALRY — No. 175.
No. 176.

RIFLE. — No. 177.
No. 178.

ENGINEER. — No. 179.
No. 180.

TOPOGRAPHICAL ENGINEER. — No. 181.
No. 182.

ORDNANCE. — No. 183.
No. 184.

No. 185. Navy Coat.
No. 186. Navy Jacket.
No. 187. Navy Vest.
No. 188.
No. 189. Shield Button.

No. 190. Marine Coat.
No. 191. Marine Jacket.
No. 192. Marine Vest.
No. 193.
No. 194. N. Y. State Line Button.

No. 195. Revenue Coat.
No. 196. Revenue Jacket.
No. 197. Revenue Vest.
No. 198.
No. 199. N. Y. State Staff Button.

28 inches long, and an ornate brass hilt with black fishskin grips with twisted brass wire wrapped around them.

The overcoat was dark-blue with four silk frogs and loops that closed it across the chest. Rank was indicated by flat black silk braid, something like an Austrian knot, on each sleeve. Generals had five braids.

A staff officer wore basically the same uniform. His frock-coat had a plain collar and cuff. A field grade officer wore two rows of seven buttons each on his coat front, while a company grade officer wore one row of nine buttons. Black velvet shoulder-straps edged with gold embroidery were worn for all but dress occasions, when gold epaulettes were

worn. Department insignia was worn on the epaulette in only a few departments and included the Old English letters 'P.D.' for Pay Department, and the flaming bomb for Ordnance officers. Shoulder insignia of rank included, for a colonel, a silver eagle; a lieutenant colonel, a silver oak leaf at each end of the strap; a major, a gold oak leaf; a captain, two gold bars; a first lieutenant, one gold bar; and a second lieutenant, a plain strap. Off duty, all officers were allowed to wear a plain dark-blue sack coat with their staff, department, or corps button, but no other insignia. Also all officers were allowed to wear a buff, white or blue vest with their assigned buttons. The blue vest was either sky- or

No. 125.—STAFF.

No. 129.—INFANTRY.

No. 126.

No. 130.

No. 127.—ARTILLERY.

No. 131.—CAVALRY.

No. 128.

No. 132.

dark-blue. Mounted officers could wear a plain dark-blue jacket with the same buttons as their frock-coat, a standing collar and shoulder-straps.

Trousers, except for Ordnance officers, were dark-blue with a gold cord one-eighth of an inch wide down each leg. Staff officers wore the same dress hat as generals save for the cords, which were intermixed black silk and gold. Moreover, company grade officers had only two ostrich feathers. Ordnance officers had a different cap badge, featuring a gold-embroidered shell and flame on a black velvet ground.

The staff officers' sword-belt was plain black and their sash was of crimson silk. The sash was worn around the waist although the officer of the day wore his from the right shoulder to the left hip. They were allowed to carry either the M1850 or M1860 staff and field officers' sword, except for Pay Department officers who carried the M1840 Pay Department sword. This was an all-gilt straight sword with

a 31-inch blade bearing the Old English letters 'P.D.' in silver on the counterguard. Military store-keepers wore the same sword without the letters. The same overcoat as that worn by generals was worn, with five silk cuff braids for a colonel, four for a lieutenant colonel, three for a major, two for a captain and one for a first lieutenant.

The military store-keeper was to wear a civilian's blue frock-coat with Ordnance Department buttons, a round black hat, and plain white or dark-blue trousers and vest (waistcoat).

Ordnance sergeants were to wear the dark-blue frock-coat with nine buttons in a single row in front and crimson piping around the standing collar and rising to a point on each cuff, which was buttoned with only two buttons. A staff non-commissioned officer's brass shoulder-scale was worn on each shoulder. The rank insignia was a chevron of three 'V's, worn points down, with a star in the angle of the 'V's, made of crimson silk and worn on both sleeves above the elbow. Also, since any ordnance sergeant had to have a minimum of eight years' service, he would wear one half-chevron of crimson silk for each five years of service on each sleeve below the elbow on the dress coat only. At the war's beginning trousers were to be dark-blue with a crimson stripe, 1.5 inches wide, on each leg. On 16 December 1861 the trouser colour was changed to sky-blue, but the stripe was retained for Ordnance sergeants.

The Ordnance sergeant's dress hat had a crimson worsted cord and only one feather. The eagle and cap badge, which was a flaming bomb, were of stamped brass. The non-commissioned officer's sword was carried on a shoulder-belt, while a red worsted sash was worn under the waist-belt which used a sword belt plate rather than the enlisted foot soldier's oval 'US' plate. The sky-blue overcoat was also worn, with chevrons on both sleeves. It had a stand-up collar and a cape that reached to the elbows when the arm was extended.

Quite against regulations, enlisted Ordnance Corps personnel apparently wore dark-blue trousers throughout the period.

A variety of US Army officers' embroidered badges. (Catalog; Schuyler, Hartley and Graham, New York)

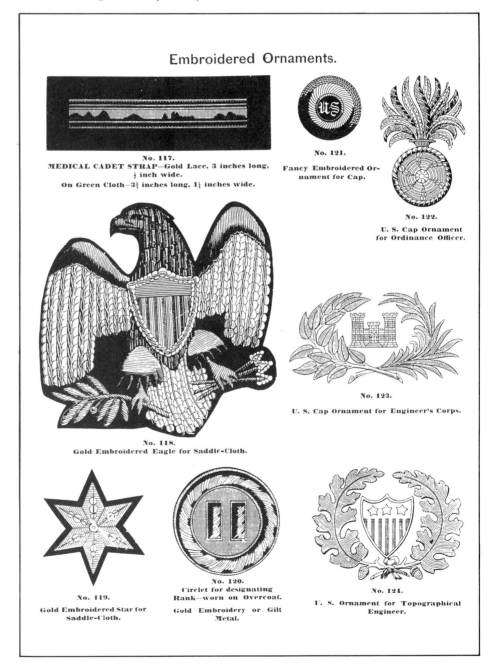

Embroidered Ornaments.

No. 117.
MEDICAL CADET STRAP—Gold Lace, 3 inches long, ½ inch wide.
On Green Cloth—3¼ inches long, 1¼ inches wide.

No. 121.
Fancy Embroidered Ornament for Cap.

No. 122.
U. S. Cap Ornament for Ordnance Officer.

No. 118.
Gold Embroidered Eagle for Saddle-Cloth.

No. 123.
U. S. Cap Ornament for Engineer's Corps.

No. 119.
Gold Embroidered Star for Saddle-Cloth.

No. 120.
Circlet for designating Rank—worn on Overcoat.
Gold Embroidery or Gilt Metal.

No. 124.
U. S. Ornament for Topographical Engineer.

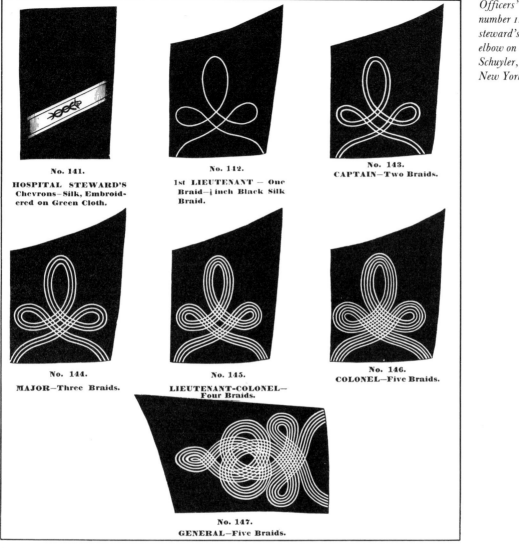

No. 141.
HOSPITAL STEWARD'S
Chevrons–Silk, Embroid-
ered on Green Cloth.

No. 112.
1st LIEUTENANT — One
Braid–⅛ inch Black Silk
Braid.

No. 143.
CAPTAIN—Two Braids.

No. 144.
MAJOR—Three Braids.

No. 145.
LIEUTENANT-COLONEL—
Four Braids.

No. 146.
COLONEL—Five Braids.

No. 147.
GENERAL—Five Braids.

Officers' overcoat cuff lace. Item number 141 is a hospital steward's chevron worn above the elbow on both sleeves. (Catalog; Schuyler, Hartley and Graham, New York)

Union troops attack their general

'[Major General J. W.] Geary frequently used to threaten to arrest us when he came across us away from our commanders, foraging, and did often take our forage. Consequently, no one liked him . . .

'This one time . . . When we halted, someone went back to hurry up our company mule, which had our pots and kettles on his back. The man leading the mule was Jerry Wallace, a big fellow. Just as he came up to us, along came General Geary and his staff and ordered Wallace to take his d---n-d mule out of the way. Wallace made a run for it and had nearly got the mule to our position on the side of the road when Geary, with an oath, drew his sword and struck Wallace with the flat of it.

'Wallace made one jump like a wildcat at Geary on his horse. Before Geary's staff could help him, Wallace had pulled him from his horse, pounded and kicked him, and had run off into the crowd of us. We during the mêlée had seized the mule, dragging him to our position, and were unloading him. When Wallace ran in amongst us, the crowd of us closed up around him so that Geary's staff could not follow him.

'Geary picked himself up from the dirt and demanded to know who we were. We told him. He said he would find Wallace and have him shot. But Geary kept away from us for a few days, and I suppose he thought better of it, as nothing came of it.'

(Robert Hale Strong, *A Yankee Private's Civil War*, Henry Regnery Co., Chicago, 1961, pp. 84–6)

US Army officers' shoulder-straps. (Catalog; Schuyler, Hartley and Graham, New York)

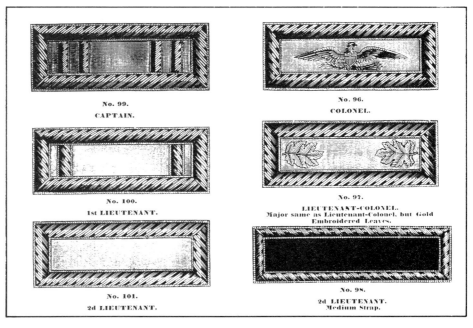

No. 99.
CAPTAIN.

No. 96.
COLONEL.

No. 100.
1st LIEUTENANT.

No. 97.
LIEUTENANT-COLONEL.
Major same as Lieutenant-Colonel, but Gold Embroidered Leaves.

No. 101.
2d LIEUTENANT.

No. 98.
2d LIEUTENANT.
Medium Strap.

Colonel Lorenzo Thomas was the adjutant general of the US Army from 1861 until 1869. Here he wears the dress uniform of his rank, and is holding the dress hat. His sword is the M1860 staff and field officer's sword. The chair behind him is unique to photographs taken by Mathew B. Brady in his Washington, DC, studio. (Atwater Kent Museum, Philadelphia)

A non-regulation regimental quartermaster's shoulder-strap with black velvet background. The letters 'QM' are embroidered in silver; the other embroidery is gold. (Author's collection)

The brass shoulder-scales with rivets worn by staff non-commissioned officers such as sergeant majors and regimental quartermaster sergeants. (Author's collection)

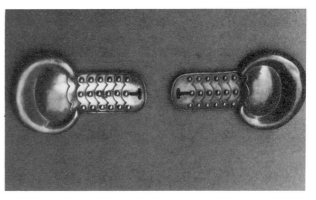

This staff officer wears the regulation officer's uniform with the single cuff braid of a first lieutenant. He was photographed in Philadelphia and the image bears a tax stamp. (Author's collection)

An unidentified staff officer with a cavalry sabre from Wilmington, Delaware, in a dress coat with undress cap and regulation cap badge. The photograph bears a three-cent tax stamp, indicating that it was taken between 1 September 1864 and 1 August 1866. (Author's collection)

The standard US Army belt-plates. The top one was cast brass with a separate silver wreath applied and was worn by officers, non-commissioned officers and mounted men. The circular one was worn on the cartridge box shoulder-belt and non-commissioned officers' sword-belt; the oval one was the enlisted man's belt-plate. (Author's collection)

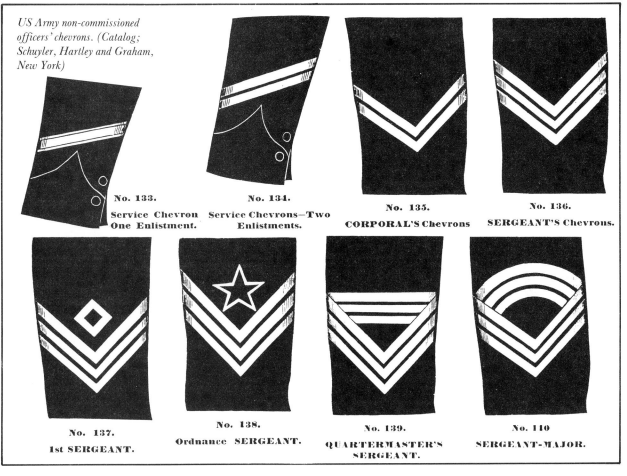

US Army non-commissioned officers' chevrons. (Catalog; Schuyler, Hartley and Graham, New York)

No. 133.
Service Chevron One Enlistment.

No. 134.
Service Chevrons—Two Enlistments.

No. 135.
CORPORAL'S Chevrons

No. 136.
SERGEANT'S Chevrons.

No. 137.
1st SERGEANT.

No. 138.
Ordnance SERGEANT.

No. 139.
QUARTERMASTER'S SERGEANT.

No. 140
SERGEANT-MAJOR.

Artillery

The basic field artillery unit was the battery. According to general orders issued on 4 May 1861 each battery was to include as a minimum, a captain, a first lieutenant, a second lieutenant, a first or orderly sergeant, a company quartermaster-sergeant, four sergeants, eight corporals, two musicians, two artificers, one wagoner and 58 privates, giving a total of 80 officers and men. At a maximum, the battery was to number one captain, two first lieutenants, two second lieutenants, a first sergeant, a company quartermaster-sergeant, six sergeants, twelve corporals, two musicians, six artificers, one wagoner and 122 privates, a total of 156 officers and men.

Batteries could be organized into regiments. Each artillery regiment was to have twelve batteries with a minimum of 960 battery officers and enlisted men plus a colonel, a lieutenant colonel, a sergeant major, a regimental quartermaster-sergeant, a regimental commissary sergeant, two principal musicians, a hospital steward; and 24 musicians in

This unidentified sergeant major wears a common variant of the regulation chevrons on his custom-made version of the issue fatigue blouse. (Author's collection)

the band, a total of 997 officers and men. The authorized maximum personnel for an artillery regiment would include the same headquarters personnel plus 1,872 battery officers and men, giving a total of 1,909 officers and men.

The same table of organization applied to heavy artillery regiments, but here the term company was substituted for battery. Generally, heavy artillery was organized at the regimental level, while field artillery served as independent batteries or as batteries organized into battalions by field headquarters. In all, the Regular US Army had five artillery regiments and nineteen batteries. There were a further 52 volunteer regiments, 22 volunteer companies, and 1,647 volunteer batteries that served in the Union Army during the war. If all the companies and batteries that served had been organized into regiments, there would have been 78 regiments and two companies of artillery.

Artillery officers wore the same uniform as that of staff officers but with slight differences. Their coat buttons featured a spread eagle with the letter 'A' on the shield in

Battery A, 4th US Artillery at Gettysburg

'When the enemy was within about four hundred yards, Battery A opened with single charges of canister. At that time [First Lieutenant Alonzo H.] Cushing was wounded in the right shoulder, and within a few seconds after that he was wounded in the abdomen; a very severe and painful wound. He called and told me to stand by him so that I could impart his orders to the battery. He became very ill and suffered frightfully. I wanted him to go the rear. "No," he said. "I stay right here and fight it out, or die in the attempt."

'When the enemy got within two hundreds yards, double and triple charges of canister were used. Those charges opened immense gaps in the Confederate lines. Lieutenant Milne, who commanded the right half battery, was killed when the enemy was within two hundred yards of the battery. When the enemy came within about one hundred yards, Lieutenant Cushing was shot through the mouth and instantly killed. When I saw him fall forward, I caught him in my arms, ordered two men to take his body to the rear, and shouted to my men, as I was left in command, to fire triple charges of canister.

'Owing to the dense smoke, I could not see very far to the front, but to my utter astonishment I saw Confederate General Armistead leap over the stone fence with quite a number of his men, landing right in the midst of our battery, but my devoted cannoneers and drivers, stood their ground, fighting hand to hand with pistols, sabers, handspike, and rammers, and with the assistance of the Philadelphia brigade, the enemy collapsed . . . '

(Thereon Wilber Haight, *Three Wisconsin Cushings*, Wisconsin Historical Commission, 1910, pp. 53–4)

Captain Charles Griffin, B Battery, 5th US Artillery Regiment, wore his dress uniform while being photographed by Mathew Brady. He is holding his dress hat and wears the enlisted pattern M1840 light artillery sabre. An excellent officer, Griffin had made the rank of brigadier general of volunteers by the Seven Days battle and served as a divisional commander in the Army of the Potomac for most of the war. (US Army Military History Institute collection)

Sergeant Major George Cole, 2nd Massachusetts Heavy Artillery Regiment, wearing his dress coat. Cole joined the regiment as a private on 23 June 1864 and was promoted to sergeant major on 16 November 1864. He was commissioned a second lieutenant on 29 March 1865. The 2nd served in various posts along the North Carolina and Virginia coast lines (Author's collection)

This first sergeant from Greenfield, Massachusetts, wears the dress frock and sash for his rank. (Author's collection)

the centre of its chest, as infantry officers wore the letter 'I' and cavalry officers the letter 'C'. Their dress gold epaulettes had an embroidered silver circle, 1.75 inches in diameter, around a scarlet centre on which the regimental number was embroidered in gold. Shoulder-straps had scarlet backing instead of black velvet. The cap badge featured gold-embroidered crossed cannon on a black velvet background, with the regimental number in silver embroidery at the intersection of the guns. Officers in heavy artillery, being foot soldiers, looped their hat brim up on the left; light artillery officers when wearing the dress hat, looped them up on the right as did all mounted men after 13 March 1861. Trousers had a scarlet welt, one-eighth of an inch in diameter, down each leg.

Unique to the branch, light artillery officers were allowed to wear a waist-length dark-blue jacket trimmed with scarlet for undress duty. The rank insignia worn with this jacket was a gold Russian shoulder-knot with the rank badge – eagle, oak leaf or bars – in silver worn on the centre of the knot.

Enlisted men of heavy and light artillery wore different uniforms. Heavy artillerymen were considered foot soldiers and wore, for dress, a single-breasted dark-blue frock-coat with a standing collar – essentially the Ordnance sergeant's uniform. The collar and pointed cuffs, which were closed with two small buttons, were edged with a scarlet welt or cord. Nine large plain eagle buttons were worn down the chest, two buttons were placed on the back along the waistline.

Officers of the 27th New York Independent Light Artillery Battery wear the Russian shoulder-knots authorized for use with short jackets. The officer standing, second from right, has a red trefoil on the top of his forage cap. The 27th served mostly in East coast cities until it joined the Army of the Potomac's IX Corps outside Petersburg in May 1864. (US Army Military History Institute collection)

A brass shoulder-scale was worn on each shoulder. There were three types of shoulder-scale. Those worn by privates and corporals had seven scalloped surfaces on a strap, 2.2 inches wide. The rounded end had a half-round crescent, four inches wide. Sergeants wore the same scale, but with a slightly larger, fully rounded crescent, 4.5 inches wide. The scale worn by staff non-commissioned officers was the same as that worn by sergeants with the addition of eighteen round-head rivets placed on six of the scallops, three in a row. Scales were slipped over a brass loop sewn down where the sleeve met the shoulder and then fastened by a brass staple near the collar that fitted through a T-shaped slot at the end of the strap and was then locked in place. The traditional belief is that these odd, brass shoulder-scales were intended to ward off saber blows.

Light artillerymen wore a uniform jacket which was cut waist length but was pointed in the front and back, while the 'shell jacket' was cut evenly all around the waist. It had one row of twelve buttons down the front and a standing collar. Two 'belt support pillars' to hold the sword belt in place were sewn to the back. On the regulation jacket, there were two buttons at each cuff and two on each side of the collar in two blind buttonholes. In fact, many jackets were made with only one blind buttonhole on the collar; others had simply one strip of lace leading from the collar to the button, rather than two that formed the false buttonhole. Many did not have functioning cuff buttons and had only eleven buttons down the front. The entire jacket was trimmed in scarlet worsted lace, around the collar, the cuffs, down the front and bottom, and up the rear seams. Brass shoulder-scales were to be worn with this jacket.

Musicians of both types of artillery had their coat or

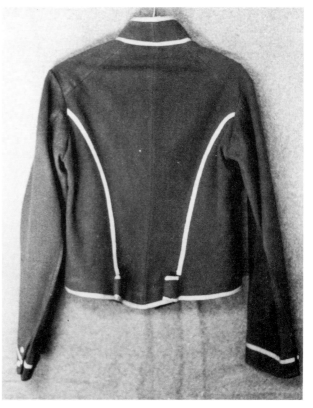

A battery quartermaster sergeant in the regulation mounted man's jacket. His non-regulation insignia had begun to make an appearance by May 1863. His mounted man's trousers have heavy reinforcement inside the legs. (Richard Carlile collection)

The back of the issue mounted man's jacket showing how it was laced, and the belt support pillars. (Author's collection)

jacket marked by bars of scarlet lace worn parallel on the chest from each button. The lace ends were connected by more lace passing up from the bottom and ending at the collar. The whole thing was to look something like the 'herring-bone form'.

For fatigue, all artillerymen were authorized a rather plain dark-blue flannel sack coat which ended half-way down the thigh. It had a falling collar and four buttons down the front with an inside pocket on the left side. These sack coats were supposed to be lined in flannel for recruits; all others were to be unlined. However, quartermaster records indicate that from 1 May 1861 to 30 June 1865, the three depots at Philadelphia, New York and Cincinnati purchased ready made sack coats of which 3,685,755 were lined, but only 1,809,270 were unlined. The New York depot also purchased another 530,144 'knit' sack coats.

Not all Union artillerymen wore regulation US Army uniform; some wore state-issued clothing. This was especially true in 1861, but some state units, in particular those from New York, continued to wear state uniforms throughout their enlistment. The New York uniform differed from the US uniform largely in that it included a dark-blue (early ones were gray) jacket with eight buttons in a single row down the front, a standing collar, a 'belt keeper' tab on the lower left side, and shoulder-straps. The collar, tab, straps, and a slit pocket on the left breast, were all piped in scarlet for artillerymen. The first four New York artillery regiments wore this jacket, as did a number of independent New York batteries. The jacket issued by Illinois to its troops was very similar to the New York jacket.

Scarlet chevrons indicating grade were worn on both sleeves, points down, above the elbow on all coats or jackets.

Sergeant majors wore three 'V's and three arcs in silk; regimental quartermaster-sergeants wore three 'V's and three bars in silk; a first or orderly sergeant wore three 'V's and a lozenge or diamond in worsted; a sergeant wore three 'V's in worsted; a corporal wore two 'V's in worsted; and a pioneer wore two crossed cloth hatchets. Prior military service was indicated by a diagonal half-chevron, a half-inch wide, worn below the elbows. One half-chevron represented five years' service. Wartime service was indicated by edging the scarlet chevrons with sky-blue; in other branches of service the edging was scarlet.

Non-regulation chevrons were also common. Starting as early as May 1863, company quartermaster-sergeants began wearing three 'V's and one bar, and battalion quartermaster-sergeants began wearing three 'V's and two bars. Chief musicians also wore non-regulation chevrons. These differed widely according to the regiment, but three 'V's and one to three bars or arcs with a star in the centre seems to have been a common chief musician's design, apparently taken from the chevron worn by chief musicians in the US Marine Corps. Sergeant majors, quartermaster-sergeants, first sergeants and chief musicians were also authorized red worsted sashes.

Heavy artillerymen's trousers were originally dark-blue, but changed on 16 December 1861 to sky-blue. Throughout the period light artillerymen wore sky-blue trousers and these were mounted men's trousers, made with a reinforcement on the inside of the legs and crotch for horseback riding. Privates had plain trousers, while corporals had a half-inch worsted lace scarlet stripe down each leg. Sergeant's stripes were 1.5 inches wide.

Enlisted heavy artillerymen wore the same dress hat as that worn by officers but with only one ostrich feather. The cord was scarlet worsted and had two tassels at the end. A stamped brass crossed cannon, the brass regimental number, $\frac{5}{8}$-inch high, and brass company letter, one inch high, made up the cap badge. Only the brass company letter was to be worn on the kepi-like dark-blue wool forage cap worn by enlisted men, although officers wore smaller versions of their embroidered dress cap badges.

Light artillerymen were to wear a dark-blue shako, edged in patent leather around the top and bottom, with a scarlet plume rising out of a brass flaming bomb, and twisted scarlet cords around the front and back, ending with a tassel on the top right (as seen from the front) side. The cord passed down and around the shoulders and across the chest and back, ending in elaborate tassels which hooked to a jacket button. A brass spread eagle was worn over brass crossed cannon on the shako front. These were obviously not suitable for field use and saw little wear during the war. Indeed, original stocks appear to have lasted until 1864 when the Quartermaster Corps began to obtain them once more.

Enlisted men's overcoats were sky-blue. Light artillerymen wore the mounted man's double-breasted overcoat which had a stand and fall collar, and a cape that reached the cuff when the arm was extended. Heavy artillerymen

---

Union Brigadier General Alexander Hays is mortally wounded

'On Saturday morning, May 3rd, about 6 o'clock, I was shot through the left side by a minnie ball, the ball passing clean through and went on its way rejoicing, having entered the small of my back, about two and a half inches from the backbone, and coming out the abdomen pretty well towards the side. Shot in the back, but no disgrace as I was mounted, and endeavouring to steady the men as we fell back to a position where we had the advantage of the "graybacks". Feeling myself wounded and unable to remain in the saddle, I checked up the horse and dismounted. The animal broke from me immediately, and I followed on after the regiment about fifty yards, but had to give it up as I was getting so weak. Down I went, face foremost, among some bed clothes upset from a medicine wagon. There I lay while the battle raged around and over me, and the demon rebels came howling on. In half an hour the fierceness of the conflict ceased directly about me; the rebels went to the right and left into the wood. Then it was that I espied a Sixty-third [Pennsylvania] boy who had come far back to look for a wounded comrade. I hailed him and got a drink of water. He got me fixed more comfortably and I had, previous to that, turned over on my back, which I found a great relief. I now discovered that some portion of my insides had run out through the hole in my abdomen. This alarmed me considerably, and I gave up entirely, had no hope of ever getting away from there alive.'

(Gilbert Adams Hays, *Under the Red Patch*, Sixty-third Pennsylvania Volunteers Regimental Association, Pittsburgh, 1908, pp. 434–5)

---

wore the single-breasted foot soldier's overcoat which had a standing collar and a cape that reached the elbow when the arm was extended. Light artillerymen were also issued with knee-length, white cotton stable frock-coats for stable duties.

Cavalry

According to General Orders issued on 4 May 1861, each Regular Army cavalry regiment was to have three battalions, each with two squadrons consisting of two companies. Each company, at a minimum, was to include one captain, a first lieutenant, a second lieutenant, a first sergeant, a company quartermaster-sergeant, four sergeants, eight corporals, two musicians, two farriers, a saddler, a wagoner and 56 privates. The maximum company strength would be 72 privates. The battalion would have 316 company officers and enlisted men, plus a major, an adjutant, a quartermaster and commissary (lieutenant), a sergeant major, a quartermaster-sergeant, a commissary sergeant, a hospital steward, a saddler sergeant, and a

Major J. H. Hazeltin, 6th Pennsylvania Cavalry, wears that regiment's unique crossed lances cap badge. The regiment was armed with lances when originally organized in mid-1861. As it turned out, lances proved useless in combat and were quickly discarded. The regiment went on to serve with distinction as ordinary cavalry in the campaigns of the Army of the Potomac and in the 1864 Valley campaign. (US Army Military History Institute collection)

The regulation coat worn by Lieutenant Colonel A. W. Corliss, 2nd Rhode Island Cavalry. There is a pointed braid cuff on each sleeve and the buttons are staff officers' button. The 2nd was organized in November 1862 and saw service in Louisiana before being merged into the 1st Louisiana Cavalry on 24 August 1863. (Christopher Nelson collection)

veterinary sergeant, with a total of 325 men as a minimum. The maximum strength battalion would have 380 company officers and men for a total of 389. The regiment would have a minimum of 975 battalion officers and men plus its colonel, a lieutenant colonel, an adjutant (a lieutenant), a quartermaster and commissary (lieutenant), two chief buglers, and a band of sixteen musicians, for a minimum total of 997 officers and men. At a maximum, its 1,167 battalion officers and men would give it a total of 1,189 officers and men.

General Orders of 4 May 1861 created a somewhat different volunteer cavalry regiment. This would consist of four, five or six squadrons. Each squadron was to consist of two companies with, at a minimum, a captain, a first lieutenant, a second lieutenant, a first sergeant, a company quartermaster-sergeant, four sergeants, eight corporals, two buglers, two farriers and blacksmiths, a saddler, a wagoner and 56 privates for a total of 79 officers and men. The regiment would also include a colonel, a lieutenant colonel, a major, a lieutenant serving as an adjutant, a regimental

Captain John Hobensack, 1st New Jersey Cavalry, wore this regulation company-grade officer's coat and belt. The collar is turned down to show the black velvet lining. Charging a Confederate cannon at Brandy Station, Hobensack saw the cannoneer ready to fire some 50 yards away. He grasped the hand of a fellow officer, saying, 'We must shut our eyes and take it. Good-bye.' The shot went over their heads. (Christopher Nelson collection)

quartermaster, an assistant surgeon, a sergeant major, a regimental quartermaster-sergeant, a regimental commissary sergeant, a hospital steward, two principal musicians and a band of sixteen musicians. To save money, in October 1861 new regiments were forbidden to recruit bands and in July 1862 all regimental bands were ordered to be discharged within 30 days. A chaplain, receiving the pay and allowances of a cavalry captain, could also be appointed by the colonel.

The Union Army mustered 258 regiments and 170 independent companies of cavalry. Only one of these regiments was armed and trained in tactics differently from the others. This was the 6th Pennsylvania Cavalry, 'Rush's Lancers', which was formed in the summer of 1861 and armed with a 9-foot lance with a blade eleven inches long and three inches wide. These also had small red-and-white pennants. Lances were worthless in the terrain of Northern Virginia, even if the lancers had been able to close with infantry armed with rifle-muskets, and they were finally abandoned, after seeing virtually no use, in June 1863, the regiment serving the rest of its enlistment as ordinary cavalry.

On 28 July 1863 the Cavalry Bureau was formed in Washington for the purpose of inspecting all cavalry units and co-ordinating the purchase and supply of horses. On 1 August 1863 the Bureau was given the task of appointing Veterinary Surgeons of Cavalry, ranking as farriers, who were assigned by regimental commanders to each company. It was responsible for cavalry depots, of which the largest was at Giesboro near Washington. Western cavalrymen went to St. Louis, Missouri. Dismounted cavalrymen were sent to the depots to be remounted and returned to their units.

Cavalry officers wore the same uniform as that worn by artillery officers, but their branch of service color was yellow and their cap badge was a pair of gold-embroidered crossed sabers, edges upward, with a silver regimental number in the upper angle. They often wore the regulation short jacket in the field.

This farrier wears a representation of a saddler's knife on the sleeves of his fatigue blouse. This was not a regulation insignia but was widely worn. He is also wearing spurs on his boots. (Richard Carlile collection)

Many men made additions to their plain blue fatigue coats. Making a stand-up collar by adding hooks and eyes was common. This member of the 16th Illinois Cavalry, photographed in St. Louis, has apparently yellow braid (which often photographed black) on his collar, around his jacket edges and in small knots on each cuff. (Author's collection)

Enlisted cavalrymen wore the uniform jacket and mounted men's trousers of light artillerymen with the dress hat of heavy artillerymen. Their branch of service colour, too, was yellow, and their cap badge was a stamped brass pair of sabres with the regimental number and company letter. Against regulations, enlisted cavalrymen also wore a dark-blue jacket with either a small amount of yellow trim around the collar edge and down the front, or wholly plain.

In addition to the mounted man's overcoat, they were also authorized a rubberized talma, a kind of raincoat with long sleeves that reached to the knee. It was made without a cape. A cheaper, rubber-coated sheet called a poncho, made with a slit for the head in the middle and grommets around the outside for use as a temporary shelter, was issued in other branches of service. In 1862 the Quartermaster suspended the issue of talmas to the cavalry, and issued the poncho instead. Quartermaster records show that the three main depots at Philadelphia, New York and Cincinnati acquired, from 1 May 1861 to 30 June 1865, 1,596,559 rubber or painted ponchos and only 34,710 talmas.

Colonel Charles Devens Jr., commander of the 15th Massachusetts Infantry, was wounded at Balls Bluff when a bullet struck a coat button. He was promoted to the rank of brigadier general on 15 April 1862. (Atwater Kent Museum, Philadelphia)

Captain John H. Symonds, 22nd Massachusetts Infantry, wears the officer's overcoat, the quilted lining showing plainly. His belt-plate is a state one. Symonds was commissioned on 1 October 1861 and discharged on 26 August 1863; his regiment was in V Corps, Army of the Potomac. (Author's collection)

Infantry

According to General Order Number 16, 4 May 1861, each Regular Army infantry regiment was to have two or more battalions, each with eight companies. Each company had a captain, a first lieutenant, a second lieutenant, a first or orderly sergeant, four sergeants, eight corporals, two musicians and, a minimum of 64 or a maximum of 82 privates, giving a total of some 82–100 officers and men. Each battalion would also have a major, a lieutenant, serving as battalion adjutant, another lieutenant serving as battalion quartermaster and commissary, a sergeant major, a quartermaster-sergeant, a commissary sergeant and a hospital steward. All told, the battalion would have between 663 and 800 officers and men. The regiment would include its colonel, a lieutenant colonel, a lieutenant serving as regimental adjutant, another lieutenant serving as regimental quartermaster and commissary, a drum major, two principal musicians, and 24 musicians in a band. The regiment would total between 2,020 and 2,452 officers and men.

This officer of the 10th Iowa Infantry wears the field-grade officer's body coat with his collar turned down to expose its black velvet lining. The 10th saw action at Vicksburg, Atlanta, the March to the Sea and the campaign in the Carolinas. (Author's collection)

First Lieutenant William Stauffer, 195th Pennsylvania Infantry, shows how rank insignia was worn on the collar in the field when shoulder-straps were dispensed with. Officers in the Western Theatre often wore their rank badges within a gold circle on their coat breast. The 195th was first raised for 100 days' service on 24 July 1864. It was re-organized for a year's service in February 1865, serving mostly in West Virginia. (Author's collection)

Orders issued on 15 April 1861 for volunteer forces mustered into Federal service called for each infantry company to include its captain, a first lieutenant, an 'ensign' (the rank did not officially exist), four sergeants, four corporals, a drummer, a fifer, and 64 privates. Ten companies would make up a regiment. The regimental staff would include its colonel, a lieutenant colonel, a major, an adjutant, a regimental quartermaster, a surgeon, an assistant surgeon, a sergeant major, a quartermaster-sergeant, a drum major and a fife major. On 4 May 1861 General Order, Number 15 revised this by changing the designation of ensign to that of second lieutenant, adding a first sergeant, four more corporals, and a wagoner, and making the minimum number of privates 64, maximum, 82. At the regimental level, the surgeon's position was eliminated but a hospital steward was added as were 24 bandsmen. The bandsmen's jobs were eliminated in July 1862. A chaplain was authorized at the regimental commander's pleasure.

Infantry officers wore the same uniform and insignia as did staff officers save that their branch of service color on the epaulette, shoulder-strap and trouser welt was sky-blue. Their cap badge was a gold-embroidered bugle with the regimental number in silver within the horn's loop.

In the field, infantry officers often preferred wearing the enlisted-style fatigue blouse. General Order, Number 286 issued on 22 November 1864 authorized all officers in the field to pin the devices used on their shoulder-straps directly to their shoulders so as to make them less conspicuous in battle. This practice had, in fact, been adopted by many officers for some time before it was officially authorized. The order also authorized officers to wear the enlisted man's overcoat and allowed them to leave off their sashes and epaulettes when in the field. While this order applied to all officers serving in the field, it most affected infantry officers.

Enlisted infantrymen wore the same uniform as did heavy artillerymen, with sky-blue chevrons and trim instead of scarlet. Their cap badge was the same bugle, in stamped brass, with the regimental number and company letter, as was worn by officers. However, there was more variety in enlisted infantry dress than in any other corps.

Many volunteers arrived in pre-war volunteer uniforms. Most of these whose regiments had any history wore a claw-tail style coatee with standing collar heavily trimmed in lace and worsted fringed epaulettes, with some form of shako or busbee. More modern units wore the frock-coat. Both types often had a jacket for fatigue duty. Ethnic dress styles were also common, including kilts worn by 'Scottish' units, spiked helmets by 'German' units and Polish caps by some lancers. Colors varied tremendously with many volunteers preferring grey because blue was the color worn by Regulars. Dark-green was often preferred by rifle companies. These uniforms were widely seen in 1861, and when local volunteer militia were called up for various emergencies.

State uniforms, such as the dark-blue jacket with sky-blue trim issued by Illinois and New York, were common. New York infantry regiments, numbered between 1 and 105, received these jackets and men from other regiments, such as the 120th New York in October 1864, wore them, too. A plain dark-blue waist-length, single-breasted jacket was also issued in large numbers by Pennsylvania, Ohio, Illinois and Missouri. Many veteran volunteers from all the states also appear to have worn this plain jacket. Wisconsin issued the 9th to 16th Infantry Regiments a dark-blue sack coat with standing collar edged with sky-blue. In 1861, too, Pennsylvania, Iowa, Maine, and Indiana issued large numbers of grey frocks and jackets. These were mostly of poor quality material and wore out quickly.

This corporal of the 23rd New York Infantry is wearing the dress frock-coat. There was no regulation enlisted man's vest or waistcoat; most men bought them or had them sent from home. The 23rd, the 'Southern Tier Regiment', saw service at the 2nd Bull Run, Antietam, and Fredericksburg before being assigned provost duty in January 1863. It was mustered out on 22 May 1863. (Author's collection)

Musician Andy Kuhl was a drummer in the 49th Pennsylvania Infantry, enlisting in August 1863 and dying of disease in December of that year. He wears the dress frock-coat with shoulder-scales and the musician's braid across the chest. An M1840 musician's sword hangs from his shoulder-belt. (Ronn Palm collection)

A regimental quartermaster sergeant with a state issue jacket, chevrons indicating at least three years' service, and a non-commissioned officer's waist-belt. He is holding the M1840 non-commissioned officer's sword. (Author's collection)

This infantry private, photographed in Philadelphia, wears the dress hat with a branch-of-service cap badge. Since the regulations were vague as to whether the hat brim should be turned up as seen from the front or as worn, some wearers turned up one side and some the other. His overcoat is the issue foot soldier's overcoat. (Author's collection)

State Infantry Uniforms of 1861

State	Regiments	Uniform
Connecticut	1st–3rd	Plain blue frock and trousers, gray overcoat
Illinois	1st	Gray shirt, blue cap
	7th–12th	Gray coat trimmed blue with short skirts, gray trousers and slouch hats
	13th–22nd	Gray frock and jacket, some blue jackets, gray trousers and slouch hat
Indiana	7th, 9th	Light-blue jacket and trousers, slouch hat
	8th, 10th	Gray jacket and trousers, slouch hat
Iowa	1st	Gray overshirt, trimmed red or green, gray trousers with matching stripe, slouch hat
Maine	1st–3rd	Gray frock coat, trousers and forage cap
Massachusetts	7th, 9th–11th	Gray jacket, trousers, and slouch hats
	3rd, 4th, 6th, 8th	Guernsey frock
Michigan	1st	Dark-blue jacket and trousers
Minnesota	1st	Chequered flannel shirt, black trousers, slouch hat
New Hampshire	2nd	Gray tailcoat trimmed red, gray trousers, light-blue Whipple hat
New Jersey	1st–9th	Dark-blue frock-coat, sky-blue trousers, black Army dress hat
New York	1st–105th	Dark-blue jacket trimmed sky-blue, sky-blue trousers, dark-blue cap
Ohio	15th, 17th, 19th 20th	Gray jacket and trousers
	16th, 18th, 22nd	Dark-blue jacket, gray trousers
Pennsylvania	12th, 27th, 28th, 29th, 62nd, 71st	Gray jacket, trousers, forage cap

The 12th New York State Militia wore an imitation of the French chasseur uniform, with baggy red trousers and kepi and a dark-blue coat with red trim. Gaiters were dark leather. (David Scheinmann collection)

State	Regiments	Uniform
Rhode Island	1st–2nd	Dark-blue overshirt, gray trousers, slouch hat
Vermont	2nd–3rd	Gray tailcoat trimmed sky-blue, gray trousers and cap trimmed sky-blue
Wisconsin	1st–2nd	Gray frock-coat, gray trousers with black stripe, gray cap piped black
	3rd	Dark-gray overshirt, light-gray trousers, gray slouch hat
	4th–8th	Gray jacket trimmed black, gray trousers with black stripe, gray forage cap

Many of these early uniforms were issued because the government couldn't equip all the volunteer infantrymen quickly enough. In September the Quartermaster even ordered 10,000 French *chasseurs à pied de la ligne* uniforms and equipment. These dark-blue uniforms with yellow trim and

---

A Union trooper hates his first issued uniform

'Something happened that I was unable to be present the first forenoon that clothing was issued, and, when I did call upon the quartermaster-sergeant, there was only two or three suits left . . . I can remember now how my heart sank within me, as I picked up a pair of pants that was left. They were evidently cut out with a buzz-saw, and were made for a man that weighed three hundred [pounds]. I held them up in installments, and looked at them. Holding them by the top, as high as I could, and the bottom of the legs of the pants laid on the ground. The sergeant charged the pants to my account, and then handed me a jacket, a small one, evidently made for a hump-backed dwarf. The jacket was covered with yellow braid. O, *so* yellow, that it made me sick. The jacket was charged to me also. Then he handed me some under-shirts and drawers, so coarse and rough that it seemed to me they must have been made of rope, and lined with sand-paper. Then came an overcoat, big enough for an equestrian statue of George Washington, with a cape on it as big as a wall tent. The hat I drew was a stiff, cheap, shoddy hat, as high as a tin camp kettle . . . The hat was four sizes too large for me. Then I took the last pair of army shoes there were, and they weighed as much as a pair of anvils, and had raw-hide strings to fasten them with.'

(George W. Peck, *How Private Geo. W. Peck Put Down The Rebellion*, Belford & Clarke, Chicago, 1887, pp. 178–9)

Colonel Rush C. Hawkins, 9th New York Infantry, wears an officer's version of his regiment's zouave dress. His kepi is red with a blue band and gold braid. The jacket, vest and trousers are dark-blue. Braiding on the sleeve, shoulders and trim, is red with gold edges. The vest braid is also gold. Two thin silver strips outside a green stripe are worn on each trouser leg. This uniform is in the Brown University collection. (National Archives collection)

epaulettes were issued to the 18th Massachusetts, 49th and 72nd New York, and 62nd and 83rd Pennsylvania Infantry Regiment.

Zouaves

Many volunteers, however, preferred to wear a version of French zouave dress. Typically, the zouave jacket was trimmed in lace and cut short, hooking away at the throat and falling to the sides to expose a fancy vest and shirt. Trousers were quite baggy, usually trimmed around the side pockets. A sash was worn under the waist-belt, usually edged with a facing color. Often, the cartridge box shoulder-belt was worn under the jacket. Gaiters held the trouser ends and covered the shoe tops; they often had leather *jambières* (shin-guards) on their tops. Fezzes, with turbans for dress and without for field duty, had tassels at their ends. Not all so-called zouave units wore all the components of the original zouave dress; some wore a kepi instead of a fez, some wore chasseur-cut trousers which were less baggy than true zouave trousers, and some had a false vest which was simply a strip of cloth attached to the jacket front.

Zouave units were often accompanied by women known as *vivandières* (sutlers, or canteen-managers). They wore a version of the male dress that included a short, cut-away jacket, a skirt that reached just below the knees, trousers worn under the skirt, and boots. The colors usually matched those worn by the males of the regiment. Union Army zouave colors were as follows:

> ### Union troops alter their uniforms to fit
>
> 'One of the amusing incidents in the earlier camp experience transpired when Quartermaster Smith issued to the future soldiers the stock of clothing furnished by the government for their use. It was clear that Uncle Sam's contracting tailor who made the garments had no idea of measuring the man and then fitting his suit; he seemed rather to expect that, having made the uniforms according to certain patterns, it would be the duty of the officers who distributed them to fit each wearer to his clothes, as Procrustes, the Attic highwayman, fitted victims to his bed. As a fact, however, when the time came to exchange the citizen's dress for the soldier's garb, it provoked a deal of hilarious mirth to see a square-shouldered, portly man struggling to encase his ample limbs in trousers scant enough to please a dude; while a lean, light-weight comrade fairly lost his corporal identity in the baggy capacity of a fat man's coat. Nor were the seams of these new garments always equal to the strain to which they were subjected, so that in the course of the first week after they were donned, many of the wearers had to resort to the spools and cushions thoughtfully provided by a loving wife or mother . . . '
>
> (George N. Carpenter, *History of the Eighth Regiment Vermont Volunteers, 1861–1865*, Boston, 1886, p. 20)

Unit	Jacket	Trim	Vest	Trousers	Sash
11th Indiana (1st uniform)	Gray	Red, sky-blue	—	Gray	—
11th Indiana (2nd uniform)	Black	Sky-blue	Dark-blue	Sky-blue	—
33rd New Jersey	Dark-blue	Red, sky-blue	Dark-blue	Dark-blue	Dark-blue
35th New Jersey	Dark-blue	Red, sky-blue	Dark-blue	Dark-blue	Dark-blue
3rd New York	Dark-blue	Magenta	Dark-blue	Dark-blue	Turquoise
5th New York	Dark-blue	Red	Medium-blue	Scarlet	Red
9th New York	Dark-blue	Magenta	Medium-blue	Dark-blue	Turquoise
10th New York	Dark-brown	Red	Scarlet	Sky-blue	Sky-blue
11th New York	Dark-blue	Red	Dark-blue	Dark-blue	Blue
17th New York	Dark-blue	Magenta	Dark-blue	Dark-blue	Turquoise
44th New York	Dark-blue	Red	—	Dark-blue	—
53rd New York	Dark-blue	Yellow	Dark-blue	Sky-blue	Sky-blue
62nd New York	Dark-blue	Deep-red	Dark-blue	Sky-blue	Blue
74th New York	Dark-blue	Yellow	Dark-blue	Red	Light-blue
140th New York	Dark-blue	Red	Dark-blue	Dark-blue	Dark-blue
146th New York	Sky-blue	Yellow	Sky-blue	Sky-blue	Red
164th New York	Dark-blue	Dark red	Dark-blue	Dark-blue	Turquoise
165th New York	Dark-blue	Medium-blue	Medium-blue	Scarlet	Red
34th Ohio	Dark-blue	Red	Dark-blue	Sky-blue	—
23rd Pennsylvania	Dark-blue	Red	Dark-blue	Dark-blue	—
72nd Pennsylvania	Dark-blue	Red	—	Sky-blue	—
91st Pennsylvania	Dark-blue	Yellow	Dark-blue	Sky-blue	—
95th Pennsylvania	Dark-blue	Red	—	Sky-blue	—
114th Pennsylvania	Dark-blue	Red	Dark-blue	Red	Light-blue
115th Pennsylvania	Dark-blue	Yellow	Dark-blue	Dark-blue	Red

Co A, 23rd Massachusetts Infantry, wore a version of the zouave uniform shown here. The uniform is dark-blue with a sky-blue sash and trim. The 23rd was in XVIII Corps at Southeastern coastal stations. (Richard Carlile collection)

Sergeant Augustus M. Hinsdale, Co K, 28th Iowa, wears a *strange-looking version of zouave dress worn in different variants by a number of Western regiments. The 28th served at Vicksburg, the Red River Campaign, the Shenandoah Valley Campaign of 1864, and ended up performing garrison duty in Southeastern states until mustered out on 31 July 1965. (Robert L. Kotchian collection)*

US Colored Troops

Originally, few Northern whites, except the small, abolitionist minority, thought of blacks as being anything other than 'property'. Indeed, soldiers such as Major General George B. McClellan felt that it was their duty to preserve property and return escaping slaves to their owners. Major General Benjamin Butler, however, recognized that slaves, by their labor, were an asset of the rebelling states, and declared them to be 'contraband of war'. As such, they would not be returned to Southerners claiming to own them.

In the deep South, however, Major General David Hunter first abolished slavery in the District of the South, which he commanded. When Lincoln repudiated that move, on the grounds that Hunter lacked the necessary authority, Hunter raised the 1st South Carolina (African Descent) in 1862. It was first ordered to be disbanded, but was later authorized by Congress. Two more South Carolina (African Descent) regiments were authorized in the following year.

Although the issue of allowing blacks to fight was controversial among Union military men, the need to fill depleted ranks caused blacks to be recruited into combat units. The 5th Massachusetts (Colored) Cavalry Regiment, and 54th Massachusetts (Colored) and 55th Massachusetts (Colored) Infantry Regiments were joined by the 29th Connecticut (Colored) Infantry Regiments as the only state-designated black units of the war. Other regiments were taken under direct War Department control and designated

Southern blacks say they'd rather fight for Confederates

'The Confederate Congress had enacted that negro troops, captured, should be restored to their owners. We had several hundreds of such, taken by [General N. B.] Forrest in Tennessee, whose owners could not be reached; and they were put to work on the fortifications at Mobile [Alabama], rather for the purpose of giving them healthy employment than for the value of the work. I made a point to visit their camps and inspect the quantity and quality of their food, always found to be satisfactory. On one occasion, while so engaged, a fine-looking negro, who seemed to be the leader among his comrades, approached me and said: "Thank you, Massa General, they give us plenty of good victuals; but how do you like our work?" I replied that they had worked very well. "If you will give us guns we will fight for these works, too. We would rather fight for our own white folks than for strangers."'

(Richard Taylor, *Destruction and Reconstruction*, Longmans Green and Co., New York, 1955, pp. 256–7)

US Colored Troops. Hunter's 1st South Carolina (AD) was redesignated the 33rd US Colored Infantry in 1864. Other redesignated Southern state units were the 1st Mississippi Cavalry (AD) which became the 3rd US Colored Cavalry; the 1st North Carolina Heavy Artillery (AD) which became the 14th US Colored Heavy Artillery; and the 1st Kansas (Colored) Infantry which became the 79th US Colored Infantry.

In all, six regiments of US Colored Cavalry, eleven regiments and four companies of US Colored Heavy Artillery, ten batteries of US Colored Light Artillery, and 100 regiments and sixteen companies of US Colored Infantry were raised during the war. They saw service in both Eastern and Western theatres, serving well at such actions as the assault on Battery Wagner, South Carolina and the siege of Petersburg.

Enlisted men were escaped slaves or freed blacks living in either the North or South. Officers, however, were whites, most of whom had seen enlisted service in other combat units. To receive their commission they had to pass tests of military knowledge, mathematics, geography and history given by an examining board. A Free Military School for Applicants for Commands of Colored Troops was set up in Philadelphia to help officer candidates prepare for this test. So white officers of USCT units were both intelligent and, generally, had combat experience, making them a cut above the average volunteer unit officer, but many felt that, socially, there was a certain lack of prestige in commanding black troops.

A guard detail of the 107th US Colored Troops in front of their guard house. The 107th was raised in Louisville, Kentucky and saw service at the Siege of Petersburg, the capture of Fort Fisher and Wilmington, North Carolina and the surrender of Johnston's army. (Black Spear Historical Productions)

After the war, USCT units were used to garrison the South, the last USCT regiments being disbanded in December 1867.

The first two South Carolina (AD) Infantry Regiments received red trousers with their regulation blouse and cap. The 1st Kansas (Colored), later the 79rd USCT, had an initial issue of a blue jacket, gray trousers, and forage cap. The 20th USCT, recruited in New York in 1864, initially received a blue chasseur uniform. Other than that, USCT units received the regulation uniform and insignia of their various branches of service.

US Veteran Volunteers

General Order 91, issued on 25 June 1863, stated that soldiers who had served one three-year enlistment would be designated 'Veteran Volunteers' on re-enlistment. On 26 November 1864 Major General William S. Hancock, seasoned commander of the II Corps and one of the Army's best soldiers, was offered command of an entire corps of 'Veteran Volunteers which would be called the US Veteran Volunteers. According to *Harper's Weekly* of 10 December 1864, 'General Hancock has orders to organize in the District of Columbia, a new corps, which is to consist of 20,000 men who have been in the service for at least two years. The corps is to be raised by January 1, 1865.'

Recruiting was slow since Hancock was not able to draw on serving officers in active units to staff his new Veteran Volunteer regiments. Moreover, bounty brokers were not given as free a hand in filling the new units as they were in ordinary volunteer units. Since they controlled five-sixths of recruiting, their help was needed but not received. The first Veteran Volunteer unit actually raised was the Veteran Volunteer Engineer Regiment, which was formed in July 1864 from men from the Department of the Cumberland's Pioneer Brigade.

Eventually, the engineer regiment was joined by nine infantry regiments. On 28 November 1864 General Order Number 287 organized these regiments into the I Corps (the old I Corps had been merged with the II Corps earlier) under Hancock's command. But by the time they had been equipped with the promised Henry repeating rifles and were ready to serve, the war was over. They saw some garrison duty before the Corps was disbanded on 11 July 1866. The last member had been discharged by August 1866.

Veteran Volunteers wore the regulation Army uniform of their corps, but there was a special cap badge, the sealed pattern of which had been deposited with the Quartermaster Department on 10 May 1865. It was a red, seven-pointed star or 'septagon', which was to be worn on the cap top, hat top or left breast of the coat. The badge had an oval in the centre; the regimental number was to be worn in the oval. Presumably white and blue badges would have been issued had other divisions been completed.

US Volunteer Infantry Regiments

In late 1863 Major General Benjamin Butler had the idea of recruiting disenchanted Confederate prisoners into infantry regiments which would be designated US Volunteer Infantry Regiments, or US Volunteers for short. These regiments had the standard infantry table of organization. Officers were battle-trained Union Army veterans, with one exception, Captain John T. Shanks, Company I, 6th US Volunteers. A Texan who had been a captain in Morgan's Cavalry, he co-operated with Union officials to thwart a Confederate scheme to free prisoners in Camp Douglas, Illinois. His Union commission was his reward.

Butler formed the 1st US Volunteers at the prison camp at Point Lookout, Maryland, on 28 March 1864. In all, 40 per cent of its men came from North Carolina, 15 per cent from Virginia and 10 per cent were foreign-born. Butler sent it into action for the first time at Elizabeth City, North Carolina, on 27 July 1864. There they fired a few shots at fleeing local defence forces, burned some cotton, and captured some horses. Grant, however, didn't want ex-Confederates fighting Confederates and on 15 August had them sent to the northwest frontier. There they garrisoned small posts in Minnesota and along the Missouri River, fighting in many skirmishes against Indians. They were mustered out at Fort Leavenworth, Kansas, on 22 May 1866.

On Lincoln's instructions the 2nd and 3rd US Volunteers were formed at Rock Island, Illinois, on 1 September 1864. The 1,797 recruits Lincoln's representatives raised were sent to Fort Leavenworth, Kansas, where they were formed into two regiments on 2 February 1865. They were sent to the Department of the Plains in March, detachments being posted to protect overland mail routes and they, too, fought Indians. An Ohio cavalryman who was stationed near them wrote home that they were 'all a quiet civil set of fellows'.[1] They were mustered out on 7 November 1865.

The 4th US Volunteers was raised at Port Lookout in October 1864. Only six companies (of less than wholly reliable men) could be recruited. They were sent to the Dakotas in May 1865 where they replaced the 1st US

Volunteers. They were mustered out at Fort Leavenworth from 18 June to 2 July 1866.

In April 1865 the 5th US Volunteers was recruited at Alton, Illinois, where were held suspected spies, political prisoners and former Union Army men who had been captured and recruited by the Confederates only to be recaptured by Union forces. As a result, many Northerners served in its ranks. They were stationed in Kansas and Colorado in May 1865 with Companies C and D in Nebraska and Company D in Denver. They were mustered out at Forts Kearny and Leavenworth from 11 October to 13 November 1866.

The 6th US Volunteers had two companies from Champ Chase, Ohio, six from Camp Douglas, and two from Camp Morton, Illinois. They arrived on the frontier in June 1865 and were posted along mail and telegraph routes, and garrisoned Salt Lake City, Utah in October 1865. The regiment's last members were mustered out at Fort Leavenworth on 3 November 1866.

The US Volunteers all wore standard Union infantry uniform and insignia.

US Sharpshooters

Colonel Hiram Berdan was authorized to raise a regiment of marksmen as the US Sharpshooters on 14 June 1861. By 24 September the regiment had been organized, each of its ten companies from a different area, and arrived in Washington. A second regiment of eight companies of US Sharpshooters was authorized on 28 September 1861 since there had been so many volunteers who passed a shooting test for the first regiment. The test required the applicant to place ten shots in a 10-inch circle from 200 yards. Any long arm could be used for the test.

Originally armed with Colt revolving rifles, which tended to discharge all its rounds simultaneously, they were next armed with Sharps breech-loading rifles in May–June 1862. In terms of organizational assignments, the regiments tended to be treated as typical infantry, but serving tactically as skirmishers rather than fighting in regular battle lines. At Antietam, for example, the 2nd US Sharpshooters were listed as an independent unit reporting directly to the headquarters of the 1st Brigade, 1st Division, I Corps which also had four volunteer New York infantry regiments in it. Later the 2nd was moved around, serving with the I, II and III Corps and spending much time serving alongside the 1st Sharpshooters.

At Antietam the 1st US Sharpshooters were listed as an independent unit reporting directly to 1st Division Headquarters, V Corps. In 1863 the regiment was transferred to III Corps, fighting at Chancellorsville and Gettysburg. It was assigned to II Corps in 1864.

Both regiments fought well in the Army of the Potomac's campaigns. Of the 1,392 officers and men in the 1st US Sharpshooters, 546 became casualties. The 2nd US Sharpshooters lost 462 killed and wounded out of 1,178 all ranks.

In August 1864 companies of the 1st US Sharpshooters began to be disbanded, the term of enlistment of many of the

Colonel Francis Peteler, 2nd US Sharpshooters, wears the dark-green uniform of his regiment with one version of its unique cap badge. (David Scheinmann collection)

men having expired. In September a greatly reduced 1st US Sharpshooters was formed into a battalion which lasted until December when most of its men, save for those from Michigan, who were sent to the 5th Michigan Infantry Regiment, were re-assigned to the 2nd US Sharpshooters. On 20 February 1865 that regiment was disbanded, members with time left to serve being assigned to units bearing their native state designations.

The US Sharpshooters wore regulation infantry uniform, but of dark-green cloth. Piping on enlisted men's frock-coats was a lighter, emerald-green, as were shoulder-straps,

One version of the US Sharpshooters' officers' cap badge, worn by Colonel Peteler. The wreath and rifles are gold, the letters are silver. Another version simply had the Old English letters 'USSS' in a straight line within the wreath. (Author's collection)

A sergeant of US Sharpshooters in his dark-green coat and cap, early war blue trousers and leather gaiters. He holds the issue Sharps rifle. (Richard Carlile collection)

chevrons and trouser stripes for those authorized to wear them. Buttons were of the same design as regulation buttons, but were made of a black plastic substance. Originally trousers were light-blue, but these were replaced by dark-green trousers in 1862. Dark-green fatigue blouses of regulation cut were issued from the start. Blue uniforms appear to have been worn from time to time when green ones were unavailable. Brass roman letters 'USSS' were sometimes worn with a corps badge on the left breast of the blouse.

The first head-dress issued was the Whipple pattern light-blue/gray hat which had a black peak and a light-blue/gray brim around the side and back to protect against rain and sun. These were discarded in early 1862 for fear of drawing fire from Union troops behind the Sharpshooters' skirmish line. They were replaced by standard-design dark-green forage caps, some of which were worn by enlisted men with the brass roman letters 'USSS' on the top. Early in the war black ostrich plumes were sometimes worn on cap sides, but these were later discarded. Also discarded quickly was the gray felt, seamless overcoat which became stiff as a board when soaked. It was replaced by the standard foot soldier's overcoat. Gaiters were of russet leather, but were only worn for a short time. Knapsacks were of Prussian design, covered with hair and complete with an attached cooking kit.

Officers wore dark-green regulation infantry officers' uniform, and had several unique hat insignia. Berdan and other officers wore a gold-embroidered wreath with a pair of gold crossed rifles and the silver Old English letters 'US' above the rifles and 'SS' beneath them. Other officers simply wore the embroidered Old English letters 'USSS' in a straight line within a wreath. Captain Francis D. Sweetser, commander of Company E, 2nd USSS, was photographed with a staff officer's cap badge with the Old English 'US' within a wreath on his cap front.

Veteran Reserve Corps

On 7 April 1862 in an effort to ease staffing problems, the War Department authorized each hospital's chief medical officer to employ convalescents as nurses, cooks and hospital attendants. But, men who were unfit for active duty received a discharge from the army, even if they were still fit for light duty, so on 20 March 1863, General Order Number 69 called for the organization of patients unfit for field duty into detachments to serve as guards, clerks, nurses and cooks, and to perform other extra duties. On 28 April 1863 the War Department went even further, issuing General Order Number 105 which created the Invalid Corps.

The new Corps was to be staffed at company level by officers and men who were either convalescent and still in the Army, or volunteers who had been discharged because of wounds received during honourable service. They had to pass not only a medical examination but one that determined their intelligence, industry, sobriety and attention to duty. Command of what later came to be called the Veteran Reserve Corps Bureau fell to a colonel appointed by the Provost Marshal General who held overall command responsibility for the Bureau.

Companies were described as being in one of three battalions. Companies in the First Battalion had men who were able to bear a musket and do garrison duty. They were fully armed and equipped. Men of companies in the Second Battalion had lost an arm or hand or were otherwise so severely injured or weakened through illness that they could only serve as hospital guards and attendants. They were given pistols and non-commissioned officers' swords, and the weapons often were not of the first-class. Company K of the 2nd Regiment received Lefaucheux revolvers, while the 6th Regiment skirmished with smoothbore muskets against Early's Confederates armed with rifle-muskets near Washington. Originally, men even worse off than Second Battalion men were to be assigned to companies in the Third Battalion; in fact there never was a Third Battalion and anybody unfit for the First Battalion ended up in the Second Battalion. On 27 December 1864 command of the Second Battalion was passed to the Surgeon General.

According to New York's *The Evening Post* of 30 October 1863, 'The duties of the invalids have been so much extended that the second battalion, whose members are all permanently disabled – men who have lost an arm or leg – are now necessarily kept actively at work; and it is an interesting fact that they are found serviceable.'

Each company was to include men from different states and was to be kept intact. The Corps grew rapidly: on 1 November 1863 there were 10,540 enlisted men in the First Battalion and 7,225 in the Second. By 1 October 1864 there were 27,974 enlisted men in 236 First Battalion companies and 159 Second Battalion Companies. On 5 September 1863 the Adjutant General authorized the combining of the companies into regiments with colonels and lieutenant colonels being authorized on 26 September. Originally, these regiments were to have both First and Second Battalion companies but the two types were separated when Second Battalion commanded passed to the Surgeon General.

Officers and men alike hated the designation Invalid Corps; one reason was that condemned equipment was stamped 'IC' and hence men from other units called Invalid Corps members 'condemned yanks'. On 18 March 1864, therefore, the Corps name was changed to Veteran Reserve Corps by General Order Number 111. After March 1864 the only troops in Washington were in the Corps. The last

Colonel Charles M. Prevost commanded the 116th Pennsylvania Infantry before being transferred to the Veteran Reserve Corps due to wounds. He then commanded the 16th VRC Regiment. He is wearing the uniform of a field-grade VRC officer, in sky-blue with black velvet collar and cuffs. (US Army Military History Institute collection)

Crippled Union veterans can't run

'On the 20th of June [1864] it [the 18th Regiment Veteran Reserve Corps] took part in the successful defense of the post [White Horse, Virginia] against Hampton's raid. Several of the men had been discharged and were on transports about to sail for the North; they returned to the camp, borrowed arms and accoutrements, and begged to go into line of battle with their old comrades. Twice during the engagement an aide rode up to Colonel Johnson with the question, "Will your invalids stand?"

'"Tell the general", was the answer, "that my men are cripples, and they can't run."'

(J. W. DeForest, official report, *The War of the Rebellion: A Compilation of the Official Records of the Union and Confederate Armies*, Series III, Vol. V, Washington, D.C., 1900, pp. 554–6)

This unidentified Veteran Reserve Corps second lieutenant shows the two black velvet stripes worn down each leg as well as the black velvet collar and cuffs. He is holding his regulation foot officer's sword. (Author's collection)

Private Eli Nichols served in Co C, 114th New York Infantry from August 1862 until he was transferred into the Veteran Reserve Corps on 1 March 1864, having been 'sick in quarters' for the preceding month. Serving in Co K, 9th VRC, he was part of the defences of Washington during Early's attack on the city in 1864. (Author's collection)

Union Army enlisted volunteer, Private William Sadler, Company B, 9th Veteran Reserve Corps Regiment, was mustered out of service on 4 October 1868.

Veteran Reserve Corps Regiments as of 30 November 1864 were as follows:

Regiment	Primary Station	Primary Duty
1st	Elmira, New York	Prison guards
2nd	Detroit, Michigan	Guard duty
3rd	Washington, DC	Garrison, guards
4th	Rock Island, Illinois	Prison guards
5th	Indianapolis, Indiana	Guard duty
6th	Johnson's Island, Ohio	Prison guards
7th	Washington, DC	Garrison duty
8th	Camp Douglas, Illinois	Prison guards
9th	Washington, DC	Garrison duty
10th	Washington, DC	Garrison duty
11th	Point Lookout, Maryland	Prison guards
12th	Alexandria, Virginia	Guard duty
13th	Gallupe's Island, Massachusetts	Guard duty
14th	Washington, DC	Garrison duty
15th	Camp Douglas, Illinois	Prison guards
16th	Various Eastern cities	Hunting deserters
17th	Indianapolis, Indiana	Guard duty
18th	Washington, DC	Garrison duty
19th	Elmira, New York	Guard duty
20th	Point Lookout, Maryland	Prison guards
21st	Various Eastern cities	Guard duty
22nd	Various Midwestern cities	Guard duty
23rd	Various Western cities	Hunting deserters
24th	Washington, DC	Garrison duty

From the start, officers and men of the Invalid, later Veteran Reserve, Corps were disinguished by a unique uniform. According to General Order Number 158 of 11 June 1863, officers wore the standard staff officer's uniform, but made from sky-blue cloth and having a dark-blue velvet collar and cuffs. Some officers wore a sky-blue shell jacket, usually left open to display a sky-blue vest. Their sky-blue trousers had two half-inch-wide dark-blue velvet stripes three-quarters of an inch apart down each leg. Shoulder-straps had a dark-blue velvet background. They wore the cap insignia of infantry officers. The jacket was found to soil easily and towards the end of the Corps' existence, officers were allowed to wear standard infantry officers' uniform.

According to General Order Number 124 of 15 May 1863, enlisted men wore sky-blue trousers and dark-blue forage caps, distinguished in some regiments by the enlisted infantry man's hat insignia. Their coat was a sky-blue kersey jacket with a standing collar with one false button-hole and button, trimmed with dark-blue, like the light artillery jacket. Dark-blue lace edged the front and bottom of the jacket, its shoulder-straps, and decorated the pointed cuffs. Two buttons opened and closed each cuff. There were two versions of the jacket: one was cut like the light artillery jacket, the other was longer in the waist, with a slit on each side, like the chasseur jacket. Non-commissioned officers wore a dark-blue stripe down each leg. According to a member of the 6th Regiment, 'When out on pass, we must have our jackets buttoned up to our chin, waist-belt on and also white gloves.'[2] It was a handsome uniform, but the men did not like it because it marked the wearer as a man who was unable to keep up with field soldiers, and seemed to suggest that his was an easy life in garrison.

To entertain patients, many regiments had bands. There was no regulation musician's uniform, so they varied according to each colonel's taste. 'Our band were getting along nicely', a 6th Regiment veteran wrote, 'and were handsomely uniformed in blue jackets trimmed with black facings and three rows of brass buttons, shake [sic] hat with plume, and brass eagle ornament, epaulettes, and black pants with blue, black and gilt stripe down the seam. They looked very gay, but the company funds had to sweat in rigging them out. The officers paid an assesment [sic] for that purpose and the funds did the rest.'[3] The shakos referred to were dress French chasseur hats, made with an Americanized shako plate that featured a spread eagle over a hunting horn within an oak leaf wreath. A red, white and blue cockade was attached just under the eagle's head.

Coast Guards

Several states on the Atlantic seaboard organized local units to serve along the coast. These units generally did not last long, heavy artillery and naval units soon taking their places.

The 1st New York Regiment of Marine Artillery was organized from November 1861 to August 1862. It served in the Department of North Carolina soon after its first companies arrived in New Berne, North Carolina in April 1862, the last company arriving there in August. Later service was in the XVIII and X Corps. It was disbanded on 31 March 1863.

The Massachusetts Coast Guard started to be organized in April 1861. It was to serve not only as artillerymen, but to be equipped with a steamer and armed with breech-loading carbines, bayonets, cutlasses and Colt revolvers. Authority for the unit was passed from the state's governor to the Navy Department which let the unit die through benign neglect.

Pennsylvania's Independent Battalion (Marine Artillery) was mustered in to service in January 1862 and was sent to garrison Fort Delaware, on the Delaware River. On 17 February 1863 the battalion's four companies were merged into the 3rd Pennsylvania Heavy Artillery.

Officers of the 1st New York wore a double-breasted dark-blue frock-coat with Army artillery officers' shoulder-straps and sashes, Army officers' belt plates, Navy officers' swords and Navy officers' caps with a gold band and a crossed cannon and anchor badge. Trousers were plain dark-blue. Enlisted men wore a Navy jumper and shirt, gray trousers with red stripes, and a blue forage cap, with a blue jacket for cold weather wear.

The uniform of the Massachusetts Coast Guard was described in the 20 April 1861 issue of the *Boston Daily Advertiser* as ' . . . a suit of plain uniform of blue cloth, with bright buttons, similar in general style to the Navy, overcoat, with suitable cap, belt and accoutrements'.

Pennsylvania's Marine Artillerymen wore regulation heavy artillery uniform.

Indian Home Guards

Some Native Americans, Indians, rallied to the cause of the United States, while others sided with the South. In April 1861 Hole-In-The-Day, a Chippewa chief, offered himself and 100 of his braves for United States service. On 9 May the offer was declined by the Secretary of War, since the situation, he wrote, 'forbids the use of savages'.[7] As early as July 1861, however, Congress grew concerned about reports of Native Americans serving in the Confederate forces, and authorized the raising of Native American troops.

In 1862 three mounted Regiments of Indian Home Guards were raised from among the Cherokees, Creeks, Wichita and Seminoles. The 1st Regiment Indian Home Guards was organized in Leroy, Kansas on 22 May 1862. Serving in VII Corps, it fought a number of battles in Arkansas, Missouri, and the Indian Territories before being mustered out on 31 May 1865.

The 2nd Regiment Indian Home Guards was organized in Big Creek and Five-Mile Creek, Kansas from June to July 1862. Also in VII Corps, it saw essentially the same service as the 1st Regiment and was mustered out on the same date. The 3rd Regiment was organized on 16 September 1862 in Carthage, Missouri. Initially unattached in the Department of Kansas, it later served in VII Corps and saw much the same action as the first two regiments, being mustered out on the same day. Organization for a 4th Regiment was

Colonel Barton S. Alexander commanded the Volunteer Engineer Brigade in the Army of the Potomac. He wears the cap badge of the Corps of Engineers with canvas leggings designed to protect the trousers from mud when in the field. (Library of Congress collection)

Artificer David H. Cole, 50th New York Engineers, joined the regiment in December 1863 as a laborer and mustered out on 13 June 1865. Photographs indicate that New York's volunteer engineers wore a frock-coat that appears to be plain, although since yellow often photographed as if black, it may be that the regulation trim is not visible. (Author's collection)

started but never completed, and the officers and men served in other regiments.

There were no unique uniforms or insignia for the Indian Home Guards. Although issued regulation clothing, including the cavalry dress hat, most Native Americans wore a mixture of their own civilian clothing and regulation dress, often with war paint and ceremonial gear.

Corps of Engineers

In 1861 the Corps of Engineers was novel in that it contained more officers than enlisted men. The officers were trained engineers, responsible for the design and building of fortifications and other public works, superintending the passage of rivers, and surveying. There was only one company of enlisted men, which in 1861 was stationed at West Point, New York.

On 3 August 1861 Congress authorized an enlarged Corps to include a colonel, two lieutenant colonels, four majors, twelve captains, fifteen first lieutenants, fifteen second lieutenants, 40 sergeants, 40 corporals, eight musicians, 256 artificers, and 256 privates, giving a total of 49 commissioned officers and 600 enlisted men. The men were organized into a four-company battalion, the 1st Engineer Battalion. Two more companies were added to the 1st Engineers in late 1862, and another two companies in the winter of 1863/4.

The 1st Engineers worked on the defences of Washington until March 1862 when the battalion was assigned to the Army of the Potomac. Its officers and men served in more than 30 engagements with this army, including Seven Days, Antietam, Fredericksburg, Chancellorsville, Gettysburg, the Wilderness, and Petersburg. In July 1865 two of the Battalion's companies were disbanded and the others were sent to various posts around the country.

By September 1863, the Regular Corps of Engineers was headed by Brigadier General Joseph G. Totten, the Chief Engineer. Under him he had four colonels, ten lieutenant colonels, 20 majors, 30 captains, and sixteen first lieutenants. Several volunteer Corps of Engineers units were also raised.

The Army of the Potomac maintained the 1st Engineers as an independent command, but also had its Volunteer Engineer Brigade formed of the 15th and 50th New York Volunteer Engineer Regiments. These two regiments were formed in October 1861 and initially worked on Washington's defences before being assigned to the Army of the Potomac, becoming its permanent engineer force throughout its existence. They were mustered out in June and July 1865.

The 1st New York Volunteer Engineer Regiment was an eight-company regiment raised in late 1861–early 1862. It saw service along the Atlantic Coast in X Corps and then the Army of the James, ending up at Petersburg, while a detachment remained in the Department of the South. It was mustered out of service on 30 June 1865. A 2nd New York Volunteer Regiment was started but not completed, its officers and men ending up in the 15th New York Volunteer Engineer Regiment on 9 October 1863.

In the Army of the Cumberland, ordinary infantry troops were assigned to make up the Engineer Brigade and the Pioneer Brigade. On 30 April 1864 the Engineer Brigade included, the 13th, 21st and 22nd Michigan Infantry Regiments, and the 18th Ohio Infantry Regiment. The Pioneer Brigade had men assigned to it in the 1st and 2nd Pioneer Battalions and the Pontoon Battalion.

The Army of the Cumberland did have an independent engineer regiment, the 1st Michigan Engineers and Mechanics. It was mustered into service on 11 December 1861 with an initial strength of 1,032 officers and men. Two more companies of 150 officers and men each were soon added to the regiment. The 1st Michigan served in the Western Theatre, seeing action at Mill Springs, Shiloh, Corinth, Perryville, Lavergne, the siege of Chattanooga, the Atlanta campaign, the March to the Sea, and Bentonville. Original enlistments expired on 2 November 1864 and many officers and men went home then, but recruits kept the regiment up to strength. The final muster out came on 1 October 1865.

Another Western unit was Patterson's Independent Company of Engineers and Mechanics, also known as

---

Pickets on both sides salute a Union general

'One morning he [Major General U.S. Grant] started toward our right, with several staff-officers, to make a personal examination of that portion of the line. When he came in sight of the Chattanooga Creek, which separated our pickets from those of the enemy, he directed those who had accompanied him to halt and remain out of sight while he advanced alone, which he supposed he could do without attracting much attention. The pickets were within hailing distance of one another on opposite banks of the creek. They had established a temporary truce on their own responsibility, and the men of each army were allowed to get water from the same stream without being fired on by those on the other side. A sentinel of our picket-guard recognized General Grant as he approached, and gave the customary cry, "Turn out the guard – commanding general!" The enemy on the opposite side of the creek evidently heard the words, and one of his sentinels cried out, "Turn out the guard – General Grant!" The confederate (*sic*) guard took up the joke, and promptly formed, facing our line, and presented arms. The general returned the salute by lifting his hat, the guard was then dismissed, and he continued his ride toward our left. We knew that we engaged in a civil war, but such civility largely exceeded our expectations.'

(General Horace Porter, *Campaigning With Grant*, Indiana University Press, Bloomington, Indiana, 1961, pp. 10–11)

Morgan's Sappers and Miners. It was raised in Camp Haskins, Kentucky in October 1861 to build the camp's defences. It then served in the old XII Corps, on the Yazoo Expedition, and ended the war with the new XIII Corps before being mustered out in January 1865.

Edwin P Howland's Independent Company of First Grade Mounted Engineers, also known as the Battle Creek Engineers, was raised in Michigan on 16 September 1861 but saw little service before being mustered out on 8 January 1862.

The Engineer Regiment of the West, also known as Bissell's Engineers, was mustered into service in Missouri from mid- to late-1861. On 4 June 1862 it was placed into the Engineer Brigade with the 1st Michigan in the Department of the Mississippi. It was consolidated with the 25th Missouri Infantry on 17 February 1864, whereupon a 1st Missouri Engineers Regiment was formed from re-enlistees of the two units and recruits. Part of the District of Nashville, it was posted along the Nashville and Northwestern Railroad. It was mustered out on 22 July 1865.

Balz's Company of Sappers and Miners from Missouri saw little service, being mustered in at St Louis on 1 September 1861 and mustered out on 10 December. Wolster's Company of Sappers, Miners and Pontoneers, also from Missouri, saw service from 10 May to 1 September 1861.

The Independent Company Acting Engineers was mustered into service in Philadelphia on 9 August 1862. Its members were civil engineers, draughtsmen, artisans, mechanics and sailors. It worked on the defences of Washington, with detachments serving with the Army of the Potomac and the Army of the Cumberland. It was mustered out on 20 June 1865.

The Corps of Engineers was considered a staff department and its officers wore staff officers' uniform. Their cap badge was a silver turreted castle within a gold-embroidered wreath of laurel and palm. The turreted castle was also worn on the epaulettes.

Enlisted men wore the uniform of the heavy artillery with yellow trim, chevrons and trouser stripes. Their cap badge was the stamped brass turreted castle. They received a work costume consisting of white cotton overalls which covered the whole body. A narrow wristband fastened with one button, and the overalls were fastened at the back of the neck with two buttons. A pair of tabs on the small of the back, along the waist-line, was fastened with a buckle and tongue to adjust for size. From May 1861 to June 1865 the Army acquired 31,001 sets of overalls at its depots in Philadelphia and New York.

In 1861 enlisted engineers in Washington appear to have worn a blue shell jacket made with shoulder-straps, a standing collar, two buttons at each cuff and nine buttons down the front. Their trousers were the regulation dark-blue.

Some volunteers wore other uniforms. The 15th New York had New York state fatigue dress. Initially the 50th New York had a gray uniform trimmed with green cords. These uniforms rapidly wore out, however, and the common Engineer uniform in the field was the dark-blue fatigue blouse, sky-blue trousers turned muddy brown, and a black slouch hat with the Corps' cap badge on its front.

Corps of Topographical Engineers

The Corps of Topographical Engineers, which was entirely composed of officers, was responsible for reconnaissance, surveying and map production. According to the *Official Army Register* for August 1862, the Corps at that time was commanded by Colonel Stephen H. Long who had received his second lieutenant's commission on 12 December 1814. He commanded three lieutenant colonels, eight majors, ten captains, and thirteen first lieutenants. However, thirteen of these officers were serving in higher ranks in volunteer organizations. George Meade, for example, was listed as a major in the Corps but was serving as a major general and would soon command the Army of the Potomac.

Therefore, at times when large quantities of maps were needed, civilians were hired. Many of them were supplied to the Corps by the Superintendent of the Coast Survey. In action, it was found unrealistic to divide the duties of the Topographical Engineers and Corps of Engineers, and officers from both corps did essentially the same types of job. As a result, General McClellan merged the Topographical

Trains were virtually the Union Army's secret weapon for they enabled them to move troops and supplies rapidly and in large numbers. (Robert Kotchian collection)

Engineers and Engineers, both of which reported directly to his headquarters, into one organization within the Army of the Potomac's headquarters during the Antietam campaign. Topographical Engineers in the Western Theatre were assigned to headquarters of brigades and higher formations. This was largely due to the distances between headquarters, which were greater than those in the East. However, the combined Topographical Engineer/Engineer organization later became official as the Corps was merged into the Corps of Engineers on 31 March 1863.

As staff officers, Topographical Engineers wore the regulation staff officers' uniform. The cap badge was a gold-embroidered shield within a gold-embroidered oak leaf wreath. The gold-embroidered shield above the Old English letters 'T.E.' were also worn on the epaulettes.

Military Railroads

During the early months of the war Confederate raiders attacked Northern railroads, the arteries carrying men and supplies from industrial centres to the front lines, and by mid-1861 some 50 Baltimore & Ohio Railroad locomotives had been destroyed. This private company could not afford such losses. Therefore, on 31 January 1862 Congress created the US Military Railroads (USMRR) system and author-ized the president to nationalize any railroad or telegraph system, and this took the employees into federal service. Daniel C. McCallum was named the Military Director and Superintendent of Railroads and Colonel Henry Haupt was appointed Chief of Construction and Transportation. In fact, Haupt devoted his time to railroads in the Eastern Theatre while E. C. Smeed oversaw railroad construction in the Western Theatre.

Confederates get hats from train riders

'Hats, however, were not to be had until some inventive genius – a member of the First Texas, it was said – hit upon a novel scheme of securing them from the passengers on trains that passed through the [Texas] brigade camp.

'A high bridge across the creek insured the slowing up of the train at the point on the track most suitable for the execution of the scheme. A train due, all men in need of hats, and many that did not need them and only went along to assist their friends, would form in line on one side of the track, each with a brush made of the tops of young pines in his hands. As the train came by, a shout would be raised that, sounding high above the roar and rattle of the train, would excite the alarm or curiosity of the passengers who, springing to the windows, would stick their heads out, and as at that moment the brushes were brought into play, off the hats of the poor innocents would tumble.'

(J. B. Polley, *Hood's Texas Brigade*, Morningside Book-shop, Dayton, Ohio, 1976, p. 141)

At first, the USMRR simply managed railroads in recaptured Southern territory, but it soon built a short railroad between Washington and Alexandria, Virginia. Shortly after this it extended railroads further into Virginia to support the Army of the Potomac. Levies from volunteer regiments were formed into the USMRR Construction Corps to carry out the work. It was soon found, however, that soldiers did not do this kind of job well – they had joined up to fight, not lay ties and tracks – and civilian mechanics and laborers were hired to replace them. They were supervised by engineers and formed into divisions, gangs and squads. The lower formations were commanded by supervisors, foremen and sub-foremen, respectively.

In the Western Theatre, however, men of the 1st Missouri and 1st Michigan Volunteer Engineers did do some railroad construction work although most was done by the Con-struction Corps of the Military Division of the Mississippi, which at its high point had more than 6,000 men available. It was organized into 777-man-strong Divisions, each headed by the Divisional Engineer, aided by an Assistant Engineer. The Division had five subdivisions, each headed by a supervisor: Bridges and Carpentry Work, Track, Water Stations, Masonry and the Ox Brigade. Also, it had a train crew of conductors, brakemen, locomotive engineers, firemen and a cook. As in the rest of the USMRR Construction Corps, subdivisions were divided into gangs, each under a foreman, while each gang was divided into squads, each under a sub-foreman.

At its largest, the USMRR had 24,964 men operating 419 locomotives with 6,330 cars on 2,105 miles of tracks. They had built or rebuilt 137,418 feet of bridges and laid 641 miles of track. By executive order of 8 August 1865 roads and rolling-stock operated by the USMRR were ordered to be returned to their original owners. Lines that the USMRR had built were sold to private companies. As an odd side effect, railroads in the South that had been run by USMRR were in better shape when returned to their original Southern owners than they had been in 1861.

The USMRR was essentially a civilian organization and did not have uniforms or insignia. The letters 'U.S.M.R.R.' were painted on the sides of its rolling-stock. Military personnel assigned to it wore the uniforms of their old branches of service.

Signal Corps

Major Albert J. Myer, who before the war had experi-mented in the west with sending messages by waving flags, was appointed Signal Officer of the Army on 27 June 1860. In 1861 he gathered volunteers at a Signal Camp of Instruction at Georgetown, DC, to teach them to use flags, torches, or lights to pass messages over some distance. Seeing how well his system worked, Congress authorized formations of the Signal Corps on 3 March 1863, although it was not fully organized until August 1864.

The Signal Corps was to consist of the Signal Officer of the Army, who ranked as a colonel, a lieutenant colonel, two majors, who served as Inspectors, and a captain, the Chief

A Signal Corps officer's embroidered cap badge. The stars, left flag, centre of the right flag, and letters are silver; the

poles and right flag are gold; the centres of both flags are red. (Author's collection)

Captain Lucius M. Ross, 11th Illinois Infantry and Acting Chief Signal Officer, XVII Corps. Critically wounded at Fort Donelson, he served as Chief Signal Officer for the Army of Tennessee during the

siege of Vicksburg and was mustered out in 1864. The canteen behind him appears to be the type used in the Corps to hold turpentine which was burned in torches for night signalling. (Richard K. Tibbals collection)

Signal Officer, at each department, army and corps headquarters. The captain commanded from 10 to 20 signal parties in his Signal Department. Divisional departments, under a first lieutenant, were sometimes called Signal Detachments. Each signal party had a lieutenant, a sergeant and two to four privates. On 1 November 1864 the Corps mustered 102 Signal Corps officers, 66 Acting Signal Corps officers, 84 non-commissioned officers, and 1,266 privates.

Officers had to be well educated and officer candidate examination boards were set up on 28 April 1863 to screen potential officers for their knowledge in mathematics, surveying, natural philosophy, chemistry, topography, geography, field signals, field telegraphs and military procedures.

Although the Signal Corps did not operate telegraphic equipment, the Corps was initially responsible for maintaining telegraphs in the field. To do so, the Corps developed the use of wagons filled with telegraphic equipment to

accompany field headquarters. On 30 December 1862 the Office of the Signal Officer in Washington notified Captain Jesse Merrill, Acting Signal Officer at General Rosecrans' headquarters in Nashville, Tennessee, to expect three of these wagons. 'The organization you will need for each train will be four intelligent sergeants and twelve privates with one commissioned officer', Merrill was told. 'The sergeants need to be quick, intelligent, and of good education . . . The signal officer of the army deems it advisable that you inform General Rosecrans of the early expectation of these trains, that you apply for the additional details you will need to manage them, and that you cause the three officers and six of the sergeants to be ordered to report here where they will be instructed while the trains are preparing, and will then, so soon as they are completed, leave in charge of the trains to report to you at General Rosecrans' headquarters. Instruction in the use of these trains will now be made a part of the regular course at the Signal Camp of Instruction, which is now organizing on a more complete basis at Georgetown, D.C.'[4]

Signal Corps officers were staff officers and wore the regulation staff officers' uniform. Their cap badge, according to General Order 36, HQSC, 22 August 1864 was: ' . . . a gold-embroidered wreath in front, on black velvet ground, encircling crossed signal flags, with lighted torch, and supported by the letters "U.S." in silver in Old English characters. *Color of Flags*: one red, with white centre; the other white, with red centre, one-eighth of an inch square; length of staff, one and one-sixteenth inches.' In fact, physical examples of Signal Corps officers' cap badges differ

from that described in that the wreath and torch have been omitted and thirteen silver stars have been embroidered over the crossed flags. Sergeants also sometimes wore this cap badge.

Prior to these orders, Acting Signal Officers wore either the cap badge of their previous branch of service or the staff officers' 'US' within the wreath. They also often wore the sky-blue trousers of their previous branches of service instead of the staff officers' dark-blue trousers. Signal Officers wore the staff officers' cap badge and staff officers' trousers.

Enlisted men wore the mounted man's sky-blue trousers and dark-blue shell jackets without trim, but with two buttons at each cuff. On the left sleeve, according to General Order 36, they wore, 'Crossed signal flags, red and white, on dark-blue cloth. *Size of flags*: three-fourths of an inch square; centre, one-quarter of an inch square; length of staff, three inches. Sergeants will wear the designation of the corps placed in the angle of the chevron upon the left sleeve. Privates will wear the designation of the corps in the same position on the left sleeve as the chevron of sergeants.' Photographs, however, clearly show the sleeve insignia being worn on the right, not the left sleeve. There was no branch of service color given for the Corps; sergeants may have worn yellow chevrons as mounted personnel.

Military Telegraph Corps

In the chaos of the early months of 1861, on 19 April the War Department seized the commercial telegraph systems around Washington and control of them was given to Assistant Secretary of War Thomas A. Scott. Congressional approval was given to this action, and, indeed, the control of

Private Lyman B. Sweeney enlisted in the Signal Corps on 28 December 1863 and was assigned to the Middle Military Division. He was captured on Fisher's Hill, Virginia on 13 May 1864 and died in captivity in Millen, Georgia that November. (Author's collection)

A military telegraph wagon is being set up as Signal Corpsmen string telegraph wire to another telegraph wagon or a fixed base. This is another of A. R. Waud's drawings. (Harper's Weekly)

This military telegraph wagon was equipped as a mobile command centre – a far cry from the first days of the war when mounted couriers were the only means of battlefield communications. (Library of Congress collection)

every telegraph system in the US was assigned to the War Department. Anson Stager was commissioned a colonel and assistant quartermaster and appointed Military Superintendent of telegraphic lines on 25 November 1861. He reported directly to the Quartermaster General. Reporting to him were Assistant Superintendents assigned to each Military District who controlled all telegraphy in that district. They were assigned civilian operators and construction workers as needed.

The Corps was responsible not only for operating telegraphic equipment, but running its lines to where new stations would be needed. From its beginning until the end of the war, Stager figured that the Corps had built and operated about 15,000 miles of military telegraphic lines. The Corps was disbanded in 1866.

Quartermaster officers in the Corps wore their regulation staff uniforms. Operators and laborers who erected poles and strung wire were civilians and wore civilian clothing.

A Texan saves his friends from a booby-trap

'Wandering through the station and warehouse, filled with stores, a Texan came upon a telegraphic instrument, clicking in response to one down the line. Supposing this to be some infernal machine for our destruction, he determined to save his friends at the risk of his own life, and smashed the instrument with his heavy boots; then rushed among his comrades, exclaiming: "Boys! they is trying to blow us up. I seen the triggers a-working, but I busted 'em."'

(Richard Taylor, *Destruction and Reconstruction*, Longmans Green and Co., New York, 1955, p. 169)

However, as such they would not be treated as prisoners of war if captured in a raid, as happened particularly frequently in the Western Theatre. Therefore, in the Department of the Tennessee, General Order Number 14 dated 5 July 1864 authorized members to wear a uniform of a light-blue blouse with staff officers' buttons, light-blue trousers with a silver cord, one-eighth of an inch in diameter, down each leg, and a white or blue vest. An officer's forage cap with a silver cord around the band completed the uniform. This uniform, minus the cap's silver cord, became regulation in the Department of the Cumberland on 26 March 1864.

Army Aeronautics

During the decade before the war, ballooning had become quite popular across the country. When war broke out, professional balloonists, who had put on exhibition flights at events such as county and state fairs, offered their services to the Army. A number of offers were accepted and the men, balloons and gas-generating equipment were assigned to the Corps of Topographical Engineers, although the men remained civilians. Thereafter, Army Aeronautics became a bit of an orphan, being transferred to Quartermaster Corps command after the Peninsular Campaign and finally to control of the Corps of Engineers on 7 April 1863.

The first use of the balloon was from a tugboat deck off Newport News, Virginia. However, Thaddeus S. C. Lowe soon became the leading balloonist in the Army of the Potomac as Chief of Army Aeronautics, with the pay of a colonel. The War Department provided civilian labourers to his group which had some seven balloons in operation by January 1862. These observed Confederate camps in Northern Virginia. Lowe's balloons were equipped with telegraph keys and connected to the ground by wires so

The balloon Intrepid *is being inflated to reconnoiter the Battle of Fair Oaks. The small figure on the far right, resting his right hand on the balloon, is T. S. C. Lowe, Chief of Army Aeronautics. (Library of Congress collection)*

information could be transmitted immediately. Members of the Military Telegraph Corps manned the keys. On 24 September 1861, using this equipment, Lowe became the first aerial observer to provide indirect artillery fire control. Some balloon operators, when there was no time to set up telegraph lines, communicated with the ground by means of small coloured balloons during the day and flares at night. Balloons were even used as platforms to take photographs of enemy positions.

Army Aeronautics saw action during the Peninsular Campaign, where Lowe incorrectly reported that the Confederates had assembled too large a force to beat; missed Antietam; and were present at Chancellorsville, where they did not see much service. On 8 May 1863 Lowe resigned his position because of differences with General Hooker, and his unit was disbanded while the Army was en route to Gettysburg. After the war some Confederates suggested that it had been a mistake to disband the Army Aeronautics since their presence had been a bother to the Confederates who were forced to conceal their movements.

Strictly civilians, Army Aeronautics members wore ordinary civilian clothing. Some wore the brass company letters 'AD', for Aeronautic Department, or 'BC' for Balloon Corps on their caps, but these only drew amused remarks from soldiers and were largely discarded.

Medical Department

At the war's outset the Medical Department was headed by Surgeon General Thomas Lawson, who ranked as a colonel and had been the Surgeon General for almost 25 years. He died on 15 May 1861 and was replaced by someone almost as ancient, Clement A. Finley, who had spent 40 years on frontier posts in the Army. An incompetent, Finley was

retired on 23 April 1862 and replaced by a 35-year-old first lieutenant, William A. Hammond.

Besides the Surgeon General, the Department in 1861 included 30 surgeons, ranking as majors, and 84 assistant surgeons, who ranked as captains or first lieutenants, all in small post hospitals as the Army lacked any general hospitals. The Surgeon General was also in charge of the surgeon, assistant surgeon and hospital steward assigned to each volunteer regiment, as authorized by Congress in May. In July, Congress further authorized a surgeon to be assigned to each brigade headquarters, and an additional ten surgeons and 20 assistant surgeons were authorized for the Medical Department.

On 16 April 1862 the Medical Department was authorized to include an Assistant Surgeon General, a Medical Inspector of Hospitals, a number of medical purveyors and as many enlisted hospital stewards as the Surgeon General thought necessary. In early 1862 the Army built its first general hospital, two long, well-ventilated sheds in Parkersburg, West Virginia. By the last year of the war the Medical Department had built, and was operating, 204 hospitals with 136,894 beds across the country, even in far-away Las Vegas, Nevada.

On 21 May the Department established the Army Medical Museum to collect data for in-depth military medical studies. This included a Photographic Gallery in which were stored photographs of unusual injuries, the results of wounds, operations, and peculiar amputations, together with models of unusual surgical equipment and dressings. The department hired a number of Contract Photographers, stationed at various general hospitals, to take these pictures. Besides medical pictures, the photographers were also to take pictures of all men discharged on certificates of disability to ensure against fraud.

A Union soldier develops gangrene

'I was getting along nicely until December 27th, when the nurse lost my sponge, went for a new one, which happened to be a washed one. That day I got gangrene, the wound sloughed open the arteries, and that night I had two severe bleeding spells, the second of which had to be stopped by putting a roll of bandage over the artery, then a strap and buckle tight around the leg, and a screw above the roll, fastening it down to the artery. The next day gangrene developed, and by the 28th it had greatly extended, my right side, from the knee to the ribs being entirely black. The surgeon then decided on amputation, but I argued with them that I was already so weak from loss of blood that I could not stand an operation; that the gangrene being way up to my ribs, an amputation at the hip would be sure death ... I had written my mother, and expected to see her soon. Bob Strohm and Paul Knox came up to see what was the matter, and after I explained to them, and showed them my condition. Paul ... brought two revolvers, and threatened to shoot any one who would touch me before my mother came. The nurses were taken away from me, and my mother came, two days after. By that time the gangrene was reduced, and was confined only to the inside of the thigh, a piece of flesh sloughing out an inch deep, and the size of the whole hand, leaving muscles and nerves exposed. This commenced healing again in a few days.'

(Unk, *History of the 127th Regiment Pennsylvania Volunteers,* Regimental Association, Lebanon, Pennsylvania, 1902, pp. 252–4)

Surgeon Alexander Mott, from New York, wears the major's leaf of his rank with the US within a wreath cap badge which was regulation for medical officers. (David Scheinmann collection)

In July another 40 surgeons and 120 assistant surgeons of volunteers were authorized, but there were still simply nòt enough doctors to go around. Civilian doctors were hired to staff hospitals. Under a contract between them and the War Department, usually calling for pay of between $80 and $100 a month, these were known as Contract Surgeons. Their quality varied greatly.

Congress also authorized the recruiting of medical cadets. These were men between the ages of 18 and 23 who had had some medical training, but were not yet qualified. They had to pass an examination administered by a medical board, received the pay of a cadet of the US Military Academy and, in the military order of things, rated between a brevet second lieutenant and a sergeant major.

The lowest military grade in the Medical Department was that of hospital steward, a non-commissioned officer on a regimental or hospital staff. According to the 1861 *Army Regulations*, hospital stewards had to be 'temperate, honest, and in every way reliable, as well as sufficiently intelligent, and skilled in pharmacy'.

In early 1862 a civilian Hospital Corps was also formed. Corpsmen were to serve at general hospitals and perform nursing and related tasks. These men would be civilians unsuited for active duty, but intelligent and interested in the work. They were organized into 11-man squads, each under a squad chief. They did not turn out to be well motivated or intelligent men and by and large volunteers did much of the nursing.

In June 1861 the War Department authorized Dorthea Dix, who was known for her pioneering work in humane treatment of the insane, to review and have general supervision of all women nurses. Her title was Superintendent of Female Nurses. She insisted that nurses had to have certificates from two physicians and two clergymen, be over 30 years old, healthy, of good moral character, unattractive and modest in dress, and be able to cook. More than 3,000 women volunteers served as nurses in Union hospitals during the war. Many were nuns.

Assistant Surgeon William F. Reiber, 47th Pennsylvania Infantry, was mustered in on 30 October 1862 and resigned on 23 January 1865. His sword is of an obsolete style and probably was a family heirloom. The 47th saw service along Southern coasts, in the Red River campaign and in the 1864 Valley campaign. (Author's collection)

brigade's ambulances were then commanded by a second lieutenant; a division's ambulances by a first lieutenant; and a corps' ambulances by a captain. Two more ambulances were assigned to each corps headquarters.

Surgeons were placed together in divisional hospitals, replacing the earlier regimental hospitals where they became administrators, wound-dressers, or four-man surgical teams.

At Gettysburg, Dr Letterman commanded a Medical Corps that included 650 medical officers, 1,000 ambulances and almost 3,000 ambulance drivers and stretcher-bearers. The system stood the test of battle so well that it was adopted in other field armies. The Ambulance Corps of the Army of the Cumberland was set up on 2 January 1864, and this differed in that the lieutenant at divisional level also served as the train quartermaster. He had a staff that included a blacksmith and a saddler. On 11 March 1864 Congress authorized a permanent Ambulance Corps under Medical Department supervision and control which was essentially identical with the one that Letterman had set up. In the Army of the Potomac, that spring, it was made up of 60 officers and 2,300 enlisted men.

Surgeons and assistant surgeons were considered to be staff officers and wore the regulation staff officers' uniform. However, their sash was of emerald-green silk instead of crimson. Their epaulettes bore the Old English letters 'M.S.' within a wreath. In fact, many volunteer medical officers wore an emerald-green background on their shoulder-straps instead of the regulation black. Many, also against regulations, had the silver Old English letters 'M.S.' embroidered in the centre of their shoulder-straps and in the wreath on their cap badges. Their sword was the same M1840 used in the Pay Department, with the Old English letters 'M.S.' instead of 'P.D.'

As civilians, contract surgeons were not authorized uniforms, but most of them seem to have adopted a form of dark-blue frock-coat and trousers like that worn by officers, but without rank badges.

The medical cadet wore the same uniform as a staff lieutenant. His shoulder-strap consisted of a strip of half-inch-wide gold lace, three inches long, centered on a piece of green cloth three and three-quarters of an inch long by one and a quarter-inch wide. Medical cadets were not authorized to wear the black felt dress hat, but wore forage caps on all occasions.

Hospital stewards wore the uniform of the heavy artillery with crimson piping and a crimson stripe down each leg. The insignia worn on each sleeve, above the elbow, consisted of an emerald-green half-chevron, 1.75 inches wide, running obliquely downward from the outer to the inner sleeve seam. It was edged with yellow silk embroidery, an eighth of an inch wide, placed an eighth of an inch from each edge. In the centre was embroidered a yellow silk caduceus, two inches long, the head toward the outer sleeve seam. Their dress hat had mixed buff and green hat cords and a brass wreath around silver roman letters 'US' for a cap badge. While all hospital stewards were to wear this

What the Army in the field lacked was a systematic method of getting soldiers off the field into the doctors' hands. Bandsmen, and later pioneers, were originally given this task but proved to be not up to it, lacking training and motivation. In the Army of the Potomac on 2 August 1862 the Army's Medical Director, Dr Jonathan Letterman, set up a system that assigned privates to stretcher-bearer and ambulance driver details on a permanent basis. In the Army of the Potomac three light, two-horse ambulances commanded by a sergeant, would be assigned to each regiment. Two stretcher-bearers and a driver were assigned to each ambulance which was equipped with two stretchers. All the

'. . . the undress uniform of a private soldier, with a green half-chevron on the left fore-arm'.

Most nurses apparently wore plain, dark civilian dress. However, Eliza Wilson, who was present with the 5th Wisconsin Regiment in 1862, was described, ' . . . in clothes of such pattern as the military board have ordered for nurses in the army, which is the Turkish costume. The color is bright brown; no crinoline; dress reaches halfway between the knee and ankle; upper sleeve loose, gathered at the wrist; pantalettes same color, wide but gathered tight around the ankle; black hat with plumes; feet dressed in Morocco boots.'[5] Volunteer nurse Adelaide W. Smith wore a female version of an officers's dark-blue coat with infantry buttons and medical cadet shoulder-straps.

In at least one Western hospital, convalescents and men detailed from other units to serve as hospital attendants had to wear a white armband on their left sleeve in March 1864. In much the same way, musicians assigned in 1864 to stretcher-bearer detail in the 105th Illinois Infantry wore yellow armbands.

The first Ambulance Corps uniform was described in Special Order 147, Army of the Potomac, in August 1862: 'The uniform of this corps is – for privates, a green band, two inches broad, around the cap, a green half-chevron, two inches broad, on each arm above the elbow, and to be armed with revolvers; non-commissioned officers to wear the same band around the cap as privates, chevrons two inches broad, and green, with the point toward the shoulder, on each arm above the elbow.' This was revised in General Order 85, Army of the Potomac, issued in August 1863, which made the green cap bands and half-chevrons only an inch and a quarter wide. The same insignia was adopted in the Army of the Cumberland in January 1864. On 30 December 1862 ambulance corpsmen in XVIII Corps were ordered to wear a broad red band with a knot on the right side around the cap. In the XII Corps from 5 April 1863 Ambulance Corpsmen wore a 'green badge' on the left breast.

Chaplains

According to General Order Number 15 dated 4 May 1861: 'There will be allowed to each regiment one chaplain, who will be appointed by the regimental commander on the vote of the field officers and company commanders on duty with the regiment at the time the appointment is to be made. The chaplain so appointed must be a regularly ordained minister of some Christian denomination, and will receive the pay and allowances of a captain of cavalry.' General Order Number 49 of 3 August 1861, required the chaplain to report to the regimental commander, at the end of each quarter, on the unit's moral and religious condition and suggest ways to better the 'social happiness and moral improvement of the troops'. In April 1864 Congress further ordered them to perform regular church services. In late 1864 Lincoln began commissioning chaplains to serve at general hospitals, too.

Although Congress made it quite clear that none but

This hospital steward wears the dress coat with tabs to hold shoulder-scales on each shoulder; a veteran's service stripe on each cuff; and the chevron of his *grade. He wears the M1840 non-commissioned officer's sword on his waist-belt under the scarlet worsted sash. (Richard Carlile collection)*

uniform, in volunteer regiments there seem to have been considerable variants. Many wore a company grade officers' plain coat; the hospital steward of the 72nd Pennsylvania Infantry was photographed in that regiment's zouave jacket.

According to Surgeon General Orders, Circular 4 dated 5 June 1862, members of the Hospital Corps were to wear

Chaplain Sullivan H. Weston, 7th New York State Militia, wears his interpretation of the chaplain's uniform which is black with black velvet collar, cuffs, trousers stripes and covered buttons. The photograph was taken in Brady's Washington studio in April 1861 when the regiment was the first to arrive in that city. (Daivd Scheinmann collection)

periods, some 2,300 chaplains served in the Union Army, of whom 66 died in service and three earned Medals of Honor.

The first regulation uniform for chaplains was spelled out in General Order Number 102 of 25 November 1861. According to this, chaplains were to wear a plain black frock-coat with standing collar with one row of nine black buttons, plain black trousers, and either a black felt hat, plain dark-blue forage cap, or a plain *chapeau-bras* for dress. On 25 August 1864 General Order Number 247 added a ' . . . herring bone of black braid around the buttons and button holes' of the coat. Also, chaplains thereafter were authorized to wear the staff officers' cap badge.

However, chaplains actually wore a variety of clothing from civilian clerical garb to Rhode Island-issue overshirts to clothing that reflected their position as being equal to that of a cavalry captain. The arrival of the 127th Pennsylvania Infantry's chaplain was noted by the unit historian: 'Chaplain Gregg, arrayed in a new uniform, with prominent shoulder-straps, a regulation hat with a golden circlet, and a

regularly ordained ministers from Christian denominations could serve as chaplains, the 5th Pennsylvania Cavalry, which was heavily Jewish, appointed a rabbi as its chaplain in 1861. When discovered, he was forced to resign. On 17 July 1862, however, Congress changed the law to allow any rabbi, with proper recommendations, to become a chaplain.

Although many regiments lacked chaplains for long

A Union chaplain finds the range

'When the [2nd US Sharpshooters] regiment first got into the line, they found themselves confronted by a rebel battery, off to their left quartering, near a farm house, and the question was asked, "How far was it across the valley to that battery?" Chaplain (Lorenzo) Barber, who had his telescope rifle sights marked for every 50 yards, cried out: "Hold on boys, I'll tell you how far it is." He saw some Virginia razor-back hogs near the farm house. Raising his sights to 650 yards he fired at a hog and wounded it. The men could hear it give a good squeal clear across the valley. Word was at once passed along the regimental line, "650 yards". It was but a few minutes before the Confederate gunners limbered up and got out of range.'

(Captain C. A. Stevens, *Berdan's United States Sharpshooters in the Army of the Potomac*, Morningside Bookshop, Dayton, Ohio, 1972, p. 388)

Cadet George A. Custer, US Military Academy Class of 1861, wears the gray dress coatee, and an officer's dark-blue forage cap with a cap badge of a wreath around the letters 'USMA'. This was the most common cadet dress. The weapon is a Colt Root revolver. The photograph was taken in mid-July 1861. (National Portrait Gallery, Smithsonian Institution)

gold cord, sashed, belted and spurred, and with a sword dangling at his side, was seen approaching headquarters, but was then to them a stranger. [The] Lieutenant Colonel said, "What damn fool is that?"[6]

Military Academy

Leaders on both sides received their initial military training at the United States Military Academy at West Point, New York. In 1861 the Corps of Cadets consisted of 278 cadets in all four classes of the four-year school. Of these, 86 came from the South; 65 resigned rather than fight their states or were discharged for refusing to take the oath of allegiance, while 21 remained in the Army.

Students were basically trained as engineers, although they also studied such subjects as French, tactics, history, mathematics, and natural and physical sciences. To get these trained officers into the field when the war broke out, classes were accelerated so that two classes graduated in 1861 ahead of their normal time. Throughout the war, the Academy graduated 159 officers, while maintaining a student body of just over 200 cadets at any given time.

The Corps of Cadets was organized by classes. First Classmen, those who were to graduate that year, were in their fourth year at the Academy. Second Classmen, known as 'Cows', were in their third year; 'Yearlings' were in their second year; and 'Plebes' were in their first year.

When on parade all the cadets were organized as the 'Brigade of Cadets' with cadets serving as the Brigade's commander, adjutants, sergeant major, and similar ranks that paralleled those of the regular army.

All instructors were Army officers and wore the uniforms of their branch of service. For dress and most duties, cadets wore a cadet-gray tail-coat, cut single-breasted but with three rows of brass bullet buttons on the chest connected by narrow black silk cord that ended in crow's feet. Three inverted black silk cord chevrons ending in crow's feet with three ball buttons at the apex decorated each cuff. The standing collar also had a black silk cord with crow's-feet decoration. Gold lace chevrons worn points up marked the various cadet ranks. Trousers were gray with a black stripe in the winter and plain white in the summer. The sashes for cadet officers was of crimson silk. A black shako with the Corps of Engineers' brass turreted castle under a spread eagle was worn for dress (with black cock feather plumes being worn by cadet officers).

For undress, cadets wore a plain dark-blue forage cap. They also wore a gray uniform jacket decorated with black lace and two buttons on the standing collar and a single row of eight gilt Academy buttons down the front for riding and, later, classroom wear. On leave cadets could wear a company grade officer's uniform without any insignia. Graduated cadets also wore a unique class ring, the

The temporary quarters of the US Naval Academy at the Atlantic House Hotel, Newport, Rhode Island. Four boat howitzers decorate the front porch where once visitors rested in easy chairs. (Author's collection)

Academy being the first school in the country to adopt such a ring.

The Navy

The Navy was headed by Secretary of the Navy Gideon Welles who reported directly to the President, constitutionally the Commander-in-Chief. Welles was assisted by Assistant Secretary of the Navy Gustavus V. Fox, who handled the day-to-day military operations, and Chief Clerk William Faxton who was reponsible for all the Navy's business operations. On 2 March 1865 their staff was joined by that of the Solicitor and Naval Judge-Advocate General, an office created by Congress on that date.

The various functions needed to maintain an armed fleet at sea to protect US commerce were divided among various bureaux, each headed by a Chief of Bureau who was assisted by a chief clerk. According to a Congressional Act of 5 July 1861 the bureaux included, in order of seniority, the Bureau of Yards and Docks; the Bureau of Equipment and Recruiting; the Bureau of Navigation; the Bureau of Ordnance; the Bureau of Construction and Repair; the Bureau of Steam Engineering; the Bureau of Provisions and Clothing; and the Bureau of Medicine and Surgery. The additional task of 'Hydrography' was assigned to the Bureau of Ordnance in the following year when it was called the Bureau of Ordnance and Hydrography.

On 16 July 1862 Congress set the strength of the Regular Navy's commissioned officers at nine rear admirals, eighteen commodores, 36 captains, 72 commanders, 144 lieutenant commanders, 144 lieutenants, 144 masters and 144 ensigns. At the same time, ships were divided into four rates, the first rate ships to be commanded by commodores, the second rate by captains, the third by commanders, and the fourth by lieutenant commanders.

In many cases Navy officers reported to their bureau chiefs under a chain of command that paralleled the chain of command of line officers. These officers were said to have 'relative rank' with the line officers. The chiefs of the different bureaux ranked as commodores; fleet surgeons, paymasters and engineers ranked as captains as did surgeons, paymasters and chief engineers with more than fifteen years and naval constructors more than twenty years' service. Surgeons, paymasters and chief engineers with more than five years, and naval constructors, chaplains, and professors of mathematics with more than twelve years' service ranked as commanders. Surgeons, paymasters and chief engineers with less than five, and naval constructors, chaplains and professors of mathematics with less than twelve years' service ranked as lieutenant commanders, when that rank was introduced. Passed assistant surgeons ranked as lieutenants. Assistant surgeons, paymasters and naval constructors, first assistant engineers and secretaries ranked as masters. Second assistant engineers ranked as ensigns and third assistant engineers and clerks ranked as midshipmen. Officers wore the insignia of their relative rank but were called by their true titles.

Enlisted petty officer titles also explained the owner's function. Line petty officers, roughly in terms of precedence, included: masters-at-arms, boatswain's mates, gunner's mates, seamen gunners, chief or signal quartermasters, coxswains to commander-in-chief, captains of forecastle, quartermasters, coxswains, captains of tops, captains of afterguard, quarter-gunners, second captains of forecastle, and second captains of tops. Staff petty officers were: yeomen, surgeon's stewards (later apothecaries), paymaster's stewards (later paymaster's writers), masters of the band, schoolmasters, carpenter's mates, armourers, sailmaker's mates, painters, coopers, armourer's mates, ship's corporals, captains of hold, ship's cooks, and bakers. Ratings were: seamen, ordinary seamen, first class firemen, second class firemen, landsmen, coal heavers and boys. The enlistment of these ratings was set at three years by Congress on 5 August 1861.

The Navy's ships were distributed in squadrons, each commanded by a flag officer. As of 1 December 1862 the squadrons were: North Atlantic Squadron, which patrolled the Virginia and North Carolina coasts; South Atlantic Squadron, which patrolled the coast from the tip of Florida to the South Carolina border; East Gulf Squadron, which patrolled the eastern Florida coast; West Gulf Squadron, which patrolled from Pensacola, Florida, to Brownsville, Texas; Mississippi Squadron, which served on Western Theatre rivers; Pacific Squadron, which served in that ocean; East India Squadron, which hunted Confederate cruisers until disbanded 3 October 1864.

Squadrons varied in size according to ships and personnel available and size of job to be performed. The Gulf Squadron in 1861 had three frigates, two sloops of war and eight steamers. During the Siege of Vicksburg, the Mississippi River Squadron included twelve iron-clad steamers, two steamer gunboats, ten steamers, one mail boat, one hospital ship, four tugboats and a number of mortar boats.

Smaller units were known as Flotillas. The Potomac Flotilla patrolled the Potomac River between Maryland and Virginia, while the Western, or Mississippi, Flotilla operated in the upper Mississippi. It was later enlarged to become the Mississippi Squadron.

Regular Navy officers were trained at the US Naval Academy. Students there were ranked as midshipmen and were appointed by Congressmen or the President and had to be between the ages of 14 and 18. At the beginning of the war the Academy was situated at Annapolis, Maryland, but fearing possible attack by Confederates or their supporters, it was transferred to the Atlantic House Hotel at Newport, Rhode Island, where staff, Corps of Midshipmen and training ships arrived on 9 May 1861. Originally, training stressed seamanship and navigation, but during the war classes were started in such subjects as analytical geometry, calculus, mechanical drawing and chemistry. Shore drills included infantry and field artillery tactics. The Academy returned to Annapolis on 1 September 1865.

On 4 July 1864 Congress, in recognition of the growing technical nature of naval service, ordered that technically minded Academy recruits be designated 'cadet engineers' and trained with a view to commissioning as naval constructors or civil or steam engineers. They were to receive only two years of training before being commissioned, as opposed to the four years of training midshipmen received.

By law the Academy could have 515 midshipmen. In fact, numbers varied from 376 in December 1862 to 463 in November 1863. As in the US Military Academy, upper classmen were rushed to early graduation, but there were not nearly enough Navy officers; some 20 per cent had left the service to fight for the South in 1861. It was necessary to

This passed midshipman, marked by the collar badges, wears the short jacket rarely worn by any higher ranking officer. His cap is covered with a rubberized waterproof cover and his overcoat is on the chair next to him. (Author's collection)

give temporary commissions to volunteers, and on 24 July 1861 Congress authorized the Secretary of the Navy to appoint as many acting lieutenants, paymasters, assistant surgeons, masters, and master's mates as would be needed to man a greatly enlarged Navy during the war. These temporary commissions would go to men from the merchant marine who had passed examinations to show that they had the necessary qualifications for the job. In all, some 7,500 volunteers were appointed to acting rank. Also, on 31 July 1861 Congress authorized the Navy to have 80 surgeons and 120 passed and other assistant surgeons.

Two sailors photographed in Brooklyn in their winter dress. Each has a white handkerchief in his shirt pocket and white tape on the edge of his falling collar. The seated able seaman appears to be John D. Thomas who served in the USS Ohio *from September 1862 until transferring to the USS* Sabine *in October. Thomas was discharged as captain of the hold on 15 September 1863. He was commissioned an acting ensign on 23 December 1864. (Author's collection)*

To train these officers taken on 'temporary service', the Navy set up schools of gunnery and seamanship at different Navy yards, the first officer training schools in the nation's history. Navy yards were located at Boston; Mare Island, California; Pensacola, Florida: Philadelphia; Portsmouth, New Hampshire; New York and Washington. The Navy Yard at Portsmouth, Virginia, had been destroyed in 1861 but was later recaptured and rebuilt. In addition, a Navy Yard was set up at Mound City, Illinois, in 1862, initially under Army control, to build gunboats.

Naval hospitals were set up in Annapolis, Boston, Mare Island, Mound City, Norfolk, Philadelphia and Ware Island. Naval magazines were located at Portsmouth and Boston. A 'Navy Asylum' for retired Navy personnel had been long established in Philadelphia. Finally, an observatory existed in Washington under Navy Department control.

Throughout the period, enlisted Navy personnel wore the same uniform. It consisted of a dark-blue wollen overshirt, often worn over a red flannel undershirt, tucked into dark-blue woollen trousers. The shirt was worn with a large black handkerchief. At times, white tape or embroidery was used to decorate the shirt's large, falling collar and cuffs. A visorless cap completed the basic uniform. The name of the wearer's ship was often painted in gold or yellow on a band worn on the cap. A white cap cover was worn in summer months, as were straw sennit hats which had visors. A double-breasted jacket was worn in cold weather. In summer, the same uniform but made of white duck was authorized.

This petty officer is either a coxswain, captain of forecastle, mechanist, quartermaster or signal quartermaster, judging from the sleeve on which his insignia is placed. The straw hat was authorized in hot climates; the woven straw floor mat and painted background suggest that the photograph was taken in Havana, Cuba. (Author's collection)

The petty officer's sleeve badge. (Author's collection)

Rank for petty officers was indicated by a 3-inch-long eagle and anchor set one inch below a half-inch diameter star, worn on one arm above the elbow. Boatswain's mates, gunner's mates, carpenter's mates, sailmaker's mates, ship's stewards and ship's cooks wore this badge on their right sleeve; all other petty officers wore it on their left.

While the Navy officers' uniforms of the Civil War are easy enough to describe, their insignia was rather complicated, because three entirely different rank badge systems were employed during the period, each changing sleeve insignia and cap badges.

Most uniform worn during the period was undress uniform, the dark-blue frock-coat being double-breasted, with nine buttons in each row, a rolling collar, three small buttons on each cuff, and rank insignia worn on shoulder-straps and as gold lace around the cuff. Also a dark-blue double-breasted jacket with rolling collar was authorized for wear at sea, but was rarely worn by any officers above the rank of passed midshipman. Trousers were plain dark-blue. The cap was between 3.5 and 4 inches high, with a slight overhang, a gold cap band and a patent leather visor. In hot climates a straw hat was authorized. In foul weather a dark-blue, double-breasted overcoat with a rolling collar insignia was authorized. The same shoulder-straps as worn on the undress coat were worn on the overcoat. A dark-blue cloak was also authorized for boat or cold or wet weather wear.

The dress regulations allowed for a full dress uniform, although this was not required to be owned by officers appointed to temporary service after 6 September 1861. Its use was abolished on 31 July 1862. The dress coat was also dark-blue with two rows of nine buttons down the front. Its stand-up collar was edged in gold lace, with different widths for different ranks. Gold epaulettes were worn on each shoulder and rank lace around each cuff. A gold stripe, of the same width as the stripe around the front and top of the dress coat collar, was worn on each trouser leg.

Commander Charles H. Davis, who served as fleet captain in the capture of Port Royal before being transferred to command in Western waters, wearing the

1852 full dress uniform. This was a Brady studio photograph hundreds of which were sold to the public by Anthony in New York. (Atwater Kent Museum)

Captain Silas H. Stringman commanded the Atlantic Blockading Squadron. He is wearing the 1852 regulation

uniform with a regulation naval officer's sword. (Atwater Kent Museum)

Collar insignia on the dress uniform was as follows: a captain had an inch and a half-wide stripe around the top and front with a half inch wide stripe on the collar bottom. The captain's pocket flaps were also edged in ¾-inch lace; all lower ranks had plain pocket flaps. The commander's top collar lace was three-quarters of an inch wide around the top and front and the lieutenant's and master's was one inch wide. Passed midshipman had plain collars and midshipmen had a three-inch long embroidered foul anchor. Surgeons wore three sprigs of live oak embroidered in gold on their collars; paymasters wore a wreath of live oak; and engineers wore a silver anchor and gold wreath. The

engineer's dress coat was also single-breasted until 8 February 1861. Chaplains had a black single-breasted coat with black velvet-covered buttons. Professors and commodores' secretaries wore a plain single-breasted coat with eight buttons in front. Clerks wore a plain single-breasted coat with seven buttons in front.

The dress hat was the *chapeau-bras* bound in black silk lace with a black silk cockade, five inches wide, and five gold and five blue bullions at each end of the hat. Captains and commanders wore a loop of six gold bullions, half-an-inch in diameter, the two inner bullions twisted together, with a small Navy button at the lower end of the loop over the cockade. All other officers wore four bullions.

Insignia on the frog of the gold epaulettes worn on each shoulder indicated rank. A captain wore an eagle and an anchor with a silver-embroidered star above. An additional star was worn by every squadron commander as well as the Navy's senior captain. A commander wore two crossed foul

This lieutenant's hat sits on the table next to him and shows the cap badge clearly. He was photographed in Boston wearing the 1852 regulation uniform. (Atwater Kent Museum)

The clerk's uniform was marked by a single row of six buttons down the coat front and a plain wreath on the cap front. (Author's collection)

Because assistant surgeons, such as this man, did not receive the relative rank of master, indicated by the buttons on the cuffs, until March 1863, and the master's rank was indicated by gold cuff lace after May 1863, this photograph must have been taken at some time between those two dates. The cap badge identifies the man as a surgeon. (Atwater Kent Museum)

A master in the 1852 regulations had his rank indicated by the shoulder-strap lacking any insignia inside and four buttons around each cuff. The cap badge was the same as that worn by a lieutenant. (Author's collection)

This engineer is wearing a mixture of 1852 and 1861 regulation dress. His cap has the early badge with a silver anchor over a gold wheel within a gold wreath while his coat has the three cuff buttons of a first assistant engineer. His narrow shoulder-straps, however, were not authorized until 1861, probably dating this photograph to very early in the war. (Author's collection)

anchors; a lieutenant, one foul anchor; and masters had plain epaulettes. Surgeons had the Old English letters 'M.D.', while paymasters had 'P.D.' on theirs and chief engineers had a strap of silver with the gold-embroidered Old English letter 'E'.

Rank was also indicated by gold lace worn around the cuffs. A captain had three ¾-inch stripes of gold lace, a half-inch apart, with another stripe of gold lace that ran at right angles to the parallel stripes along the outer seam from the top lace stripe to the cuff edge. A commander had two stripes, a lieutenant one, a master had three medium-size Navy buttons, and midshipmen, plain cuffs. Officers from other bureaux wore the rank insignia of equivalent line officers, except engineers. A chief engineer had three large Navy buttons around each cuff; a first assistant engineer three medium-size Navy buttons, and second and third assistant engineers had plain cuffs.

Warrant officers – boatswains, gunners, sailmakers and carpenters – wore a silver anchor over two parallel gold bands on their cap. Their coat had a rolling collar with a false buttonhole of gold lace and three medium-size buttons on each cuff.

The plainer, undress coat had the same cuff insignia to indicate rank. Instead of epaulettes, officers wore shoulder-straps with gold embroidery against a dark-blue background with the same rank badge as worn on their epaulettes embroidered on the shoulder-straps.

The undress cap was also worn with a different cap badge for every rank. Line officers had their epaulette insignia embroidered within an oak and olive leaf wreath. Surgeons and paymasters had 'M.D.' and 'P.D.' within an oak leaf wreath. Engineers wore a gold-embroidered wheel under a silver-embroidered anchor.

On 25 February 1861 it was ordered that lieutenants serving as ships' executive officers were to wear a gold-embroidered star, 1.25-inch in diameter, half-an-inch above their gold cuff stripe. It was also ordered that all engineers wear a cross of four oak leaves within an oak and laurel leaf wreath for a cap badge. Chief engineers with more than twelve years' service wore the same cross within their shoulder-straps, with an acorn at each end and a half-inch wide stripe of gold on the top of the dress coat collar. First

Commander John L. Worden, who was wounded while commanding the USS Monitor *in its fight with the CSS* Virginia, *wears the cuff insignia of his rank, with its combination of narrow and wide stripes, authorized in 1862. (Author's collection)*

Following the creation on 16 July 1862 of the new ranks of rear admiral, commodore, lieutenant commander and ensign, a new system of rank insignia was adopted on 28 July. This gave a rear admiral a cap badge of a silver star within a gold laurel and oak leaf wreath. A captain wore the same cap badge he had worn before, but that cap badge was now worn by commodores, commanders, and lieutenant commanders as well. Lieutenants, masters, and the rank of ensign, which had been created on 16 July 1862, wore a diagonal silver foul anchor within the wreath. A midshipman wore a vertical anchor within the wreath, while masters' mates and other warrant officers wore the plain vertical anchor.

Lieutenant William F. Stewart, commissioned a lieutenant on 16 July 1863, wears the star of an executive officer above his cuff lace. At first assigned to the *Gulf Blockading Squadron, in 1863 he was serving in the USS* St Louis *on patrol duty in the Atlantic. (Author's collection)*

and second assistant engineers wore narrow shoulder-straps edged in gold with no insignia within them.

On 17 July 1861 Congress authorized a new grade when it called for 36 assistant paymasters. On 6 September 1861 it was stipulated that these new officers would have plain epaulettes and cuffs.

On 18 July 1862 Congress authorized warranted masters' mates to wear a single-breasted coat with nine buttons, and plain cuffs and a plain rolling collar. The cap bore a blue and gold band with a silver foul anchor cap badge. The shipped or rated masters' mates, who were enlisted rather than warranted, wore a waist-length jacket with two rows of six medium Navy buttons down the front. Their cap had the anchor but no bands.

Acting Master William P. McCann first served aboard the USS Sabine, *then became executive officer of the USS* Maratanza *in September 1862, hence the executive officer's star.* *In January 1863 he took over command of the USS* Hunchback, *then the USS* Kennebec *in October 1863. He wears an officer's boat cape. (Author's collection)*

The tedium of blockading duty

'Blockading was desperately tedious work, make the best one could of it. The largest reservoir of anecdotes was sure to run dry; the deepest vein of original humor to be worked out. I remember hearing two notorious tellers of stories being pitted against each other, for an evening's amusement, when one was driven as a last resource to recounting that "Mary had a little lamb."'

(A. T. Mahan, *From Sail To Steam, Recollections of a Naval Life*, Harper & Brothers, New York, 1907, p. 174)

Rear admirals had a silver star at each end of the shoulder-strap with a foul anchor in its centre. A commodore wore a silver star at one end and the foul anchor at the other. A captain wore an eagle on an anchor. All other ranks wore a silver foul anchor in the centre of the shoulder-strap with the insignia of the equivalent Army rank at each end, i.e., a silver oak leaf for a commander, a gold oak leaf for a lieutenant commander, two gold bars for a captain, one gold bar for a lieutenant and plain straps for an ensign. Lower ranks did not wear shoulder-straps.

Cuff lace became a mixture of quarter-inch wide and three-quarter-inch wide gold stripes. An ensign wore one narrow stripe; a master, one wide stripe; a lieutenant, one

Although not authorized until 14 January 1865, the sack coat was a popular fatigue dress among Navy officers. This man is wearing the plain uniform of a master's mate as war regulation from 31 July 1862 until 28 January 1864. (Author's collection)

This man's cap with two gold bands and a single anchor, combined with the plain coat, indicates that he is a boatswain, gunner, sailmaker or carpenter according to the 1862 dress regulations. (Author's collection)

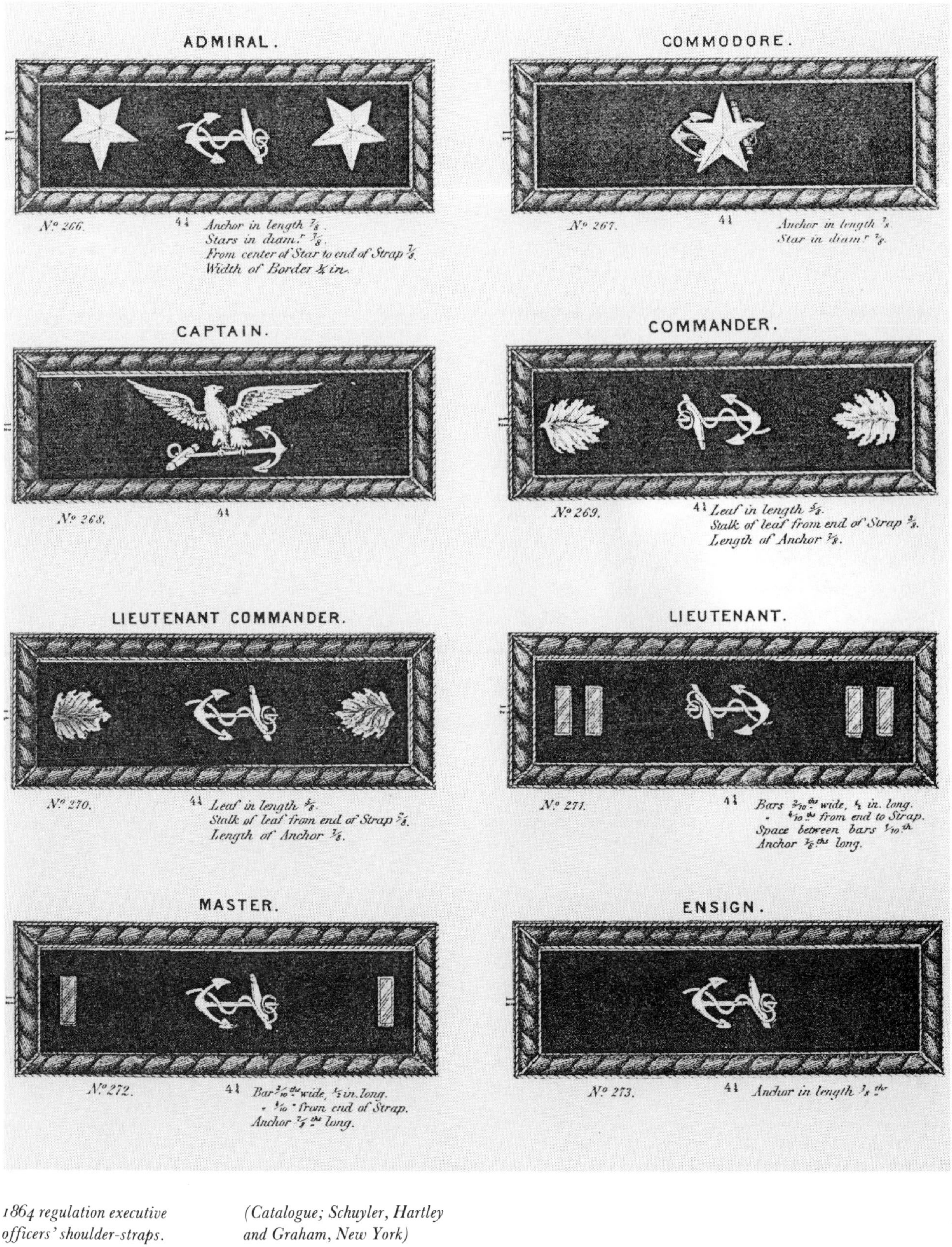
ADMIRAL.
No. 266.
4¼ Anchor in length 7/8.
Stars in diam.r 7/8.
From center of Star to end of Strap 7/8.
Width of Border ¼ in.
COMMODORE.
No. 267.
4¼ Anchor in length 7/8.
Star in diam.r 7/8.
CAPTAIN.
No. 268.
4¼
COMMANDER.
No. 269.
4¼ Leaf in length 5/8.
Stalk of leaf from end of Strap 3/8.
Length of Anchor 7/8.
LIEUTENANT COMMANDER.
No. 270.
4¼ Leaf in length 5/8.
Stalk of leaf from end of Strap 3/8.
Length of Anchor 7/8.
LIEUTENANT.
No. 271.
4¼ Bars 2/10ths wide, ½ in. long.
" 4/10ths from end to Strap.
Space between bars 1/10th.
Anchor 7/8ths long.
MASTER.
No. 272.
4¼ Bar 3/10ths wide, ½ in. long.
" 3/10 " from end of Strap.
Anchor 7/8ths long.
ENSIGN.
No. 273.
4¼ Anchor in length 7/8ths

1864 regulation executive officers' shoulder-straps. *(Catalogue; Schuyler, Hartley and Graham, New York)*

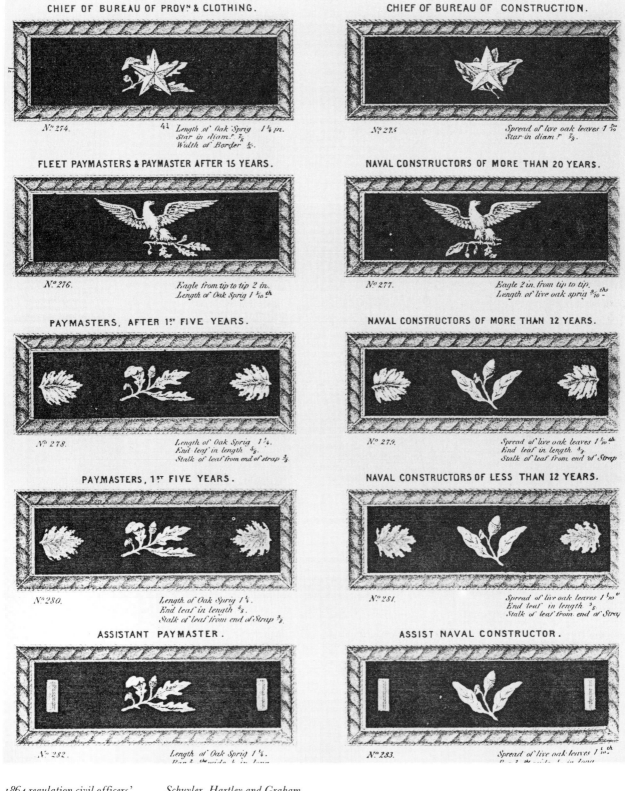

CHIEF OF BUREAU OF PROV.ⁿ & CLOTHING.

N.º 274. Length of Oak Sprig 1¼ in.
Star in diam.ʳ ⅞.
Width of Border ½.

CHIEF OF BUREAU OF CONSTRUCTION.

N.º 275. Spread of live oak leaves 1¾.
Star in diam.ʳ ⅞.

FLEET PAYMASTERS & PAYMASTER AFTER 15 YEARS.

N.º 276. Eagle from tip to tip 2 in.
Length of Oak Sprig 1⁴⁄₁₀ᵗʰ

NAVAL CONSTRUCTORS OF MORE THAN 20 YEARS.

N.º 277. Eagle 2 in. from tip to tip.
Length of live oak sprig ⁹⁄₁₀ ᵗʰ

PAYMASTERS, AFTER 1ˢᵗ FIVE YEARS.

N.º 278. Length of Oak Sprig 1¼.
End leaf in length ⅜.
Stalk of leaf from end of strap ⅔

NAVAL CONSTRUCTORS OF MORE THAN 12 YEARS.

N.º 279. Spread of live oak leaves 1⁴⁄₁₀ᵗʰ
End leaf in length ⅜.
Stalk of leaf from end of Strap

PAYMASTERS, 1ˢᵗ FIVE YEARS.

N.º 280. Length of Oak Sprig 1¼.
End leaf in length ⅜.
Stalk of leaf from end of Strap ⅜.

NAVAL CONSTRUCTORS OF LESS THAN 12 YEARS.

N.º 281. Spread of live oak leaves 1⁴⁄₁₀ᵗʰ
End leaf in length ⅜.
Stalk of leaf from end of Strap

ASSISTANT PAYMASTER.

N.º 282. Length of Oak Sprig 1¼.

ASSIST NAVAL CONSTRUCTOR.

N.º 283. Spread of live oak leaves 1⁴⁄₁₀ᵗʰ

*1864 regulation civil officers'
shoulder-straps. (Catalogue;* *Schuyler, Hartley and Graham,
New York)*

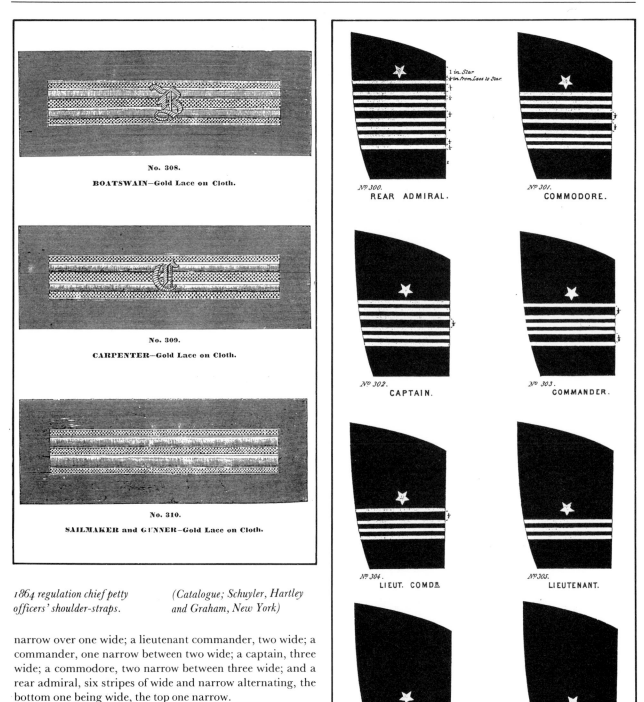

No. 308.
BOATSWAIN—Gold Lace on Cloth.

No. 309.
CARPENTER—Gold Lace on Cloth.

No. 310.
SAILMAKER and GUNNER—Gold Lace on Cloth.

1864 regulation chief petty officers' shoulder-straps. (*Catalogue; Schuyler, Hartley and Graham, New York*)

Nº 300. **REAR ADMIRAL.**

Nº 301. **COMMODORE.**

Nº 302. **CAPTAIN.**

Nº 303. **COMMANDER.**

Nº 304. **LIEUT. COMDR**

Nº 305. **LIEUTENANT.**

Nº 306. **MASTER.**

Nº 307. **ENSIGN.**

1864 regulation officers' cuff stripes. (Catalogue; Schuyler, Hartley and Graham, New York)

narrow over one wide; a lieutenant commander, two wide; a commander, one narrow between two wide; a captain, three wide; a commodore, two narrow between three wide; and a rear admiral, six stripes of wide and narrow alternating, the bottom one being wide, the top one narrow.

Officers of equivalent rank wore their bureau insignia on their cap badge, within the wreath, and on their shoulder-straps. Medical officers wore an oak leaf cap badge but plain shoulder-straps. Paymasters wore a sprig of three oak leaves and two acorns. Engineering officers wore a cross of four oak leaves. Naval constructors wore a sprig with two oak leaves and two acorns. Chaplains wore a Latin cross. Professors of mathematics wore the Old English letter 'P' in silver on a gold disc. Secretaries wore the silver Old English letter 'S'.

1864 regulation officers' cap badges. (Catalogue; Schuyler, Hartley and Graham, New York)

For some reason, this system did not please, and it was replaced by yet another rank badge system on 28 July 1864. This directed all line officers below the rank of rear admiral to wear the same cap badge, a silver vertical foul anchor within a wreath. The gold cap band was ordered to be removed. However, for each line officer, a gold star, one inch in diameter, was to be placed a quarter-inch above the top lace stripe on each cuff. All cuff lace stripes were a quarter-inch wide and one lace stripe was added for each rank, although spacing between the stripes changed. A rear admiral wore eight stripes, the bottom one a half-inch from the next, then three a quarter-inch apart, then a half-inch, then three more a quarter-inch apart, then a half-inch until the top one. A commodore had two groups of three, closely grouped and separated by a single stripe a half-inch from the top and bottom group. A captain wore two sets of three. A commander wore a group of three, a half-inch from one next to the cuff and a half-inch from the one over it. A lieutenant commander wore a set of three on the bottom and then a half-inch to a single stripe. A lieutenant wore a group of three; a master, two; an ensign, one.

Shoulder-straps remained what they were in 1862, although the design of the captain's eagle was changed to resemble more closely that worn by the Army's colonel. Also the warrant officers received four-inch-long gold stripes three-quarters of an inch wide for shoulder-straps. Those

Lieutenant Commander Richard W. Meade, Jr., wears the 1864 rank insignia with epaulettes for a full dress uniform. (US Army Military History Institute)

worn by boatswains and gunners had the Old English 'B' or 'G' on their centres. All warrant officers, midshipmen, boatswains and gunners were to wear the line officers' star above their cuffs and nine buttons on each row of their coat front. Masters' mates were allowed the line officers' star but retained the single-breasted coat.

On 14 January 1865 insignia for the newly created rank of vice admiral was authorized. This consisted of three silver stars over the line officers' cap badge and three silver stars over the foul anchor on the shoulder-strap. The cuff insignia was a piece of two-inch gold lace with two half-inch stripes at half-inch intervals over it. With this came a change in the rear admiral's cuff lace, giving him the two-inch stripe and one half-inch stripe.

The sack or pilot coat, which was already being worn by Navy officers, was officially authorized on the same date. It was similar to the Army's body coat or fatigue blouse and had five buttons down the front. It could be worn with any combination of cuff lace and shoulder-straps.

Marine Corps

The US Marine Corps was created to serve as the police of the US Navy and as naval infantry for amphibious landings. Its officers and men reported to the Colonel Commandant who, in turn, reported to the Secretary of the Navy.

On 25 July 1861 Congress set the authorized strength of the US Marine Corps at one colonel commandant, one colonel, two lieutenant colonels, four majors, one adjutant and inspector, one paymaster, one quartermaster, two assistant quartermasters, 20 captains, 30 first lieutenants, 30 second lieutenants, one sergeant major, one quartermaster sergeant, one drum major, one principal musician, 200 sergeants, 220 corporals, 30 musicians in the band, 60 drummers, 60 fifers and 2,500 privates. In fact, at the beginning of the war the Corps consisted of 1,892 officers and men.

While all the Corps' field officers remained loyal to the Union in 1861, half the captains and two-thirds of the lieutenants resigned to fight for the South. After strenuous recruiting, however, the Commandant was able to report by October 1861 that the Corps consisted of 2,964 officers and men.

The Corps was usually sent in small detachments to serve aboard the Navy's ships and at installations such as Navy yards. At sea they served as the ship's police, manned a

Gulf Squadron officers in 1864 are Lieutenant Commander George A. Bigelow (left), commander of the USS Calhoun and Surgeon Thomas M. Potter. (Author's collection)

Acting Gunner William E. Keyes served aboard the USS Chillicothe in Western waters in 1864–5. He wears the plain gold shoulder-strap of his rank. (Author's collection)

Acting Assistant Surgeon A. H. McGuinn was photographed in Cairo, Illinois, site of the important Western naval base.

His cap with its surgeon's cap badge sits on the chair next to him. (Author's collection)

cannon or two, sniped at enemy sailors with their rifle-muskets and participated in any landings the crew might make. They could also serve under Army control during land operations. A Marine battalion served under Army command during the First Bull Run campaign. It consisted of 350 officers and enlisted men, mostly new recruits, and suffered nine killed, nineteen wounded and sixteen missing.

The Corps participated in every naval action along the coast and rivers. Marines even helped put down the New York draft riots. By the war's end, the Corps had reached a peak strength of 4,167 officers and men. In the four years it

had lost 148 officers and men killed, and 312 dead of other causes. However, the Corps was not a major contributor to the Union's success. In 1864 a resolution was introduced in Congress to merge the Corps into the Army. It was tabled after some debate.

The officers' dress frock-coat was dark-blue with two rows of eight buttons on the chest. The Commandant was distinguished by wearing his buttons in pairs, all other ranks having evenly spaced buttons. Field officers wore four false button holes of gold lace on each cuff; captains and staff officers wore three; and lieutenants wore two. All ranks had a standing collar edged in scarlet with two false button holes of gold lace on each end. A gold epaulette was worn on each shoulder with a silver bugle, the Old English letter 'M' in its loop, on the crescent and a rank badge on the strap. Rank badges were the same as Army rank badges, save that they were embroidered in silver; a major had no rank badge on his epaulette. Epaulette fringes varied according to rank: field officers had half-inch wide fringes, three and a half inches long; captains and staff officers had quarter-inch-wide fringes two and a half inches long; lieutenants wore one-eighth of an inch fringes two and a half inches long.

Trousers were sky-blue with a scarlet welt down each leg. Officers not serving with troops, i.e., staff officers, wore

Second Lieutenant Julius E.
Meire served from 1855 to 1861
when he resigned to join the
Confederate Marine Corps. He
holds his cap with its silver Old

English letter 'M' within the
horn; a Russian knot is worn on
each shoulder. (Offiical USMC
photograph)

silver Old English letter 'M' in its loop, centred on the shield.

For dress, the sword-belt was white with the regulation Army officer's belt plate. The sword was the Army M1850 foot officers' sword worn with a gold sword knot. The sash was of crimson silk (Commandant, buff silk) and was knotted over the left hip. As in the Army, the Officer of the Day wore his sash across the chest, from the right shoulder to the left hip.

For undress, officers wore the same trousers but had the choice of three coats. The first was a plain dark-blue double-breasted frock-coat with a standing collar and three small buttons at each cuff. Rank was indicated by a gold Russian shoulder-knot about seven inches long. Those worn by field grade officers had twisted straps of four gold cords; those by captains and lower ranks, three gold cords. The same silver insignia worn on the epaulette strap was worn at the end of the shoulder-knot. A similar white linen coat with shoulder-knots was allowed shipboard wear in hot weather. The shoulder-knot was also worn on the fatigue jacket. This was buttoned down the front with a single row of twelve small buttons. It was lined with scarlet and edged all around in gold lace a half-inch wide, with gold lace forming pointed cuffs. At times these cuffs were as much as a foot long.

The undress cap was a dark-blue French-style kepi with three rows of narrow black silk worn up the front and back and up the sides. As well, a quatrefoil black silk knot was worn on top of the cap. The badge was a gold-embroidered bugle horn, the silver Old English letter 'M' in the centre of its loop over scarlet backing.

Although belts were still to be white, in practice the Army officers' black sword-belt was commonly worn by Marine officers in undress wear. Also Marines wore the Army officers' overcoat, but lined in scarlet, the Commandant wearing five braids on the cuff.

The enlisted men's dress uniform was identical with that worn by officers save that the lace was yellow worsted tape rather than gold and only seven buttons were worn on each row down the chest. Members of the Marine band and musicians wore this coat in scarlet instead of dark-blue. The Sergeant Major of the Corps, quartermaster sergeants, and drum and fife majors wore four lace loops on each cuff; sergeants wore three; corporals and below wore two. Non-commissioned officers wore the same chevrons as did their Army counter-parts, but theirs were made of yellow worsted or silk edged with red and the chevrons were worn points up rather than down. The drum major wore three chevrons and a tie with a star in the centre in silk. These chevrons were also worn on overcoat cuffs. Brass shoulder-scales of the Army pattern, but made with yellow detachable fringe and a strap half an inch longer than the Army scales, were worn on each shoulder. The fringe was three and a half inches long and 0.375 inches wide for senior sergeants, a quarter of an inch wide for sergeants, and 0.0625 inches for corporals and below. First sergeants and above wore a red worsted sash with a white belt, an Army officers' belt plate, and M1850 Army foot officers' sword.

dark-blue trousers with a scarlet welt. In hot weather white linen trousers were authorized.

A French pattern *chapeau-bras* was authorized for dress. It was five and a half inches tall, with a black cockade and gold lace loop worn on the left, and a gold fringe tassel at each end. The Commandant wore a yellow swan feather plume, other officers wore red cock or vulture feather plumes. For dress, officers were also authorized to wear shakos with gold net pompoms. The black shako had a large cap badge with a gold wreath around a national shield with a bugle horn, the

This squad of Marines in full dress at the Washington Navy Yard is commanded by a sergeant (left). The yellow in their fringe and other trim has photographed black. (Library of Congress collection)

These Marines on duty at the Boston Navy Yard wear summer-weather white trousers with fatigue frock-coats. (US Army Military History Institute)

Winter trousers were sky-blue with a narrow scarlet cord worn by the sergeant major, quartermaster sergeants, the drum major, and musicians. Plain white linen trousers were worn by all enlisted grades in hot weather. The hat was the same shako as worn by officers, with a red pompom, except for the drum major who wore an astrakhan busby with a red pompom and bag hanging down the left side and a yellow cord and tassel.

For fatigue, enlisted men wore a single-breasted frock coat, its standing collar edged in scarlet along the bottom, and seven buttons down the front. Two small buttons were at each cuff, with two large buttons at the rear. The officers' kepi was also worn, but without black silk decoration, and with a brass stamped bugle horn over a piece of scarlet leather backing in the loop and the silver Old English letter 'M'. Marines could wear a pullover-style dark-blue flannel overshirt, fastened with four small buttons down the front. It was only a little shorter than the frock and was worn with chevrons over a white cotton shirt. This 'fatigue sack' was worn by Marines at sea, on parades and by shore parties.

The enlisted Marines' overcoat was of blue/gray mixture, single-breasted, with seven large buttons down the front. A detachable cape came down to the upper ends of the five-inch, turn-over cuffs. A heavier greatcoat was occasionally issued to Marines at sea.

Marine equipment was similar to that used by soldiers, but belts were of white buff leather and a plain rectangular belt-plate was worn. Marines were issued with a double-bag pattern knapsack that was unique to the Corps, marked 'U.S.M.' in an oval on the back.

Mississippi Marine Brigade

Neither fish nor fowl, the Mississippi Marine Brigade was an Army formation created to serve on the Western rivers. On 1 November 1862 it was authorized to consist of one infantry regiment, one light artillery battery and four cavalry squadrons for service under Brigadier General Alfred W. Ellet with the Mississippi ram fleet which had been built by the Army. Among other inducements, the unit offered prospective recruits the chance of service without any foot-slogging or rough camping, as they would be quartered in riverboats. By March 1863 the Brigade mustered 527 infantrymen, 104 artillerymen with six guns, and 368 cavalrymen, with another 200 recruits ready for assignment. Control of the Brigade passed to the Navy when that service took over riverine warfare, but was returned to Army control in October 1863. It was disbanded in August 1864.

Uniform was standard dress according to the wearer's Army branch of service. Caps, however, were different, being made like those worn by a Navy officer with a wide green band edged with gold lace. Photographs of Brigade members show cap badges including two foul anchors for officers, an infantry bugle for infantrymen, and crossed cannon for artillerymen.

Revenue Cutter Service

In peacetime the Revenue Cutter Service, sometimes called the Revenue Marine Service or Revenue Marine Cutter Service, came under the civilian command of the Secretary of the Treasury. Its duties were to enforce customs regulations and see that import duties were paid; enforce immigration laws, especially on the west coast where Chinese were being imported as cheap labour; assist distressed mariners at sea, and ensure that all vessels complied with navigation regulations. They also provided ceremonial crews for the official greetings accorded to visiting dignitaries arriving by ship.

To accomplish these duties the Service had, at the outbreak of the war, 24 revenue cutters dispersed throughout the country's ports. All but one were wooden sailing vessels, mostly crewed by one or two officers and six or seven ratings. Only one, *Harriet Lane*, was a steam-driven side-wheeler. When hostilities broke out, the Service was almost immediately reduced, *William Aiken, Cass, Washington, Robert McClelland, Henry Dodge* and *William J. Duane* being either captured or turned over to Southern officials, leaving only eighteen cutters on duty.

In time of war command of the service and its individual cutters could pass from the Treasury Department to the Navy Department if necessary, and on 5 April 1861 *Harriet Lane* was transferred to Navy control. Control of the remaining cutters, however, together with some newly purchased ones and some transferred from the Coastal Survey, remained in Treasury Department hands so the Service had to expand its fleet. In June a board consisting of a Service captain, a Navy lieutenant, and a merchant marine captain was convened in New York to examine

The Revenue Cutter Caleb Cushing *is blown up by a*   *Confederate raiding party in Maine. (*Harper's Weekly*)*

prospective candidates for Service third lieutenant commissions in navigation and seamanship. Also, larger cutters had a squad of ratings assigned as 'marines' who were responsible for the cutter's defence if needed. A drummer and a fifer were also added to each crew. These new officers and units were needed; by April 1865 the Service had 35 cutters, mostly steam-propelled.

Jerry J. Benson was commissioned a second lieutenant in the Revenue Marine on 12 November 1861 and was promoted to first lieutenant on 11 July 1864. He is wearing the Service's 1862 uniform. Benson served on various cutters during the war, including the Floyd, Toucey *and* Dobbin. *(Author's collection)*

On 4 February 1863 Congress ruled that Service officers had equivalent rank with Navy officers. Captains rated with lieutenant commanders; first lieutenants with lieutenants; second lieutenants with masters; and third lieutenants with passed midshipmen. The only other type of officer in the Service was the engineering officer; Congress did not assign them relative rank. However, as indicated by cuff insignia, chief engineers rated with first lieutenants; first assistant engineers, with second lieutenants; and second assistant engineers, with third lieutenants. Enlisted ranks were confined to petty officers, seamen, firemen, coal-passers, stewards, cooks and boys.

Revenue Cutters in 1861 were as follows:

Cutter	Station
Andrew Jackson	Eastport, Maine
Caleb Cushing	Portland, Maine
Morris	Boston, Massachusetts
James Campbell	New London, Connecticut
Harriet Lane	New York, New York
Walter B. Forward	Wilmington, Delaware
Philip Allen	Baltimore, Maryland
William J. Duane	Norfolk, Virginia
William Aiken	Charleston, South Carolina
James C. Dobbin	Savannah, Georgia
John Appleton	Key West, Florida
Robert McClelland	New Orleans, Louisiana
Washington	New Orleans, Louisiana
Henry Dodge	Galveston, Texas
William L. Marcy	San Francisco, California
Joseph Lane	Astoria, Oregon Territory
Jefferson Davis	Port Townsend, Washington Territory
Howell Cobb	Oswego, New York
Jeremiah S. Black	Erie, Pennsylvania
Aaron V. Brown	Milwaukee, Wisconsin
Isaac Toucey	Michilimackinac, Michigan
John B. Floyd	Marquette, Michigan

Ratings throughout the period wore essentially the same dress as did those of the Navy. Throughout 1864 their overshirt or 'frock' was to have a collar and falling collar of a facing colour; dark-blue on the summer white frock and white on the dark-blue winter frock. Trousers were dark-blue or white, according to the season, and a visor-less mustering cap or straw sennet hat was worn as needed. Petty officers, who were not given a unique insignia, this being thought unnecessary in the small craft the Service used, were allowed a blue cloth jacket with nine Revenue buttons on each lapel, three under each pocket flap, and three on the cuff, with white or blue trousers according to the season.

On 20 August 1861 Service Captain William A. Howard, who was then in overall charge of arming, equipping and assigning cutters to their stations, wrote to the Secretary of the Treasury that the Service's uniforms were obsolete. Moreover, he said, no two officers wore the same uniform. The uniform of 1861 included a dark-blue, double-breasted

This Revenue Marine second assistant engineer is wearing the 1864 regulation uniform. The cap badge includes a wheel within a wreath for engineers;

executive officers would wear a shield over the cuff lace in much the same way as Navy executive officers wore a star. (Author's collection)

Two rows of nine Service buttons were worn down the front of the Navy officers' frock-coat. Rank was indicated by two stripes of gold lace around each cuff for a captain and two gold epaulettes on dress. For undress, a captain had Navy officers' shoulder-straps with two gold crossed foul anchors instead of the epaulettes. A first lieutenant had one stripe on each cuff and a single foul anchor over a shield and two bars at each end of the shoulder-strap for undress. A second lieutenant had the same, but with only one bar at each end of the shoulder-strap. A third lieutenant had no bars on his straps. A chief engineer had a gold wheel surmounted by an anchor on his shoulder-straps and a single stripe around each cuff. A first assistant engineer had three buttons around each cuff and lacked the anchor on his shoulder-straps. A second assistant engineer had plain shoulder-straps.

The hat was the Navy officers' model with a gold lace band an inch and a half wide and cap badge featuring the Treasury Department shield within a gold wreath. A lieutenant had a foul anchor over the shield as well. An engineer had a cap badge featuring gold wheel within a wreath; a chief engineer also had a star over the wheel. Officers gained a gold lace stripe down each leg in dress trousers, but wore plain trousers for undress. Also the distinctive sword was replaced by the Navy officers' sword, although engraving on it had the letters 'USRM' instead of 'USN'.

On 20 August 1864, further in an endeavour to bring the Service into line with Navy practices, the insignia was changed, to give each captain four half-inch-wide stripes on each cuff under a gold-embroidered Treasury Department shield, much as Navy line officers wore a gold star over their cuff stripes. First lieutenants wore three stripes; second lieutenants, two, and third lieutenants, one. Engineer officers also wore one, two, or three stripes, without the shield, according to their rank. Engineer officers all wore a gold-embroidered wheel within a wreath for their cap badges. Gold lace was removed from cap bands.

Civilian Organizations

Sanitary Commission

No sooner had the Civil War started than civil aid groups began to spring up in Connecticut, Massachusetts, New York and Ohio, inspired by the activities of Florence Nightingale and other civilians in the Crimea. A group of doctors and reformers met on 12 June 1861 to establish a national aid group which they called the 'Sanitary Commission'. They became its board of commissioners. On 19 June they appointed a secretary and chief executive officer, Frederick Law Olmsted. Several board members made up the smaller Executive Committee which took over Commission administration in 1862.

Olmsted created a modern, professionally managed organization. Initially he divided the Commission into two parts, inquiry and advice. He hired General Inspectors and Special Inspectors, mostly doctors, and helpers, called

tail-coat with eight buttons down each row. Captains were marked by a row of four buttons parallel with the edge of each cuff; lieutenants had three buttons. Captains had two gold epaulettes; first lieutenants wore one on the right shoulder; second lieutenants wore one on the left shoulder; third lieutenants had no epaulettes. Engineers had a gold-embroidered shield, the arms of the Treasury Department, on each falling collar. Trousers were of the same color in winter, with an inch-wide black stripe down each leg, and plain white in summer. Swords were the M1835 regulation Revenue Cutter Service sword which had an all-metal grip with a gilt pommel and guard and a silver grip with a straight blade, 30.75 inches long.

In 1862, apparently in answer to Howard's complaint, the uniform was revised to look more like that of the Navy.

*A peaceful-looking scene, the headquarters of the Sanitary Commission on the battlefield of Gettysburg. (*Harper's Weekly*)*

Agents, for them. General Inspectors and Agents distributed medical supplies and educated Army doctors as to the latest medical and hygienic practices.

Special Inspectors observed military medical field practices and gathered information on deaths and illness which was sent to the three associated secretaries who supervised the inspectors in their assigned geographic areas. From them it passed to the Commission's Bureau of Vital Statistics which was headed by a Chief Inspector. In addition to inspecting all general hospitals, a total of 1,482 inspections of some 870 regiments was made.

Another associate secretary was responsible for dealing with local aid societies that funnelled contributions into the Commission. Much of this money came from Sanitary Fairs held in most large Northern cities throughout the war. He was assisted by a team of canvassing agents, who accepted donations in the field and forwarded supplies; clerks; storekeepers, who were responsible for supplies in depots; messengers, who accompanied shipped supplies to prevent loss or delay; and watchmen. Olmsted himself and other board members spent much of their time lobbying Army officials and Congress to get basic improvements made in the Army's medical organization. Improvements such as the Ambulance Corps were in large part due to the lobbying work of the Commission.

The Commission operated 'Homes' in Washington, Boston, Nashville, Cairo, Memphis, Louisville, Cleveland and Cincinnati, providing food, care and assistance to honorably discharged soldiers without funds; they also provided railroad tickets home for these soldiers. In the vicinity of Washington the Commission maintained Lodges near railway stations to serve the travelling soldier's immediate needs. In association with the Army Paymaster's

Department it operated a Pension Agency to handle paperwork for discharged soldiers and make sure that they received everything due to them. Other Commission agents specialized in ensuring that back pay was paid in full.

On 16 September 1862 the Commission established a hospital directory. Agents in the field gathered the names and units of patients and where they were sent, and recorded this information so that friends and relatives could apply to one source to learn the whereabouts of missing loved ones. Next of kin were kept informed of patients' whereabouts, and the transferral of patients was recorded and updated. More than 600,000 names were recorded in the directory.

The Commission operated Nurses' Homes in Washington and Annapolis where sick and exhausted female nurses could recuperate. They also looked after soldiers' wifes and mothers who came to the hospitals to tend the patients.

The Commission appeared on the field after every major battle to help the survivors. At Gettysburg, for example, a Commission depot was set up at nearby Westminster when first news of the battle arrived at Commission headquarters. From there, supplies were sent to field hospitals. When the battle was over, the Commission set up a Lodge near the railroad station with hospital tents, a field kitchen and storage tents. It had ten cooks and 30 to 40 attendants working there full time, as well as agents who helped administer first aid. Other agents made sure that every wounded man put on a train to be evacuated to a general hospital had a full canteen of water and a cup of hot soup or coffee.

In the spring of 1864 the Commission set up the Auxiliary Relief Corps to administer first aid on the field, serve as nurses in hospitals, and set up temporary hospitals. By 14

The Sanitary Commission raised much of its funds through giant fairs. This is the outside of the buildings on 14th Street, New York which housed the Metropolitan Fair in early 1864. (Harper's Weekly)

July the Corps numbered almost 200 members. While these were dedicated workers, those in the Field Relief Corps were noted as being the sweepings of the city streets.

At the end of the war, the Commission sent supplies South to aid not only Union soldiers but poor Southern families as well. The latter activity, however, was quickly stopped by the Executive Committee. One of its most important post-war tasks, however, was handled by its Bureau of Information and Employment. This sent out questionnaires to soldiers soon to be discharged, beginning 14 June 1865, asking such things as jobs held before the war, military service, skills, references, the soldier's local relief agencies, the effect of a long absence on the applicant's children, the influence of army life on the applicant, 'industrial habits' and habits 'temperate or otherwise'. Completed questionnaires were sent to its offices in every major city in the east and two west of the Alleghenies, in Detroit and Cleveland, where discharged soldier abilities were matched with civilian jobs. Job offers were also posted on a blackboard outside the office doors. Tools and materials needed to return to civilian life were lent and training in schools and commercial colleges was provided as needed. The effort was moderately successful; the Cleveland office, for example, reported 170 employers needing help and placed 108 able and 98 disabled veterans out of 411 who asked for help. Of the 411, 80 did not return after the initial interview to take the job offered so the placement rate could have been higher.

The Commission had competitors in other organizations such as the Western Sanitary Commission, headquartered

in St. Louis, Missouri. However, it remained the most influential civilian aid organization in existence throughout the war.

The Commission's New York and San Francisco offices were closed in August 1865, the London office in September, the Chicago office in November, and the Washington headquarters in December. On 26 January 1866 the Sanitary Commission was reborn as the American Association for the Relief of Misery on the Battlefield with many of its old personnel in the new organization.

As a civilian organization, Sanitary Commission employees and volunteer were forbidden by the War Department to wear uniforms, although photographs indicate that they wore something like the officer's body coat. Field Relief Corps members, as probably did other Commission workers, wore an officer's brass-type button with the shield and the Old English letters 'U.S.' on the top and beneath this in roman letters, 'SANITARY COMMISSION'. Auxiliary Relief Corps members wore a white Greek cross surrounded by an oval silver band on cap front or coat breast. In April 1863 all Commission members were ordered to wear a cap badge consisting of the Commission's name within a wreath. A flag including the United States shield with the letters 'U.S.S.C.' floated over each Commission establishment.

Christian Commission

Organizations such as the Young Men's Christian Association (YMCA) and American Tract Association began working to meet the spiritual needs of the volunteers from the war's beginning. The YMCA then called a meeting of concerned clergy to be held in its New York headquarters on 14 November 1861. Delegates there formed the Christian Commission with the mission of promoting soldiers' and sailors' spiritual and temporal welfare, collecting and transmitting civilian contributions, and holding services in the field. A five-man Executive Committee was appointed on 11 December 1861 with George H. Stuart of Philadelphia as its chairman.

The Committee set up a three-man General Committee which, with the treasurer, would take in contributions and get them to the field as needed. The country was divided into districts, each under control of a three-man committee. They were to work with regimental chaplains in their district; if a regiment lacked a chaplain they were to try to get its officers to form a religious association to hold meetings. They were also to pass out tracts and religious books. Each district committee was authorized to hire clerks as needed.

On 14 May 1862 the Commission sent its first agents into the field to serve for at least six weeks. Later called delegates, these were clergymen and laymen who set up chapel tents for religious services and worked in hospitals helping the wounded and on battlefields burying the dead. A General Agent (with assistants) was named to command the agents within each field army. He reported to the Commission's General Field Agent. A permanent station agent, who also reported to the General Field Agent, was appointed to headquarters at corps level. The Navy was served by agents sent by the New York Committee.

In more permanent locations, the Commission maintained diet kitchens, each with two or three female managers, for soldiers unable to eat standard hospital fare. In all, it employed 157 female diet kitchen managers. It maintained 215 full loan libraries for the soldiers. These were standardized with 125 volumes of history, biography, fiction, science and religion selected by the Executive Committee and packed in a standard case for easy transport to the troops. There were another 70 half-size libraries. The Committee distributed medical supplies, clothing and small items such as housewife, soap and ink to both medical officials and individual soldiers.

The Commission closed its offices on 1 January 1866, its Executive Committee meeting for the last time on 10 February. During its existence it had distributed 328,879 Bibles, 6,818,994 religious newspapers and 159,781 hardback and 2,611,028 paperback books. In all, 1,079 delegates had been sent into the field.

However, it should be said that many, perhaps the majority, of the soldiers did not appreciate the work of these men who appeared to be more interested in proselytizing than in offering practical assistance. Many soldiers noted using the Commission's tracts for something other than reading, regarding them as little more than 'moral pap', of small redeeming social value but of real physical usefulness.

As civilians, Commission members wore ordinary clothes, clergymen wearing the garb of their denomination. Agents

Delegate George J. Mingins was one of the first Christian Commission members to arrive at Fortress Monroe, Virginia in May 1862. After helping the wounded in the Peninsula Campaign and at Antietam, he was named General Agent of the New York Army Committee. He was one of two organization representatives sent to San Francisco in April 1864 to organize a branch of the Commission there, and did not return East until January 1865. (Author's collection)

or Delegates wore a silver badge, two inches long, in the form of a scroll bearing the legend 'U.S. Christian Commission PHIL.' The latter indicated the Commission's headquarters in Philadelphia. Female diet kitchen managers wore a silver badge in the shape of an open book, the legend 'U.S. Christian' appearing diagonally on the left page and 'Commission' on the right.

Union Commission

The Union Commission was set up in St. Louis, Missouri, in June 1864 to handle the flood of refugees fleeing the war. Through contributions, it purchased seeds and agricultural equipment to give to farmers who had lost all. It re-opened schools, and got displaced persons back to their homes. It was closed in February 1865 after handling some 100,000 refugees.

As civilians, Union Commission members wore no special uniform or insignia.

This soldier in a state issue jacket wears the Whipple hat as worn by troops from New Hampshire and New York as well as by other units. (David Scheinmann collection)

Notes

1. William E. Unrau, *Tending The Talking Wire*, University of Utah Press, Salt Lake City, Utah, 1990, p. 262
2. David H. Donald, ed., *Gone For A Soldier*, Little Brown and Co, Boston, 1975, p. 261
3. Ibid., p. 266
4. *OR*, Series I, Vol. LII, Part I, p. 317
5. Harriet A. Engler, 'Women in the Civil War,' *Living History*, Fall, 1984, p. 41
6. Regimental Association, *History of the 127th Regiment Pennsylvania Volunteers*, Report Publishing Co, Lebanon, Pennsylvania, 1901, p. 223
7. *OR*, Series III, Vol. I, p. 184

References

George W. Adams, *Doctors in Blue*, Collier Books, New York, 1952

Alphaeus H. Albert, *Record of American Uniform and Historical Buttons*, A. H. Albert, Heightstown, New Jersey, 1976

D. Alexander Brown, *The Galvanized Yankees*, University of Illinois Press, Urbana, Illinois, 1963

John R. Brumgardt, ed., *Civil War Nurse*, University of Tennessee Press, Knoxville, Tennessee, 1980

Jane T. Censer, ed., *The Papers of Frederick Law Olmsted*, Vol IV, John Hopkins University Press, Baltimore, 1986

Dudley T. Cornish, *The Sable Arm*, University Press of Kansas, Lawrence, Kansas, 1987

Gordon Dammann, *Pictorial Encyclopedia of Civil War Medical Instruments and Equipment*, Vol. II, Pictorial Histories Publishing Co, Missoula, Montana, 1988

Frederick H. Dyer, *A Compendium of the War of the Rebellion*, Morningside Bookshop, Dayton, Ohio, 1978

William K. Emerson, *Chevrons*, Smithsonian Institution Press, Washington, 1983

Robert Garofalo and Mark Elrod, *A Pictorial History of Civil War Era Musical Instruments & Military Bands*, Pictorial Histories Publishing Co, Charleston, West Virginia, 1985

Joseph T. Glatthaar, *Forged in Battle*, The Free Press, New York, 1990

P. C. Headley, *Massachusetts in the Rebellion*, Boston, 1866

Edgar M. Howell, *United States Headgear 1855–1902*, Smithsonian Press, Washington, DC, 1975

Philip Katcher, *American Civil War Armies (2): Union Artillery, Cavalry and Infantry*, Osprey Publishing, London, 1986

— *American Civil War Armies (3): Staff, Specialist and Maritime Services*, Osprey Publishing, London, 1986

— *American Civil War Armies (4): State Troops*, Osprey Publishing, London, 1987

— *Union Forces of the American Civil War*, Arms & Armour Press, London, 1989

Francis Kern, *The United States Revenue Cutters in the Civil War*, US Coast Guard, ndg

Bertram W. Korn, *American Jewry and the Civil War*, Jewish Publication Society of America, Philadelphia, 1951

Francis A. Lord, *They Fought for the Union*, Stackpole, Harrisburg, Pennsylvania, 1960

Francis A. Lord and Arthur Wise, *Uniforms of the Civil War*, Thomas Yoseloff, Cranbury, New Jersey, 1970

Michael J. McAfee, *Zouaves . . . The First And The Bravest*, US Military Academy, West Point, New York, 1979

William Q. Maxwell, *Lincoln's Fifth Wheel*, Longmans Green & Co, Toronto, 1956

Lemuel Moss, *Annals of the United States Christian Commission*, J. B. Lippincott & Co, Philadelphia, 1868

Official, *Laws Relating To The Navy And Marine Corps And The Navy Department, July 1, 1865*, Government Printing Office, Washington, 1865

Official, *Register of Officers and Agents, Civil, Military, and Naval in the Service of the United States on the Thirtieth September, 1863*, Government Printing Office, Washington, 1864

Official, *Revised Regulations of the Army of the United States*, J. B. Lippincott & Co, Philadelphia, 1862

Frederick Phisterer, *Statistical Record of the Armies of the United States*, Jack Brussel, New York, ndg

David D. Porter *Naval History of the Civil War*, Castle, Secaucus, New Jersey, 1984

Thomas C. Railsback and John P. Langellier, *The Drums Would Roll*, Arms & Armour Press, London, 1987

Robert H. Rankin, *Uniforms of the Marines*, G. P. Putnam's Sons, New York, 1970

Schuyler, Hartley and Graham, *Illustrated Catalog of Arms and Military Goods*, New York, 1864 (reprinted by Dover 1985)

Edwin H Simmons, *The United States Marines*, The Viking Press, New York, 1976

Randy Steffen, *The Horse Soldier 1776–1943*, Vol. II, University of Oklahoma Press, Norman, Oklahoma, 1978

C. A. Stevens, *Berdan's United States Sharpshooters in the Army of the Potomac*, Morningside Bookshop, Dayton, Ohio, 1972

Frank H. Taylor, *Philadelphia in the Civil War 1861–1865*, City of Philadelphia, 1913

James C. Tily, *The Uniforms of the United States Navy*, Thomas Yoseloff, Cranbury, New Jersey, 1964

Frederick P. Todd, *Cadet Gray*, Sterling Publishing, New York, 1955

— *American Military Equippage 1851–1872*, Company of Military Historians, Vol. II, Providence, Rhode Island, 1977; Vol. III, Westbrook, Connecticut, 1978

V
THE FORCES OF
THE CONFEDERATE
STATES

THE FORCES OF THE CONFEDERATE STATES

General Officers and Staff Departments

The Confederate Army had four types of general: brigadier general, major general, lieutenant general and general. All four were appointed by the President, but their commissions had to be approved by the Senate as was the case in the Union Army. However, since for much of the war communications between the Senate in Richmond and the field forces west of the Mississippi River were difficult at best, General E. Kirby Smith named generals who were 'assigned to command' in the Trans-Mississippi Command.

In all, the Confederate Army had 425 general officers. Of these 77 were killed or mortally wounded, nineteen resigned, fifteen died accidently or from disease, two were killed in duels, one was murdered, one committed suicide, one retired because of wounds and one was demoted to colonel. Five had their commissions cancelled and three refused to accept their commissions. A total of 146 of them were graduates of the US Military Academy, while another ten had attended the Academy. The Virginia Military Institute produced seventeen Confederate generals; the South Carolina Military Academy produced four. Another nineteen, although not Academy graduates, had held US Army commissions.

Assisting the generals were the various staff departments and corps which had been designated in the Act passed by the Congress on 6 March 1861 creating the Provisional Army of the Confederate States.

Adjutant and Inspector General's Department This was reponsible for the assignment of all officers of engineers, ordnance and staff departments to their duty stations; and

Major General William Mahone wears the general's rank badge on his collar. The short jacket with a collar insignia but without the Austrian knot on the sleeve was common among all ranks of commissioned officers. Mahone's jacket is unusual, however, in that it has a laydown collar and pleated front. (National Archives)

engineer and artillery officers to various headquarters; handling officers' resignations; recruiting; and care of deceased soldiers' effects. The department essentially issued all War Department orders and commands, maintained Army records and inspected all Army personnel and installations. The Adjutant and Inspector General, who was also the Army's ranking general, was Samuel Cooper who had been named the US Army's Adjutant General in 1852, but had resigned on 7 March 1861; he was appointed a Confederate general on 31 August 1861, the rank taking effect from 16 May 1861. An adjutant on the staff of every regimental or larger unit reported to this Department as well as to his unit commander.

Quartermaster's Department This was headed by Colonel Abraham C. Myers, the Quartermaster General. His pre-war service had been in the US Army's Quartermaster Department. His Richmond-based staff included a colonel in the post of Assistant Quartermaster General and a staff of Assistant Quartermasters and store-keepers. Of the assistant quartermasters, one captain was in charge of transportation; another, of officer's quarters, commutation and fuel; another, of payments to civilian railroads and stage lines; a major, responsible for the pay of the Army of Northern Virginia; two captains, of army-wide pay; two more, of pay to discharged and detached service soldiers; one, of miscellaneous items including stationery and soldiers' burials; a major, of horses, mules, wagons, and harness; another captain, of arranging railroad troop movements; and two captains, of issuing clothing, shoes,

tents, etc. Two majors titled Quartermasters were in charge of the Clothing Bureau which oversaw Shoe Manufactories and Clothing Manufactories across the South. At the field level, the Quartermaster General was served by a quartermaster at each regimental headquarters and at each higher command headquarters. Despite all this actvity, there was much criticism of Myers' operation by troops who were sometimes in rags. Too often, however, the fault lay in the inadequate Southern infrastructure which made the transportation of clothing and equipment very difficult. In August 1863, however, Jefferson Davis named Brigadier General Alexander R. Lawton, who was recovering from wounds received at Antietam, as Quartermaster General over Myers, and when the appointment was confirmed by Congress on 17 February 1864, Myers resigned. Lawton remained in the post until the war's end.

Commissary General's Department Better known as the **Subsistence Department**, was responsible for feeding the Army's men and livestock. It was commanded by Lucius B. Northrop, the Commissary General, aided by a major serving as Assistant Commissary and a lieutenant serving as Assistant Commissary and Store-keeper. Each general's staff had a lieutenant named Assistant Commissary of Subsistence, and each regiment had its own commissary

Regulation Confederate Army buttons. Some British-made varieties had Old English lettering. (1861 Army Dress Regulations)

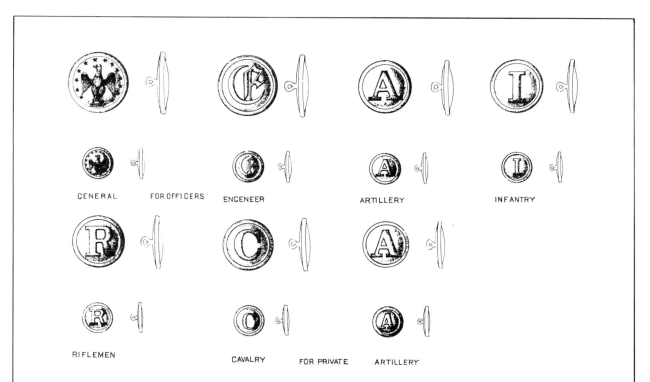

GENERAL   FOR OFFICERS   ENGINEER   ARTILLERY   INFANTRY

RIFLEMEN   CAVALRY   FOR PRIVATE   ARTILLERY

officer, a lieutenant. Widespread hunger in individual units from time to time, due as much to inadequate transportations as to inept Subsistence Department management, led to Northrop's removal on 15 February 1865. He was replaced by Brigadier General Isaac M. St-John who served until the war's end.

Indian Bureau Reporting to the Secretary of War, this dealt with those Native Americans who were fighting for the Confederacy. It was headed first by David Hubbard and later by S. S. Scott.

Bureau of Ordnance Created on 8 April 1861, this was responsible for arsenals, armouries and depots and the acquisition and issuing of small arms, artillery and munitions. Colonel Josiah Gorgas served as Chief of the Ordnance Bureau. Under him, the Chief of Foreign Supplies was responsible for obtaining and importing military supplies from overseas. A Superintendent of Laboratories was named in May, and a Superintendent of Armories in September, each also reporting to Gorgas. Both men had staffs of artillery officers and store-keepers at each ordnance installation, with ranks according to the size and importance of the unit. Additional officers were assigned to the Ordnance Bureau under an 1862 Congressional Act which authorized the appointment of 40 first lieutenants of

Regulation Confederate Army and Marine Corps officers' collar badges. (1861 Army Dress Regulations)

A Confederate general expects to die in battle

'I found [Brigadier] General [Elisha] Paxton very much depressed; he had been so for several days. We had a long conversation late at night. At the conclusion, he repeated what he had stated to me in the beginning, that he was convinced he would not survive the next day's battle. He did not seem morbid or superstitious but he spoke with earnest conviction . . . He concluded by asking me to write to his wife as soon as he was killed and to see that his body was sent to Lexington by Cox, his faithful orderly, who had recently been made his aide-de-camp. I was never so impressed by a conversation in my life. Paxton was not an emotional man but one of strong mind, cool action, and great force of character. He was the last man to give way to a supersitition . . .

'The next day was Sunday and we were ordered to be ready to move forward at daylight . . .

'After a while we became hotly enaged . . . We soon had some warm work and my time and attention were fully occupied. At the first lull, I was informed that General Paxton had been shot in the first movement and had died almost instantly.'

(Henry Kyd Douglas, *I Rode With Stonewall*, Fawcett Publications, Greenwich, Connecticut, 1961, pp. 217–18)

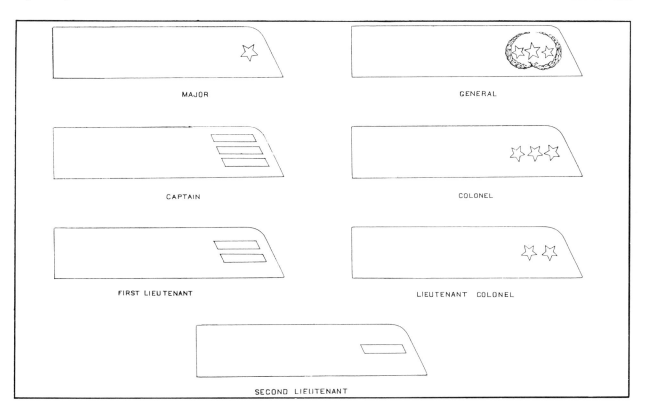

MAJOR

GENERAL

CAPTAIN

COLONEL

FIRST LIEUTENANT

LIEUTENANT COLONEL

SECOND LIEUTENANT

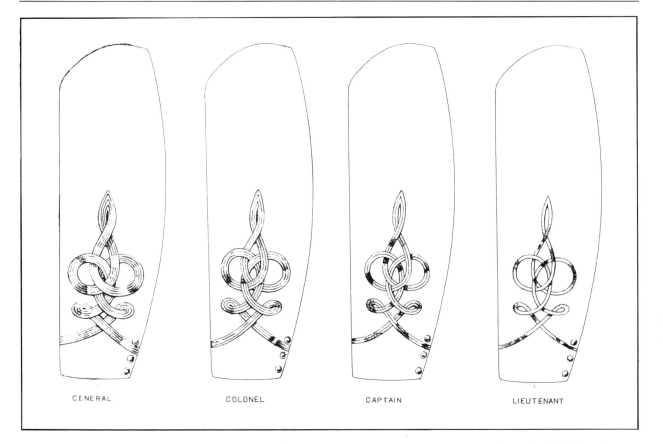

GENERAL COLONEL CAPTAIN LIEUTENANT

artillery for assignment as ordnance officers. Additionally, each major command's staff had an ordnance officer on it. Gorgas was promoted to the rank of Brigadier General on 10 November 1864 and served in the Bureau until the war's end.

Regulation Confederate Army and Marine Corps officers' sleeve insignia. (1861 Army Dress Regulations)

Niter and Mining Bureau Created on 11 April 1862 and placed under War Department control as an independent bureau on 16 June 1863, this was responsible for the supply of nitrates, coal, lead, iron and saltpeter for the production of munitions. Headed by Major Isaac M. St-John of the Corps of Engineers, it had a staff of 20 officers who oversaw mining operations and foundries, surveyed niter and sulfur caves, and even collected human waste in chamber-pots for use in nitrate filter-beds. At its height, in December 1862, nitrate production had reached some 500,000 pounds a year; even by the war's end the Bureau was producing some 180,000 pounds annually. Officers' pay-scale was that of cavalry officers. Outside contractors were hired to run the mines. When St-John was transferred to the Subsistence Department, he was replaced by his second in command, Lieutenant Colonel Richard Morton, who retained the position until the war's end.

Conscript Bureau This was created by the War Department to administer the draft authorized by the first Conscription Act passed by Congress on 16 April 1862. Brigadier General Gabriel J. Rains, previously a combat soldier, was named the Bureau's first Superintendent, with a lieutenant colonel as his Assistant Superintendent. Conscription in each state was overseen by a state Commandant of Conscripts, generally a colonel, who reported to the Bureau. Rains was replaced in May 1863 by Colonel John S. Preston, who had been Commandant of Conscripts for South Carolina. Preston was promoted on 10 June 1864, despite criticism about his heavy-handed enforcement of the unpopular law, and served until the Bureau was abolished in March 1865. The job of overseeing conscription was turned over to each state's Reserve Force commander.

Reserve Force This was created by Congress on 17 February 1864. It consisted of men under 18 and over 45 years old in each state who reported to the state's Reserve Force commander, a general officer, who was appointed by the central government's Secretary of War. Those under 18 went into Junior Reserve units, those over 45 went into the Senior Reserves. The purpose was to make sure that local militia conformed to Confederate Army organizational tables and were trained according to national standards. The effect was further to violate the principle of 'states rights' for which the South was presumably fighting by centralizing control of what previously had been the exclusive property of each state's governor, its militia.

Torpedo Bureau This was authorized by Congress in October 1862. It was headed by Brigader General Gabriel J. Rains, who had devised land-mines or 'torpedos' for use during the Peninsula Campaign, in June 1864.

Bureau of Examination This was created to interview and approve candidates for officers' commissions. According to complaints from field commanders, it was unable to commission needed officers rapidly enough and many officers never faced the Board.

Other Staff Departments While the Confederate Army lacked a judge-advocate general, in February 1864 President Davis appointed a clerk in the War Department to act as the Department's 'military judge'. The judge was given the rank and pay of a colonel of cavalry.

Separate from the military judge were the Provost Marshal's men. These came in two varieties, provost guards in the field armies and provost guards in areas under martial law.

Each field army developed its own system of provost guards. On 5 June 1862 a Department of Northern Virginia order stated that provost marshals had to be chosen according to reliability and efficiency. Each divisional provost guard was to consist of an officer, a non-commissioned officer and ten men drawn from different regiments. The Army of Northern Virginia's First Corps assigned the 1st Virginia Battalion as its provost guards; its Second Corps assigned the 1st North Carolina Infantry; and the Third Corps assigned the 5th Alabama Infantry. On 9 April 1863 a Provost Marshal Department was established in the Army of Tennessee to consist of a provost marshal general with one assistant at army headquarters; a field grade officer with an assistant at each corps headquarters; a captain at each divisional headquarters; and a lieutenant at brigade headquarters. On 27 September 1864 the provost guard in the Army of Missouri was to consist of four officers and 50 men in each brigade.

On the civilian side, on 22 June 1861 Brigadier General John H. Winder was appointed inspector general of military camps in the Richmond area and his post was enlarged in 1864 to become commissary general of prisoners east of the Mississippi. Winder became the *de facto* provost marshal general, as he was given responsibility for maintaining order among troops in the Richmond area. He appointed Captain A. C. Godwin to serve as provost marshal and assigned him a staff of civilian detectives to close down illegal drinking establishments, arrest spies and issue passports for travel North. Winder even tried fixing prices to control inflation. He and his men, many of who were Marylanders like Winder, were highly unpopular among the press and citizens of the city, since they made both drinks and passports difficult to obtain. On 6 February 1865 Winder died while inspecting the prison camp in Florence, South Carolina. The actual post of provost marshal general was not officially accepted until 20 February 1865 when a bill creating that title was introduced in the Senate with the idea of confirming Brigadier General Daniel Ruggles in the post.

Other cities also had their own provost guards. The 25th Georgia Battalion (Atlanta Provost Battalion) policed Atlanta. Other units were detailed from field armies to patrol nearby cities for short periods as needed. Army officers hired civilian provost marshals in other cities when regular units were unavailable. On 9 March 1865 provost guard membership was limited to officers over the age of 45, or retired or unfit for field service, and enlisted men who were invalids or Reserve Force troops. At the same time, the appointment of provost marshals was limited to places adjudged as essential by generals commanding departments or field armies.

According to General Order Number 9 of 6 June 1861, all officers and men were to wear a cadet-gray, double-breasted frock-coat. Brigadier generals were to wear their eight buttons in pairs; all other ranks had seven buttons worn evenly down each row. In fact, major generals and above often followed US Army practice and wore nine buttons in threes on each row. The coat's pointed cuffs and collar were to be in a branch-of-service facing color, which was buff for staff officers and enlisted men and red for artillery officers in the Ordnance Bureau. Each cuff was to be fastened with three small buttons with a pointed cuff ending four inches from the cuff. The coat's pocket was to be hidden in the skirt folds, with one button at the hip, placed level with the bottom front button, and one at the end of each pocket.

Officers' insignia was worn on the collar and sleeves; all generals wore three gold stars within a gold wreath, the centre one 1.25 inches in diameter and the others .75 inches in diameter; three large gold stars marked a colonel; two gold stars, a lieutenant colonel; one gold star, a major; three parallel horizontal gold bars, a half-inch wide and the top one three inches long, a captain; two gold bars, a first lieutenant; and one gold bar, a second lieutenant. Also, a gold Austrian knot was worn on each sleeve over the cuff. Lieutenants had one gold braid; captains had two; field grade officers three; and generals four. At the start, however, many officers wore US Army officers' shoulder-straps of their rank, a practice that carried well into mid-1862. On 21 March 1862 the Richmond *Daily Dispatch* had to warn against this practice, but Confederate officers with shoulder-straps were photographed some months later.

Non-commissioned officer grade was indicated by chevrons, worn points down above the elbows of both sleeves, made in the same facing colors as worn on cuffs and collars. A sergeant major wore three 'V's and arcs in silk; a quartermaster-sergeant, three 'V's and ties in silk; an ordnance sergeant, three 'V's and a star in silk, probably red for artillery; a first or orderly sergeant, three 'V's and a lozenge in worsted; a sergeant, three 'V's in worsted; a corporal, two 'V's in worsted. In practice, many Confederate non-commissioned officers never bothered with chevrons; others applied tape directly to their coat sleeves rather than on pieces of material that were later sewn to the sleeve as was done in the Union Army. The tape was often black regardless of the actual branch of service color required.

In fact, uniform coats generally tended to be more informal than regulations indicated. Lee himself was described as usually wearing a loose sack or frock-coat of the type commonly worn by businessmen. The three stars of a colonel were sewn to his laydown collar.

For enlisted men, the waist-length jacket was almost immediately issued instead of the regulation frock-coat which used more material. Indeed, from 1862 when enlisted men's coats are mentioned in official documentation, 'jackets' are referred to more often than 'frocks'. For the three months ending 31 December 1862 the Clothing Manufactury in Atlanta produced 37,150 jackets and no frock-coats. Even generals preferred a waist-length jacket as being more comfortable in the saddle; Stonewall Jackson was photographed in a plain version of this jacket, while General Wilcox in the Army of Northern Virginia and Cleburne in the Army of Tennessee were described by contemporary observers as wearing short jackets. Finally, a circular from the Adjutant and Inspector General's office dated 3 June 1862 stated that officers in the field were allowed to wear a plain frock-coat or jacket without 'embroidery', apparently with rank insignia worn only on the collar. First Lieutenant Joseph V. Bidgood, adjutant of the 32nd Virginia Infantry, wore such a jacket, of a brownish/olive-green (now in the Museum of the Confederacy) which is totally plain save for the two gold bars on each collar and a single row of US Army staff officers' buttons. This was an extremely common dress for all Confederate officers in the field, although certainly grays and even browns were more commonly seen than green.

All staff officers were to wear dark-blue trousers. Generals were to have two-inch wide stripes of gold lace, an eighth of an inch apart, down each leg. Staff officers were to have a gold stripe, an inch and a quarter wide, down each leg. The Museum of the Confederacy owns a pair of trousers worn by Major John Hughes, quartermaster in Hoke's Division, which are sky-blue with a one-inch-wide gold stripe down each leg. Sergeants and staff non-commissioned officers were to have a branch-of-service colored cotton webbing or braid stripe, an inch and a quarter wide, down each leg of their sky-blue trousers. Privates were to have plain sky-blue trousers. On 21 September 1864, however, the quartermaster purchasing agent in charge of buying clothing for the Army in England was notified that ' . . . you need not contract for blue cloth for pants, as the gray makes up to more advantage.'[11]

Again, in practice, a great variety of trousers was worn. At first, Lee continually wrote home requesting plain blue trousers, but he was photographed in 1864 and 1865 in the gray trousers worn generally by then. Other staff officers wore trousers made with a welt of the branch-of-service colour inset into the outer leg seams or a plain stripe sewn over them. A look at some original trousers in the Museum of the Confederacy shows examples of how even generals wore other than regulation dress. Major General Joseph Wheeler's trousers are cadet-gray with two half-inch gold stripes down each leg. Brigadier General Martin W. Gary

---

Confederates learn to dress light and comfortably

'The volunteer of 1861 made extensive preparations for the field. Boots, he thought, were an absolute necessity, and the heavier the soles and longer the tops the better. His pants were stuffed inside the tops of his boots, of course. A double-breasted coat, heavily wadded [lined], with two rows of big brass buttons and a long skirt, was considered comfortable. A small stiff cap, with a narrow brim, took the place of the comfortable "felt", or the shining and towering tile worn in civil life.

'Then over all was a huge overcoat, long and heavy, with a cape reaching nearly to the waist.

'Experience soon demonstrated that boots were not agreeable on a long march . . . And so, good strong brogues or brogans with broad bottoms and big, flat heels, succeeded the boots . . .

'A short-waisted and single-breasted jacket usurped the place of the long-tailed coat, and became universal. The enemy noticed this pecularity, and called the Confederates gray jackets . . .

'Caps were destined to hold out longer than some other uncomfortable things, but they finally yielded to the demands of comfort and common sense, and a good soft felt hat was worn instead . . .

'Overcoats . . . grew scarcer and scarcer; they were found to be a great inconvenience . . . '

(Carlton McCarthy, *Detailed Minutiae of Soldier Life in the Army of Northern Virginia 1861–1865*, Carlton McCarthy and Company, Richmond, 1882, pp. 16–21)

---

wore dark, cadet-gray trousers with a buff woollen stripe, one-eighth of an inch wide, down each leg. Brigadier General Bryan Grimes' trousers are plain cadet-gray. And the trousers worn by poor Brigadier General Benjamin G. Humphreys are plain butternut homespun jeans.

General and staff officers were authorized a *chapeau*, or cocked hat. Major General John B. Magruder was photographed holding such a uniform item, but these must have been extremely rare; those wearing them probably brought their old US Army dress *chapeaux*. Otherwise, they were to wear a forage cap which was like a French kepi. On 24 January 1862 General Order Number 4 ordered that these were to be all dark-blue for generals and staff officers and red for artillery officers in the Ordnance Bureau. For generals, the tops were to be made with four quatrefoils and four gold braids running up the side, front and back. Field officers were to wear three such gold braids; captains, two; lieutenants, one. Enlisted men wore plain forage caps. In practice, all officers and men often wore plain forage caps or wide-brimmed slouch hats. Also, gray cloth was often substituted for the regulation branch-of-service color. A branch-of-service color band was often worn with the gray forage cap; artillery officers and ordnance sergeants often wore these gray caps with red bands.

All officers were to wear a silk sash under their sword belt, knotted and hanging over the left hip. Generals were to wear a buff silk net sash; staff officers were to wear red silk. Ordnance sergeants would wear red worsted.

No regulations overcoats were ordered for officers. The few surviving examples are similar to the overcoat worn by General Gary which was cadet-gray, with two rows of US Army staff buttons down each front, and a detachable cape made with a single row of small US Army buttons down the front. No insignia of any sort was worn on this, or other, surviving overcoats. Major General John B. Hood's overcoat was similar, but had Confederate staff officers' buttons.

Artillery

On paper, the organization of Confederate artillery was essentially the same as that of Union artillery. On 10 May 1861 President Davis was authorized by Congress to muster in any company with a complement of officers and men that seemed 'proper', without spelling out any exact organization. A War Department circular issued in November 1861 put the minimum number of privates in each artillery company or battery at 70, with ten companies in a regiment. This number was raised by a Congressional Act dated 11 October 1862 which called for a minimum of 150 enlisted men in each company or battery.

Heavy artillery was organized into regiments, of which some sixteen were raised, five from Louisiana, two from North Carolina, three from South Carolina, two from Texas and four from Virginia.

The light artillery picture is a bit more confusing. The basic light artillery organization was the battery, just as in the Union army. However, many – indeed, the average – Confederate light artillery batteries had only four guns; only four horses were allowed to each gun and caisson; guns were often mixed as to type and calibre within a given battery. It even is difficult to say exactly how many light artillery batteries served the South; the numbers calculated by historians vary between 227 and 261. Most batteries had some 90 men in them.

Until the winter of 1862 batteries were assigned to each brigade headquarters in the Army of Northern Virginia. This situation, which made for poor artillery concentration, was revised when the artillery was then re-organized. The

While the uniforms shown here do not conform wholly to the printed Confederate dress regulations, they were said to have been of 'regular Confederate troops'. There must have been some reason for this. The sergeant with the zouave-style jacket and sword (right) is an artilleryman and he is talking to a cavalryman. The others are all infantrymen. (Harper's Weekly)

UNIFORMS OF REGULAR CONFEDERATE TROOPS.

INFANTRY.   CAVALRY.   ARTILLERY.

212 THE FORCES OF THE CONFEDERATE STATES

A artillery captain's fine coat with three bars on the red collar and two rows of gold lace as an Austrian knot on each sleeve. The

buttons are British-made with the Old English letter 'A' on each. (Smithsonian Institution collection)

battalion is complete in itself, with a quartermaster, adjutant, ordnance officer, surgeon, etc. The whole is under the control of the chief of artillery of the army, but assigned at convenience of the corps commanders, one of whose staff-officers is chief of artillery of the corps, and another chief of ordnance.

'The chief of artillery places them in action, and commands them there.

'The chief of artillery to an army is a brigadier general; to a corps, a colonel; and to a division, a major.'[2]

Each Army of Tennessee artillery battalion had a staff that included a major, the commanding officer; a quartermaster; a commissary; a surgeon; and an adjutant. The Army of Nothern Virginia added an ordnance officer to each staff. Also, the Eastern army divided its artillery reserve at corps level, although the Army of Tennessee retained its army-level artillery reserve of some 36 guns.

On 14 October 1862 fourteen light batteries in the Army of Northern Virginia were ordered disbanded as being unnecessary, while another four batteries were merged into two larger ones.

The first dress regulations described for the regular Confederate Army was dated 19 April 1861 and included a dark-blue smock worn as an overshirt, steel-gray trousers, a forage cap of an unspecified color and a red or white flannel shirt.

When the regulations of 6 June 1861 appeared, however, artillery officers and enlisted men were given the same uniforms as staff officers save that their branch-of-service color was red. The orders of 6 June also called for a red pompom worn on the forage cap, but this was changed on 24 January 1862 when the forage cap was now to be scarlet with a dark-blue band. Gold lace worn on the officers' caps was the same as that worn by staff officers. Trousers were to be sky-blue instead of dark-blue, those of officers marked by a red cloth stripe an inch and a quarter wide down each leg. Sergeants and staff non-commissioned officers wore the same in cotton braid. Buttons all bore the letter 'A'. Regulations also allowed a double-breasted light-gray fatigue blouse with seven buttons down each row and a small, turnover collar. It does not appear as if this blouse was ever issued in any quantities, if at all. Finally, according to regulations, heavy artillerymen, as all foot soldiers, were authorized a cadet-gray double-breasted overcoat with a stand-up collar and a cape that reached the elbow fastened with eighteen buttons. Light artillerymen, as all mounted troops, were to receive a cadet-gray overcoat that differed from the foot model in that the cape was to reach the cuff.

In practice, the same lack of uniformity noted among generals and staff officers existed among artillery officers. Frock-coats sometimes had red cuffs and collars and sometimes were plain; sometimes had the gold lace Austrian knot, sometimes not; sometimes were made of gray cloth and sometimes of brown. Gray and brown jackets, especially among light artillery officers, were quite popular. Although many of these lacked the gold lace Austrian knot, some had it and indeed the jacket worn by Captain G.

same situation existed in the Army of Tennessee until March 1864 when its artillery was re-organized.

According to a visitor to the Army of Northern Virginia in mid-1863, 'The artillery is organized into battalions; five battalions in a corps of three divisions, one to each division, and two in reserve. They always mass the artillery now, and commanders of battalions say that they lose no more men in a battalion than they formerly did in a single battery. Each

Gaston Otey, Battery A, 13th Battalion, Virginia Light Artillery, has the regulation Austrian knot made of red, not gold, braid on each sleeve.

An artillery officer later described his first uniform, something close to, but not exactly according to regulations: 'It is so long since and these things are so soon forgotten, that it may not be out of place to mention here that my new uniform was a gray tunic with scarlet cuffs and scarlet collar; an Austrian knot of gold braid on each arm; two bars of gold lace, denoting the rank, on each side of the standing collar; gray trousers with broad red stripes; a scarlet kepi, trimmed with gold braid, and commonly known, by the way, as the "Woodpecker cap".'[3]

Enlisted men usually wore a jacket instead of a frock-coat. Today, it is quite common to think of Confederate soldiers as being dressed in rags and tatters, poorly supplied, shivering against the cold. During certain short periods especially after a long, hard campaign, this was an accurate picture. On the whole, however, the image of the ragged soldier is a distorted one, partly created to prove that the South was overwhelmed by the material wealth of the North, partly to show how brave the individual Confederate soldier was in soldiering on despite his miserable condition. The bravery of the Confederate soldier needs no such false boost; he was heroic enough irrespective of whether he was well-enough clothed.

During the early war period, Confederate manufacturing and purchasing resources were stretched to the limit and civilians were called upon to help by donating clothing during the winters of 1861–2 and 1862–3 in what were known as 'Great Appeals'. Depots for receiving this clothing were set up at Richmond, Nashville and in the Trans-Mississippi department to forward the clothing to the troops as needed. J. B. Jones, a War Department clerk, noted in his diary on 9 October 1861 that Southerners contributed as much as $20,000 worth of clothing and food a day to the Army during that appeal. The next year, on 29 November, he noted, 'The Quartermaster-General publishes a notice that *he* will receive and distribute contributions of clothing, etc. to the army, and even *pay* for the shirts $1 each! Shirts are selling $12. The people will not trust him to convey the clothing to their sons and brothers, and so the army must suffer on.'[4]

These uniforms conformed to general specifications, but varied in color, cut, and material. Color especially varied from the regulation gray. A New Yorker, after South Mountain, in September 1862, noted the dead after that battle: 'All around lay the Confederate dead – undersized men mostly, from the coast district of North Carolina, with shallow, hatchet faces, and clad in "butternut" – a color running all the way from a deep, coffee-brown up to the whitish brown of ordinary dust.'[5] In May 1863 a foreign military observer described Confederates as having good clothes 'though they look very coarse, being made of a yellowish-brown homespun'.[6] British Coldsteam Guards Colonel A. J. L. Fremantle noted a parade of Arkansas troops in early 1863: 'The men were good sized, healthy and

A typical enlisted man's jacket with artillery buttons. This one was worn by Private John P. Lyle, 63rd Tennessee Infantry; Confederate inspectors complained about infantrymen in the Army of Tennessee wearing artillery jackets. (John D. Lyle collection)

well clothed, though without any attempt at uniformity in color or cut; but nearly all were dressed in gray or brown coats and felt hats.

'I was told that even if a regiment was clothed in proper uniform by the government, it would become parti-colored again in a week, as the soldiers prefered wearing the coarse homespun jackets and trousers made by their mothers and sisters at home. The generals very wisely allow them to please themselves in this respect, and insist only upon their arms and accoutrements being kept in proper order.'[7]

As if to prove his point, Virginian William H. Routt wrote home on 13 March 1863: 'I sold my pants, vest, shoes, &

More artillerymen apparently wore the regulation double-breasted coat than did members of any other branch of service, possibly because so many were stationed in permanent posts where they could obtain enough cloth for such a coat. Although this man's insignia would seem to indicate that he is an ordnance sergeant, many color sergeants wore the star over three 'V's until the rank of ensign was created for those who carried the regimental standard. (US Army Military History Institute)

drawers for sixtyone dollars so you can see I am flush again ... You will have to make me more pants and drawers, if you can raise the material make two pair of pants & four pair of drawers & I will have A pair of pants & two pair of drawers for sale in that way will get mine clear.' He added that if his wife made enough clothing, he could get himself detailed to go home and bring it back.[8]

However, by late 1863–early 1864 the Quartermaster General was able successfully to clothe all the troops under Confederate command. For example, Quartermaster General Lawton was able to report to Congress on 27 January 1865 – when the Union blockade was in full strength and many valuable manufacturing sites were in

Union hands – that, 'It will be found, I think, that with the exception of overcoats, which have not been made up, owing to the great consumption of woolen material for jackets and pants, and the item of flannel undershirts, but partially supplied, the armies have been fully supplied.' Lawton's figures showed that the Army of Northern Virginia from the last half of 1864 up to 21 January 1865 received 104,199 jackets, 140,578 trousers, 167,862 pairs of shoes, 74,851 blankets, 27,011 hats and caps, 21,063 flannel shirts, 157,727 cotton shirts, 170,139 drawers, 146,136 pairs of socks, and 4,861 overcoats from Confederate quartermasters. Furthermore, North Carolina made special clothing issues to its men as did Georgia which provided 26,795 jackets, 28,808 trousers, 37,657 pairs of shoes, 7,504 blankets, 24,942 shirts, 24,168 drawers and 23,042 pairs of socks during 1864.[9] Meanwhile, Lee's Adjutant General, Walter H. Taylor, reported that on 10 January 1865 the entire Army of Northern Virginia consisted of only 57,535 enlisted men and 3,716 officers [who should not have received issued supplies since they were responsible for buying their own uniforms].[10] Clearly, if Lawton's figures were correct, even at this late date, the Confederates had more than enough clothing to uniform their troops. However, there were still complaints that the soldiers weren't uniform in appearance and, indeed, still often ragged. Lawton felt that any poor clothing condition was the fault of 'the improvidence of the soldiers, who too often dispose, by sale and barter, of what they have received'.[11]

By late 1864 the major depots seem to have had more than enough cloth so that only gray cloth was used for their uniforms. In fact, War Department clerk Jones noted in his diary on 1 December 1864 that he was able to buy four yards of dark-gray cloth for personal use because it was a bit too dark for army use. Such a reason for rejecting the cloth was a far cry from the time when any color was acceptable.

Moreover, there do appear to have been specific types of uniforms issued by various government agents. Generally, all jackets were cut very much the same, with a short standing collar and a single row of buttons down the front. There are several specific jacket pattern variants issued that can be traced to specific Quartermaster Department depots.

Three types have been traced to the Richmond Depot. 'Type I' was made with a short standing collar edged in the branch-of-service color, red for artillery. Pointed cuffs were also edged in branch-of-service colors as were the epaulettes sewn on each shoulder. A single row of nine brass buttons was worn on the front. A belt loop was sewn on each side just over the hip. These appear to have been produced as early as February 1862. The Richmond Depot 'Type II' was similar but lacked the branch-of-service trim. Surviving examples show them to have been made of both a rough wool/cotton combination as well as dark- and cadet-gray kerseys and other wools with osnaburg linings. These were produced from early 1862 until at least mid-1864 and some examples were in service until the end of the war. The 'Type III' was the same but lacked epaulettes. They were made during the last twelve months of the war.

Jackets made by Peter Tait, a ready-made clothing manufacturer in Limerick, Ireland, date from 1864. They were made of fine cadet-gray kersey with eight brass English-made regulation buttons down the front, and standing collars and pointed cuffs in branch-of-service colors. Some came with epaulettes sometimes edged and sometimes wholly in branch-of-service colors. Jackets made at the Charleston Depot were quite plain, made of dark-gray kersey, lined with unbleached cotton osnaburg, with six buttons down the front, and a belt loop on each side. In the West, Columbus, Georgia Depot jackets were made of a grey wool/unbleached cotton warp with six wooden buttons on the front (five and seven button examples are also known). They often had branch-of-service colored standing collars and jampot cuffs. Some had external pockets. These were made from November 1862 until the war's end. In 1864 the Atlanta Depot provided quite plain jackets made of a roughly woven gray wool lined in unbleached cotton osnaburg with six buttons down the front. Jackets provided by the Department of Alabama in 1865 were made of woollen jean lined with cotton osnaburg with a branch-of-service coloured collar and five wooden buttons. They came with a single belt loop on the left side.[12]

Even when issued with the type of jacket that had branch-of-service trim, artillerymen seem not always to have worn the correct color. On 18 August 1864 the artillery of the Army of Tennessee was inspected, the inspectors reporting that, 'On very few occasions have I seen articles of clothing issued to the artillery with the proper (red) trimmings for that branch of service. In nearly every instance it has been the uniform of the infantry, although occasionally I have seen jackets with artillery trimmings in the infantry.'[13]

Finally, as Lawton noted, overcoats were rarely issued. Union Army overcoats were common among front-line troops able to capture them. At times these were dyed black, but they were usually left sky-blue. Confederate-made overcoats were made from British medium blue cloth as well as in coarse butternut wool.

Cavalry

On 6 March 1861 Congress created an army, on paper, of 100,000 volunteers for a year's service, to be organized in companies of, at a minimum, 64 privates, or a maximum of 100 privates and from 12 to 14 non-commissioned officers, musicians and officers. The regular Confederate Army was authorized at the same time; each cavalry company in it was to include 72 officers and men in a regiment of ten companies. That same organization was ordered for volunteer cavalry regiments on 8 May 1861. A War Department circular issued in November 1861 called for each cavalry company to include 60 privates in a regiment of ten companies. The final change came on 11 October 1862 when Congress placed the minimum number of privates in each cavalry company at 80.

While the basic organization of Confederate cavalry regiments and battalions was similar to that of the US Army, the Confederate high command was quicker to group it into large organizations to use as a hard-hitting force on its own. At its best, during the Chancellorsville campaign in May 1863, cavalry of the Army of Northern Virginia was organized into the Cavalry Corps under Major General J. E. B. Stuart. Its first brigade had five regiments; the second, four; the third, six; and the fourth, seven. Also, the Corps had its own Horse Artillery Brigade of four batteries. Wheeler's Cavalry Corps of the Army of Tennessee at Stone's River in December 1862 was made up of Wheeler's Brigade with six regiments or battalions and an artillery

battery; Buford's Brigade with three regiments; Pegram's Brigade with two regiments; and Wharton's Brigade with nine regiments or battalions, one detachment, two escort companies and a horse artillery battery.

In all, there were between 127 and 137 cavalry regiments and 47 to 143 cavalry battalions. The latter discrepancy can be attributed to the fact that not every so-called 'cavalry battalion' was a regular cavalry battalion. A Prussian officer wrote during the war, 'The Confederate cavalry was divided into four quite distinct classes, the functions of which differed completely . . .

'1. *Regular Cavalry*. Combined into regiments, brigades, and divisions for skirmishes, battles, and raids in force. Stuart's, Van Dorn's and Morgan's cavalry belong in this group. 2. *Partisan Rangers*. A kind of free corps that was not limited with respect to numbers. Their raids under a well-known commander [Mosby was the most famous one] are the most adventurous and the most stirring events of recent times. Their pay was their booty, which they were required to sell to the War Department at a fair price. 3. *Scouts*. Drawn mostly from the Indian states of the West, they acted on their own responsibility. They had to be in enemy

Regulation Confederate Army non-commissioned officers' chevrons. (1861 Army Dress Regulations)

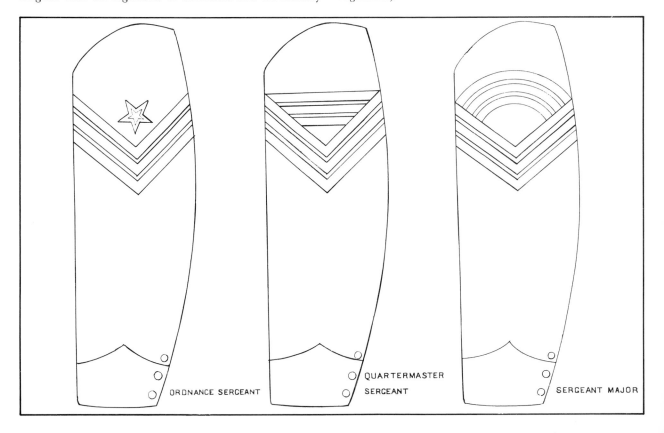

ORDNANCE SERGEANT   QUARTERMASTER SERGEANT   SERGEANT MAJOR

*Major, later colonel, John S.
Mosby was the best-known and
most effective partisan unit
commander the Confederates
had. He commanded the 43rd*

*Virginia Cavalry Battalion
which operated behind Union
lines in Northern Virginia.
(Library of Congress collection)*

territory from time to time and to report on all movements
of the enemy. They usually rode through the outposts at
night and hid in the daytime in dense thickets or in houses
occupied by Southern sympathizers. They always had to be
in uniform, and they differed from spies in this respect. 4.
Couriers. Young, skilled, nimble horsemen on excellent
mounts performed orderly service and were attached to
headquarters, so that the commanding general had sixty, a
corps twelve, a division six, and a brigade three, each ready
for duty.'[14]

Cavalry officers and men wore the same uniforms as did
artillerymen save that their branch-of-service color on coats,
trouser stripes and chevrons was yellow. Cavalry officers
and sergeants were also to wear yellow sashes. According to
the 16 June orders, enlisted cavalrymen were to wear their
regimental numbers on their buttons; in fact this never

*Regulation Confederate Army
non-commissioned officers'
chevrons. (1861 Army Dress
Regulations)*

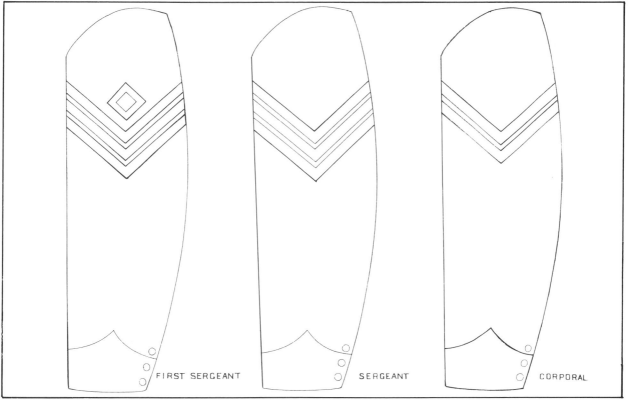

FIRST SERGEANT   SERGEANT   CORPORAL

These sky-blue trousers were worn by Colonel Thomas Ruffin, 1st North Carolina Cavalry Regiment. Notice the 'mule ear' pocket flaps which button shut; there are no back pockets. Lining is of white cotton. (North Carolina Museum of History collection)

Private J. J. Dodd, Co C, 4th South Carolina Cavalry, holds an M1833 dragoon sabre in one hand and a revolver in the other. The 4th was formed in January 1863 from members of the 10th and 12th Cavalry Battalions and saw service in the deep South and with the Armies of Northern Virginia and Tennessee, with whom it surrendered. (Library of Congress collection)

◀

Private George Hawkins, Co H, 2nd Kentucky Cavalry, was photographed while a prisoner of war at Camp Douglas, Illinois. His jacket has pointed cuffs, although they appear to lack branch-of-service colors. (John Sickles collection)

▲

Captain William F. Curry, assistant quartermaster of the 8th Kentucky Cavalry Regiment, wears a common variant of the frock-coat, with a laydown collar on which the rank insignia has been applied. Curry was captured on a raid in Cheshire, Ohio, and confined in the Western Penitentiary in Pennsylvania. While being transferred to another prison in October 1864, he slipped out of a train window and escaped, spending the rest of the war in the Army of Northern Virginia. (Robert L. Kotchian collection)

First Lieutenant Philip B. Jones, adjutant, 10th Kentucky Cavalry Regiment, wears a plain set of gold lace inverted 'V's on each cuff instead of the full Austrian knot. This was a common variant; another had a crow's-foot on the back at each top cuff button. (John Sickles collection)

was to consist of not less than 64 or more than 100 privates with from 12 to 14 non-commissioned officers, musicians and officers. In addition, in the regular Confederate Army, each regiment should consist of ten companies, each with 104 officers and men, with appropriate staffs. According to a War Department circular issued in November 1861, each volunteer regiment was to conform to the regular army organization, with not less than 64 privates in each company. This was revised on 11 October 1862 when each company was ordered to consist of at least 125 privates.

There were between 259 and 642 infantry regiments and 85 and 163 infantry battalions that served with the active Confederate Army during its existence, plus another 62 independent companies of infantry. The exact numbers, however, are confused because of the consolidation of large numbers of units as they shrank in combat and were later merged. Moreover, many units changed their designations during their service, making accurate tracing difficult if not impossible.

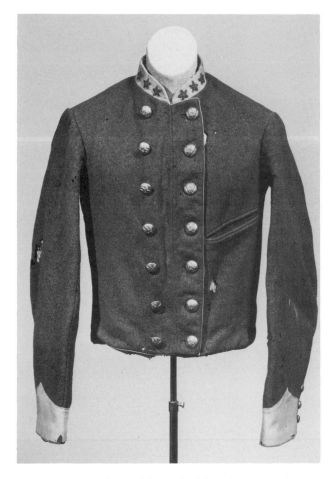

The jacket worn by Colonel John S. Mosby bears US cavalry officers' buttons, a common practice since regulation

Confederate buttons were hard to find. The facings are cavalry-yellow. (Smithsonian Institution Collection)

Colonel James Kemper, 7th Virginia Infantry, was promoted to brigadier general on 3 June 1862 and was wounded and captured during Pickett's Charge. He is wearing a plain sack coat field uniform. (Library of Congress collection)

happened and in June 1862 all cavalrymen were allowed to wear buttons with the letter 'C' on them.

Considering themselves a bit above the riff-raff who had to go on foot, cavalrymen tended to try to get somewhat better uniforms, preferring to use yellow trim as much as possible. A Texas cavalry sergeant wrote home in October 1863 for his wife to make him a coat: 'The coat I want has a band around the waist and a pleated body, infant waist I believe they call it. They are all the fashion among the Cavalry for even dress uniform.'[15] He mentioned that December taking his coat to a local tailor to ' . . . have the cuffs and collars trimmed with yellow flannel (Cavalry stripes)'.[16] And, next April wanted ' . . . some more yellow trimming for cuffs and collar'.[17]

Infantry

The Confederate Army's infantry was organized essentially the same as was that of the US Army. According to a Congressional Act of 6 March 1861 each infantry company

Confederates threaten Union pickets with a log

'The North Carolinians had found a pair of immense wheels with a tongue attached, probably used for hauling timber, which at a distance looked not unlike a gun carriage, although it would have carried a piece of great calibre. Upon this they mounted a huge hollow log, and providing themselves with a rammer and some large round stones, they suddenly dashed out with it from the house half way to the river, wheeled into position and pointed it at the opposite house, rammed with loud words of command a stone into the log, and seemed about to knock the enemy's headquarters about their ears. For a time there was considerable commotion on the other side. The picket line hurriedly prepared for action and the house was speedily emptied, the inmates, or some of them, not standing in any order going but making for the woods at once. The joke was presently appreciated and, with much laughter, the lines resumed their status.'

(McHenry Howard, *Recollections of a Maryland Confederate Soldier and Staff Officer under Johnston, Jackson and Lee*, Morningside Bookshop, Dayton, Ohio, 1975, p. 256)

One observer noted in 1863 in the Army of Northern Virginia that ' . . . many of the regiments had little bands of three or four musicians, who played rather discordantly. The Southerners are said to be extremely fond of music though they seldom take the trouble to learn to play themselves, and seem not very particular as to whether the instruments they hear are in tune or not. The bandsmen are almost all Germans.'[18]

Infantry officers and men wore the same uniforms as did artillerymen save that their branch-of-service color on coats, trouser stripes and chevrons was light-blue. Sashes were red. According to the 16 June orders, enlisted infantrymen were to wear their regimental numbers on their buttons; in fact this never happened and in June 1862 all infantrymen were allowed to wear buttons with the letter 'I' on them.

Confederate sergeants charged with carrying the regimental color – and there was but one in each regiment – often wore a star above their three 'V's as a unique grade

Captain James Tucker, 9th Florida Infantry, apparently had himself photographed in his old uniform after the war. It is the regulation dress, although the slouch hat he holds is a gesture towards comfort rather than dress regulations. (Fritz Kirsch collection)

First Lieutenant W. H. Young, from North Carolina, wears the common short jacket worn in the field, but has decorated his not only with collar rank badges but an Austrian knot on each sleeve.

His apparently dark-blue cap is trimmed with a lighter facing braid, perhaps sky-blue or white. (US Army Military History Institute)

Union troops kill a Southern partisan

'Captain Stump was one of McNeil's scouts, with the reputation of hanging and cutting the throats of Union prisoners . . . Running up as fast as we could, we discovered Captain Stump in the act of mounting his horse, I ordered him to surrender. While in the act of mounting his horse, we fired several shots, and he fell forward to the ground. He tried to regain his feet, and reached for his revolver. But we were upon him before he could use it, and I pointed my revolver in his face and forced him to his knees . . . We then made him ride between us, and told him that if he attempted to get away, we would make a sieve out of him . . .

'After we caught up with the column, Major Young asked me, "Whom have you there?" . . . Captain Stump then said, "I might as well own up to it: I am Captain Stump." Major Young then said, "I suppose you know that we kill you. But we will not serve you as you have served our men, cut your throat or hang you. We will give you a chance for your life. We will give you ten rods start on your own horse, with your spurs on. If you get away, all right. But remember, my men are dead shots." Captain Stump smiled, rode out, and we gave him the word "Go." We allowed him about ten rods start, then our pistols cracked, and he fell forward, dead.'

(H. P. Moyer, *History of the Seventeenth Regiment Pennsylvania Volunteer Cavalry*, Sowers Printing Co., Lebanon, Pennsylvania, 1911, pp. 226–8)

chevron. On 17 February 1864, however, Congress created the rank of ensign who wore a first lieutenant's uniform and carried the regimental color.

There were only a handful of zouave units in the Confederate Army and virtually none of them wore their imitation French dress far into 1862. From Louisiana, the 1st Zouave Battalion, better known as 'Coppens' Zouaves', wore a dark-blue jacket trimmed with yellow lace, a blue sash, red pantaloons and a fez, russet leather greaves and white canvas gaiters. Louisiana's 1st (Wheat's) Special Battalion wore a dark-blue jacket trimmed with red lace, a red shirt and sash, blue-and-white striped pantaloons and stockings, and white gaiters. By late 1861 these jackets were described as brown, possibly having faded and possibly being Virginia-made replacements for worn-out originals. The Richmond Zouaves (Co E, 44th Virginia Volunteers) appear to have worn a dark-blue jacket with yellow trim, scarlet pantaloons also with yellow trim, a blue sash with scarlet fringe, white gaiters, and a patented oil-cloth-covered knapsack. One Union soldier writing home on 26 June 1862 about the Peninsular Campaign stated that, ' . . . we were opposed by the Fourth Georgians. The Georgians were dressed in a fancy French zouave uniform, which caused our men to hesitate'.[19] While the 4th Georgia does

The most common Confederate infantryman's belt-plate was a frame buckle of some sort, but these two types of plate were fairly common. The cast rectangular type was most common in the Army of Tennessee, most being produced in the Atlanta Arsenal and by Francis Minchemer of Griffin, Georgia. The oval plate is of stamped copper with a lead backing and wire attachments. It was found along the southeastern coast of Virginia. (Author's collection)

appear to have been known as 'band-box soldiers', none of the pre-war volunteer companies that made it up are known to have worn zouave dress. Moreover, its 1862 uniform was apparently a gray cap and jacket and sky-blue trousers.[20]

The same type of white cotton duck gaiters, fastened with buttons or leather straps and buckles, worn by zouaves were worn by regular infantry from time to time. The entire brigade that included the 6th to the 9th Louisiana Infantry Regiments was described by its commander as having new gray uniforms with white gaiters in early 1862. Infantry from Hampton's Legion received a complete issue of gaiters on 30 September 1863, but it is unlikely that many gaiters were issued after that.

In the field, Confederate infantry presented a rather unkempt, and certainly unmilitary, appearance. Officers and non-commissioned officers sometimes removed their insignia so as to be inconspicuous in battle. Observers noticed that most of the privates stuck a toothbrush through one jacket button hole; few carried knapsacks, instead wrapping up their belongings in a piece of carpet or blanket and slinging that from their left shoulder to their right hip, horseshoe fashion. These carpets, which often came in bright colors, were often slit in the centre for use as a poncho. Captured Federal uniforms also saw much use; trousers were accepted as they were, but coats often were required to be dyed or bleached out before issue.

Sharpshooters

In 1862 Congress authorized a Confederate sharpshooter regiment to be structured much along the lines of the 1st and 2nd US Sharpshooters. In fact, a number of Southern sharpshooter units was raised and saw much service although none of them bore a 'Confederate' designation or served in the regular army. Most of them were simply battalions of about three companies, although some had as few as two and some, as many as six companies.

Most were simply used as regular infantry, but at times they were used as individual skirmishers armed with heavy-barrelled target rifles. For example, expert marksmen from

Although faded, this photograph is important in that it shows a Confederate infantryman in the rarely issued overcoat. The wearer is Private Andrew G. Walton, Co A (Louisia Rifles), 23rd Virginia Infantry. He enlisted on 1 March 1862 and died of pneumonia on 10 July 1862 at Stanton, Virginia. (Michael Dan Jones collection)

Sniping at the siege of Port Hudson, Louisiana

'Directly in front of the position occupied by Company B, but nearly over to the river, was a large round tent standing by itself, but so far off and so situated, that with the naked eye it was almost impossible to see if it was occupied, the opening being on the side. Corporal W. E. Halladay, of Company B, had a small telescope, which he used to amuse himself by watching anything which might attract his attention inside the enemy's lines. One day while in the pit with Samuel O. Horn, a movement at the opening of the tent attracted his attention and he remarked to Horn that a man was standing just inside the tent at the opening, and described to him the exact position. Horn, who was a good shot, immediately sighted his Enfield rifle to the highest notch, and aiming at the part of the tent indicated, asked Halladay to tell him if the man made his appearance again. After waiting a few minutes the man came and stood in the same place where first seen, holding the flap of the tent back with his hand. At the word Horn fired, and in a very few seconds afterwards the flap of the tent suddenly closed. We never learned if the shot took effect on the man at whom it was fired, but in the course of fifteen or twenty minutes an ambulance displaying the hospital flag drove up to the tent, thus advertising that some one got hurt.'

(George N. Carpenter, *History of the Eighth Regiment, Vermont Volunteers*, Deland & Barta, Boston, 1886, pp. 129–31)

the 2nd, 5th and 9th South Carolina Infantry Regiments were transferred into a new unit, the Palmetto Sharpshooters, in early 1862, but instead of being assigned at a headquarters level, as were the US Sharpshooters, the Palmetto Sharpshooters were named the sixth regiment in Jenkins' Brigade of Jones's Division of Longstreet's Corps. At Antietam, they were simply placed on line with the other regiments. On this occasion, as with many others, the Confederates failed to use the special qualities that their unique units offered.

Most units, as listed below, were designated with their state names, e.g., 1st Battalion Texas Sharpshooters. The battalions that are indicated as having served 'In Mississippi' surrendered at Vicksburg.

Confederate sharpshooter units were as follows.

Unit	State	Raised	Service
1st Bn	Arkansas	mid-62	In Mississippi
1st Bn	Georgia	spring 62	Army of Tennessee
1st Bn	Mississippi	fall 62	Army of Tennessee
1st Bn	South Carolina	summer 62	In South Carolina
1st Bn	Texas	spring 62	Trans-Mississippi
2nd Bn	Georgia	mid-62	Army of Tennessee
3rd Bn	Georgia	spring 63	Army of Northern Virginia
4th Bn	Georgia	spring 63	Army of Tennessee
9th Bn	Mississippi	fall 62	Army of Tennessee
9th Bn	Missouri	winter 62	Trans-Mississippi
12th Bn	Arkansas	spring 62	In Mississippi
14th Bn	Louisiana	summer 62	Army of Tennessee
15th Bn	Louisiana	summer 64	Trans-Mississippi
15th Bn	Mississippi	spring 63	In Mississippi
23rd Bn	Alabama	fall 63	Army of Northern Virginia
24th Bn	Tennessee	spring 63	Army of Tennessee
30th Bn	Virginia	spring 61	Army of Northern Virginia
Palmetto	South Carolina	spring 62	Army of Northern Virginia

Sharpshooters wore the same uniforms and insignia as ordinary infantrymen.

Invalid Corps

The Confederates were a bit slower off the mark than the Federals to organize their men, wounded in battle or wasted with disease, who could still be of service although unable to remain in the field. The Confederate Invalid Corps was finally established on 17 February 1864, but it was never organized as completely into units as was the US Veteran Reserve Corps. Instead, officers and men 'retired' into the Corps, as the Confederates put it, being sent individually to companies at relatively stable posts such as hospitals and prisons. The Corps register, maintained in the Adjutant and Inspector General's office, listed 1,063 officers and 5,139 enlisted men. Co H, 1st Invalid Battalion garrisoned the

Confederate States Barracks, Richmond, which housed and fed recovered soldiers on transit between hospitals and field commands.

The Confederates put officers and men into the Invalid Corps who would not have passed US Veteran Reserve Corps standards; Major James C. Holmes, 30th North Carolina, was retired into the Corps 'with paralysis' on 19 August 1864.

Disabled men were also used in the President's Guard, a company formed to guard the executive mansion and its inhabitants in 1864.

There were no special uniforms or insignia for the Corps, although there was at least one issue of frock-coats to Corps enlisted men. Men from both Co H and the President's Guard received a gray jacket, trousers and cap.

Men of the Invalid Corps were issued with a frock-coat, such as worn by this unidentified private. His light-colored collar and cuffs suggest that his branch-of-service is infantry. (US Army Military History Institute)

Foreign Battalions

As the number of Federals held in Confederate prison camps grew and the exchange of prisoners stopped, the Confederate high command began to realize that they could possibly use some of these ill-fed, unhappy men. Knowing many were of foreign birth, with possibly less than total loyalty to the United States, the recruitment of prisoners into the Confederate Army was allowed. In March 1863 Lieutenant General John C. Pemberton in Mississippi was first authorized to recruit Federal prisoners, but it was not until 1864 that recruiting began in earnest. In September 1864 the Confederates recruited more than 800 prisoners at the prison camp in Florence, South Carolina, while instructions went to the prison camp at Andersonville, Georgia, to make a roster of foreign-born Federal prisoners there for recruiting purposes. Several hundred prisoners volunteered for the ranks of the 5th and 47th Georgia and 10th Tennessee Infantry Regiments where they served in the ranks with Southerners. Eventually, however, two Foreign Battalions were created entirely from prisoners who volunteered in order to escape prison life. Officers were native-born Southerners; non-commissioned officers and enlisted men were of foreign birth, largely Irish, and had been in the US Army.

The 1st Foreign (Tucker's) Battalion was organized in a camp near Columbia, South Carolina, in December 1864. It was converted to a pioneer regiment and assigned to the Army of Tennessee, participating in the retreat through North Carolina and surrendering with that army on 26 April 1865.

The 2nd Foreign (Brooks's) Battalion was organized in Summerville, South Carolina, in November 1864 and had five companies. Four companies were sent to Savannah in December, to join the troops awaiting Sherman's arrival. Shortly after arriving, some 60 men deserted. On 15 December, as the unit was about to be withdrawn from the lines because of unreliability, a first sergeant reported a plot led by the other first sergeants to mutiny and lead a mass desertion that night. The Battalion was surrounded by Georgia troops, disarmed, and disbanded. Several ring-leaders were shot, while the rest of the Battalion's enlisted men became prisoners of war in Florence again. The officers were returned to their old units.

Officers and men of the Foreign Battalions wore standard infantry dress with no special insignia.

Negro Units

Blacks presented the South with its biggest threat and greatest possibility for success. Threat, in that if the slaves were to revolt *en masse* there would be no way the outnumbered whites could re-enslave them, especially if they were to be helped by Northern forces. Possibility for success, in that if the great numbers of blacks could be put into use for the Confederacy, a gap between Northern and Southern military population sizes would be greatly filled.

The 1860 Census gave the following statistics for the South.

State	Slaves	Whites
Alabama	432,132	529,164
Arkansas	111,104	324,323
Florida	61,753	78,686
Georgia	462,232	595,097
Kentucky	225,490	930,223
Louisiana	333,010	376,280
Mississippi	436,696	354,700
Missouri	114,965	1,167,352
North Carolina	331,081	661,586
South Carolina	402,541	301,271
Tennessee	275,785	834,056
Texas	180,683	421,750
Virginia	490,887	1,105,192
Total	3,860,357	7,579,689

It was, of course, the soldiers in the field who saw the potential use of black soldiers long before politicians would admit their value. On 2 January 1864 Major General Patrick Cleburne, a brilliant, Irish-born officer in the Army of Tennessee, signed a petition circulated and signed by three other generals, four colonels, two lieutenant colonels, three majors, and one captain which called for arming the slaves. 'As between the loss of independence and the loss of slavery, we assume that every patriot will freely give up the latter – give up the negro slaves rather than become a slave himself,' the petition read, in a long plea for recruiting slaves into the Confederate army. 'This measure will at one blow strip the enemy of foreign sympathy and assistance, and transfer them to the South; it will dry up two of his three sources of recruiting; it will take from his negro the only motive it could have to fight against the South, and will probably cause much of it to desert over to us; it will deprive his cause of the powerful stimulus of fanaticism, and will enable him to see the rock on which his so-called friends are now piloting him.' But, the petition went much further than just calling for armed slaves: 'If we arm and train him and make him fight for the country in her hour of dire distress, every consideration of principle and policy demand that we should set him and his whole race who side with us free.'[21]

The politicians were horrified. Howell Cobb, freely admitting the cause of the war was slavery, pointed out that ' . . . the moment you resort to negro soldiers your white soldiers will be lost to you . . . The day you make soldiers of them is the beginning of the end of the revolution. If slaves will make good soldiers our whole theory of slavery is wrong.'[22]

Davis had Cleburne's petition suppressed, but the idea would not go away.

As the twilight of the Confederacy deepened, more and more politicians came around to the idea as a desperate measure to win the war. In February 1865 Lee himself wrote to Davis asking for authorization to recruit slaves with the consent of their owners, saying they were already fit physically, and mentally conditioned to be well disciplined. In March the Congress passed a law allowing blacks to be recruited and it went to the President's desk. They were to be freed after their tours of duty. While it was sitting there, Lee wrote to Davis on 10 March saying, 'I do not know whether the law authorizing the use of negro troops has received your sanction, but if it has, I respectfully recommend that measures be taken to carry it into effect as soon as practicable.'[23] With the South's top soldier pushing for it, Davis signed the measure into law on 13 March and the first advertisements in the newspapers for black volunteers appeared in Richmond on 16 March. On 1 April Colonel K. Otey, 11th Virginia Infantry, was assigned to duty in Lynchburg, Virginia, to recruit, muster, and organize black units for the army.

However, it was far too late for the handful of blacks who actually joined the Confederate army to affect the course of history. Their only major event was a parade of Chambliss's Battalion of two companies recruited from blacks already working at government installations through Richmond's Capital Square on 22 March 1865, an event which War Department clerk Jones noted in his diary: 'The parade of a few companies of negro troops yesterday was rather a ridiculous affair. The owners are opposed to it.'[24]

Black troops were to be furnished with a gray jacket and trousers, blanket and pair of shoes. Although the trousers and shoes, together with shirts, drawers and socks appear to have been issued, there is no evidence that jackets were supplied. The units had no special insignia.

Indian Regiments

Quite a few Native Americans in the Indian Territories, now Oklahoma, and Southern states such as Missouri and Texas were slave-holders and, as such, sided with the Confederacy. The Confederate government appointed Brigadier General Albert Pike special commissioner in charge of treaty-making with the Five Civilized Tribes: the Cherokees, Creeks, Choctaws, Chickasaws, and Seminoles. Predicting that he could raise a large number of troops from among the tribes, he signed the last treaty with them on 7 October 1861. Pike reported to the Secretary of War on 27 November 1861: 'We have now in the service four regiments, numbering in all some 3,500 men, besides the Seminole troops and other detached companies, increasing the number to over 4,000. An additional regiment has been offered by the Choctaws and another can be raised among the Creeks.'[25]

Pike was optimistic, however, because the number of Native Americans serving the Confederacy had peaked and was now ebbing. On 25 December he was forced to report: 'The Creek and Choctaw regiments were raised in August and the Cherokee regiment in October; but it was a long time before Colonel Cooper's regiment was even partially armed. No arms were furnished the others; no pay was provided for any of them, and with the exception of a partial supply for the Choctaw regiments, no tents, clothing, or camp and garrison equipage were furnished to any of them . . .

'Since the disbanding of Colonel Drew's regiment there are but three indian regiments, averaging, perhaps 700 men each, and only partially and indifferently armed. Of these the Cherokee regiment of Col. Stand Watie, composed of original Southern-rights men, mostly half-breeds . . . is on the neutral land between Missouri and Kansas. This leaves me two weak regiments only, badly armed and poorly supplied with ammunition.'[26]

Pike brought his Native American troops to their only major battle, Pea Ridge, on 7 March 1862. There they proved difficult to control, Pike complaining later about how they wandered about, talking to everyone and taking orders from no one. They also could not stand up under artillery fire. None the less, they successfully charged and took a Union battery before being flanked and driven from the field. Thereafter, they returned to the Indian Territory, which was re-occupied by US forces in early 1863, their service being as scouts or in the particularly brutal guerrilla warfare between pro-Southern and pro-Northern Native Americans and US forces.

As noted above, Confederate Native American units were poorly clad and wore a mixture of native garb, white civilian clothing and whatever military dress was available. A Cherokee soldier described his dress in September 1863 as only a threadbare gray shirt and a pair of pants.[27]

Indian Regiments were as follows.

Regiment	Formed	Disbanded
Cherokee Mounted Rifles	spring 61	summer 62
Drew's Cherokee Mounted Rifles	spring 61	summer 62
1st Cherokee Cavalry Battalion	summer 62	spring 65
1st Cherokee Mounted Rifles	summer 61	spring 65
2nd Cherokee Mounted Rifles	fall 61	spring 65
Faye's-Scales' Cherokee Cavalry Battalion	summer 64	spring 65
1st Chickasaw Cavalry Battalion	fall 62	spring 65
1st Chickasaw Cavalry Regiment	spring 63	winter 64
1st Choctaw and Chickasaw Mounted Rifles	spring 61	spring 65
1st Choctaw Cavalry Regiment	spring 62	spring 65
1st Choctaw Cavalry Battalion	summer 62	spring 63*
2nd Choctaw Cavalry Regiment	summer 62	spring 65
3rd Choctaw Cavalry Regiment	fall 63	spring 65
1st Creek Infantry Regiment	summer 61	spring 65
2nd Creek Infantry Regiment	fall 61	spring 65
1st Seminole Cavalry Battalion	fall 61	spring 65
Osage Battalion	spring 63	spring 65
The Indian Battalion	winter 61	fall 62**

* Raised in Mississippi and only served in that state.
** Raised in Arkansas/Missouri and merged into the 9th Missouri Infantry.

Corps of Engineers

Originally the Corps of Engineers was to have been composed only of commissioned officers, trained engineers, under the direction of the Chief of the Engineer Bureau as well as a company of sappers, miners and pontoniers authorized 6 March 1861 and another company of sappers and bombardiers authorized on 16 May 1861. At first Brigadier General Josiah Gorgas was head of both Bureaux of Ordnance and Engineers, but the job was too much even for someone as able as he was, and thereafter Major General Danville Leadbetter, Captain Alfred L. Rives and Major General Jeremy F. Gilmer served as Chiefs of the Engineer Bureau. Engineer officers were to be assigned to headquarters staffs of armies, corps, divisions and detached brigades.

The actual labor was to be performed by men detailed from line regiments, requisitioned by the staff engineer, as needed. In the Army of Northern Virginia, these details were gathered on a relatively permanent basis into the Pioneer Corps which was officered by Engineer Corps members.

Eventually, it was seen that a trained, skilled Engineer Corps capable of building or destroying bridges, field works, or permanent fortifications was needed, and full battalions with complements of enlisted, as well as commissioned, personnel were authorized and raised.

The 1st Engineers Battalion had four companies organized in the Trans-Mississippi Department in the winter of 1863/4. Two companies were in the Galveston area, while two served in Missouri and Louisiana.

The 1st Engineers Regiments was assigned to the Army of Northern Virginia after its organization in the fall of 1863. Co D served in the Richmond and Petersburg Lines during Butler's abortive attempt to take Richmond before the siege of Petersburg. At Appomattox the entire regiment surrendered, 213 all ranks.

The 2nd Engineers Regiment was organized in the summer of 1863 and never served as one unit. Companies A and B were at Fort Fisher, North Carolina; Companies B, F and I were at Fort Gaines and Morgan, Alabama; Companies C, G, H and K served in the field with the Army of Northern Virginia; and Co D was at Fort McAllister, Georgia.

The 3rd Engineers Regiment was organized in the summer of 1863 with nine companies, of which Co E served in the Valley of Virginia. The other companies served in the Army of Tennessee, Companies A, D and the Company of Sappers and Miners being assigned to army headquarters; Co B to Cheatham's Division; Co C to Stewart's Division; Co F to Cleburne's Division; and Co G to Hindman's Division, as of 30 April 1864.

The 4th Engineers Regiment, apparently only three companies strong, was organized in Shreveport, Louisiana in the summer of 1864. It was attached to headquarters, Trans-Mississippi Department.

Engineers were staff officers and as such wore the regulation uniform for the rank. Colonel T. M. R. Talcott,

This unidentified private wears the Richmond Depot Type II jacket. These jackets were among the types of uniform issued to the 1st and companies of the 2nd Engineers Regiments. (Author's collection)

commander of the 1st Engineers Regiment, wore a staff officer's dark-blue forage cap with only two bars of gold lace up the sides, front and back (none at the top), and as a cap badge a silver Gothic letter 'E', like the letter on the regulation button, on a black velvet background about an inch and a half square. However, Captain William H. Echols of the Engineers was photographed holding a plain dark-blue forage cap with the insignia of the US Corps of Topographical Engineers on the front.

Echols's otherwise regulation frock-coat is piped in buff rather than having all-buff collar and cuffs. This piping arrangement is also to be seen on the otherwise regulation frock-coat worn by Major Conway R. Howard, Chief of Engineers on A. P. Hill's staff. The star on each collar is edged in white on Howard's coat. General Gilmer had his three stars and wreath embroidered on black velvet.

Presumably, non-commissioned officers, being assigned to a staff department, would have used buff or white tape for their chevrons and trouser stripes.

Signal Corps

A second lieutenant of US Engineers, Edward P. Alexander, a Georgian, had assisted US Signal Officer Myers in testing his flag and torch signalling system in the West prior to the Civil War. When war broke out, he resigned and accepted a Confederate commission. During the First Bull Run the men he had trained passed the word of McDowell's flanking march and greatly helped the South to win the war's first big battle. After that battle, Alexander went on to train more Southern signalmen.

On 19 April 1862 Congress authorized a Signal Corps, but Alexander turned down its command, wishing to use his US Military Academy training in a combat role. The job of Chief Signal Officer went to Captain William Norris. The new Corps was to consist of ten officers ranking no higher than captains and ten sergeants with sufficient privates detailed to the Corps as necessary. In November 1862 the Corps establishment was enlarged to a major (William Norris), ten captains, ten first lieutenants, ten second lieutenants and 30 sergeants. A squad of from three to five Corps privates under the command of a sergeant or lieutenant was assigned to each division and cavalry brigade headquarters.

At the same time that Alexander was organizing his signallers, an old sailor and serving officer in the Virginia State Navy, James F. Mulligan, was training men in signalling by means of coloured balls hoisted on poles. The system was used along Virginia's rivers. The Department of Norfolk commissioned Mulligan as a captain, although he didn't relinquish his Virginia Navy commission, and on 22 April 1862 authorized him to raise two signal companies. Mulligan resented Norris and in the political infighting that followed Mulligan managed to get his organization recognized as the Independent Signal Corps and Scouts (ISCS). After the fall of Norfolk the ISCS headquarters moved to Petersburg and served along the eastern seaboard as far south as North Carolina.

Both the Signal Corps and the ISCS reported directly to the Adjutant and Inspector General, and men from both organizations went into an organization unofficially known as the Marine Signal Corps. They served aboard blockade-runners with the intention of communicating with coastline forts. In all, some 1,500 officers and men saw service in the various Confederate Signal Corps organizations.

The Signal Corps in the Army of Tennessee was started when in late 1862 1st Lieutenant W. N. Mercer Otely from Texas was ordered by the Secretary of War to join that army to organize a signal corps, with power to detail any man from any branch of service who was intelligent and acquainted with the area's topography. His unit was established and trained in time for the Battle of Stone's River on 31 December.

In Richmond the Confederate Signal Corps was responsible not only for internal army communications but intelligence-gathering through a division known as the Secret Service Bureau. This responsibility began with Corpsmen reading signals sent by the US Signal Corps. In September 1862, however, it took over the 'Secret Line', a route of safe houses used by messengers, spies and smugglers between Washington, DC and Richmond. Secret Service personnel brought current Northern newspapers to Richmond which were studied for orders of battle and similar information, as well as bringing mail for Confederate agents. Finally, the Signal Corps was responsible for monitoring all movements of the Army of the Potomac. To handle delicate affairs, two Signal Corps sergeants engaged in the Secret Service were attached directly to the Secretary of State's office.

In November 1864 Co A, Secret Service, commanded by Captain Z. McDaniel, was set up. This organization, which was to have no more than 50 men, apparently was responsible for placing the coal torpedo which caused the great explosion at City Point, Virginia. However, it appears to have reported to the Torpedo Bureau rather than to the Secret Service Bureau.

Signal Corps officers were staff officers and wore appropriate uniforms, while enlisted men wore standard dress. Non-commissioned officers may have used white or buff tape for their chevrons and trousers stripes, as befitted members of a staff department. It is quite possible that officers wore a unique cap badge consisting of the same type of signal flags worn by US Signal Corps officers, but in metal. A Signal Corps member wrote a letter on 2 October 1863 requesting, ' . . . a pair of silver-plated cross flags w'h can be gotten on Wall St., or near the Columbian Hotel'. A second letter, sent on 1 May 1864, refers to obtaining 'the signal badge'.[28] Interestingly, there was at that time a silversmith, Francis La Barre, on Wall Street in Richmond who did produce cipher discs for the Corps. There exists in a private collection a ¾-inch-wide brass badge, consisting of crossed flags, the flags being mounted on poles one-inch long.

Partisan Rangers

Given that much of the South quickly came under Federal control and that Southerners characteristically took to mounted, undisciplined warfare, it was only natural that bands of partisan rangers would spring up to attack Union forces in their rear. In April 1862 Congress authorized the formation of partisan units to serve behind Union lines. The men in them were required to wear regulation Confederate uniform, to be mustered into Confederate service under the Articles of War, and to turn over all captured weapons and munitions.

Many of these units adhered to these requirements. Leading among these was Colonel John S. Mosby, 43rd Battalion of Virginia Cavalry, Co A of which was established on 10 June 1863. According to his orders, Mosby was authorized to create a company when he had gathered sufficient men who were willing to serve unconditionally in the Confederate Army. Eventually, the 43rd mustered seven companies. The unit served in Northern Virginia, so controlling the area that it was known as 'Mosby's Confederacy'. Mosby disbanded his unit on 21 April 1865.

Some of the men in the units were outlaws plain and simple, taking advantage of civil chaos to rob for their own good. William C. Quantrill was one of these, early receiving a captain's commission, but in November 1862 murdering unarmed teamsters during a raid in Missouri. Refused a major command because of his reputation in Richmond, he went on to destroy Lawrence, Kansas, on 21 August 1863, killing more than 150 men, women and children there. He was fatally wounded in Kentucky in 1865, but others of his band, including the infamous James Brothers, went on to careers as outlaws in the post-war West.

Southern partisans hang a Union man

'We came suddenly upon the corpse of a man suspended over a creek by the neck, who, our guide informed us, had been hung the night before by the guerrillas. The body was that of a man apparently forty years old, with an immense muscular frame, and the ground around the tree indicated that a severe struggle had taken place between the poor man and his executioners.

'We cut the rope, took down the body, and carried it about a fourth of a mile up to the valley to his house, which was a rude hut built of logs. On entering, we discovered on a cot in one corner an old man with a minnie ball in his side. The same party of guerrillas had shot him at the same time they had compelled his son to go with them, and whom they afterwards hung. The dead man's wife and four or five small children met us at the door, and their grief was intense. The old man was suffering intensely, but from him we learned all the particulars. His son had been accused of being a Union Man, and the guerrillas had tried to impress him into the Rebel service, but his steady refusal to fight against the old flag, his unswerving loyalty, had cost him his life. They took him by main force, but he probably resisted, and they hung him like a dog.

'The old man's interference provoked the leader of the party, who, from his horse, shot him while standing in the door.'

(Otto F. Bond, ed., *Under the Flag of the Nation*, Ohio State University Press, Columbus, Ohio, 1961, pp. 20–1)

On 23 March 1864 the Adjutant and Inspector General of the Army sent a circular to field commanders inquiring about partisan rangers. Lee replied on 1 April that he approved of the 43rd Virginia, but otherwise, 'Experience has convinced me that it is almost impossible, under the best officers even, to have discipline in these bands of Partisan Rangers, or to prevent them from becoming an injury instead of a benefit to the service, and even when this is accomplished the system gives licence to many deserters & marauders, who assume to belong to these authorized companies & commit depredations on friend & foe alike.

Another great objection to them is the bad effect upon the discipline of the army from the great licence allowed in these bands. With the single exception mentioned, I hope the order will be issued at once disbanding the companies & battalions serving in this department.'[29] Following that, Congress repealed the Partisan Ranger Act but allowed organizations approved by the Secretary of War to stay in existence. Most did, with or without his approval.

When all was said and done, the partisan rangers did little to advance the Southern cause or even prolong the war, but created animosities that would take years to erase.

Unit	State Raised	Organized
1st Regiment	Texas	summer 62
1st Battalion	Virginia	summer 62
2nd Regiment	Maryland	spring 62
2nd Regiment	Texas	fall 61
5th Regiment	Texas	spring 63
8th Battalion	North Carolina	spring 63
10th Regiment	Kentucky	summer 63
12th Battalion	Mississippi	spring 63
12th Battalion	North Carolina	spring 63
13th Battalion	Alabama	fall 62
15th Battalion	Alabama	spring 63
18th Battalion	Alabama	summer 62
20th Battalion	Georgia	summer 62
27th Battalion	Virginia	fall 62
37th Battalion	Virginia	summer 62
43rd Battalion	Virginia	spring 63
51st Regiment	Alabama	summer 62
53rd Regiment	Alabama	fall 62
56th Regiment	Alabama	summer 63
62nd Regiment	Georgia	fall 62
McNeil's Rangers	Virginia	spring 62
Patton's Battalion	Kentucky	spring 63

By regulations, Partisan Rangers were to wear cavalry uniforms. Mosby's men seem to have done so, actually being better dressed than regular cavalrymen since they could get good Northern-made cloth and supplies from which to have them made locally. Otherwise, Partisans wore a mix of civilian clothing and US Army uniforms.

Medical Department

Following the US Army's Medical Department organization, the head of the Confederate Army's Medical Department was the Surgeon General, Dr Samuel P. Moore, who ranked as a brigadier general of cavalry. He was aided by two assistant surgeon-generals, one in the Trans-Mississippi Department and the other at Richmond, with five surgeons assigned to his office. Additionally, in September 1864, the department was staffed with eighteen medical directors who were assigned to every independent corps or command, eight medical directors of hospitals, six medical inspectors in the field in various departments, seven medical inspectors of hospitals, and a varying staff of medical purveyors, all of whom ranked as colonels. Five medical boards examined prospective surgeons to ascertain their medical and surgical expertise.

Under them all were surgeons, who ranked as majors, assigned to each regiment and hospital. About 1,000 surgeons served in the Confederate Army. Under them were assistant surgeons, ranking as captains, of whom about 2,000 served. The War Department also hired a number of contract surgeons or acting assisting surgeons who were paid and rated as second lieutenants of cavalry. All Confederate Army medical officers had to pass a medical board examination to retain their commissions. All surgeons were exempt from capture as non-combatants according to Confederate General Order Number 45 dated 26 June 1862 and Union General Order No. 60 dated 6 June 1862.

A foreign observer in mid-1863 summed up the organization of the Army of Northern Virginia's Medical Department: 'The medical department is organized thus: – Medical director of the army; medical director of each army corps, chief surgeon of division; senior surgeon of brigade. Each regiment has a surgeon, an assistant-surgeon, two ambulances and a medical waggon, belonging to it. Two men from each company are detailed to act as litter-bearers and attendants upon the wounded; those follow the troops on the field of battle, and convey men to the hospitals in the rear.'[30]

The senior regimental surgeon became the senior surgeon of brigade to whom other regimental surgeons reported. His regiment was assigned an additional assistant surgeon to serve in his absence. The senior surgeon of brigade reported to the chief surgeon of division, who reported to the corps medical director.

Two privates from each line company made up the Army of Northern Virginia's Ambulance Corps. One company commander later recalled that ' . . . each company had two men detailed as litter-bearers who were excused from all company drill and the regimental drill. Their principal duty was to pick up wounded men and carry them back to the surgeon and assist the surgeon after the battle. The captains selected the strongest and bravest men for this duty. Often the litter-bearer had to carry a man on his back or in his arms, which called for greater strength, and to return to the firing line was more trying than to stay and shoot.'[31] Originally, the litter-bearers were bandsmen, but as bands were discontinued for lack of personnel they were replaced by permanently assigned and trained Ambulance Corpsmen. These men were the only troops allowed to leave the battlefield.

Each regiment also had an enlisted staff which included a hospital steward who had to have had medical or pharmaceutical schooling. A private was usually assigned the job of hospital clerk. He had to be present at sick call each morning to handle necessary paperwork.

Surgeons, hospital stewards and hospital clerks were also assigned to each permanent hospital. As of 27 September 1862 each hospital was authorized two matrons, two

These three surgeons were accompanied by a black servant when they had their photograph taken. Two wear the regulation coat with black facings and the rank badges of a major; one wears the common sack coat with the rank badge on his laydown collar. (US Army Military History Institute)

assistant matrons and two ward matrons for every 100-bed ward. Each hospital was responsible for assigning one skilled surgeon per five hundred beds to the Reserve Surgical Corps which could be called up by field armies for temporary duty in emergencies. In hospitals near the front, convalescents and attendants were organized and armed as infantry companies for local defence.

The major Confederate hospital was the huge Chimborazo Hospital in Richmond which was made up of five hospitals each under the direction of a surgeon with 45–50 assistant and acting assistant surgeons under each surgeon. The hospital covered 125 acres and could deal with 4,800 patients at a time. But, in Richmond there were also 32 hospitals open to other needy individuals, as well as special hospitals maintained for patients from Louisiana and South Carolina, a hospital for members of the Engineers Bureau, and regimental hospitals maintained by the 1st to 3rd

Alabama Regiments and 1st to 4th Georgia Regiments stationed in the city. This chaos led to a law which closed private hospitals unless commanded by a commissioned officer no lower in rank than an assistant surgeon.

Medical Department officers wore staff officers' uniform with black collar and cuffs. The trousers were to be dark-blue with a black velvet stripe, an inch and a quarter wide, and edged with a gold cord down each leg. The sash was to be green silk.

While thre was no regulation cap badge, one surgeon later recalled ' . . . on the front of the cap or hat were the letters "M.S." embroidered in gold, embraced in two olive branches'.[32] One acting assistant surgeon recalled in April 1862 wearing the ' . . . dress of an assistant-surgeon, with the M.S. upon my cap'.[33] This badge was far from universal. In his photograph Surgeon William H. Philpot, 4th Georgia Infantry, wore an officer's dark-blue cap with the Old English letters 'M' on one side of the two gold stripes down the front and 'S' on the other side and no wreath. Surgeon William F. Steuart wore the entire badge with the Old English letters 'MS' within the gold wreath when he was photographed, and Surgeon William B. Wise's forage cap was plain dark-blue with no decoration of any sort.

The hospital steward, who rated between a first sergeant and a sergeant major, also had no authorized unique insignia. However, recalled a surgeon, ' . . . the chevrons on the coat sleeves and the stripe down the trousers of the hospital steward were similar to those worn by an orderly or first sergeant, but were black in color'.[33] Ambulance Corps members wore a red badge on their hat or cap. The exact design, if there was one, is unknown.

A Confederate chaplain decides not to go to heaven

'One of our chaplains, Rev. Dr. L----, who had fallen heir to Gen. Stonewall Jackson's sorrel mare, was riding at the head of our column as we marched down the valley, when suddenly we ran into the enemy's pickets, and the rifles began to crack at a very lively rate, whereupon the aforesaid chaplain turned the sorrel's head the other way, and began to pace rapidly to the rear. Just then General Early appeared, and seeing Dr. L----, he called out in that high-pitched drawling voice which was so peculiar to him, "Hello, Parson L----, where are you going? You've been praying for forty years to get to heaven, and right down this road there's a first-rate chance to go there quick, and you won't take it!"'

(Randolph H. McKim, *A Soldier's Recollections*, Zengler Publishing Co., Washington, DC, 1983, p. 226)

A Disembowelled Confederate officer lives

'It was in this battle [Slaughter Mountain] that Major Snowden Andrews of the artillery, also from Maryland, received one of those fearful wounds from which recovery is thought to be an impossibility. Struck by a piece of shell he was disembowelled and his abdomen and viscera rolled in the dust where he fell: he was left without hope. Dr. McGuire, passing and seeing him, stopped to say he was grieved to see he could not be any help to him.

'"Yes, that's what you fellows all say," said Andrews.

'Stung a little by this, McGuire, who greatly liked him, sprung to the ground to do what he could. He washed off and restored his viscera to their proper place, stimulated him, sewed him up, gave him all the benefit of his skill and sent him to a hospital. Meeting McGuire a few minutes afterwards, I said, "McGuire, is Snowden Andrews mortally wounded?"

'"Well – if the good Lord will let the rest of the world take care of itself for a time and devote his attention exclusively to Andrews, he may be able to pull him through, but no one else can!"

'"Snowden Andrews still lives [he died in 1903].'

(Henry Kyd Douglas, *I Rode With Stonewall*, Fawcett Publications, New York, 1961, pp. 129–30)

Chaplains

Each regiment was authorized a chaplain, to be appointed by the unit commander and, indeed, most regiments had chaplains. Additionally, a number of chaplains served with the armies 'at large' or as 'missionary chaplains'. Generally each hospital had a post-chaplain in attendance. In all, some 600 ministers served as Confederate chaplains, fourteen being killed in action and another 25 dying in service.

On 16 March 1863 Chaplains in the Army of Nothern Virginia's II and III Corps formed a joint Chaplains' Association to work together towards common goals. An army-wide Chaplains' Association was also formed in the Army of Tennessee.

Chaplains generally wore civilian ministers' dress in black. On 14 April 1863 the II and III Corps Chaplains' Association appointed a committee of three to choose a unique badge for its members. In June they finally chose the letter 'C' within a half-wreath of gold-embroidered olive leaves on a black velvet background, the whole about two and a half inches wide. Chaplains in the Army of Tennessee wore a Maltese cross on their coat collar or lapel.

Military Academies

The Confederates did not establish a national military academy, but the South was served by a number of private military academies that had been established long before the Civil War.

The Virginia Military Academy (VMI) was founded at Lexington, Virginia, in 1839, and had graduated 455 men prior to the Civil War. On 4 July 1861 the class of 1861 received an early graduation so as to leave for service in the

Confederate armed forces. The class of 1862 was graduated early on 6 December 1861. The school reopened on 1 January 1862 when cadets still not actively serving in the Army and new first-year men, or 'rats' at they were called, arrived. The Civil War gave a boost to enrollment at the school, 818 cadets attending during the war period.

The Corps of Cadets was called into action during the Valley Campaign in 1862 although they did not see action then. In May 1864 they were again called out to oppose Union forces under Major General Franz Sigel driving South through the Valley. The 258 cadets and their instructor officers were part of a force that met Sigel's men at New Market, Virginia, on 11 May where they stopped a Union assault and then went on the counter-attack, capturing a Union cannon. Five cadets were killed in action, five more were mortally wounded and 47 were wounded. Thereafter, the Corps of Cadets served a short time in Richmond's local defence force before being returned to the Valley and the defence of Lexington on 11 June. The school was destroyed when that city was overwhelmed. Even so, on 27 June 1864 VMI graduated fourteen cadets amid the school's ruins, and the other cadets were granted leave. In October 1864 the Corps was reunited in Richmond at the city almshouse, continuing classwork there. In March 1865 they were called out for the city's defence. On 2 April the Corps was given leave of absence as the city fell, only to resume classes that October.

The South Carolina Military Academy had its origins when the state legislature created two military schools at the Arsenal in Columbia and the Citadel and Magazine in Charleston. By the Civil War, cadets attended the Arsenal for their first year and the Citadel for their last three, although the two schools did not become The South Carolina Military Academy until 28 January 1861. As a whole, cadets were in the Battalion of State Cadets, a two-company-strong organization of some 200 cadets. The Battalion was mustered into the State Militia in November 1861 but never served together during the war. However, Citadel cadets manned the four-gun battery that opened fire on the *Star of the West* as it was coming to the relief of the garrison at Fort Sumter on 9 January 1861, and on 1 May 1865, South Carolina's first-year cadets probably fired the last shots of the war.

The Arsenal was destroyed when Columbia burned in 1865, but the Citadel was allowed to continue in operation after the war, although not as a military academy.

The Georgia Military Institute was set up in Marietta in 1851. Its students formed the Cadet Battalion which served as part of the permanent force created to defend the state capital of Milledgeville. During Sherman's march through the state the Institute was burned and the school was then closed.

The North Carolina Military Institute, located in Charlotte, had been established in 1859 but was closed in 1861 as its student and teaching bodies left to join the serving forces. Cadets from the Arkansas Military Institute, which had been opened in Tulip in 1850, formed Co I, 3rd Arkansas

Infantry in 1861 when the school closed. Florida's West Florida Seminary, which opened in 1851, had its own Cadet Corps which saw a month's active service in the dying days of the war in 1865.

The University of Alabama, in Tuscaloosa, formed a cadet corps in 1860 which stayed in existence until 1865 at which time it included three companies of cadets. It saw no active service. Other military schools in Alabama included the Southern Military Academy in Wetumpka, the La Grange College and Military Academy, and the Glenville Military Academy. La Grange had been founded in 1858 and the other two in 1860 and all three closed for lack of students during the war.

Mississippi trained cadets at the Mississippi Military Institute, Pass Christian; Brandon State Military Institute, Brandon; and Jefferson College, Natchez. These were never large groups, with only 175 muskets being needed for the entire cadet company of the Mississippi Military Institute before 1860. They did not survive the war's early years.

At the outbreak of war, VMI cadets wore a uniform virtually the same as that worn by US Military Academy cadets, of gray with three rows of brass ball buttons connected by black silk piping, three black chevrons at the cuff, and crow's-feet at the end of each line of lace. Trousers were gray in the winter and white in the summer. A gray forage cap with a single line of black lace up the sides, front and back and a black band was worn for undress while a black shako with a pompom for cadet privates and cock feathers for cadet officers was worn for dress.

Service in the 1862 Valley campaign wore out this elaborate uniform for most cadets. A cadet described their uniforms thereafter: 'Then we had to resort to coarse sheep's gray jacket and trousers, with seven buttons and a plain black tape stripe ... We were content with a simple forage cap, blue or gray, as we could procure it. The cadet of today disports himself in white cross-belts, shining plates, and patent-leather accoutrements. Then, we had a plain leather cartridge box, and waist-belt with a harness buckle ...

'As the war progressed, our uniforms ceased to be uniforms; for the difficulty of procuring cloth increased we were permitted to supply ourselves with whatever our parents could procure, and in time we appeared in every shade from Melton gray to Georgia butternut.'[35]

During the war South Carolina's cadets wore the regulation school fatigue dress which consisted of a gray uniform jacket with a standing collar and a single row of nine state buttons down the front, with gray trousers with a black stripe down each leg for winter and white trousers for summer. The plain forage cap was dark-blue.

The dress uniform worn by Georgia cadets apparently included a single-breasted dark-blue frock-coat with sky-blue standing collar, pointed cuffs, and worsted fringed epaulettes. Trousers matched, and the hat was a version of the 1839 US Army forage cap. Belts were white.

North Carolina's cadets wore copies of the US Military Academy cadet uniform with the US Army Corps of Engineers' cap badge on their black shako. Cadets at the

Arkansas Military Institute wore copies of the VMI fatigue uniform. West Florida Seminary cadets wore essentially the basic US Military Academy cadet uniform with a 'chasseur' cap. All Alabama's cadets appear to have worn a gray coatee, trousers, and a forage cap trimmed with black. Mississippi's cadets wore standard copies of the US Military Academy uniform.

The Navy

The Confederate Navy was created by Congress on 16 March 1861 when the President was authorized to appoint four captains, four commanders, 30 lieutenants, five surgeons, five assistant surgeons, six paymasters, and two chief engineers to the new Confederate Navy. He was also allowed to recruit as many masters, midshipmen, engineers, naval constructors, boatswains, gunners, carpenters, sailmakers and other warrant and petty officers and seamen as needed, not to exceed 3,000 men. Many of these officers and men came as already organized groups from the state navies of Georgia and Virginia. On 24 December 1861 four admirals were authorized.

The President appointed Stephen R. Mallory to the post of Secretary of the Navy, civilian head of the organization. Mallory created a body similar to the US Navy, with Captain Franklin Buchanan as Chief, Bureau of Orders and Detail; Commander George Manor, Chief, Bureau of Ordnance and Hydrography; Paymaster James A. Semple, Chief, Bureau of Provisions and Clothing; and Surgeon W. A. W. Spotsword, Chief, Bureau of Medicine and Surgery. E. M. Tidball became Chief Clerk of the Navy.

Recognizing the need of a larger navy, on 21 April 1862 Congress created several new ranks and authorized four admirals, ten captains, 21 commanders, 100 first lieu-tenants, 25 second lieutenants, 20 masters in line of promotion, twelve paymasters, 40 assistant paymasters, 22 surgeons, fifteen passed assistant surgeons, 30 assistant surgeons, an engineer-in-chief and twelve engineers. All the admirals, four captains, five commanders, 22 first lieutenants, and five second lieutenants were to receive their commissions solely because of gallant or meritorious conduct rather than seniority. Besides the commissioned officers, the navy was to have these warrant officers: 20 passed midshipmen, 106 acting midshipmen, 50 first assistant engineers, 150 second assistant engineers, 150 third assistant engineers, ten boatswains, 20 gunners, six sailmakers, and 20 carpenters. A Bureau of Naval Constructors was also set up at this time; John L. Porter was its chief.

The Confederate Navy at the Battle of Sailor's Creek

'The Union soldiers were greatly astonished at the miscellaneous uniforms in our small division and under other circumstances we would have found amusement in listening to their comments. One of them pointed out an officer in a naval uniform with wide gold lace on it and asked me who he was. When I told him that he belonged to the navy, his jaw dropped and he said, "Good Heaven, have you gunboats way up here too?" I might have answered, as some one said earlier in the war, that we had them wherever there was a little dew on the grass had I not been in too serious a frame of mind.'

(McHenry Howard, *Recollections of a Maryland Confederate Soldier and Staff Officer under Johnston, Jackson and Lee*, Morningside Bookshop, Dayton, Ohio, 1975, pp. 386–7)

Executive officers' cap badges.
(1861 Dress Regulations)

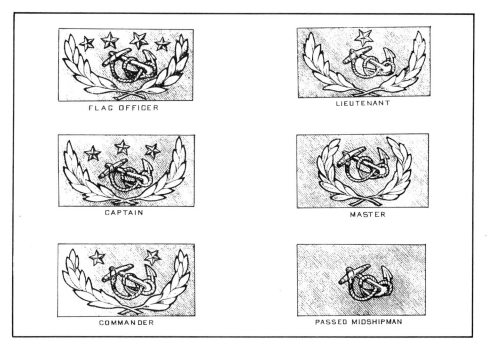

FLAG OFFICER   LIEUTENANT

CAPTAIN   MASTER

COMMANDER   PASSED MIDSHIPMAN

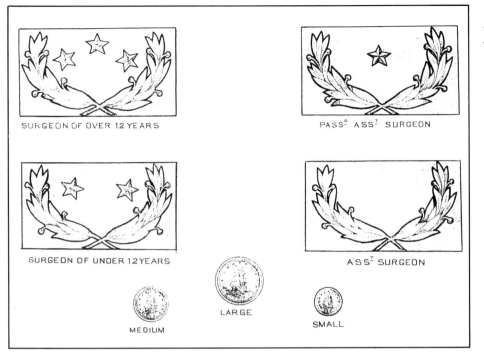

SURGEON OF OVER 12 YEARS

PASS^D ASS^T SURGEON

SURGEON OF UNDER 12 YEARS

ASS^T SURGEON

MEDIUM

LARGE

SMALL

Civil officers' cap badges and button showing a ship under full sail. (1861 Dress Regulations)

In April 1863 a Volunteer Navy was authorized essentially to commission those serving on privateers. In May 1863 Congress separated the Regular Navy from a newly created 'Provisional Navy'. The Provisional Navy served as the active navy, with lower-ranking Regular Navy officers being promoted to higher rank on the Provisional Navy list over the heads of older, less active officers who remained in their Regular Navy ranks. Essentially, it turned the Regular Navy into a retired list. In January 1864 both navy lists were merged.

As in the US Navy, Confederate Navy officers assigned to different bureaux had relative rank with line officers. At first Chiefs of Bureaux rated as captain, later commodores as the Navy was enlarged. Commanders and first lieutenants commanding rated with surgeons, paymasters, engineers and naval constructors with more than twelve years' service; the same ranks with less than twelve years' service rated with first lieutenants; passed assistant surgeons, assistant paymasters, naval constructors and first assistant engineers rated as masters; assistant surgeons and second and third assistant engineers rated as passed midshipmen.

The Navy had ordnance works in Richmond; Augusta, Georgia: Selma, Alabama; and Charlotte, North Carolina; a powder mill in Columbia, South Carolina; and a laboratory in New Orleans. A rope-walk was built in Petersburg, Virginia.

The Naval Submarine Battery Service was set up in October 1862 to construct and deploy mines, or 'torpedoes', in Southern rivers and harbours. Torpedo stations were established in Charleston; Mobile, Alabama; Richmond; Savannah, Georgia; and Wilmington, North Carolina.

The Congressional Act of 16 March 1861 authorized the

Secretary of the Navy to set up a naval academy. This was organized on 23 March 1863 when Secretary Mallory appointed a board of officers to examine acting midshipmen for appointment to the academy. The school was headquartered in the CS Steamship *Patrick Henry*, a 10-gun ship with a complement of 150, then part of the James River Squadron. Only 52 midshipmen could berth aboard the ship. Nine instructors were named, giving classes in astronomy, navigation and surveying; seamanship; gunnery; mathematics; physics; French and Spanish; English; history; artillery and infantry tactics; and swordsmanship. The school opened with a class of 50 acting midshipmen between 14 and 18 years old, divided into four classes. Examinations were held every June and December, those passing their December examinations being promoted and assigned to duty stations. The Corps of Midshipmen took part in the defence of nearby Drewry's Bluff. When Richmond fell, the Corps accompanied some $500,000 in Confederate and Richmond bank gold and silver coins and bars ($86,000 of which was given to Clerk Tidball and Paymaster Semple to smuggle out of the country and was never seen again in one of the war's great mysteries) and the Confederate archives south until sent on leave in Abbeville, South Carolina, on 2 May 1865.

Despite a lack of naval yards or trained naval carpenters or builders, the Confederate Navy managed to commission more than 130 vessels and craft. Its greatest problem was manning its ships. Conscripts went into the Army which was loath to transfer them into the Navy. Exceptions for seamen and ordinary seamen to be transferred into the Navy were passed by Congress on 16 April 1862, 2 October 1862 and 1 May 1863. As of November 1863, the

Executive officers' cuff lace. (1861 Dress Regulations)

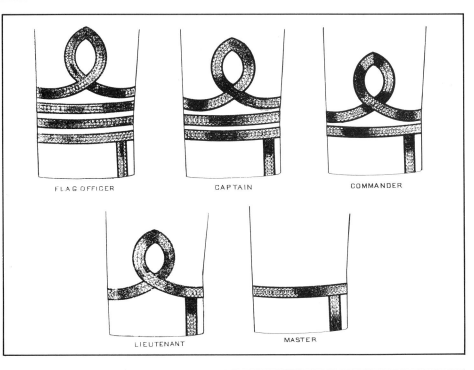

FLAG OFFICER   CAPTAIN   COMMANDER

LIEUTENANT   MASTER

Confederate Navy consisted of 753 officers and 2,700 enlisted men. Not until 20 March 1864, when the Army's Adjutant and Inspector General called for 1,200 soldiers to be transferred to the Navy, of which some 960 actually were, that the problems was somewhat resolved. At its peak, by the end of 1864, the Navy had 3,674 enlisted men on active duty.

When the Army's Invalid Corps was created, seamen were to be allowed to transfer to it, but it was under the command of the Secretary of the Army, something that did not sit well with the Navy. On 7 June 1864 the Navy and Marine Corps Invalid Corps was created for sailors and Marines who, though disabled by injury or disease, could nevertheless perform light duties. The Corps reported directly to the Secretary of the Navy.

Most commissioned officers originally served in the US Navy and brought their old uniforms with them. Many changed their buttons to state buttons. In November 1861 Raphael Semmes, commander of the CSS *Sumter*, described her officers as wearing new navy-blue uniforms with gold epaulettes for lieutenants and gold-embroidered anchors for midshipmen. Her seamen wore white duck frocks and trousers, he wrote. Photographs show Semmes' lieutenants wearing a single stripe of gold lace on each cuff, a loop both above and below the lace strip. Semmes himself, as a commander, wore two lace stripes, a loop going towards the elbow from the top stripe and a lace going down towards the cuff from the bottom stripe.

Sometime after Semmes had left the South with the *Sumter* on 30 June 1861 and before 21 April 1862, when the rank structure was changed, the Navy Department issued a full set of dress regulations. According to these, officers were to

---

A Confederate sailor is forced to fight

'During the afternoon when the battle [of Roanoke Island] was at its height I ordered the engineer to send me all the men he could spare from the fire-room to work at the gun; one of the men sent up was my green coal-passer, who evidently did not like the appearance of things on deck. However he went to the side tackles of the gun as ordered; after awhile a shell bursting overhead I called to the men to lie down, and when it was over I ordered them to jump up and go at it again. All promptly obeyed but the coal-passer, who still lay flat on his stomach. "Get up," I called to him from the hurricane deck just above him: he turned his head like a turtle and fixed his eye on me, but otherwise did not move. "Get up", I said, "or I will kill you," at the same time drawing a pistol from my belt and cocking it. He hesitated a moment and then sprang to the gun, and behaved well during the rest of the engagement.'

(Captain William H. Parker, *Recollections of a Naval Officer*, Charles Scribner's Sons, New York, 1883, p. 250)

---

wear a frock-coat such as worn by US Navy officers but of steel-gray cloth; steel-gray cloth or white drill trousers; and a steel-gray double-breasted overcoat with rolling collar. Coats were double-breasted save for chaplains, who had one row of nine buttons; professors and commodore's secretaries who had eight buttons in a single row; and clerks who had a single row of six buttons. A steel-gray double-breasted jacket was also authorized but was largely worn by midshipmen.

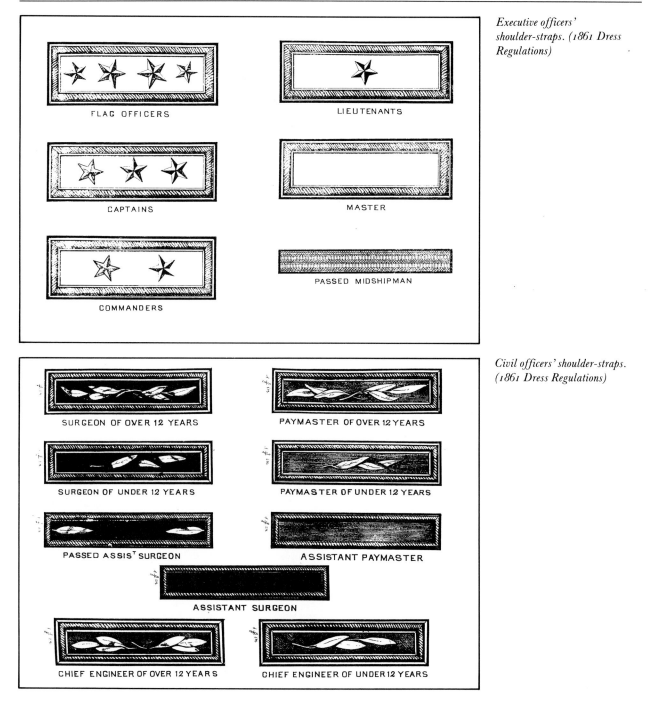

Executive officers' shoulder-straps. (1861 Dress Regulations)

Civil officers' shoulder-straps. (1861 Dress Regulations)

Rank was to be distinguished by gold lace stripes on the cuff and shoulder-straps. Executive officers had a loop of lace on the top lace stripe, while civil officers wore plain parallel lace stripes. Flag officers had four stripes of half-inch-wide gold lace, a stripe also running along the buttoned cuff edge. A captain had three lace stripes; a commander, two lace stripes; a lieutenant, one. A master had a quarter-inch-wide lace stripe, without the loop. Passed midshipmen had three large-sized (the printed

regulations apparently incorrectly said 'medium') Navy buttons running parallel with the cuff, while midshipmen had three medium-sized buttons. After April 1862 admirals were to wear five gold lace stripes on each cuff.

Rank was also indicated by shoulder-straps that looked much like those worn in the US Army. These came in branch-of-service color backs edged in gold with gold insignia embroidered in their centres. Executive officers had a sky-blue background with five stars worn by admirals, four by flag officers (commodores), three by captains, two by commanders, one by lieutenants and plain straps by masters. Passed midshipmen wore a four-inch-long strip of gold lace a half-inch wide. Surgeons had a black background for their shoulder-straps with two olive sprigs for a surgeon with more than twelve years' service; one olive sprig for a surgeon with less than twelve years' service; an olive leaf at each end for a passed assistant surgeon, and a plain strap for an assistant surgeon. Paymasters had a dark-green background and wore the same insignia as surgeons of equivalent rank. Engineers had a dark-blue background. A chief engineer with twelve years' service wore two sprigs of live oak; a chief engineer with less than twelve years' service wore one sprig of live oak; a first assistant engineer wore a live oak leaf at each end of the strap (after April 1862), second assistant engineers wore plain shoulder-straps (after April 1862), and third assistant engineers wore nothing on their shoulders. After April 1862 naval constructors were to wear the same shoulder-straps as the equivalent engineer officer ranks, but with a buff background.

The cap was also steel-gray with a patent leather visor and a slight overhang. A gold lace band an inch and three quarters wide was worn with the cap. Rank and branch of service was also indicated by cap badge. An admiral wore a gold foul anchor within a live oak leaf wreath under five stars; a commodore's or flag officer's badge had four stars; a captain's, three stars; a commander's, two stars; a lieutenant's, one star; and a master had a plain foul anchor within the wreath. A passed midshipman had a plain foul anchor, a midshipman had a plain cap. Surgeons and paymasters had the wreath and same number of stars as their equivalent rank, but lacked the anchor. Engineers had the same but added the Old English letter 'E' within the wreath while naval constructors had the Old English letter 'C'. Volunteer Navy officers were also to wear the ¾-inch-long gilt letters 'VN' on their cap front as of 19 June 1863.

In April 1862 when new ranks were created the following changes were made to the uniform regulations:

'Lieutenants Commmanding will wear one stripe in addition to the number worn by First Lieutenants on the sleeve.

'First Lieutenants will wear the uniform prescribed for Lieutenants.

'Second Lieutenants will wear the same uniform as First Lieutenants except the star in the shoulder-strap.

'Lieutenants for the war the same as Second Lieutenants.'[36]

Officers were also authorized to wear a straw hat in hot climates, as well as light-weight gray frock and trousers. Officers of the Mobile, Alabama Squadron were allowed to wear a gray flannel frock- or sack coat with gray trousers and vest from 1 June until 1 October, according to a Squadron order of 1 June 1864.

Despite regulations, gray was an unpopular color for naval officers, all of whom were used to the dark-blue used by virtually all the world's navies (save Russia which wore dark-green). Many officers continued to wear dark-blue on

An admiral is wounded on the CSS *Tennessee*

'One of these missiles had struck the iron cover of the stern port and jammed it against the shield so that it became impossible to run the gun out for firing, and Admiral [Franklin] Buchanan, who superintended the battery during the entire engagement [of Mobile Bay, Alabama], sent to the engine room for a mechanist to back out the pin of the bolt upon which the port cover revolved. While this was being done a shot from one of the monitors struck the edge of the port cover, immediately over the post where the machinist was sitting, and his remains had to be taken up with a shovel, placed in a bucket, and thrown overboard. The same shot caused several iron splinters to fly inside of the shield, one of which killed a seaman, while another broke the admiral's leg below the knee. The admiral sent for me, and as I approached he quietly remarked, "Well, Johnston, they've got me. You'll have to look out for her now. This is your fight, you know." I replied, "All right, sir. I'll do the best I know how."'

(James D. Johnston, 'The Ram "Tennessee" At Mobile Bay', *Battles & Leaders of the Civil War*, Thomas Yoseloff, New York, 1956, p. 404)

A British-made Navy button. The foul anchor over the crossed cannon badge was used on all British-made Confederate Navy items, ranging from buckles to leather equipment box flaps. (Author's collection)

A Confederate officer is saved by a dictionary

'Our river steamers went down to City Point [Virginia] occasionally with prisoners to exchange. As we had torpedoes [mines] in the river anywhere from Drewry's Bluff to Trent's reach, and below, their captains ran great risks. On one occasion two of our boats were returning from City Point, fortunately with no passengers, when one of them struck a torpedo and immediately went down. A boat went from the other steamer and found the captain struggling in the water, with a Webster's *Unabridged Dictionary* in his arms. As he was pulled into the boat he said: "I did not have time to get it on." He thought he had seized a life-preserver!'

(William H. Parker, *Recollections of a Naval Officer*, Charles Scribners' Sons, New York, 1883, pp. 350–1)

Flag Officer French Forrest, head of the Bureau of Orders and Detail, holding a British-made regulation Confederate Navy officer's sword. His cap peak is edged in gold metal. (US Army Military History Institute collection)

Crew members aboard the CSS Alabama. *The officer with the buttons on his cuff and no cap badge, although he wears an officer's cap, appears to be a midshipman, despite the beard. He does not appear to have shoulder-straps, which would make him a civil officer such as an assistant surgeon, or a lace loop on the collar that would make him a warrant officer. (Peabody-Holmes collection, Cape Archives, South Africa)*

service. The waist-length jacket worn by First Lieutenant Robert D. Minor of the CSS *Virginia* when he was shot in an open boat in March 1862 was dark-blue without a loop on his cuff lace. First Lieutenant George Gift, CSS *Gaines*, wrote that he wore a dark-blue flannel uniform in September 1863, as did Master's Mate I. Dutton Graves in April 1864.

Warrant officers – boatswains, gunners, carpenters and sailmakers – were to wear a steel-gray double-breasted coat, with eight buttons in each row; rolling collar; pointed pocket flap with three large buttons underneath each; three medium-sized buttons around each cuff and two small ones on the sleeve openings; and four buttons on the back of the coat. Rank was indicated by a loop of ¾-inch gold lace, an inch and a half wide and four inches long, with a small button at the point of each loop.

According to the late 1861 regulations, boatswain' mates, gunner's mates, carpenter's mates, sailmaker's mates, ship's stewards and ship's cooks were to wear a three-inch-long black embroidered foul anchor in their gray jacket's right sleeve. The same badge in dark-blue was to be worn on the white frock. Other petty officers except for yeomen and stewards were to wear the same badge on the left sleeve.

Originally, Confederate sailors were clothing that was very much like that worn by US sailors. An Englishman who shipped from England in the *Nashville* in late 1861 recalled his first dress: 'I wore a blue woollen shirt open at the neck; a black silk handkerchief, with ample flowing ends, tied loosely around the neck; blue trousers made very tight at the knee and twenty-two inches in circumference at the bottom, and on my head a flat cloth cap ornamented with long black ribbons. I had besides, in the famous sea-chest, a pea jacket, sea boots, and the necessary under-clothing.'[37] Semmes's largely foreign-born and recruited crew in the *Alabama* wore blue flannel shirts and trousers in winter and white duck in summer. Indeed, the first uniforms ordered in England included dark-blue flannel overshirts, undershirts and underdrawers, blue cloth caps, black silk handkerchiefs, wool and duck trousers, cloth jumpers, Barnsley shirting frocks, wool socks, blankets and pea jackets for 1,000 enlisted men.

However, the late 1861 regulations changed the basic color for cold-weather-issue shirts and trousers to steel-gray, although the design did not change. Cuffs and collars were to be of white duck; hats were to be black. In warm weather the white frock, the collar and cuffs to be lined with blue cotton cloth and stitched round with thread, and trousers, with white or black hats were authorized. Gray, visorless caps were to be worn at sea, save when at muster or on leave.

Honorably discharged seamen were authorized a foul anchor, two and a half inches long, embroidered in blue or white above the elbow on the left sleeve.

Marine Corps
On 16 March 1861 Congress authorized a Marine Corps to consist of six companies, each with a captain, a first lieutenant, a second lieutenant, four sergeants, four corporals, two musicians and 100 privates. The Corps staff was to include a major, the Commandant; a quartermaster; a paymaster, an adjutant, the Sergeant Major of the Corps; and a quartermaster sergeant.

On 20 May the Corps was enlarged to number 46 officers and 944 enlisted men with a headquarters staff including a colonel, a lieutenant colonel, a major, a major serving as quartermaster, a major serving as adjutant, a major serving as paymaster, a sergeant major, a quartermaster sergeant and two principal musicians. At the line level, the Corps

First Lieutenant David G. Raney, Jr., was appointed a second lieutenant in the Corps on 22 April 1861. Serving at a variety of seaports, Raney was captured aboard the CSS Tennessee on 5 August 1864. Escaping in October, he rejoined Mobile's garrison only to surrender on 10 May 1865. After the war he suffered from Post Traumatic Stress Disorder, his last days being spent as a recluse in the family home in Apalachicola, Florida. (Mrs. Margaret Key/Apalachicola Historical Society via David M. Sullivan)

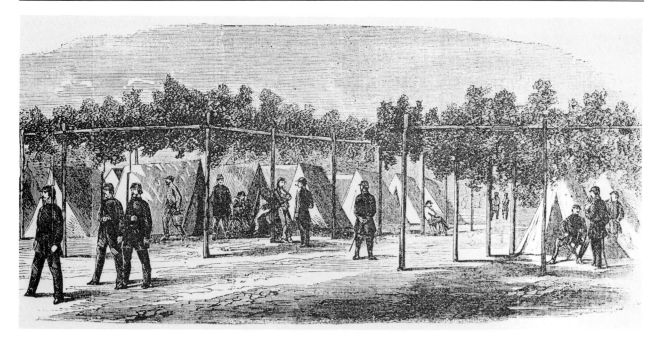

British artist Frank Vizetelly drew this Marine camp at Drewry's Bluff, Virginia. The Marines on guard detail wear

frock-coats. Just visible are two 'V's, points up, worn by the corporal leading the guard detail. (Harper's Weekly)

was to consist of ten captains, ten first lieutenants, 20 second lieutenants, 40 sergeants, 40 corporals, ten drummers, ten fifers, and 840 privates. Although of proper strength for a regiment of ten companies, no company organization was detailed in this organizational plan. Lloyd J. Beall was appointed the Colonel Commandant on 23 May. On 6 March 1862 a 'writer', in fact a civilian secretary, was authorized to be hired for the Commandant's office. Another clerk was authorized for the quartermaster's office on 30 April 1863.

On 24 September 1862 an additional 20 sergeants, 20 corporals, 20 drummers and 20 fifers were added to the Corps, made necessary by the fact that the Corps served as small detachments on shipboard and at Navy installations rather than as a regiment, so more non-commissioned officers were necessary than in Army infantry regiments.

In late 1864 all officers of the Corps signed a petition asking Congress to transfer command of the Corps to the Army as a brigade of three regiments, one of which would be designated 'Marine Infantry'. Guards for Navy installations and ships would be assigned from the Marine Infantry as needed. On 6 February 1865, the Congressional Committee on Naval Affairs was directed to look into the proposal, but there was no time to do anything about the idea before the war was over. In the meantime, Marines did serve in Tucker's Naval Battalion created from Navy Department personnel and assigned to the Army of Northern Virginia during the Appomattox campaign.

Actual strength of the Marine Corps was always lower than Congress authorized. The Corps included some 350 officers and men in 1861; 500 in 1862; 560 in 1663; and 571 in 1864. All told, some 1,200 men enlisted throughout the war.

First Lieutenant Becket K. Howell was commanding a detachment of 20 Marines in the CSS *Sumter* when it left the South in June 1861. He was photographed with the ship's officers in what appears to be his old US Marine Corps officer's uniform. Indeed, he had served as a USMC Lieutenant from 1 August 1860 to 1 March 1861 when he resigned to join the CSMC. Early issues to enlisted men included blue and grey flannel shirts, white and blue trousers, and white shirts or jumpers. Jackets were also issued to men in Co A on 25 July 1861.

Thereafter, Marines seem to have been dressed according to regulations, but no copies of these regulations have been found to date. External evidence must be used to describe the CSMC uniform. On 9 May 1861 an order was sent to Navy buyers in England for jackets, trousers, overcoats and watch coats, woollen socks, flannel shirts, shoes, flannel drawers, linen and cotton shirts and fatigue caps. Accoutrements ordered in September 1861 included black leather waist-belts with cartridge boxes, cap boxes and bayonet scabbards, knapsacks with straps to connect to the waist-belts, bugles, and non-commissioned officers' swords. All were to be the same as used in British service. In March 1863 the Secretary of the Navy reminded his buyer that cloth for Marine uniforms was grey.

Deserter descriptions printed in Southern newspapers in 1863 mention gray coats trimmed with black and black or blue trousers. Drawings show frock-coats worn by enlisted Marines, and photographs show them worn by Marine officers. On 9 June 1863, Captain J. E. Meiere wanted some blue cloth of the type used for Marine trousers, while blue cloth was issued to make a drummer's trousers on 10 September 1864. White trousers were issued in hot climates in deep South ports such as Mobile and New Orleans. A Richmond newspaper item dated 26 May 1862 mentions a Marine's blue cloth cap, while the commander of the Marines aboard the CSS *Richmond* requisitioned a blue cap on 17 May 1864.

The picture then is of a blue forage cap with gray frock-coat probably trimmed around the collar and cuffs with black; blue trousers in winter and white in summer worn by enlisted Marines. Chevrons were worn points up and appear to be the same as worn in the US Marine Corps. Most officers, according to photographs, wore a dark-blue collar and cuffs with a uniform coat that looked like an

Marine Private A. P. Hamm chose the Corps after being conscripted in June 1863. He served in Co E, surrendering at Charleston on 26 April 1865. His equipment is British-made and includes an expense pouch or ball bag on the right front hip as well as a brass 'snake buckle'. (Brooks Hamm via David M. Sullivan)

Army officers' coat, using Army officers' collar insignia and Austrian knots. US Marine Corps shoulder-knots were often worn with this coat. Buttons that have been dug up from sites occupied by Marines were British-made, looking like Army buttons but with the roman letter 'M' in their centre. Accoutrements were also British.

On 25 January 1864 a new pattern of coat and cap was ordered for the Corps, but the design is unknown. Some coats made then were to be of a 'Blue Gray Army Cloth' while other coats were made of one yard and four inches of blue jeans with four buttons a coat.

Finally, on 3 April 1865 the CSS *Shenandoah* captured a Northern ship carrying 70 muskets and two dozen US Army infantry coats and trousers which were intended to be used for trade with islanders in the Pacific. The ship's captain issued them to his Marines.

Revenue Cutter Service

One of the first things Congress did was to pass a law that made all prior US laws that did not conflict with the Confederate constitution once more the law of the land. Among other things, this created a Confederate Revenue Cutter Service with the same organization as that of the United States. US Revenue Cutters which had been turned over to Southern state authorities at the war's outbreak were then assigned to the Confederate Revenue Cutter Service, under the Treasury Department, and many of the USRCS officers and men were taken into the new service.

For example, the USRC *William J. Duane* became the CSRC *Duane* in Norfolk, Virginia; The USRC *Morgan* and *Lewis Cass* changed sides but not names in Mobile; the USRC *Gallatin* became a CRCS cutter (later a privateer) in Georgia; the USRC *William Aiken* became the CRCS *Petrel* (later commissioned as a privateer) at Charleston; the USRC *Minot* became the CSRC *Manassas* off the North Carolina coast; and the USRC *Henry Dodge* became the CSRC *Dodge* (later becoming a blockade-runner) in Galveston.

Officers held the same ranks as in the US Revenue Cutter Service, captains and first, second and third lieutenants, and chief and assistant engineers. However, the blockade severely limited the need for an organization to prevent smuggling and most of the Service's officers and men were seconded to Army seacoast defences and Navy boats while its cutters took on new duties.

At first officers probably wore their old US Revenue Cutter Service uniforms. There are no known copies of CRCS dress regulations, but they probably wore uniforms similar to those worn by CS Navy personnel. Interestingly, in 1834 the US Revenue Cutter service wore a dark-gray uniform with black braid trim in response to US Navy demands that the Service's officers be dressed in any other color than navy-blue so that officers of the two services would not be confused. Although this gray uniform lasted only until 1836 when blue uniforms were returned in response to Service officers' complaints, there was some tradition of gray uniforms in the Service before the war.

Civilian Aid Societies

Although a great many civilian aid societies sprang up to assist the Confederate war effort, none had the overall impact, or was as well organized, as the US Sanitary Commission.

In 1861 Felicia Grundy Porter of Nashville formed the Woman's Relief Society in Tennessee and it soon spread throughout the South. The Society raised money through concerts and spent it largely on artificial limbs for amputees.

In early 1862 Richmond's citizens set up the Richmond Ambulance Committee. Its almost one hundred members organized the transportation in 39 ambulances of the wounded from nearby battles to Richmond's hospitals throughout the war.

Almost every town had its Ladies' Aid Society which usually directed its efforts to help troops from that town in the field. The *Dallas Herald* on 10 November 1861, for example, reported that the Lancaster, Texas, Ladies' Aid Society had sent $1,676.50 worth of coats, jeans, flannel and linsey shirts, winter drawers, winter vests, boots, shoes, woollen mittens, blankets and 'bed comforters' to the men of the 6th Texas Cavalry Regiment during the first 'Great Appeal'.

On their own, too, many Southern women spent a great deal of time working as volunteer nurses in Confederate hospitals.

Civilian Southern aid societies do not appear to have worn any unique uniforms or insignia.

Notes

1. *OR*, Series 2, Vol. IV, p. 986
2. FitzGerald Ross, *Cities and Camps of the Confederate States*, University of Illinois Press, Urbana, Illinois, 1958, p. 131.
3. Francis W. Dawson, *Reminiscences of Confederate Service*, Louisiana State University Press, Baton Rouge, Louisiana, 1980, p. 55
4. Earl S. Miers, ed., *A Rebel War Clerk's Diary*, Sagamore Press, New York, 1958, p. 125
5. Robert U. Johnson and Clarence C. Buel, eds., *Battles and Leaders of the Civil War*, Thomas Yoseloff, New York, 1956, Vol. II, p. 558
6. Ross, op. cit., pp. 33–4
7. Walter Lord, ed., *The Framantle Diary*, Capricorn Books, New York, 1954, p. 124
8. William H. Routt to wife, manuscript department, Confederate Museum, Richmond
9. 'Resources of the Confederacy in February, 1865,' *Southern Historical Society Papers*, Vol. II, No. 1, pp. 117–20
10. Walter H. Taylor, *Four Years with General Lee*, Bonanza Books, New York, 1962, p. 184
11. 'Resources of the Confederacy in February, 1865,' op. cit.
12. Leslie D. Jensen, 'A Survey of Confederate Central Government Quartermaster Issue Jackets,' parts I and II, *Military Collector & Historian*, Journal of the Company of Military Historians, Washington, DC, Fall 1989–Winter 1989, pp. 109–22, pp. 162–71
13. *OR*, Series I, Vol. XXXVIII, p. 121
14. Justus Scheibert, *Seven Months in the Rebel States During the North American War, 1863*, University of Alabama Press, Tuscaloosa, Alabama, 1958, pp. 43–4
15. Edwin H. Fay, *This Infernal War*, University of Texas Press, Austin, TX 1958, p. 344
16. Ibid., p. 374
17. Ibid., p. 392
18. Ross, op. cit., p. 40
19. Gilbert A. Hays, *Under the Red Patch*, Regimental Association, Pittsburgh, 1908, p. 420
20. Thomas G. Rogers and Richard M. Harrison, *Never Give Up This Field*, The Wordsworth Groups, Norcross, Georgia, 1989, p. 32
21. Irving A. Buck, *Cleburne And His Command*, McCowat-Mercer Press, Jackson, Tennessee, 1959, pp. 191–7
22. James M. McPherson, *Battle Cry of Freedom*, Oxford University Press, New York, 1988, p. 835
23. Clifford Dowdey and Louis H Manarin, eds., *The Wartime Papers of R. E. Lee*, Bramhall House, New York, 1961, p. 914
24. Miers, op. cit., p. 522
25. *OR*, Series I, Vol. VIII, p. 697
26. Ibid., p. 721
27. James Bell to Caroline Bell, 2 September 1863, Cherokee letters in the Frank Phillips Collection, Library of the University of Oklahoma
28. Charles E. Taylor papers, University of Virginia Manuscript Collection
29. Dowdey and Manarin, op. cit., p. 689
30. Ross, op. cit., pp. 132–3
31. James C. Nisbet, *Four Years on the Firing Line*, McCowat-Mercer Press, Jackston, Tennessee, 1963, p. 78
32. Francis T. Miller, ed., *The Photographic History of the Civil War*, Thomas Yoseloff, New York, 1957, Vol. VII, p. 350
33. William G. Stevenson, *Thirteen Months in the Rebel Army*, A. S. Barnes and Co, New York, 1959, p. 134
34. Miller, op. cit., p. 350
35. H. Charles McBarron Jr. and Frederick P. Todd, 'Virginia Military Institute, 1864', *Military Collector & Historian*, Vol. III, No 2, p. 44
36. Official, *Register of the Commissioned and Warrant officers of the Navy of the Confederate States to January 1, 1863*, MacFarlane & Ferguson, Richmond, 1862, p. 2
37. Dawson, op. cit., pp. 8–9

References

William A. Albaugh III, *Confederate Faces*, Verde Publishers, Solana Beach, California, 1970
— *More Confederate Faces*, ABS Printers, Washington, DC, ndg
Joseph H. Crute, Jr., *Units of the Confederate Army*, Derwent Books, Midlothian, Virginia, 1987
William C. Davis, *The Commanders of the Civil War*, Gallery Books, New York, 1990
Ralph W. Donnelly, *The Confederate States Marine Corps*, White Mane Publishing, Columbia, Maryland, 1989
Tucker Hill, *Catalogue of Uniforms*, The Museum of the Confederacy, Richmond, 1987
J. William Jones, *Christ in the Camp*, Sprinkle Publications, Harrisonburg, Virginia, 1986
Philip Katcher, *American Civil War Armies (1): Confederate Artillery, Cavalry and Infantry*, Osprey Publishing, London, 1986
— *Confederate Forces of the Civil War*, Arms & Armour Press, London, 1990
Offiical, *Regulations for the Army of the Confederate States*, J. W. Randolph, Richmond, 1863
Official, *Uniforms and Dress of the Army and Navy of the Confederate States*, C. H. Wynne, Richmond, 1861
Kenneth Radley, *Rebel Watchdog*, Louisiana State University Press, Baton Rouge, Louisiana, 1989
J. Thomas Sharf, *History of the Confederate States Navy*, Crown, New York, 1962
Charles E. Taylor, *The Signal and Secret Service of the Confederate States*, Toomey Press, Harmans, Maryland, 1986
William A. Tidwell, *Come Retribution*, University Press of Mississippi, Jackson, Mississippi, 1988
Frederick P. Todd, *American Military Equippage 1851–1972*, Company of Military Historians, Vol. II, Providence, Rhode Island, 1977, Vol. III, Westbrook, Connecticut, 1978
V&C, *The City Intelligencer or Stranger's Guide*, MacFarlane & Ferguson, Richmond, 1862
Ezra J. Warner, *Generals in Gray*, Louisiana State University Press, Baton Rouge, Louisiana, 1959
Jeffry D. Wert, *Mosby's Rangers*, Simon and Schuster, New York, 1990
Edward Younger, ed., *Inside the Confederate Government*, Oxford University Press, New York, 1957

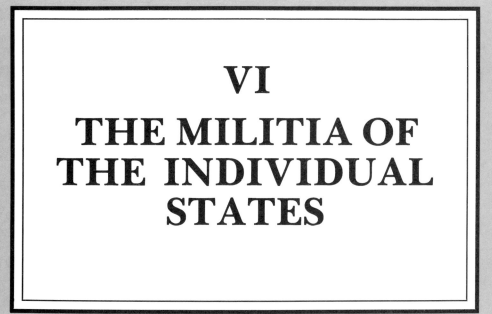

VI
THE MILITIA OF
THE INDIVIDUAL
STATES

THE MILITIA OF THE INDIVIDUAL STATES

Alabama

Before the war, Alabama had, on paper, 108 regiments of 'enrolled militia', but these untrained and unequipped men rarely met to drill and the state depended on its 40-odd companies of uniformed volunteers for real emergencies. On 24 February 1860 Alabama created the Volunteer Corps of the State of Alabama, commonly called the Alabama Volunteer Corps (AVC), to consist of 8,000 men under the governor. He was assisted by the State Inspector General, Quartermaster General, and Adjutant General. The volunteer militia was declared officially abolished in November 1861. In early 1862 the government formed its State Guard, mostly for deserter hunting, from men not liable for conscription. In August 1863 the governor reactivated the enrolled militia, with mandatory weekly drills, to serve as the final defenders of the state.

On 28 May 1861 the AVC uniform was described as a dark-blue frock-coat, double-breasted for field-grade officers and single-breasted for all lower ranks, with nine eagle buttons marked 'A.V.C.' (Buttons bearing the state seal were also used.) The enlisted men's coat was slightly shorter. There were three small buttons on each cuff, and the collar was standing; collars of officers higher than the rank of captain were of dark-blue velvet. Company-grade officers had their collar and pointed cuffs trimmed in light-blue (sometimes white) for infantry, scarlet for artillery, orange for dragoons and emerald-green for riflemen. Rank badges were those of the US Army. Chevrons, also of US Army pattern, were in the branch-of-service colors.

In 1861 the Independent Blues of Selma, Alabama, wore a dark-blue uniform with sky-blue trim and gray trousers. The cap badge was brass with a dark-blue circle in the centre. The company became Co D, 8th Alabama Infantry. (Alabama Department of Archives and History collection)

Although there are no known printed California dress regulations, photographs show that the uniform worn by Captain John B. Dawes, Co A, 1st State Militia Infantry Regiment, was also worn by enlisted men of the 5th and 7th State Militia Regiments in about 1864. The coat was dark-blue with sky-blue cuffs and standing collar with white piping. Enlisted men had sky-blue shoulder-tabs with white piping. Trousers were sky-blue with a white welt. Non-commissioned officers wore the hat shown here; a private of the 5th Regiment wore a felt US Army dress hat in his photograph. (Richard Tibbals collection)

Trousers were cadet-gray, plain for generals but with a one and a quarter-inch wide branch-of-service colored stripe down each leg for company-grade officers and enlisted men. The dress shako was a copy of the US Military Academy shako and had the brass letters 'AVC' over an eagle for its badge. The US Army dress hat was often worn by officers instead of the shako. A forage cap was worn for undress. This uniform appears to have been worn by some Alabama troops at least until July 1863.

However, the state government also called for uniforms fitting Confederate specifications in an appeal for clothing issued on 31 August 1861 in the *Montgomery Weekly Advertiser*. The uniform described in it included a gray woollen jacket with seven brass military buttons down the front, a double-thickness standing collar lined with osnaburg, a shoulder-strap on each shoulder, and a belt strap on each side which could button at the top and be sewn to the bottom over the side seam. Trousers were plain gray and the gray woollen overcoat had seven brass military buttons down the front and a detachable cape attached to the collar's bottom with six hooks and eyes. The cape was to be lined with checked or striped osnaburg, and two straps along the waistline would be adjusted for size. Shirts were to be of checked or striped cotton, while drawers were to be of wool cotton flannel or osnaburg.

Arkansas

Before the war, Arkansas had only inactive, untrained enrolled militia. The convention that declared the state out of the Union also created the Army of Arkansas, made up of the 1st to 5th State Infantry Regiments, two mounted rifle regiments, and four or five batteries all of which would see six months' active service in the state's defence. The convention also created a 'home guard of minute-men' to serve for three months when needed. Control of one Army of Arkansas regiment passed to the Confederate government in July 1861; the rest refused to transfer and were disbanded. The state had no regulation uniform.

California

California's militia consisted of just under 75 active companies in 1861. These were organized in twelve brigades, but in 1862 they were re-organized into regiments or battalions. There was no regulation state uniform described in print.

Colorado Territory

Colorado, which was formed as a territory on 26 February 1861, had no militia prior to the war. While several volunteer regiments were formed for US service, the territory raised no permanent militia during the war save for some short-lived companies raised during the threat of Native American attacks. Six of these were formed into the 1st Regiment Volunteer Mounted Militia in February 1865 to guard the Overland Stage Route. There was no regulation state uniform.

Connecticut

When war broke out the militiamen on Connecticut's rolls were totally disorganized. Power over the militia rested in the legislature, according to the state's 1818 constitution, rather than with the governor as was more typical. The governor could call our four independent regiments of 'foot guards' which were really ceremonial organizations unfit for field service. The legislature controlled eight Active Militia Regiments arranged by geography. Under prompting from the governor, the legislature improved the militia's organization, ending with the formation of the state's National Guard in 1865.

In 1856 the state prescribed a uniform for its militia that was quite like the US Army's 1851 uniform, with a dark-blue frock-coat with gold epaulettes for officers and branch-of-service colored worsted epaulettes for enlisted men. Branch-of-service colors were light-blue for infantry, scarlet for artillery, orange for cavalry, and emerald-green for riflemen. Trousers were dark-blue for generals and staff officers and sky-blue for everyone else. Generals had a gold welt down each leg; general staff and field officers, a white welt; and a branch-of-service stripe for everyone else. The shakos had the US Army branch-of-service cap badge under the state seal in front with a branch-of-service colored pompom.

Delaware/District of Columbia

Neither Delaware nor the District of Columbia had enrolled militia during the war nor any regulation uniforms. The US Government formed the War Department Rifles, the Quartermaster's Volunteers and the US Treasury Guards from employees of those organizations during the period. They wore regulation US Army uniforms.

A Southerner eats $5 worth of candy samples

'Samuel Rector had gone from Loudoun county [Virginia] to Richmond in 1864 on some business. When ready to go home he thought it would be nice and the proper thing to do to take the family some little remembrances. He went into a confectionary store and asked to see some candies. The jars were taken down and he tasted first one then another. Selecting one and asking the price, he was told that it was $25 per pound. It was one of the long, red-striped variety just mentioned, worth in times of peace about 10 cents per pound. He had a pound of it wrapped up, and handed the proprietor a $50 Confederate note. Twenty dollars was handed back in change. Mr. Rector said, "I understood you to say the price was $25." "That is true," said the affable confectioner, "but you ate $5 worth." The joke was well worth $5 to Mr. Rector, and he got more pleasure out of it than he did out of the pound of candy.'

(Luther Hopkins, *From Bull Run To Appomattox*, Fleet-McGinley, Baltimore, Maryland, 1908, p. 198)

Florida

On paper Florida had 22 militia regiments when the war began, but their organization was moribund. In February 1861 the state acted to enroll all able-bodied men into a reformed militia, as well as to authorize two infantry and one cavalry or mounted rifle regiment for six months' service as needed. The 1st and 2nd Regiments of State Guards were formed in 1861 but had been disbanded by 1862. A regulation state uniform was authorized on 8 February 1861 but its design is unknown. Governor John Milton wore a standard Confederate general's coat with four, rather than three, stars on each collar, which was edged in gilt lace, and US general and staff officers' buttons.

Georgia

Georgia didn't even have an adjutant general until December 1860 although there were many volunteer militia companies in the state. A state navy was created in January 1861 and mustered into Confederate service in March. In early June 1861 Governor Joseph Brown raised a reinforced brigade for the state's defence, but it was transferred to the Confederate Army in August. Brown then began raising the First Division, State Troops to consist of three brigades serving for three months, who were later conscripted into Confederate service. In early May 1862 Brown raised a company to guard railroad bridges which grew into a Bridge Guard of several companies. On 13 December 1863 the legislature authorized Brown to enlarge the Guard to the Georgia State Line which eventually consisted of two infantry regiments whose members were exempt from Confederate conscription. A State Line cavalry company was organized in March 1864. The State Line's own hospital, with two surgeons, a hospital steward, a ward master, a matron, three cooks, ten male nurses and two slaves to do the laundry, was created in Savannah in early 1864.

According to orders issued on 15 February 1861, the state uniform included a dark-blue frock-coat and trousers for officers. Rank insignia was the same as in the US Army. Enlisted men were to wear a cadet-gray frock-coat and trousers. Infantrymen wore a black patch on their standing collar, while artillerymen had orange piping and trouser stripes. Fatigue dress was to consist of a blue flannel sack coat; a State Line private was photographed in a single-breasted, light-coloured sack coat with a laydown collar made of homespun, with plain metal buttons. The state navy uniform consisted of US Navy officers' uniform with state buttons for officers; red flannel shirt with sky-blue falling collar edged with white and an anchor at each corner, and sky-blue cuffs for enlisted men. Trousers and mustering caps were dark-blue.

Illinois

At the war's outbreak the state's effective militia consisted of an adjutant-general, a commissary, a quartermaster-general and several brigadier generals and their staffs, but virtually

Private D. R. Cessar, Co E, 1st Georgia Local Troops, wore a gray frock-coat with black trim. The waist pocket, with its flap, was used to hold percussion caps. The company was formed of *workers at the Forest City Foundry, Augusta, Georgia, who were exempt from conscription. (Lee Joyner collection)*

no privates. In 1863 the state formed its 1st and 2nd Regiments, Volunteer Militia. There was no regulation state militia uniform. The state did make and issue its volunteer troops a dark-blue uniform jacket trimmed in branch-of-service colors, with shoulder-tabs, a standing collar, nine buttons down a single row in front, and a left breast pocket. A dark-blue forage cap and sky-blue trousers were also issued.

Indiana

By 1861 the state had virtually no enrolled militia, although there were a number of volunteer militia companies in existence. On 10 September 1861 the state commissioned Major General John Love to organize the Indiana Legion of state militia. The Legion first met for training on 16 October 1862 at Indianapolis. It consisted of two divisions, each under a major general. The 3rd, 4th, 5th, 6th and 9th Brigades were in the First Division; the 1st, 2nd, 7th and 8th Brigades were in the Second. Brigades were made up of organized militia in neighbouring counties. Regiments within the brigades included a mixture of artillery, cavalry and infantry. Many of them were called out during Confederate raids in the state. Thirteen Minute-Man regiments were formed in July 1863 in the southern part of the state to defend against Confederate raiders. There was no regulation state uniform; Indiana Legion companies were free to choose their own.

Iowa

Iowa had no enrolled militia although a number of uniformed volunteer companies had been organized just prior to the war. In May 1861 the legislature authorized a militia, and in October the governor called for companies to be formed in the south of the state. A Southern Border Brigade with ten companies and a Northern Border Brigade with five were authorized in 1862 and an enrolled militia on 26 March 1864. By the war's end, more than 1,000 companies, organized by battalions or regiments, had been formed. No state uniform was authorized.

Kansas

Kansas had almost been laid waste by bands of armed pro-slavery or anti-slavery men who had been fighting for years before the war. When the war started the pro-Union legislature placed all militia and volunteer companies into either one of the five regiments of the state's Northern Division or the six regiments of the Southern Division. The Kansas River separated the two commands. On 24 February 1864 the militia was re-organized into five brigade districts. The militia saw service in October 1864 against a Confederate invasion. There was no regulation state uniform.

Two Southern girls' father is held in a Confederate jail

'While reconnoitering the neighbourhood [near Richmond, Virginia], as the pickets were being established, an officer of the brigade staff observed two young girls on a hillside, waving their handkerchiefs to him. Though a little apprehensive of a snare, he went to see what they desired. One of them told him that it had been so long since they had seen a Yankee uniform that they wanted to look at it; and then eagerly inquired of him the news. Thinking them rebels, he answered carelessly that we had taken Richmond the night before, and wondered that they had not heard it. The girls clapped their hands for joy, one of them exclaiming, "Then father is out of prison!" It was painful to have to undeceive them, with the reason for their welcoming our approach was thus revealed, and to tell them that their father was still suffering for his loyalty to the nation.'

(Henry R. Pyne, *Ride to War*, Rutgers University Press, New Brunswick, New Jersey, 1961, pp. 204–5)

Kentucky

Divided by the war, the state's 73-company-strong State Guard which was well organized, drilled and equipped, was pro-Southern, while the 66-company-strong Home Guard was pro-Northern. The State Guard was dissolved as many of its members joined the Confederate Army; the Home Guards, much poorer equipped and trained, nevertheless saw much action against partisan rangers. A regiment of State Troops, comprised of three battalions, was raised in mid-1863 for six months' duty to defend the state capital against Confederate partisan raids. There was no regulation state uniform.

Louisiana

In September 1861 the governor, in an endeavour to consolidate the various types of volunteer units in the state, registered all white males of military age in an enrolled militia. Many of the New Orleans companies went into the Provisional Regiment, Louisiana Legion. Three brigades of Volunteer State Troops although not mustered into Confederate service, were added to New Orleans' defence in early 1862. Most of them escaped when the city fell and the brigades, like the rest of the militia, fell apart. The state navy, which had been created in 1861, was also virtually destroyed when the city fell. In January 1863 the legislature called for volunteers to serve in an army to defend the state, but little came of this. A battalion of State Infantry and another of State Cavalry were raised for a year's service that year but were mustered into Confederate service. Two more battalions were raised in 1864 and also mustered into Confederate service. No regulation state uniforms were authorized. State navy officers wore US Navy officers' dark-blue uniform with state buttons.

Maine

In 1861 the Volunteer Militia of Maine ('VMM' was marked on belt plates) included 35 independent companies organized into three Military Divisions. Many of the volunteers went into the Union army and new companies, called State or Home Guards, were formed starting in 1862. These were organized in each Military Division in 1863, with a nine-company regiment being set up from the companies in the First Division. In 1865 the state made provisions for three classes of militia: active, volunteer and reserve. The state had no regulation uniform.

Maryland

Maryland's militia was virtually non-existent in 1861 save for some volunteer companies. And, since so many volunteers joined the Confederate army, while the state remained under Union control, it had virtually no militia during the war. There was no regulation state uniform.

Massachusetts

The Massachusetts Volunteer Militia (MVM) was well organized into regiments with 5,592 active militiamen at the beginning of the war. On 31 July 1863 the formal

Frock-coats issued to troops from Massachusetts were often made with piping in a parellel line to the cuff edge rather than in a point. This sergeant was photographed in Springfield, Massachusetts. (Author's collection)

Cadet corps tended to wear black trim on gray uniforms. This cadet second lieutenant is from the Highland Cadets, the corps of the Highland Military Academy, Worcester, Massachusetts, which had been founded in 1856. (Author's collection)

designation of MVM was adopted for the state's volunteer as well as militia regiments. The state uniform, like that of Connecticut, was a close copy of the 1851 US Army uniform although many regiments and companies chose to wear different uniforms. The fatigue uniform included a long gray jacket trimmed with red lace and a red fez or broad-brimmed gray or brown felt hat. On 22 May 1862 the state's adjutant general ordered MVM infantry and light artillery units to wear the regulation US Army dress uniform with buttons bearing the state seal. The two Divisionary Corps (Cadets) and cavalry remained free to choose their own dress.

Michigan

Michigan's volunteer companies had been formed into battalions on paper before the war and were under the command of the State Military Board of Officers. In January 1862 the legislature called for the militia to be reorganized but the state's two volunteer infantry regiments remained its active militia force throughout the war. In 1860 the Board recommended that its militia wear a US Army uniform of gray cloth, but in practice each company wore a uniform of its own choosing.

Minnesota

The state's militia in 1860 included 712 enlisted men in four infantry, five rifle, three artillery and one cavalry companies. A further 31 uniformed companies had been raised by December 1861, but as men went into the Union army this number had fallen to 29 by late 1863 despite problems with the Sioux. There was no regulation state uniform.

Mississippi

As war drew closer, volunteer companies sprang up all over the state, giving it a militia force of 3,927 officers and men in 78 volunteer companies by January 1860. They were assigned to one of four regiments in a division under the Commandant of Division elected by all the company captains who made up the state's Volunteer Military Board. On 9 January 1861 the state set up its Military Board, which consisted of the governor and five generals, and the Army of Mississippi with eight infantry or rifle regiments in four brigades, and ten cavalry and ten artillery companies. The staff included an adjutant and inspector general, a colonel, who was chief of staff; an assistant adjutant and inspector general, who was a lieutenant colonel, and four majors serving as assistant adjutant and inspector generals. Other staff members were the chief of ordnance, a lieutenant colonel; a quartermaster general, a colonel who also served as commissary and paymaster general; five assistant quartermasters, majors; and one surgeon general. Each regiment had an assistant quartermaster, a surgeon and an assistant surgeon. Many of these went into the Confederate army, leaving local defence to the State Troops, Minute Men and Local Defense Troops whose ranks were filled with men not liable for conscription.

In 1861 the Military Board called for a uniform consisting of a gray frock-coat, double-breasted for field-grade officers (seven buttons in each row) and single-breasted for lower ranks (with nine buttons). A general's coat had a black velvet standing collar with an embroidered star on each side, gold for major generals and silver for brigadier generals. The field-grade officer's black cloth collar was edged with half-inch gold lace. Captains and below wore branch-of-service color collar and cuffs. Branch-of-service color braid worn across the chest as rows that passed through the buttons was also worn by regimental officers. Staff officers did not wear braid on their coat. In January 1861 the original branch-of-service colors were crimson for infantry or riflemen, yellow for cavalry and orange for artillery, but according to the New Orleans *Daily Delta* of 14 March 1861, the colors were then changed to green for infantry, red for artillery and yellow or orange for cavalry. Final regulations called for blue for infantry, red for artillery and orange for cavalry.[1] Commissioned rank was indicated by gold epaulettes, a major general's being marked with a gold star; a brigadier general's, with a silver star; a colonel's, a gold crescent; a lieutenant colonel's, a gold leaf; a major, a silver leaf; a captain, two gold bars; a first lieutenant, a gold bar; and a second or third lieutenant, a plain epaulette. The same devices were used on shoulder-straps which had a dark-blue background for all officers. Chevrons were the same as in the US Army with branch-of-service color stripes. A half-chevron worn below the elbow indicated service in any previous US war.

Originally a fatigue shirt was authorized, which was red with a white star on each collar for infantry and riflemen, gray for artillery and blue for cavalry. The final regulations changed the infantry and rifle shirt to gray and the artillery shirt to red. Trousers were gray with a black cord down each leg for generals, a black inch-wide stripe for field-grade officers, and a branch-of-service stripe for all other ranks. A black broad-brimmed felt hat looped up like a tricorne was regulation, with a white plume for major generals, a white plume with a red tip for brigade generals, crimson plume with a gilt regimental number for field and staff officers, and a short branch-of-service color plume for all lower ranks.

A Union spy brings a message

'At an early hour on the morning of July 1st [1863], and before the reserves of the Seventeenth [Pennsylvania Cavalry] were ordered to the front, Colonel Kellogg and Dr. J. Wilson De Witt, acting surgeon, were about mounting their horses to make calls on relatives in the town. At this moment a plain-looking, well-dressed citizen made his appearance in the camp. He wore the garb and used the language of a Quaker. He appeared advanced in years, and carried a cornstalk cane. He desired to see one of the general officers. He was taken to Colonel Kellogg. Upon being presented he made himself known as a Union man, and then carefully taking out a closely written despatch which he had adroitly concealed in the hollow of his cornstalk cane, he handed it to Colonel Kellogg. The despatch conveyed the information that [Lieutenant General Richard] Ewell's [Confederate] Corps was concentrating on the Carlisle Road, and had gone into camp for the night of the 30th at a point within a short day's march from Gettysburg, with every indication of a movement in force on that place early on the morning of July 1.'

(H. P. Moyer, *History of the Seventeenth Regiment Pennsylvania Volunteer Cavalry*, Sowers Printing, Lebanon, Pennsylvania, 1911, pp. 61–2)

Surgeons had green plumes; officers in the adjutant general's corps, yellow plumes; quartermaster officers, blue plumes; and ordnance officers, blue tipped with red. Hat cords and tassels were to be gold for commissioned officers and worsted branch-of-service color for enlisted men. Overcoats were sack coats made of waterproofed cotton.

Missouri
According to legislation passed in 1859, the state depended on its volunteer companies as its militia, each man serving a seven years' enlistment. However, the militia, like the population, was divided in loyalties. A pro-Union Home Guard was then formed, many of its battalions seeing short service in the State Guard against pro-Southern militia. The Home Guard fell apart and was replaced by the Missouri State Militia which saw some field service. An Enrolled Missouri Militia was formed in safe areas, while the Active Militia was formed to fight pro-Southern partisans in contested areas of the state. The pro-Southern State Guard lasted until September 1862, although many of its men joined regular Confederate units while others became partisans. Neither side had a regulation uniform.

Nebraska
The state's handful of volunteer companies served against the Sioux, although the state did not have an adjutant general to supervise its militia until 1864. There was no regulation uniform.

Nevada
Nevada does not appear to have had much if anything in the way of militia – virtually all its men were armed most of the time anyway – or a state uniform.

New Hampshire
In 1861 the state's volunteer militia, consisting of one regiment, one battalion and 20 companies, received financial support from the state in return for meeting minimum training requirements. During the war, the militia existed solely as independent companies with no higher command. There was no regulation state uniform. Volunteers usually placed the roman letters 'NHV' on the top of their forage caps.

New Jersey
When the war began the state's Active Militia was largely inactive. In 1863, therefore, the state formed its Rifle Corps, an organization that numbered some 40 companies by 1865. It was trained in summer camps held in 1864 and 1865. At the same time, the Active Militia was renamed the State Guard although it was essentially unchanged. Union veterans joined special veteran units, many of which were attached to the State Guard. Most State Guard units wore regulation US Army dress, while the Rifle Corps received chasseur uniforms, complete with white gaiters, in blue and

gray for dress and blue and gray jackets, trousers and forage caps for undress. Gray was a more common colour than blue in both uniforms. The officers' forage cap had a coloured band edged with gold lace and a circular cap badge with crossed rifles and the letters 'NJ' and 'RC'.

New York

In 1861 the New York State Militia was active and large, complete with a headquarters and staff of some 532 officers to oversee almost 19,000 volunteers. The staff included the adjutant general's department, the inspector general, the

For fatigues, members of the New Jersey Rifle Corps wore a plain gray jacket, trousers and forage cap with a black or dark-blue band. Dark-blue uniforms were also worn. (Author's collection)

Lieutenant Colonel Eli R. Lyon, 43rd New York State Militia Regiment, wears the state's 1858 regulation uniform complete to the state badge over the branch-of-service insignia on the shako front. (Michael J. McAfee collection)

New Yorkers wearing the state-issue jacket in camp. The corporal (right) has poured himself a drink and is smoking a pipe; the piping on his epaulettes is visible on him and the man standing centre. (David Scheinmann collection)

commissary general's department, the department of engineers, the judge-advocate's department, the medical department, the quartermaster's department and the pay department. The NYSM was divided into regiments, a number of which saw limited service with the Union army. In April 1862 the designation of the NYSM was changed to the National Guard, of which there were 108 regiments and one battalion of infantry, one battalion and nine troops of cavalry and twelve artillery batteries in 1865.

Although most NYSM units wore distinctive uniforms of their own choosing, there was a regulation state uniform that closely copied the US Army's 1857 uniform. It had a plain dark-blue frock-coat for officers, the enlisted man's frock-coat being trimmed in standard branch-of-service colors. Rank was marked in the same way as in the US Army. Trousers for staff officers were dark-blue; sky-blue for everyone else. A dark-blue shako with a branch-of-service colored pompom over the state seal cap badge was worn for dress. Pompoms in the adjutant general's department were buff on the bottom and white on the upper third; for inspector generals, buff on the bottom and scarlet on the upper third; for commissaries, crimson; for engineers, buff on the bottom and black on the upper third; for judges-advocate, white; for quartermasters, buff on the bottom and emerald-green on the upper third; for paymasters, buff on the bottom and dark olive-green on the upper third; for aids-de-camp, buff; for artillery, scarlet; for infantry, sky-blue; for riflemen, emerald-green; and for chaplains, black.

Enlisted engineers wore yellow pompoms, while enlisted ordnance personnel wore crimson and cavalrymen, orange.

For fatigue, officers could wear a standard dark-blue forage cap, the foot soldiers' cap being in cadet-gray with a black band and a silver company letter. A cadet-gray chasseur-style jacket with nine buttons in a single row, black collar and cuffs, and grey shoulder-straps were also authorized for all foot personnel. Cavalry and light artillery wore the jacket in dark-blue piped in branch-of-service colors, with a dark-blue forage cap with the company letter on a branch-of-service colored circle.

On 22 April 1861 the state's Military Board approved a new uniform, giving enlisted men a single-breasted, dark-blue jacket with a left breast pocket, eight buttons down the front (some were made with different numbers of buttons), and branch-of-service piping around the standing collar, the pointed cuffs and shoulder-straps. Two small buttons were placed on each cuff. Trousers were light-blue as was the overcoat, and the forage cap was dark-blue, all made to US Army regulations.

On 16 May 1863 the militia was given a new dark-blue single-breasted jacket piped in white. It came in two styles, chasseur and 'polka jacket'. Trousers were light-blue with white trim when worn with the chasseur jacket. The cap was a McClellan kepi with branch-of-service piping (white for infantry) and a red-white-blue pompom for enlisted men. Belt plates throughout the period were marked 'SNY'.

Drunken Confederate thinks he's got smallpox

'There were many stills in . . . the Blue Ridge [Mountains, Virginia], and by 9 a.m. many of the boys were in a good humor . . . and apple-jack brandy could be had out of dozens of canteens. To prevent any straggling for the purpose of replenishing empty canteens [Major General John B.] Hood authorized the statement, which was industriously circulated and really believed, that small-pox was raging among the citizens . . . Riding by himself, half a mile in the rear of the brigade, he discovered, lying in the middle of the road and obviously very drunk, a member of the Fourth Texas.

'Checking his horse, the general asked: "What is the matter with you, sir? Why are you not with your company?" The stern . . . voice brought the culprit to a sitting posture, and looking at the general with drunken gravity, he said: "Nussin much, I reckon, General – I jus' feel sorter weak an' no account." "So I see, sir," said Hood; "Get up at once and rejoin your company." The fellow made several ineffectual attempts to obey, but each time fell back on the ground and a few sober stragglers coming along just then, Hood ordered to . . . conduct him to his company. But as they approached . . . the fellow found voice to say between hiccoughs: "Don't you fellers that ain't been vaccinated come near me – I've got the small-pox – tha's wha's the masser with me."

'The stragglers shrank back in alarm, and the general, laughing at the way his own chickens had come home to roost, said, "Let him alone, then – some of the teamsters will pick him up," and rode on.'

(J. B. Polley, *Hood's Texas Brigade*, Morningside Bookshop, Dayton, Ohio, 1976, pp. 35–6)

North Carolina

North Carolina's militia was in a state of chaos before the war and on 8 May 1861 her legislature authorized ten regiments of State Troops to serve for the war. Volunteer regiments were authorized, at first using the same numbers as the State Troop regiments but later being numbered from 11 on. On 7 July 1863 the state formed its Home Guards, a true militia, that served for short times in emergencies. Eventually, the state could count seven regiments and more than 50 battalions of Home Guards. The state was different from most other Southern states in that her 1864 Reserve Force units were not divided into Senior and Junior Reserves but placed on a single list.

On 27 May 1861 the state adopted a uniform consisting of a gray frock-coat, double-breasted for field-grade officers and single-breasted for lower grades, following the US Army pattern. Rank badges were the same as in the US Army. Enlisted men wore a gray sack coat with a falling collar, six buttons down the front, and a branch-of-service colored stripe on each shoulder. Branch-of-service colors

were black for infantry, red for artillery and yellow for cavalry. Branch-of-service colored chevrons were the US Army designs. Musicians also had horizontal branch-of-service colored stripes across their coat breast. Generals and staff officers had dark-blue trousers with a buff welt down each leg, others had gray trousers with a branch-of-service colored stripe down each leg. Stripes were mere cords for officers, but were an inch wide for non-commissioned officers and three-quarters of an inch wide for corporals and privates. The hat was a black broad-brimmed felt turned up on the right with the state seal in front for generals. Lower ranks wore a similar gray felt hat with US Army cap badge worn by officers and a regimental number and company letter worn by enlisted men. Off duty, a gray kepi was authorized for officers. All officers' sashes were crimson silk.

In February 1862 the state ordered a short jacket to be issued instead of the sack coat, although apparently some sack coats were made according to the 1861 regulations throughout the war.

Ohio

Ohio started the war with some 30 active uniformed volunteer companies most of which went into Union army regiments. In April 1861 the legislature created an active militia and a Militia of the Reserve. On 14 April 1863 it created the Ohio Volunteer Militia ('OVM' being marked on belt plates). By the end of the year this had 99 infantry regiments or battalions with an average strength of 500 men, six cavalry companies and sixteen light artillery batteries. The OVM was designated the Ohio National Guard in March 1864.

The state uniform was a copy of the US Army's 1857 uniform with state insignia instead of US and a sky-blue jacket for fatigue wear. This was updated to a copy of the 1861 regulation US uniform in May 1861. In that month, too, enlisted men in the Militia of the Reserve were to wear a gray zouave jacket with standing collar, trimmed on the cuffs, collar and edges with black lace. Trousers, shirts and forage cap were also gray trimmed with black. The OVM was to wear the standard US Army uniform with the state seal replacing the US seal, although there was no state button and only cross-belt plates bore the state seal.

Pennsylvania

Pennsylvania's militia was county based, one brigade for each county; the brigade was then assigned to one of twenty military divisions. The state's adjutant general was given all the staff tasks normally performed by other staff officers, making him less efficient than he could have been. On 15 May 1861 the state raised its Reserve Volunteer Corps of the Commonwealth consisting of thirteen infantry regiments, one cavalry regiment and one artillery regiment; the Corps was soon mustered into US service and served in the Army of the Potomac. Thereafter, various cities raised their own militia units as their citizens desired. Emergency militia regiments were created in 1863 during the invasion.

Private A. MacAlister Grant, described as a professional 'gentleman' in the 1863 Philadelphia City Directory, wears the uniform of Landis's Philadelphia Battery of Light Artillery on his return from the Gettysburg campaign. The battery duelled with Stuart's cavalry near Carlisle. The cap badge includes the letter 'A' over crossed cannon; the hat cord is red. (Author's collection)

In August 1864 the legislature authorized the State Guard but it was never recruited.

The regulation state officers' uniform was that of the US Army. There was no regulation enlisted men's uniform.

Rhode Island

In 1861 Rhode Island had an enrolled common militia which never met to train, but which numbered every man of military age, and an active militia of some fifteen volunteer companies each with some 120 officers and men. Each company was commanded by a colonel with a full regimental staff. A further 44 volunteer companies formed the National Guard under the State Central Military Committee, headed by the governor. In April 1863 the state organized its common militia into five infantry brigades, with 20 regiments, and another four infantry battalions; one squadron and an independent troop of cavalry; and two light artillery batteries, with ten other assorted companies. This organization was abandoned on 26 March 1864.

The uniform approved for the National Guard in September 1861 consisted of a dark-blue tunic, light-blue trousers and a blue 'army' cap. The US Army fatigue uniform was authorized for militia officers in June 1863; later they were also authorized a blue blouse with shoulder-straps, dark trousers and a forage cap.

South Carolina

South Carolina's beat, or enrolled, militia was untrained and un-equipped, while its volunteer militia companies were well equipped and trained. Most of the volunteer militia entered the regular Confederate service, so the state created two Corps of Reserve. The First was made up of men between 35 and 50 years of age and was liable for service anywhere. By August 1862 the First Corps consisted of ten regiments which were mustered into Confederate service but left in the state for local defence. The Second Corps included boys aged 16 to 18 and men over 50 and served as local district police.

The state's 1861 uniform regulations called for a dark-blue frock-coat, single-breasted for company-grade officers and double-breasted for higher grades. State buttons were gold for generals and staff officers and silver for regimental officers. However, only a handful of silvered French-made and war-time pewter Southern-made buttons with the state seal exist; the rest are gilt. Epaulettes were of the same color as the buttons. Rank badges were the same as in the US Army except that a major general wore a silver crescent between two gold stars; a brigadier general, two silver stars; and a colonel, a gold palmetto tree. The epaulette insignia was also worn on shoulder-straps for undress. Staff non-commissioned officers wore white worsted epaulettes on a company-grade officer's uniform. Trousers were dark-blue with a stripe an inch and a half wide for generals and field-grade officers, and an inch wide for staff and company-grade officers. Stripes were gold lace for generals and staff officers, silver for field-grade officers, and white for company-grade officers. A French *chapeau* was authorized for field-grade officers and above. A white ostrich feather tipped black was worn by a major general; tipped red by a brigadier general, and white cock feathers by field-grade officers. Company-grade officers wore a dark-blue forage cap with a silver palmetto tree and the regimental number on its left and letter 'R' on its right; photographs show a wreath around the tree but no numbers or letters. The same cap was authorized for other officers for undress. The general's and staff officer's cap badge had the letters 'SCV' within a gold wreath: field-grade officers wore a silver wreath around the regimental number. Regimental staff officers wore the letters 'A', 'Q', 'C' or 'S' for adjutant, quartermaster, commissary, or surgeon. Enlisted men's uniforms for other than staff non-commissioned officers were not described.

Tennessee

On 9 May 1861 the state's military and financial board created the Provisional Army of Tennessee staffed by two major generals, five brigadier generals, an adjutant general's department, an inspector general's department, a paymaster general's department, a quartermaster department, a commissary department, a medical department, the corps of military engineers, the corps of artillery and the ordnance department. This force was mustered into Confederate service when the state joined the Confederacy.

At the same time, it created its Home Guard of militia which was to arm itself and could only be called out for three months' duty.

Tennessee's regulation uniform dated back to 1836 and authorized generals and staff officers to wear the current US Army uniform, while black hunting shirts and trousers with white plumes in the broad-brimmed hat were authorized for riflemen and the same uniform in blue for infantry. Cavalry coats and trousers were also to be dark-blue.

Texas

While the militia was moribund in 1861, internal defence in Texas was provided by the Texas Rangers, a quasi-military force. Attempts to create an active militia during the war largely failed. There was no regulation state uniform.

Utah Territory

Largely a theocracy, the territory's militia consisted of the Nauvoo Legion Militia, composed entirely of Mormons. It included a Battalion of Life Guards, to serve the president of the Church of Latter-Day Saints. The Battalion provided a mounted company for three months' service in 1862. The Legion had no regulation uniform.

Vermont

In 1861 Vermont had some 22 volunteer militia companies but most of their men went into the Union army and in 1862 only thirteen of these companies were still in existence. The state then created a new enrolled militia of every able-bodied man between the ages of 18 and 45. On 2 December 1862 the legislature demobilized all the state's militia. There was no state uniform until 28 March 1865 when officers were directed to wear US Army officers' uniforms with the state button.

Virginia

On 27 April 1861 the state created the Provisional Army of Virginia consisting of two artillery regiments, one rifle regiment, one cavalry regiment and eight infantry regiments. This force was taken into Confederate service starting in June although some officers not chosen for Confederate service retained their provisional army commissions. The state also created the Provisional Navy of Virginia at the same time; this was transferred into the Confederate Navy on 6 June 1861.

On 27 March 1861 the assembly authorized between ten and 20 companies of State Rangers to operate behind Union lines in the western part of the state. Each company was to have a captain, a first lieutenant, a second lieutenant and 75 men. The rangers were transferred to Confederate service on 28 February 1863.

The state's militia was divided into two classes, active and reserve, on 29 November 1861. Men between the ages of 21 and 31 were in the active militia. So many men went into Confederate or other state organizations that whenever the militia was called out state officers did not know what to expect and results were generally small. As of 30 November the state's adjutant general reported that only a handful of active militia were still available, while reserve militia consisted of one artillery and 20 infantry companies. By 1864 Virginia's militia ceased to exist.

On 14 May 1862 citizens in each county were ordered to form Home Guard companies to serve as local police. Each company was to have a captain and two lieutenants and between 50 and 100 men. By 30 November 1863 28 infantry and seven cavalry Home Guard companies had been formed.

The Virginia State Line, made up of men not liable to the draft, was created on 15 May 1862. It was to consist of two brigades of five regiments each, but only five regiments, with some 3,338 men as of 11 January 1863, were formed. When the State Line was abolished on 28 February 1863, its men either mustered into Confederate units or went home.

The regulation uniform was that of the US Army, Navy or Marine Corps, with the state button.

West Virginia

In July 1861 West Virginians for the Union created Home Guards from local volunteer companies. There were 24 such companies in 1865, although a year earlier there had been 35. There was no regulation state uniform.

Wisconsin

Wisconsin's 1,993 volunteer militiamen were organized into 50 uniformed and equipped companies in January 1861. Another dozen companies were being formed at that time.

Many of these men went into the Union army so that by the end of 1862 there were only 20 active companies in existence. With the Sioux War in neighbouring Minnesota in 1863, the legislature called for a militia of three regiments, either by volunteers or through a draft. By that July enough men for four regiments and a battalion, together with two artillery batteries, had volunteered. Each unit was allowed to chose its own uniform.

Either the Lima Home Guard or the Sheboygan Falls Home Guard; both units were formed in Sheboygan, Wisconsin, in 1863. A company-grade officer, extreme left, front, is the only one in any type of military uniform, although one of the officers standing within the square wears an issue forage cap. (Milwaukee Public Museum collection)

The Racine Zouave Cadets wore, according to the 27 May 1863 Racine Advocate, 'a jaunty cap of red and blue, a neat blue jacket, scarlet pants and scarlet leggings'. The unit was formed in 1862 as part of the 1st Regiment, Wisconsin State Militia, and was dissolved in June 1864. (Richard K Tibbals collection)

Types of belt-plate using seals. The two-piece plate was mostly worn by officers in the North, although Southern mounted men also wore them. This particular one bears the seal of the City of Philadelphia. The stamped brass oval plate with Georgia's seal has a back filled with lead and three belt hooks. The mounted man's cast plate bears the Maryland seal and was used by Marylanders on both sides. (Author's collection)

Seals of the various states. These often appeared on buttons and belt-plates. (Harper's Weekly)

STATE INSIGNIA

Special state buttons, stamped oval brass belt plates, two-piece brass sword-belt plates, rectangular cast brass sword-belt plates, and stamped cross-belt plates used state insignia. In most case the insignia was simply the state seal; in some cases, especially with the oval belt plates, roman block capital letters were used, as indicated below. The same oval belt plate design was often used on cartridge box plates, too. Except for buttons, most of these unique state insignia items were made some years before the war although they did see wartime use. Southern states more commonly had state-insignia military items than did Northern states.

State	Button	Oval Belt plate	2-piece Belt plate	Rectangular Belt plate	Cross-belt Plate
Alabama	Seal/AVC	Seal/AVC	Seal	None	None
Arkansas	Seal	Seal	None	None	None
California	None	None	Seal	None	None
Connecticut	Seal	None	None	None	None
Florida	Seal	None	None	None	None
Georgia	Seal	Seal	Seal	None	None
Illinois	Seal	None	None	None	None
Kentucky	Seal	None	Seal	None	None
Louisiana	Seal	None	Seal	Seal	None
Maine	Seal	VMM	None	None	None
Maryland	Seal	Seal	Seal	Seal	None
Massachusetts	Seal	None	Seal	Seal	None
Michigan	Seal	None	None	None	None
Mississippi	Star	Seal	None	Seal	None
New Hampshire	Seal	NHSM	None	None	None
New Jersey	Seal	NJ (script)	None	None	None
New York	Seal	SNY	SNY	NY in wreath	None
North Carolina	Seal	NC	Seal/NC	None	None
Ohio	None	OVM	None	Seal	Seal
Pennsylvania	Seal	None	None	None	None
Rhode Island	Seal	None	None	None	None
South Carolina	Seal	SC	Seal	Seal	Seal
Tennessee	Seal	None	None	None	None
Texas	Seal	Seal	Seal	Seal	None
Vermont	Seal	None	None	None	None
Virginia	Seal	None	Seal	Seal	Seal
Wisconsin	Seal	None	None	None	None

Notes

1. Official, *Southern Military Journal*, J. L. Power, Jackson, Mississippi, and HP Lathrop, New Orleans, 1861 (Boston Athenaeum, Crandell Number 2481)

References

Adjutant General, *Indiana in the War of the Rebellion*, Vol. I, Indiana Historical Bureau, Indianapolis, 1960

Arthur W. Bergeron, Jr., *Guide to Louisiana Confederate Military Units 1861–1865*, Louisiana State University Press, Baton Rouge, 1989

William H. Bragg, *Joe Brown's Army*, Mercer University Press, Macon, Georgia, 1987

P. C. Headley, *Massachusetts in the Rebellion*, Walker Fuller, Boston, 1866

Philip Katcher, *American Civil War Armies (4): State Troops*, Osprey Publishing, London, 1987

— *American Civil War Armies (5): Volunteer Militia*, Osprey Publishing, London, 1989

J. Phillip Langellier, *Parade Ground Soldiers*, State Historical Society of Wisconsin, Madison, 1978

E. B. Long, *The Saints and the Union*, University of Illinois Press, Urbana, 1981

Harold R. Manakee, *Maryland in the Civil War*, Maryland Historical Society, Baltimore, 1961

John Nivin, *Connecticut for the Union*, Yale University Press, New Haven, 1965

No author given, *Tennesseeans in the Civil War*, Tennessee Civil War Centennial Commission, Nashville, 1964

Official, *General Regulations for the Military Forces of the State of New York*, Weed, Parsons, Albany, 1858

Offical, *Orders of the Military Board of the State of Mississippi*, E. Barksdale, Jackson, 1861

Official, *Regulations for the Uniforms Dress and Equipments of the Volunteers & State Troops of North Carolina*, NC Institute for the Deaf and Dumb and the Blind, Raleigh, 1861

Official, *Uniform and Dress of the Officers of the Volunteer Forces Raised under the 'Act to Provide an Armed Military Force'*, Charleston, SC, 1861

Duane A. Smith, *The Birth of Colorado*, Oklahoma University Press, Norman, Oklahoma, 1989

Frederick P. Todd, *American Militiary Equippage 1851–1972*, Vol. II, *State Forces*, Chatham Square Press, New York, 1983

Lee A. Wallace, Jr., *A Guide to Virginia Military Organizations 1861–1865*, M. E. Howard, Lynchburg, Virginia, 1986

VII
BIOGRAPHIES

BIOGRAPHIES

Banks, Nathaniel Prentiss (1816–94)

One of the rare important Democrats to support the Republican-led government at the outbreak of the war, N. P. Banks, earlier the governor of Massachusetts, was appointed a general to show bi-partisan support to the Union cause. He was, however, a better politician than a military man. He was defeated by Jackson in the Shenandoah Valley, Virginia, and again by the same general at Cedar Mountain. He was then given command of the Military District of Washington. One of Banks's officers later said that while he commanded there in late 1862 he had the ' . . . tact, good judgement, and experience to retain the confidence of his superiors . . . '[1]

This confidence brought him command of the Department of the Gulf in October 1862, with the mission of opening the Mississippi River from the South. His poor judgement cost the Union Army many lives at Port Hudson, Louisiana, after which he lead his men on the unsuccessful Red River Campaign. He was then replaced by Canby. Thereafter, he was elected to the House of Representatives from Massachusetts, dying at his home in Waltham, Massachusetts, on 1 September 1894.

Note

1. Richard B. Irwin, 'Washington Under Banks', *Battles & Leaders of the Civil War*, Thomas Yoseloff, New York, 1956, Vol. II, p. 544

Reference

Fred Harrington, *Fighting Politician: Major General N. P. Banks*, J. B. Lippincott, Philadelphia, 1948

Beauregard, Pierre Gustave Toutant (1818–93)

A French creole from Louisiana, Beauregard was a member of the US Military Academy class of 1838 and saw much service in the Mexican-American War as a member of the Corps of Engineers. He was twice wounded and twice breveted during that war as a member of Winfield Scott's staff.

For a short time in 1861 he was Superintendent of the US Military Academy, but he was replaced because of his Southern sympathies. He resigned his commission on 20 February 1861 and was quickly named a Confederate brigadier general. His first posting was to Charleston, South Carolina, where he commanded at the attack on Fort Sumter.

He was then ordered to take command of Confederate troops near Manassas, Virginia, commanding in the first major battle of the war, at First Bull Run. On 31 August 1861 he was named general in the regular Confederate Army. He failed to get along with Jefferson Davis, however, and was sent west as A. S. Johnston's second in command in early 1862. He replaced Johnston when the commander was fatally wounded at the Battle of Shiloh, bringing his weary troops away from that unsuccessful field. Davis's antagonism grew with that, blaming him for the retreat and subsequent withdrawal from Corinth, Mississippi. In June 1862 Beauregard became ill, passing his command on temporarily to Bragg while he went home to recover. Davis took this opportunity to replace him, charging him with leaving his post without authority.

Despite Davis's opinion, Beauregard was widely popular. At the start of the war, wrote a Southern War Department clerk, among the people, 'Beauregard is the especial favorite'.[1] And, although he lost favor with Jefferson Davis

Nathaniel Prentiss Banks (1816–94) in the full dress uniform of a major general. (Author's collection)

Pierre Gustave Toutant Beauregard (1818–93) in the uniform of a colonel of engineers in the Army of Louisiana, taken between his US Army and Confederate Army service in 1861. (Author's collection)

and others in high office in large part due to his extremely critical remarks and a personality considered by many to be excitable, he retained his popularity, the same clerk noting in October 1864 that Beauregard had been named to supervise troops in Georgia 'in response to the universal calls of the people'.[2]

On his recovery, therefore, he was placed in charge of coastal defences in the Carolinas and Georgia. In April 1864 he was brought back to Virginia to command troops south of Richmond, Virginia, and contained Butler's troops there. His command was eventually absorbed into the Army of Northern Virginia during the Siege of Petersburg, Virginia,

and he was given a largely empty title of commander of the Military Division of the West. The war's end found him in the Carolinas under J. E. Johnston.

After the war, Beauregard served as president of a railroad and supervisor of the controversial Louisiana Lottery. He was offered, and declined, the positions of commander of the armies of Roumania and Egypt. He died in New Orleans on 20 February 1893.

Notes

1. Earl S. Miers, ed., *A Rebel War Clerk's Diary*, Sagamore Press, New York, 1958, p. 28
2. Ibid., p. 431

References

Hamilton Basso, *Beauregard, The Great Creole*, Charles Scribners' Sons, New York, 1933
Alfred Roman, *The Military*

Operations of General Beauregard in the War Between the States, 1861–1865, Harper & Brothers, New York, 1884
T. Harry Williams, *P. G. T. Beauregard: Napoleon in Gray*, Louisiana State University Press, Baton Rouge, Louisiana, 1955

Bragg, Braxton (1817–76)

Graduating from the US Military Academy in 1837, Bragg gained fame as a light artillery battery commander during the Mexican-American War. He resigned from the Army as a lieutenant colonel in 1856 and became a planter in Louisiana. On 7 March 1861 he was commissioned a brigader general in the Confederate Army, receiving command of the coastal area between Pensacola, Florida, and Mobile, Alabama. Promoted in September, he was given command of A. S. Johnston's II Corps at Shiloh and the Siege of Corinth. He was promoted full general in June 1862 and was given command of the Army of Tennessee.

He was beaten at the Battles of Perryville and Murfreesboro, but won at Chickamauga. Following the unsuccessful siege of Chattanooga, he was replaced by J. E. Johnston, having lost the trust of his officers and men. He then became the chief of staff of his personal friend, Jefferson Davis. After R. E. Lee became overall Confederate commander, Bragg was given command of a division of the Army of Tennessee.

After the war, Bragg became chief engineer of the State of Alabama, later moving to Galveston, Texas, where he fell dead while walking down a street on 27 September 1876.

'Bragg', later wrote U. S. Grant, 'was a remarkably intelligent and well-informed man, professionally and otherwise. He was also thoroughly upright. But he was possessed of an irascible temper, and was naturally disputatious.'[1] The Head of the Confederate Bureau of War went further, writing in his diary, 'Prying, indirection, vindictiveness, and insincerity are the repulsive traits which mark Bragg's character.'[2]

Notes

1. U. S. Grant, *Personal Memoirs of U.S. Grant*, World Publishing, New York, 1952, p. 343
2. Robert G. H. Kean, *Inside The Confederate Government*, Oxford University Press, New York, 1957, p. 175

References

Grady McWhiney, *Braxton Bragg and Confederate Defeat*, Columbia University Press, New York, 1969
Don C. Seitz, *Braxton Bragg, General of the Confederacy*, The State Co., Columbia, South Carolina, 1924

Buchanan, Franklin (1800–74)

Entering the US Navy, as a midshipman during the last year of the War of 1812, Buchanan fought in the Mexican War, commanded the flagship in Perry's expedition to China and Japan, and helped plan the US Naval Academy. At the Civil War's outbreak, he resigned his commission, thinking that his own State of Maryland would join the Confederacy. When it did not, he tried to withdraw his resignation, but the Secretary of the Navy wanted no lukewarm supporters and had Buchanan dismissed from the service.

Commissioned a Confederate Navy captain, Buchanan was first named Chief of the Bureau of Orders and Detail. Preferring active duty, he took command of the Chesapeake Bay Squadron, including the CSS *Virginia*, the South's first iron-clad ship, in her action against the US squadron at Hampton Roads. His being wounded prevented him from taking part in the next day's action against the USS *Monitor*.

Promoted rear admiral, Buchanan then was given command of the naval forces at Mobile, Alabama, where he worked for two years to prepare for the eventual Union attack. He was wounded in that final battle while in command of the CSS *Tennessee*. Captured and later exchanged, he returned to Mobile in time to surrender the city.

After the war, he served as president of Maryland Agricultural College (now the University of Maryland) and then as an insurance executive, dying in Talbot City, Maryland, on 11 May 1874.

References

Charles L. Lee, *Admiral Franklin Buchanan, Fearless Man of Action*, The Norman, Remington Co., Baltimore, 1929

Braxton Bragg (1817–76), one of the South's most disliked officers. (Library of Congress)

Franklin Buchanan (1800–74) wears the uniform of a US Navy captain in this Mathew Brady photograph. (Library of Congress)

Ambrose Everett Burnside (1824–81) in the uniform of a major general. (Author's collection)

Burnside, Ambrose Everett (1824–81)

Burnside went straight from the US Military Academy, where he graduated in 1847, to garrison duty in Mexico City with the 2nd Artillery. Afterwards, he served in the Southwest until he resigned his commission in 1853. He then started a factory to produce the breech-loading rifles which he had designed, but this business failed when he could not secure a government contract for the weapons.

Burnside organized the 1st Rhode Island Infantry at the war's outset and served as a brigade commander at the First Bull Run. Now a brigadier general, Burnside showed

promise in capturing part of the North Carolina coast in early 1862; this earned him his major general's commission.

He returned to the Army of the Potomac, receiving command of IX Corps. His single-mindedness and precise dedication to orders resulted in his continued attacks across the stone bridge over the Antietam Creek despite the loss of hundreds of lives and priceless time. But, he was named commander of the Army of the Potomac, against his wishes, in September 1862. His planning thereafter was good, but his failure to deviate from his original plan cost thousands more lives at Fredericksburg, Virginia, where he sent his men into hopeless frontal attacks long after any purpose could be served. An attempt to salvage his reputation led to the 'mud march', and he was then removed from command of the Army. One of his private soldiers wrote home then, 'We think Burnside did all he could do and cannot understand why he was relieved of the command. Burnside appeared much like Washington to the troops that knew him best.'[1]

Burnside was then given command of the Department of Ohio where he successfully defended Knoxville, Tennessee. In early 1864 he was restored to command of IX Corps. He commanded at the bloody Battle of the Crater during the Siege of Petersburg, after which he was relieved for improper handling of troops, and resigned his commission. Thereafter, he went into politics, being elected governor of Rhode Island three times and was one of Rhode Island's senators at the time of his death on 13 September 1881.

Note
1. William G. Gavin, ed., *Infantryman Pettit*, White Mane Publishing Co., Columbia, Maryland, 1990, p. 52

References
Benjamin P. Poore, *The Life and Public Services of Ambrose E.* Burnside, *Soldier–Citizen–Statesman*, J. A. & R. A. Reid, Providence, Rhode Island, 1882

August Woodbury, *Burnside and the IX Army Corps*, Sidney S. Rider and Brother, Providence, Rhode Island, 1867

Butler, Benjamin Franklin (1818–93)

A Democratic politician from Massachusetts, Butler backed the States' Rights presidential candidate against Abraham Lincoln in the 1860 elections. However, in the week after the bombardment of Fort Sumter he arrived in Washington, DC, at the head of his 8th Massachusetts Regiment, opening communications between the capital city and the North. He was soon afterwards appointed a brigader general of volunteers. His first action, Big Bethel, ended in disaster but his second, at Hatteras Inlet, captured two Confederate forts and 615 prisoners.

Butler's legal background enabled him to solve the thorny problem of what to do with escaped slaves. He called them 'contraband of war', reckoning that they were property that aided the enemy, thereby escaping the problem of prematurely abolishing slavery, for which most Northerners were not ready to fight. In May 1862 Butler was sent to garrison New Orleans where he earned the hatred of most of the South by ordering that women who insulted his men

Benjamin Franklin Butler (1818–93) has had the collar of his major general's uniform   *embroidered to suit his own taste. (Library of Congress collection)*

should be treated as women of the streets plying their trade. For this he was nicknamed 'Beast' Butler. He was also widely rumoured to have personally plundered homes, earning him the nickname of 'Spoons' Butler.

Removed from command in December 1862, Butler was assigned the command of the Army of the James in 1863 with the task of taking Richmond from the South. Not a good fighting general, he failed to move quickly enough and ended up penned down on the Bermuda Hundred, and was removed from command in November 1864. He was then given a last chance to take Fort Fisher, North Carolina, which he also fumbled and he finally resigned his com-

mission on 30 November 1864. He returned to politics as a member of Congress and Massachusetts governor, dying in Washington, DC on 11 January 1893.

References
Benjamin F. Butler, *Autobiography and Personal Reminiscences of Major-General Benjamin F. Butler*, A. M. Thayer & Co., Boston, 1892

Canby, Edward Richard Sprigg (1817–73)

A US Military Academy graduate in 1839, Canby served as a chief of staff in the Mexican War and at various frontier posts. In 1860 he was a major in the 10th Infantry. He was named colonel of the 19th Infantry and commander of the Department of New Mexico on 14 May 1861. There he repulsed the attempted Confederate invasion of New Mexico, winning the vital battle of Glorieta Pass. As a result, he was promoted and brought to Washington where he was named Assistant Adjutant General. During this time he was sent to put down the New York draft riots. On 7 May 1864 he was again promoted and given command of the Military Division of West Mississippi. He then captured Mobile, Alabama, and accepted the surrenders of Richard Taylor and Edmund Kirby Smith. At the war's end he was commissioned a regular army brigadier general. While on a peace mission in that capacity, he was murdered by Modoc Indians at Siskiyou, California, on 11 April 1873.

Grant later wrote, 'General Canby was an officer of great merit. He was naturally studious, and inclined to the law. There have been in the army but very few, if any, officers who took as much interest in reading and digesting every act of Congress and every regulation for the government of the army as he. His knowledge gained in this way made him a most valuable staff officer . . .'[1]

Note
1. U. S. Grant, *Personal Memoirs of U.S. Grant*, World Publishing Co., New York, 1952, p. 574

Reference
Max L. Heyman, *Prudent Soldier; A Biography of Major General E. R. S. Canby, 1817–1873*, Arthur H. Clark, Glendale, California, 1959

Custer, George Armstrong (1839–76)

Graduating last in his class, and among the last in cavalry tactics in his class, from the US Military Academy in 1861, Custer began his career on the staffs of Generals McClellan and Alfred Pleasonton. His bravery and enterprise as a staff officer saw his rise to the rank of captain by 29 June 1863 when he was suddenly promoted to the rank of brigadier general of volunteers and given the 2nd Brigade of the 3rd Cavalry Division. His Michigan Brigade's heroic charge at Gettysburg stopped Stuart's attempt to reach the Union rear and greatly contributed to that victory. In October 1864 he was given command of the 3rd Cavalry Division and served with distinction in the Shenandoah Valley Campaign; at Yellow Tavern, where J. E. B. Stuart was killed during one of Custer's charges; at the Third

George Armstrong Custer (1839–76) was photographed in Mathew Brady's New York *studio in mid-February 1864, in a regulation general's uniform. (Michael F. Bremer collection)*

Winchester; Fisher's Hill; and Five Forks. It was Custer and his men who completed the entrapment of the Army of Northern Virginia at Appomattox.

He was especially noted for his long reddish-blonde hair and his unique uniform, of black velvet trimmed with gold, with a wide-collared navy-blue shirt with a silver star at each side and a crimson necktie – all quite dramatic and quite against regulations.

After the war, Custer received a regular army commission as a lieutenant colonel in the 7th Cavalry Regiment. He led this regiment, heroically and impetuously as always, to its

destruction at Little Big Horn on 25 June 1876 where he paid the final price for his failure to do better in cavalry tactics.

References

George A. Custer, 'War Memoirs', *The Galaxy: An Illustrated Magazine of Entertaining Reading*, XXI–XXII, no. 5 (Jan–Nov 1876)

Lawrence A. Frost, *The Custer Album*, University of Okhlahoma Press, Norman, Oklahoma, 1964

Margaret Merington, ed., *The Custer Story*, Devin Adair, New York, 1950

Gregory J. W. Urwin, *Custer Victorious, The Civil War Battles of General George Armstrong Custer*, Farleigh Dickinson University Press; Cranbury, New Jersey, 1983

Davis, Jefferson Finis (1808–89)

A graduate of the US Military Academy in 1828, Davis resigned his commission as first lieutenant in 1835 to become a Mississippi planter. During the Mexican War he served as colonel of the 1st Mississippi Rifles, gaining much praise for his conduct at the Battle of Buena Vista. Afterwards he went into politics, serving as Secretary of War under Franklin Pierce and senator from Mississippi, the position he was holding when the Civil War broke out.

Although he wished for a military command, he was picked as a compromise candidate for a six-year term as Confederate President in 1861. Although certainly trained for the job, both through legislative and administrative offices held before the war, he was not the perfect choice. A Union general who had known him before the war said he had 'some verbose talents, some capacity to write and speak clearly, but is a man of limited views and utterly wanting in magnanimity'.[1] A clerk in the Confederate War Department said that Davis attached 'the upmost importance to *consistency* . . .'[2] While he could be personally charming, he was also prideful and quite narrow-minded, vindictive to imagined enemies, and too often unwilling to compromise. Mostly because of these traits, he went through six Secretaries of War. At times he seemed to be more at war with the Southern state governors than the Union forces.

Despite these flaws, he did manage to oversee the Confederate war effort until final defeat. After the war he was imprisoned at Fort Monroe, Virginia, for two years while the US government deliberated whether to try him for treason or not. He was finally released on bail, going to Canada at first, then returning to a donated estate in Mississippi where he wrote his defence of secession. He died there on 9 December 1889, by which time Southerners had returned him to their favour.

Notes

1. Cecil D. Eby, Jnr., ed., *A Virginia Yankee in the Civil War*, The University of North Carolina Press, Chapel Hill, North Carolina, 1961, p. 13
2. Earl S. Miers, ed., *A Rebel War Clerk's Diary*, Sagamore Press, New York, 1958, p. 13

References

Michael B. Ballard, *A Long Shadow, Jefferson Davis and the Final Days of the Confederacy*, Jackson, Mississippi, 1986

Jefferson Davis, *The Papers of Jefferson Davis*, Louisiana State University Press, Baton Rouge, Louisiana, 1971, 1974, 1981,

1983, 1985

Varina H. Davis, *Jefferson Davis, Ex-President of the Confederate States of America*, Belford Co., New York, 1890

Paul D. Escott, *After Secession: Jefferson Davis and the Failure of Confederate Nationalism*, Louisiana State University

Press, Baton Rouge, Louisiana, 1978

Robert McElroy, *Jefferson Davis: The Unreal and the Real*, Harper & Bros., New York, 1937

Hudson Strode, *Jefferson Davis*, Harcourt Brace & Co., New York, 1950–64

Early, Jubal Anderson (1816–94)

A member of the US Military Academy class of 1837, Early resigned from the army after service in the Seminole War to practise law in Rocky Mount, Virginia. He saw Mexican War service as a major of Virginia Volunteers. Although he voted against secession in 1861, when Virginia did leave the Union he accepted a colonelcy in Virginia's army and was soon given command of the 24th Virginia Infantry. He led this regiment at the First Bull Run, being promoted to brigadier general after that. He fought well during the Peninsula Campaign where he was wounded in the shoulder.

Jefferson Finis Davis (1808–89), president of the Confederate States of America. (Library of Congress collection)

Jubal Anderson Early (1816–94). (Library of Congress collection)

On 17 January 1863 he was promoted major general, serving in the Army of Northern Virginia's campaigns thereafter. He was appointed a lieutenant general on 31 May 1864, to command the Army of Northern Virginia's II Corps. A Confederate staff officer later wrote that Early was: 'Quick to decide and almost inflexible in decision, with a boldness to attack that approached rashness and a tenacity in resisting that resembled desperation, he was yet on the field of battle not equal to his own intellect or decision.'[1]

In an attempt to take the pressure off Lee's lines at Gettysburg, Early was sent north through the Valley of Virginia to strike at Washington, DC. His troops burned Chambersburg, Pennsylvania, during the raid. He won a victory at Monocacy, Maryland, but it had cost precious time and allowed reinforcements to reach Washington and save that city. He then returned to the Valley followed by Sheridan's troops who had driven him completely from those bountiful acres by March 1865. After Lee surrendered he went abroad. In 1869 he returned to his Virginia law practice. Never one of Lee's great generals, Early nevertheless lionized his war-time leader, serving as one of the organizers of the Lee Monument Association in Richmond and later as president of the Southern Historical Society. Along with several others, it was his biased pro-Lee writings that created the image of Lee as the invincible military leader. Early, an 'unreconstructed rebel' to the end, died on 2 March 1984.

Note

1. Henry Kyd Douglas, *I Rode With Stonewall*, Fawcett Publications, Greenwich, Connecticut, 1961, p. 42

References

M. K. Bushong, *Old Jube – A Biography of General Jubal A. Early*, Carr Publishing, Boyce, Virginia, 1955

Jubal A. Early, *Lieutenant General Jubal Anderson Early, CSA, Autobiographical Sketches and Narrative of the War Between the States*, Philadelphia, 1912

Farragut, David Glasgow (1801–70)

Entering the US Navy in 1810, before the War of 1812 in which he served under Commander David D. Porter, Farragut's loyalty to the Union was at first suspect since he was a native of Tennessee and lived in Virginia. Even so, in December 1861 he was assigned command of the West Gulf Blockading Squadron with orders to capture New Orleans, Louisiana. His success here earned him promotion to the rank of rear admiral on 16 July 1862. He then led naval efforts to open the Mississippi through the capture of Vicksburg, Mississippi. After its fall he was assigned the capture of Mobile, Alabama, where he led a fleet in past enemy mines that sunk one of his ironclads within minutes of entering the harbour, and resistance from a small Confederate fleet. His success at Mobile led to his being commissioned a vice admiral on 23 December 1864. After a short period of ill health, he returned to active duty in Northern Virginia, being one of the first Northerners to enter Richmond, Virginia, after its fall. On 25 June 1866 he

David Glasgow Farragut (1801–70) in the uniform of a US Navy captain. (Author's collection)

became the first American commissioned admiral, and thereafter commanded the European Squadron. He died on 14 August 1870.

Farragut's personal bravery, together with his careful planning, sparked his triumphs at both New Orleans and Mobile, and he well earned the distinction of 'First American Admiral'.

References

Loyall Farragut, *The Life of David Glasgow Farragut, First Admiral of the United States Navy, Embodying His Journal and Letters*, D. Appleton, New York, 1879

Charles L. Lee, *David Glasgow Farragut; Admiral In The Making*, US Naval Institue Press, Annapolis, Maryland, 1941–3
A. T. Mahan, *Admiral Farragut*, D. Appleton, New York, 1892

Forrest, Nathan Bedford (1821–77)

Born to extreme poverty and then self-educated, by the war's outbreak Forrest was a well-established planter and slave trader. He immediately enlisted in the Confederate Army as a private, but his abilities had earned him a brigadier generalship by 21 July 1862, a major generalship on 4 December 1863, and a lieutenant generalship on 28 February 1865. This despite, as a fellow Confederate later wrote, the fact that 'Forrest knew nothing about tactics – could not drill a company. When first ordered to have his brigade ready for review, he was quite ignorant, but Armstrong told him what commands to give and what to do with himself . . .'[1]

Generally considered the oustanding cavalry leader on either side, Forrest escaped with his men from Fort Donelson, going on to capture the Union garrison at Murfreesboro, Tennessee. He then led his cavalry to cut Union communications in West Tennessee. One of many to fight with Braxton Bragg when under his command, Forrest was given an independent command in North Mississippi and West Tennessee where he captured Fort Pillow and fought his most brilliant battle at Brices Cross Roads, followed by the successful defence of Tupelo, Mississippi. In late 1864 he was in charge of cavalry in the Army of Tennessee and was finally overwhelmed by numbers at Selma, Alabama.

Afterwards he returned to planting, although he also helped organize and was president of the Selma, Marion & Memphis Railroad. He died in Memphis, Tennessee, on 29 October 1877, apparently of diabetes.

Note

1. Dabney H. Maury, 'Recollections of a Virginian in the Mexican, Indian, and Civil Wars', quoted in Francis Miller, *Photographic History of the Civil War*, Thomas Yoseloff, New York, 1957, Vol. IV, p. 282

References

Robert S. Henry, *'First With The Most' Forrest*, Bobbs-Merrill,
Indianapolis, Indiana, 1944
H. Harvey Mathes, *General Forrest*, D. Appleton, New York, 1902
E. W. Sheppard, *Bedford Forrest, The Confederacy's Greatest Cavalryman*, Longman, Green, Toronto, 1930
John A. Wyeth, *That Devil Forrest: Life of General Nathan Bedford Forrest*, Harper & Row, New York, 1959

Nathan Bedford Forrest (1821–77), one of the Confederacy's greatest leaders. (Library of Congress collection)

Grant, Ulysses Simpson (Hiram Ulysses) (1822–85)

Born to a doting father and a cold mother, Grant was sent to the US Military Academy against his wishes by his father (where his name was accidentally changed from Hiram Ulysses to Ulysses Simpson) in 1839. His main distinction there was as an equestrian, setting a jumping record that stood for many years. He hated the military so much that he carefully followed a debate in Congress about closing the Academy in the hope that they would do just that.

On 1 July 1843 he was graduated 21st in a class of 39, too low for the cavalry which he preferred, and was assigned as a second lieutenant to the 4th Infantry Regiment. He served as regimental quartermaster during the Mexican War, but volunteered for action, carrying ammunition to the front under fire once and manhandling a howitzer into a tower at Monterey where his fire helped decide the battle.

After the war he was assigned to the Pacific Coast, having to leave his beloved wife Julia behind. Several attempts to earn extra money through commercial enterprises there failed, and he succumbed to the habit, common to soldiers on isolated detachment, of drinking more than was good for him. A conflict with his commanding officer, apparently

Ulysses Simpson Grant
(1822–85). (David Scheinmann
collection)

however, taking increasingly larger forces on to victories at Forts Henry and Donelson, Shiloh, Champion's Hill, Big Black River Bridge, and Vicksburg. For his service in opening the Mississippi River he was commissioned a Regular Army major general. He was then sent to relieve the besieged troops at Chattanooga, driving the enemy off Lookout Mountain.

Grant was not the sort of soldier who caused his men to cheer wildly and toss their caps in the air. One of his officers later wrote that all they saw in him was a 'quiet solidity'.[2] That was enough; he was obviously a man of drive, one who, to the pleasure of Abraham Lincoln, fought and fought with what he had on hand, not forever crying for more men and equipment. Moreover, he kept his political superiors fully informed of his plans and actions, something generals like McClellan often failed to do. His enemy was the Confederate Army, not the federal government.

After his Western victories he was commissioned lieutenant general and given command of all the Union Armies. His plan then sent Sherman to drive into Georgia, Butler to take Richmond, and Sheridan into the Valley of Virginia, while he attached himself to the Army of the Potomac to destroy the Army of Northern Virginia. He was stopped by Lee in the Wilderness, but instead of retreating and rebuilding his forces, he continued to drive South, continually turning round Lee's right. Battles of Spotsylvania Court House, the North Anna, and Cold Harbour led to an eventual siege at Petersburg from which he knew Lee could not emerge victorious. Constant pressure led to Lee's being forced out of Petersburg and surrendering at Appomattox. There, Grant displayed his thoughtful, conciliatory side, allowing Lee and his men the most generous of terms.

After the final victory Grant was commissioned a full general, the first since George Washington. In 1868 he was elected president and proved to be as poor a political leader as he had been adroit a military leader. His two terms were marked by corruption. After retiring, he and his wife travelled around the world, ending up in New York, a bankrupt with cancer of the throat. At the suggestion of Mark Twain, he wrote his memoirs, which were vastly successful and, dying only a week after he had finished them on 23 July 1885, left his family a fine legacy and the world one of the best books ever written by a soldier.

caused in part by this drinking, forced him to resign his commission on 31 July 1854.

He returned home to a string of failures as a firewood peddler, farmer and real estate salesman, ending up in 1861 as a clerk in his family's tannery and leather store. At the war's outbreak he offered his service to the government, finally receiving a commission of colonel to the 21st Illinois Infantry. The 21st was sent to Missouri where Grant was commissioned a brigadier general on 7 August 1861. His first battle was at Belmont, Missouri, where his badly disciplined troops failed him. He did not look back,

Note
1. Abner R. Small, *The Road To Richmond*, University of California Press, 1957, p. 130

References
Bruce Catton, *Grant Moves South*, Little Brown, Boston, 1960
— *Grant Takes Command*, Little Brown, Boston, 1968
J. F. C. Fuller, *The Generalship of Ulysses S. Grant*, New York, 1929
Ulysses S. Grant, *The Personal Memoirs of U.S. Grant*, World

Publishing Co., Cleveland, Ohio, 1952
Lloyd Lewis, *Captain Sam Grant*, Little Brown, Boston, 1950
William S. McFeely, *Grant, A Biography*, W. W. Norton & Co, New York, 1981
Horace Porter, *Campaiging With Grant*, Century, New York, 1887
Gene Smith, *Lee And Grant*, McGraw Hill, New York, 1984
William E. Woodward, *Meet General Grant*, Horace Liverlight, New York, 1928

Halleck, Henry Wager (1815–75)

Graduating third in the US Military Academy class of 1839, Halleck was commissioned into the Corps of Engineers and sent to inspect the French military scene. On his return he published several books on the subject as well as a translation of Henri Jomini's work on Napoleon. This work earned him the nickname of 'Old Brains'. After returning home he served in a number of important posts in California where he resigned his commission in 1854 to become a San Francisco lawyer, businessman, writer and militia officer.

Henry Wagner Halleck (1815–72). (Library of Congress collection)

On 19 August 1861 he was commissioned a US Army major general in the Department of Missouri where he received laurels for victories actually won by his subordinates Grant, Buell and Samuel Curtis. His one field activity, the attack on Corinth, Missouri, showed his inability to command in the field because of his excessive caution.

In July 1862 he was named general in chief in Washington where he served as little more than a glorified clerk or adjutant to Lincoln and Secretary of War Stanton since he himself proposed little in the way of strategy. When Grant was promoted to command of the US Army, Halleck was given the new post of 'chief of staff', which he held until the war's end.

His later years were spent in the Army as commander of the Divisions of the Pacific and the South. He died in Louisville, Kentucky on 9 January 1862.

Reference
Stephen E. Ambrose, *Halleck, Lincoln's Chief of Staff*, New York, 1962

Hardee, William Joseph (1815–73)

A member of the US Military Academy class of 1839, Hardee's pre-war career included two brevets for gallantry during the Mexican War, a stint as commandant of cadets at the Academy, and the authorship of the standard infantry manual, *Rifle and Light Infantry Tactics*. A Georgian, he followed his state when it left the Union, being commissioned a Confederate brigadier general in June 1861 and a major general less than four months later. He commanded a corps at Shiloh and then another in the Army of Tennessee, where he earned a reputation as one of the South's best corps commanders. He was promoted to lieutenant general on 10 October 1862. He was offered command of the Army of Tennessee after Bragg left, but declined it. 'Hardee', a fellow Confederate general later wrote, 'was among the best of our subordinate generals, and, indeed, seemed to possess the requisite qualities for supreme command; but this he steadily refused, alleging his unfitness for responsibility. Such modesty is not a common American weakness, and deserves to be recorded.'[1] Later, he requested a transfer since he distrusted Hood who took the command. In September 1864 he accepted command of the Department of South Carolina, Georgia and Florida. There he was forced out of Savannah, Georgia and then driven through the Carolinas by Sherman, ending the war as a corps commander in J. E. Johnston's army.

Afterwards he was a planter in Selma, Alabama, dying in Wytheville, Virginia, on 6 November 1873.

Note
1. Richard Taylor, *Destruction and Reconstruction*, Longmans Green, Toronto, 1955, p. 264

Reference
Nathaniel C. Hughes Jr., *General William J. Hardee, Old Reliable*, Louisiana State University Press, Baton Rouge, Louisiana, 1965

Hill, Ambrose Powell (1825–65)

Graduated from the US Military Academy in 1847, Hill's pre-war service was with the US Coastal Survey, as well in the Army during the Mexican and Seminole Wars. At the war's outbreak, Hill resigned from the US Army to accept command of the 13th Virginia Infantry. Promoted a brigadier general on 26 February 1862, he served well during the Peninsular Campaign and earned promotion to major general on 26 May 1862. His division, which he and

Ambrose Powell Hill (1825–65) generally wore a red shirt on the battlefield; here he is wearing a 'salt and pepper' suit with the *three stars of a colonel on his collar. (Library of Congress collection)*

his men called the 'Light Division', served under Stonewall Jackson, with whom he had strained relations. His troops arrived in time to save Lee's army at Antietam, and he took over Jackson's command when Stonewall was mortally wounded at Chancellorsville, only to be wounded there himself shortly thereafter.

Promoted lieutenant general on 24 May 1863, Hill then commanded the Army of Northern Virginia's III Corps throughout its campaigns until he was killed by a skirmisher on the Petersburg lines on 2 April 1865.

Hill's medical problems kept him out of action several times when he was most needed, including Gettysburg where he did little. At Bristoe Station, Virginia, an attack he made without proper reconnaissance cost him more than 1,300 men. Apart from that, he lacked the ability to focus on the big picture, spending more time on combat leadership than on planning and organization.

'As a division commander', one of Jackson's staff officers later wrote, 'he had few equals. He was quick, bold, skillful, and tenacious when the battle had begun . . . It cannot be said he added to it [his reputation] when he commanded a corps.'[1]

Note

1. Henry Kyd Douglas, *I Rode With Stonewall*, Fawcett Publications, Greenwich, Connecticut, 1961, p. 148

References

Warren W. Hassler, *Lee's Forgotten General*, Garrett & Massie, Richmond, 1957

James I. Robertson, *General A. P. Hill, the Story of a Confederate Warrior*, Random House, New York, 1987

Martin Schenck, *Up Came Hill*, Stackpole, Harrisburg, Pennsylvania, 1958

Hood, John Bell (1831–79)

Born to an upwardly mobile Kentucky family, John Hood was a member of the US Military Academy's class of 1853. Originally an infantrymen, he was transferred to the 1st Cavalry where he served in Texas until the outbreak of the war. He resigned then and was commissioned into the Confederate cavalry, quickly gaining command of the 4th Texas Infantry in Virginia. He moved up the chain of command rapidly, first as commander of 'Hood's Texas Brigade', then as a division commander in the Army of Northern Virginia.

According to a fellow Confederate officer, 'His men were devoted to him and believed in him absolutely. There was no task too great or too dangerous for them to undertake if he led them, and he was as popular and as trusted by his officers as his men.'[1]

During his career he had the luck to be in the right place at the right time and then to seize the initiative, something many of his peers failed to do. He was badly wounded at Gettysburg where his left arm was rendered useless, and again at Chickamauga where he lost a leg. When he resumed the field it was as a commander of a corps in the Army of the Tennessee. There he aided J. E. Johnston against Sherman in the Atlanta campaign. When Johnston

John Bell Hood (1831–79).
(Library of Congress collection)

Like Ney, "the bravest of the brave", he was a splendid leader in battle, and as a brigade or division commander unsurpassed; but, arrived at a higher rank, he seems to have been impatient of control, and openly disapproved of Johnston's conduct of affairs between Dalton and Atlanta. Unwillingness to obey is often interpreted by governments into capacity for command.'[2]

Hood failed in basic logistical and tactical planning and in supervision of his subordinates. Afterwards he tried to lay blame on the shoulders of those subordinates, quite probably in conjunction with Jefferson Davis in an effort to destroy Johnston's reputation. After the war he married (1868) and became a factor and commission merchant in New Orleans. He and his wife died in a yellow-fever epidemic in 1879.

Notes
1. John Haskell, *The Haskell Memoirs*, G. P. Putnam's Sons, New York, 1960, p. 16
2. Richard Taylor, *Destruction and Reconstruction*, Longmans Green, Toronto, 1955, p. 265

References
J. P. Dyer, *The Gallant Hood*, Bobbs-Merrill, Indianapolis, Indiana, 1950
John B. Hood, *Advance and Retreat; Personal Experiences of the United States and Confederate States Armies*, Hood Orphan Memorial Fund, New Orleans, 1880
Richard McMurry, *John Bell Hood and the War for Southern Independence*, University Press of Kentucky, Lexington, Kentucky, 1982
Richard O'Conner, *Hood: Cavalier General*, Prentice-Hall, New York, 1949

Hooker, Joseph (1814–79)

Joseph Hooker graduated from the US Military Academy in 1837. He saw service along the Canadian border, in the Seminole War, and as a staff officer in the Mexican War where he reached the rank of lieutenant colonel through brevets. Assistant adjutant general of the Pacific Division, he resigned his commission in 1853 to take up farming in California. At the war's outbreak he was appointed a brigadier general of volunteers. Serving on the Peninsula, a press dispatch headed 'Fighting – Joe Hooker', earned him the nickname, which he never liked, of 'Fighting Joe Hooker'. None the less, he fought well there and at Antietam and Fredericksburg, for which he criticized Burnside publicly. Burnside told the War Department that one of them must go and Hooker was named to replace Burnside as Army of the Potomac commander.

'I believe you to be a brave and skilful soldier,' Lincoln wrote to Hooker on 26 January 1863. 'You have confidence in yourself, which is a valuable if not an indispensable quality. You are ambitious ... but ... you have taken counsel of your ambition and thwarted him [Burnside] as much as you could, in which you did a great wrong to the country and to a most meritorious and honorable fellow officer.'[1] Hooker was a morale builder, taking a badly defeated and dismayed army, after Fredericksburg, and restoring it to a fighting force. 'The soldiers are well pleased with their new commander Gen. Hooker,' one of them wrote home on 3 February 1863.[2] His plans, too, were excellent,

was relieved at Atlanta, Hood was given command of the army. It was then widely believed that he was not fit for this command, but the Confederacy, by mid-1864, had run out of its first-level generals.

Hood went on to lead the Army of Tennessee to destruction, first in failed attempts to free Atlanta and then in an attempt to lure Sherman back north by attacking at Franklin and then Nashville.

Fellow Confederate General Richard Taylor later wrote, 'It is painful to criticize Hood's conduct of this campaign.

Joseph Hooker (1814–79)
wearing a brigadier general's
uniform. (Author's collection)

and featured a flank move around Lee to destroy him. But, at the last minute, at Chancellorsville, his own nerve failed, especially after being badly stunned when the post against which he was leaning was hit by a cannon-ball, and Lee's daring overcame him.

Relieved of command, he went on to success as a corps commander at Lookout Mountain and in Sherman's campaign against Atlanta. When O. O. Howard was promoted over him, however, he asked to be relieved from command. Thereafter, he served as a commander of the Departments of the East and the Lakes until he retired from the army on 15 October 1868 after a stroke. He died in Garden City, New York on 31 October 1879.

Notes

1. Roy E. Appleman, ed., *Abraham Lincoln From His Own Words and Contemporary Accounts*, National Park Service, Washington, DC, 1946, p. 36
2. William G. Gavin ed., *Infantryman Pettit*, White Mane

Press, Columbia, Maryland, 1990, p. 55

Reference

Walter H. Hebert, *Fighting Joe Hooker*, Bobbs-Merrill, Indianapolis, Indiana, 1944

Jackson, Thomas Jonathan (1824–63)

The most beloved of Southern soldiers at the war's end was graduated from the US Military Academy in 1846. He held the brevet rank of major after his heroic service in the Mexican War. After serving in New York and Florida, on 13 August 1851 he reported to the Virginia Military Academy, having resigned his commission, to serve as professor of artillery and natural philosophy. He also joined the Virginia Militia as a major, being present at the hanging of John Brown.

At the war's outbreak, he was promoted to colonel and given command of Harpers Ferry. On 17 June 1861 he was promoted to brigadier general, commanding a brigade that earned him and his brigade the nickname 'Stonewall' for their stand at the First Bull Run. Promoted to major general on 7 October 1861, he was sent to the Shenandoah Valley where he was first beaten at Kernstown, but then turned and in rapid strokes freed the Valley from several different Union columns.

The Valley in Southern hands, he quickly marched to join Lee on the Peninsula, but there was oddly sluggish, his performance lack-lustre. None the less, he was sent against Pope once McClellan's threat had passed, and dazzled that general, capturing tons of supplies and driving Pope's army back to Washington. His hard fighting was equally vital at Antietam and Fredericksburg, but his real claim to fame was his march around Hooker's flank, under Lee's orders, to strike at Chancellorsville. Throwing the Union forces completely off balance, his troops completed a magnificent victory. That evening, however, when scouting between the lines, Jackson was wounded by his own men. His left arm amputated, he died of pneumonia on 10 May 1863.

He was not a warm man. One of his later generals later wrote that 'his ambition was vast, all-absorbing'.[1] An aide

Thomas Jonathan Jackson (1824–63). (Library of Congress collection)

thought that, among all his best points, 'Jackson was a man of strategy, and it is this quality of his mind that has attracted the admiration of military critics.'[2] But his men loved in him. 'There was something about Jackson that always attracted his men,' a private recalled. 'He was the idol of his old soldiers, and they would follow him anywhere. The very sight of him was the signal for cheers.'[3]

Notes

1. Richard Taylor, *Destruction and Reconstruction*, Longmans Green, Toronto, 1955, p. 91
2. Henry K. Douglas, *I Rode With Stonewall*, Fawcett Publications, Greenwich, Connecticut, 1961, p. 227
3. John H. Worsham, *One of Jackson's Foot Cavalry*, McCowat-Mercer Press, Jackson, Tennessee, 1964, p. 102

References

Lenoir Chambers, *Stonewall Jackson*, William Morrow, New York, 1959
John E. Cooke, *Stonewall Jackson, A Military Biography*, New York, 1866
R. L. Dabney, *Life and Campaigns of Lieut.-Gen. Thomas J. Jackson (Stonewall Jackson)*, Blelock & Co., New York, 1866
G. F. R. Henderson, *Stonewall Jackson and the American Civil War*, Longmans Green, Toronto, 1955
Mary Anna Jackson, *Life and Letters of General Thomas J. Jackson (Stonewall Jackson)*, Harper & Brothers, New York, 1892
James D. McCabe, *Life of Thomas J. Jackson, by an Ex-Cadet*, Richmond, 1864
Allen Tate, *Stonewall Jackson, The Good Soldier*, Minton Balch, New York, 1928
Frank E. Vandiver, *Mighty Stonewall*, McGraw Hill, New York, 1957

Johnston, Albert Sidney (1803–62)

An officer during the Black Hawk War, Johnston was a member of the US Military Academy's class of 1826. He left the US Army to join that of Texas, where he became senior brigadier general, chief commander, and secretary of war of the Republic of Texas. His Mexican War service was as a Texas volunteer colonel. He was named colonel of the US Army's 2nd Cavalry Regiment in Texas in 1855, leading the expedition to Utah against the Mormons in 1857 for which he was brevetted brigadier general. Thereafter he commanded the Department of the Pacific until the Civil War broke out when he returned to Texas.

Commissioned a full Confederate general to rank from 30 May 1861, he was given command of all troops west of the Alleghenies – i.e., most of the South. Concentrating his forces at Corinth, Mississippi, he attacked Grant's unfortified troops at Shiloh. There, while driving troops on near the Peach Orchard, he was hit in the leg by a bullet. He hid the fact from his men, bleeding to death unnoticed, the blood pouring into his boot.

While his friend Jefferson Davis, also an admirer of Braxton Bragg, considered him to be among the best soldiers the South had, his opponent at Shiloh, Grant, later decided he was not a good general, being 'vacillating and undecided in his actions'.[1]

Note

1. U.S. Grant, *Personal Memoirs of U.S. Grant*, World Publishing, Cleveland, Ohio, 1952, p. 187

References

William P. Johnston, *The Life of Albert Sidney Johnston*, New York, 1878

Avery C. Moore, *Destiny's Soldier*, San Francisco, 1958

Johnston, Joseph Eggleson (1807–91)

Graduating from the US Military Academy in 1829, Johnston was assigned to the 4th Artillery. He resigned from the army after eight years, but in 1838 he was commissioned a first lieutenant in the Topographical Engineers, seeing service in the Seminole and Mexican Wars.

On 22 April 1861 he resigned from the US Army and on 14 May received a Confederate brigadier general's commission. He first commanded at Harpers Ferry, then brought his troops east to join battle at First Bull Run. On 31 August he was promoted to full general. He objected, however, to the fact that he was fourth on the general's list when he had been first on the US Army brigadier general's list; he and Jefferson Davis had a falling out on this that lasted until the war's end.

Next he was in charge of stemming McClellan's thrust on Richmond until badly wounded at Seven Pines. Recovered by November, he was named commander of the Department of the West, a nebulous title with uncertain powers. After Bragg was removed, he was given command of the Army of Tennessee which he led in retreat in a dance of manoeuvre with Sherman to the gates of Atlanta. There Hood replaced him and he was out of action until Lee gave him command again of the Army of Tennessee in time for one last battle and then its surrender on 26 April 1865.

During the war Johnston was among the most popular of all Confederate generals. One artillery colonel wrote, 'As a soldier he will always rank high, though he never achieved great results, attributable to some extent to his relations with President Davis . . .'[1] The head of the Bureau of War noted in his diary on 26 July 1863: 'While I do not trust him because he is timid and because he hates Davis and Lee, I have a high opinion of his military *coup d'oeil*, derived however mainly from public reputation; for I do not think he has done anything worthy of a second-rate officer during the war.'[2] Finally, one of his privates later recalled that, 'He was loved, respected, admired; yes, almost worshipped by his troops.'[3]

Johnston was a fine organizer, but his main flaw as a general was in paying too little attention to the terrain in which he was to fight. On top of that, his main attitude was one of defence, rarely thinking of how to attack and get that major victory that was necessary if his cause were to triumph.

After the war Johnston worked in the insurance business, served in the US House of Representatives, and was US Commissioner of Railroads. He died after catching a cold while marching bareheaded in Sherman's funeral procession in March 1891.

Notes

1. John Haskell, *The Haskell Memoirs*, G. P. Putnam's Sons, New York, 1960, p. 7
2. Edward Younger, ed., *Inside The Confederate Government*, Oxford University Press, New York, 1957, p. 83
3. Sam R. Watkins, *"Co Aytch"*, Collier Books, New York, 1962, p. 126

References

Gilbert E. Govan and James W. Livingwood, *A Different Valor, The Story of General Joseph E. Johnston*, Bobbs-Merrill, Indianapolis, Indiana, 1956

Robert M. Hughes, *General Johnston*, D Appleton, New York, 1897

J. E. Johnston, *Narrative of Military Operations, Directed, During the Late War Between the States*, New York, 1874

Kirby Smith, Edmund (1824–93)

Graduating from the US Military Academy in 1845, Kirby Smith won two brevets for gallantry in the Mexican War. Commissioned a Confederate brigadier general on 17 June 1861, he led his men, at a critical stage, on to the field at First Bull Run, where he was badly wounded. Recovered, on 11 October 1861 he was promoted and assigned to command the District of East Tennessee. He won a decisive victory at Richmond, Kentucky. On 9 October 1862 he was promoted lieutenant general and given command of all troops west of the Mississippi. He almost resigned in 1863 to devote his life to the ministry, but changed his mind in time to stop Union drives into western Louisiana and Texas. Although the war's main action did not occur within his command, and he apparently did well enough with what he had, one of his generals later wrote that he 'proved unequal to extended command'.[1] Even so, his was the last major Confederate field army to surrender, which he did on 26 May 1865. Save for two years as president of the Pacific and Atlantic Telegraphic Company, his post-war years were spent as an educator at the Universities of Nashville and the South.

Note

1. Richard Taylor, *Destruction and Reconstruction*, Longmans Green, Toronto, 1955, p. 151

University Press, Baton Rouge, Louisiana, 1954

Reference

A. H. Noll, *General Kirby-Smith*, Sewanee University Press, Sewanee, Tennessee, 1907

T. N. Parks, *General Edmund Kirby Smith*, Louisiana State

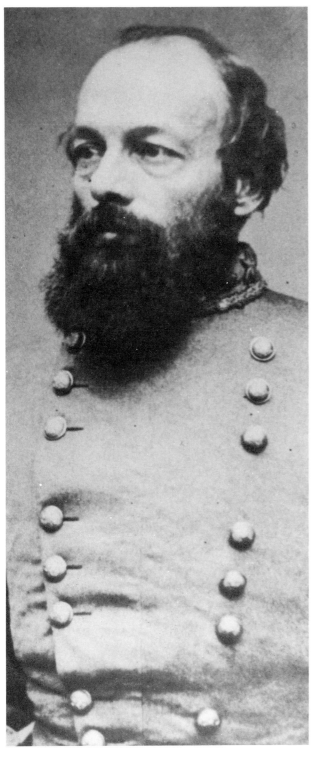

Edmund Kirby Smith (1824–93). (Library of Congress collection)

Lee, Robert Edward (1807–70)

The son of 'Light Horse' Harry Lee, a noted general of the Revolutionary War, who squandered fortune after fortune in his later years, Lee graduated from the US Military Academy in 1829 without a single demerit. Noted as an engineer in the Mexican War, 1861 found him as a lieutenant colonel in the 2nd Cavalry. He married after graduation, apparently badly although the couple did have seven children.

Lee joined Virginia when it left the US, having previously been offered, and turned down, command of the US Army. He was commissioned a Confederate brigadier general on 14 May 1861 and a full general shortly afterwards. His first campaign, in West Virginia, was a failure and he was then sent to examine South Atlantic coastal defences. In March 1862 he returned to Richmond as adviser to the president, taking over command of the Army of Northern Virginia when J. E. Johnston was wounded. He held field command of this army until its surrender on 9 April 1865 despite suffering a heart attack in early 1863. In addition, on 23 January 1865 he was given the title of General in Chief of the Armies of the Confederate States, too late to do much good even had he not been distracted by the defence of his own state which he always placed above the new 'Confederate States'.

In later years, Lee refused several lucrative offers to serve in positions where he could trade on his name as the most famous Confederate military leader of the war. Instead, he took charge of a small Virginia college, Washington, now Washington and Lee. He urged reconciliation with the North and peaceful rebuilding of the South. By the time of his death he had surpassed Jackson as the most loved soldier of the Confederacy. Indeed, one of his fellow Virginians wrote of Lee years after his death, 'It is impossible to speak of General Lee without seeming to deal in hyperbole.'[1] During his life, however, other Confederates saw him more clearly. A South Carolina colonel said that after Gettysburg the Army of Northern Virginia was ' . . . a demoralized army, and for this I hold General Lee largely responsible. He . . . had an utterly undue regard for the value of the elementary teaching of West Point . . . General Lee never went outside the regular grades, and was apparently resolute against so doing, to find officers, who might have been very Samsons to help him multiply his scant resources. He never discovered or encouraged a Forrest . . . '[2] One of his generals called him 'reserved almost to coldness'. He went on to say, 'In truth, the genius of Lee for offensive war had suffered by too long a service as an engineer.'[3] But, the common soldiers under him loved him. As one later wrote, 'He believed in his men and thought they could do anything that mortals could do. His men worshipped him, and I think the greatest man world ever saw was Robert E. Lee.'[4] Indeed, many of his opponents agreed, Grant later recalling, 'It was not an uncommon thing for my staff-officers to hear from Eastern officers, "Well, Grant has never met Bobby Lee yet."' However, Grant also ' . . . had known him

personally, and knew that he was mortal; and it was just as well I felt this'.[5]

In fact, Lee was a brilliant tactician, although less brilliant as a strategist. He often overlooked the long view, as for example in giving more emphasis to the war in his own state rather than in the West where the South actually lost the war. He was a gambler, always going for the knockout punch at battles like Chancellorsville and Gettysburg, where the more conservative tactics urged by Longstreet could have been more successful but would not actually have destroyed the Union Army. He failed to discipline his generals sufficiently, allowing men like Stuart to pursue their own interests rather than being sufficiently subordinated to the overall interests of the cause. This said, it is also true that the fact that the Army of Northern Virginia lasted as long as it did is as much due to Lee's influence over, and belief in, his troops as much as to his opponents' ineptness.

Notes

1. John S. Wise, "The End of an Era", *Confederate Veteran*, February, 1927, Nashville, Tennessee, p. 45
2. John Haskell, *The Haskell Memoirs*, G. P. Putnam's Sons, New York, 1960, pp. 55–7
3. Richard Taylor, *Destruction and Reconstruction*, Longmans Green, Toronto, 1955, pp. 111–12
4. John H. Worsham, *One of Jackson's Foot Cavalry*, McCowat-Mercer Press, Jackson, Tennessee, 1964, pp. 187–8
5. U.S. Grant, *Personal Memoirs of U.S. Grant*, World Publishing, Cleveland, Ohio, 1952, pp. 96, 453

References

Thomas L. Connelly, *The Marble Man: Robert E. Lee and His Image in American Society*, New York, 1977
J. E. Cooke, *A Life of General Robert E. Lee*, New York, 1873
Clifford Dowdey and Louis H. Manarin, eds., *The Wartime Papers of R. E. Lee*, Bramhall House, New York, 1961
Jubal Early, *The Campaigns of Gen. Robert E. Lee*, Baltimore, 1872
Douglas S. Freeman, *R. E. Lee, A Biography*, Charles Scribners' Sons, New York, 1941
Charles B. Flood, *Lee: The Last Years*, Houghton Mifflin, New York, 1981
R. E. Lee, *Recollections and Letters of General Lee*, Garden City Publishing, Garden City, New Jersey, 1924
Frederick Maurice, *Robert E. Lee the Soldier*, Houghton Mifflin, Boston, 1925
Edward Pollard, *Lee and His Lieutenants*, New York, 1867
Gene Smith, *Lee And Grant*, McGraw Hill, New York, 1984
Walter H. Taylor, *Four Years with General Lee*, Bonanza Books, New York, 1962

The Confederates trust Lee and not God

'The people [in Pennyslvania] generally were evidently greatly surprised at the devotion of our men to General Lee, and made some rough remarks about it. One old lady called out to an officer of ours as he strode by: "You are marching mighty proudly now, but you will come back faster than you went." "Why so, old lady?" he asked. "Because you put your trust in General Lee and not in the Lord Almighty," she replied.'

(Francis W. Dawson, *Reminiscences of Confederate Service*, Louisiana State University Press, 1980, p. 93)

Lincoln, Abraham (1809–65)

Born to a poor farming family and receiving little formal education ('somehow, I could read, write, and cipher to the rule of three, but that was all'),[1] Lincoln worked as a clerk in a small town store, served as a militia captain in the Black Hawk War, became a lawyer in the Illinois state capital and ran in several elections, with mixed success.

None the less, his speeches had gained him a national reputation when the new Republican Party gave him their presidential nomination in 1860. The Democratic Party split into factions, and Linoln won the election though with less than half the total vote.

When the Southern states left the US after his election, he oversaw the huge military campaign to restore the Union.

Abraham Lincoln (1809–65), President of the United States of America, in a Mathew Brady photograph. (David Scheinmann collection)

He faced re-election in 1864, in one of the few examples of a country involved in a major civil war holding a peace-time type of election, and won it against a peace-policy opposition party led by popular Union general McClellan, despite his early forebodings that he would lose. On 15 April 1865 he was murdered by a ring led by actor John Wilkes Booth which had apparently been authorized and aided by Confederate secret service officials in an attempt to kidnap Lincoln.

He was a masterful politician, balancing military necessities against political requirements. He had an intuitive sense of what should be done to win, and when. An example of this was the Emancipation Proclamation, which gave all slaves in rebelling states their freedom. He saw that turning the war into something greater than simply a war to retain one particular government would help to deter foreign governments, which would not fight to retain the wrong of human slavery, from helping the South. At the same time, he did not introduce the Proclamation too early, which would have cost the support of many common Northerners who would fight for their country but not for Black equality.

Often given to personal depression and despair, he retained the will to win throughout the war, despite heavy casualties and a great deal of political opposition from all sides. Although a poor administrator, he was a brilliant speech writer (but a bad speaker, having a high, shrill voice) and, above all, a leader in the military field and in foreign and domestic policy. He was, finally, a gentle man who wanted nothing more than to serve, 'With malice toward none; with charity for all; with firmness in the right, as God gives us to see the right, let us strive on to finish the work we are in; to bind up the nation's wounds; to care for him who shall have borne the battle, and for his widow, and his orphan – to do all which may achieve and cherish a just and lasting peace among ourselves, and with all nations.'[2]

Notes

1. Roy E. Appleman, *Abraham Lincoln From His Own Words and Contemporary Accounts*, National Park Service, Washington, DC, 1946, p. 2
2. Ibid, p. 48

References

Isaac N. Arnold, *The Life of Abraham Lincoln*, Jansen McClurg, Chicago, 1885
Albert J. Beveridge, *Abraham Lincoln*, Houghton Mifflin, Boston, 1928
John G. Nicolay and John Hay, *Abraham Lincoln; A History*, The Century Co., New York, 1904
Carl Sandburg, *Abraham Lincoln*, Harcourt Brace, New York, 1926
Ida M. Tarbell, *The Life of Abraham Lincoln*, McClure Phillips & Co., New York, 1902
Benjamin P. Thomas, *Abraham Lincoln*, Alfred A. Knopf, New York, 1952
William A. Tidwell, James O. Hall, David W. Gaddy, *Come Retribution, The Confederate Secret Service and the Assassination of Lincoln*, University Press of Mississippi, Jackson, Mississippi, 1988

Longstreet, James (1821–1904)

A graduate of the US Military Academy in 1842, Longstreet's pre-war service was in the Mexican War, in the west, and as a paymaster. It was in this latter role that he wished to serve the Confederacy, but he was given a brigadier general's commission and field command on 17 June 1861. 'Old Pete's' distinguished service as a battlefield tactician at the First Bull Run and Peninsula Campaign earned his major generalship on 7 October 1861 and lieutenant generalship on 9 October 1862.

Twice during those campaigns, however, he acted slowly when ordered to make a movement with which he did not agree. After the war many pro-Lee Southerners would have it that there was a third occasion, the second day at Gettysburg. 'It is generally conceded that General Longstreet, on this occasion, was fairly chargeable with tardiness,' one of Lee's staff officers later wrote.[1] However, another Confederate recalled seeing Lee and Longstreet at dawn that day and said he ' . . . never understood why, if General Lee wanted the fight to begin, what delayed it then. Surely he could have begun it, had he so desired.'[2] In truth, this unfair blame was placed on Longstreet in an attempt to take the defeat's blame from Lee. Still, blame for Gettysburg followed Lee's favourite general for the rest of his life.

After Gettysburg Longstreet took his corps west where he served under Bragg with whom he did not get along, at Chickamauga and then independently and unsuccessfully at Knoxville. He and his men returned to the Army of Northern Virginia thereafter to be accidentally wounded at the Wilderness by his own men and then surrender at Appomattox.

After the war Longstreet became a Republican, adding fuel to Southern dislike of the general whom Lee called 'My Old Warhorse'. He served as minister to Turkey and commissioner of Pacific Railroads before settling in Gainesville, Georgia, where he died on 2 January 1904, the last of the Confederate high command.

Notes

1. Walter H. Taylor, *Four Years with General Lee*, Bonanza Books, New York, 1962, p. 99
2. John Haskell, *The Haskell Memoirs*, G. P. Putnam's Sons, New York, 1960, p. 58

References

H. J. Eckenrode and Bryan Conrad, *James Longstreet, Lee's War Horse*, University of North Carolina Press, Chapel Hill, North Carolina, 1936
James Longstreet, *From Manassas to Appomattox, Memoirs of the Civil War in America*, J. B. Lippincott, Philadelphia, 1896
William G. Piston, *Lee's Tarnished Lieutenant, James Longstreet and His Place in Southern History*, University of Georgia Press, Athens, Georgia, 1987

McClellan, George Brinton (1826–85)

After graduating from the US Military Academy in 1846, McClellan earned two brevets in the Mexican War and was sent to observe European forces during the Crimean War. Resigning from the Army in 1857, he served as an officer for several railroads. At the war's outbreak he was commissioned a major general of volunteers and quickly cleared West Virginia. He was then brought east to head the Army of the Potomac where his care for his troops, combined with a tightened discipline and sense of purpose, won him the love of his troops. 'I never saw men have so much confidence in a man as the soldiers have in McClellan,' one

that battle for a long wait, without making any attempt to follow Lee back into Virginia, McClellan was finally removed on 7 November 1862. He ran for president on the Democratic Party ticket in 1864, was beaten, and later served as governor of New Jersey, where he died on 29 October 1885.

McClellan's main contributions during his four months as Union general-in-chief were the activist interpretation he placed on that job and the creation of a single strategy for fighting the war. Against that, however, he always believed that his enemy was superior in both numbers and ability, something which rubbed off on the rest of his army and eventually prolonged the war. He never learned from his past mistakes. He also believed that anyone who objected to his actions was either a fool or a traitor. He failed, too, because, he did not want to change the social order, something that would be required if the war were to be won. He spent more time playing politics in Washington than fighting the rebels at Richmond. Finally, his personal actions suggest that he was not especially brave in battle.

Notes

1. William G. Gavin, *Infantryman Pettit*, White Mane Press, Columbia, Maryland, 1990, p. 36
2. Cecil D. Eby, Jnr, ed., *A Virginia Yankee in the Civil War*, The University of North Carolina Press, Chapel Hill, North Carolina, 1961, p. 129

George B. McClellan, *McClellan's Own Story: The War for the Union*, Charles L Webster, New York, 1887
William Myers, *General George Brinton McClellan*, Appleton Century, New York, 1934
Stephen M. Sears, *George B. McClellan, the Young Napoleon*, Tickner & Fields, New York, 1988

References

G. S. Hillard, *Life and Campaigns of George B. McClellan, Major- General U.S. Army*, J. B. Lippincott, Philadelphia, 1865
Clarence E. McCarthy, *Little Mac, The Life of General George B. McClellan*, Dorrance, Philadelphia, 1940

George Brinton McClellan (1826–85) in a major general's *uniform. (National Archives collection)*

of his privates wrote on 13 November 1862.[1] The following day, a staff officer noted in his diary, 'My opinion of McClellan is that he is the most capable man we have in military affairs.'[2]

He led the Army against Richmond in the Peninsula Campaign, where he lost his nerve at the last minute, giving way to fantasies of huge enemy armies. Relieved of overall command of the Union Armies, he watched Pope's Army get smashed without making an effort to aid him. Nevertheless, as the best-known and loved US soldiers, Lincoln again gave him command of the Army of the Potomac, which he led to a stand-off battle at Antietam. Settling down after

McDowell, Irvin (1818–85)

Graduating from the US Military Academy in 1838, he served as an instructor of tactics there from 1841 to 1845. Thereafter he saw staff service in the Mexican War and in Washington. Appointed a brigadier general of volunteers on 14 May 1861, he was given the unhappy assignment of rushing raw troops, whose confidence he did not inspire, southward to take Richmond in response to popular demand. Although his plans were good, his troops, many of whom distrusted McDowell and even suspected him of treason, were unable to break the Confederate defence at First Bull Run, and were thrown back in confusion to Washington. McDowell was left in charge of the defence of Washington during the Peninsula Campaign, then joined Pope's army as a corps commander. After the battle of Second Bull Run, he was removed from all field command until 1 July 1864 when he was given command of the Department of the Pacific. Staying in the army after the his men to a successful defence at Gettysburg. Although he failed to pursue Lee's beaten army aggressively, he remained in command of the Army of the Potomac through Appomattox.

Grant reported on 13 May 1864 that Meade was one of the fittest officers 'for large commands I have come in contact with'.[1] Despite this Meade, with some reason, felt himself overshadowed by Grant and thought that he did not receive sufficient credit for his work. His commission as a regular army major general did not come until after his wartime subordinate, Sheridan, had been promoted, which greatly irritated the hot-tempered Meade. But he remained in the army, commanding various departments, as well as holding the position of Commissioner of Philadelphia's Fairmont Park. He died in that city on 6 November 1872, partly as a result of old war wounds.

Note

1. U.S. Grant, *Personal Memoirs of U.S. Grant*, World Publishing, Cleveland, Ohio, 1952, p. 424

References

Richard M. Bache, *Life of George Gordon Meade, Commander of the Army of the Potomac*, 1897

Theodore Lyman, *Meade's Headquarters, 1863–1865: Letters of Colonel Theodore Lyman*, Atlantic Press, Boston, 1922

Irvin McDowell (1818–85).
(Library of Congress collection)

war, he became a regular army major general on 25 November 1872, having commanded several departments until his retirement in 1882. He died in San Francisco on 4 May 1885.

Meade, George Gordon (1815–72)

Born in Spain, where his father served as US naval agent, Meade was graduated from the US Military Academy in 1835. He resigned the following year but rejoined the Army in 1842, seeing service in the Mexican War. On 31 August 1861 he was commissioned a brigadier general of volunteers, serving in the Peninsula Campaign where he was twice wounded. He returned, although far from recovered, to lead his brigade at the Second Bull Run. He commanded a division at South Mountain and Antietam and V Corps at Fredericksburg and Chancellorsville. He was given command of the Army of the Potomac on 28 June 1863 and lead

George Gordon Meade (1815–72). (Library of Congress collection)

Pemberton, John Clifford (1814–81)

Pennsylvania-born Pemberton was graduated from the US Military Academy in 1837. While there he made friends with many Southern-born cadets and, afterwards, married a Virginia native. Brevetted twice for gallantry during the Mexican War, he resigned to go South on 24 April 1861 and received a Confederate brigadier general's commission on 17 June 1861. His first command was the Department of South Carolina, Georgia, and Florida, in which he earned promotion to major general on 14 January 1862 and to lieutenant general on 10 October 1862. Although he was not an inspiring leader, he handled this job well, being an able administrator. On 14 October 1862 he received command of the Department of Mississippi and East Louisiana, with his main defence centered around Vicksburg. His superior, J. E. Johnston, ordered him to abandon the city, while President Davis told him to defend it at all costs. He chose to obey the latter, allowing himself to become besieged and finally surrendering on 4 July 1863. On being exchanged, he resigned his commission, but accepted a commision as a colonel and inspector of artillery, a job he filled well until the war's end. He returned to Pennsylvania after the war, and died in Pennllyn on 13 July 1881.

References

John C. Pemberton III, *Pemberton, Defender of Vicksburg*, University of North Carolina Press, Chapel Hill, North Carolina, 1942

Pope, John (1822–92)

Graduating from the US Military Academy in 1842 at the age of 16, Pope was a collateral descendant of George Washington and connected by marriage to the family of Mary Todd Lincoln. A captain by brevet in the Mexican War, he was appointed a brigadier general of volunteers on 14 June 1861 although before the war he had never even commanded a platoon. However, he made a name for himself for the capture of Island No. 10 on the Mississippi. He was then offered a command in Northern Virginia, which at first he turned down, but Lincoln, whom he had known before the war, pressed it on him. His eventual acceptance was followed by a bombastic proclamation about seeing the backs of his enemies in the West, which cost him the respect of both South and North. One of his soldiers said that his orders were unfortunate 'because they incited a degree of contempt for him which greatly impaired his usefulness'.[1] A staff officer noted in his diary that 'There seems to be a furious and universal outcry against Pope.'[2] The eventual result was the Second Bull Run. 'In this campaign', a staff officer noted, 'Pope was entirely deceived and outgeneralled. His own conceit and pride of opinion led him into these mistakes. On the field his conduct was cool, gallant, and prompt.'[3] The battle was followed by a banishment to Minnesota where he was given the task of subduing the Sioux Indians. Thereafter, he commanded a

number of departments until his retirement in 1886. He died in the Old Soldiers' and Sailors' Home, Sandusky, Ohio, on 23 September 1892.

Notes

1. Julian W. Hinkley, *Service With The Third Wisconsin,* Wisconsin Historical Commission, Madison, Wisconsin, 1912, p. 31
2. Cecil D. Eby, Jnr., *A Virginia Yankee in the Civil War*, The University of North Carolina Press, Chapel Hill, North

Carolina, 1961, p. 100
3. Ibid, p. 97

Reference

Wallace J. Schutz and Walter N. Trenerry, *Abandoned By Lincoln*, University of Illinois Press, Urbana, Illinois, 1990

John Pope (1822–92). *(Harper's Weekly)*

Porter, David Dixon (1813–91)

Born into a seafaring family, Porter's first service was in 1827 as a midshipman in the Mexican Navy, spending time as a prisoner of war. He joined the US Navy in 1829, accepting command of the USS *Powhatan* as a commander in April 1861. Commander of a fleet of mortar boats at the capture of New Orleans, he was promoted to acting rear admiral in the fall of 1862 and given command of the Mississippi Squadron. A member of the commanding staff at the capture of Vicksburg, he was promoted to the rank of

David Dixon Porter (1813–91) in the 1861 uniform of a commander; a Brady studio photograph. (Author's collection)

Rosecrans, William Starke (1819–98)

A US Military Academy graduate in 1842, Rosecrans missed Mexican War service and resigned from the Army in 1854. A Democrat and a Roman Catholic, Rosecrans was the type of person courted by a Republic administration and was quickly given a regular army brigadier general's commission in May 1861. His first service was in West Virginia, where he won the Battle of Rich Mountain against Robert E. Lee. His next command was in the Army of the Mississippi at Corinth, which he then commanded in the Battles of Iuka and Corinth. On 17 September 1862 he was commissioned a major general of volunteers, to rank from 21 March, and given command of the Army of the Cumberland. He commanded at Stones River and Chickamauga, where he made a tactical blunder which opened a gap in his lines and almost caused total defeat. Thereafter, he was besieged in Chattanooga where he was relieved by Grant on 19 October 1863. He then commanded the Department of Missouri until December 1864 when he went on leave until he resigned on 28 March 1867. 'Rosecrans', one of his officers noted in his diary, 'is an educated officer, who has rubbed much against the world, and has experience.'[1]

Named minister to Mexico in 1868, he was later elected in California to the US House of Representatives, then later served as Registrar of the Treasury. He died at his California ranch on 11 March 1898 and was buried in Los Angeles.

Note
1. John Beatty, *The Citizen Soldier*, Wilstach Baldwin, Cincinnati, Ohio, 1879, p. 235

Reference
William M. Lamers, *The Edge of Glory: A Biography of General William S. Rosecrans*, Harcourt, Brace & World, New York, 1961

Scott, Winfield (1786–1866)

Little known today, Winfield Scott was possibly America's finest soldier. Appointed to the Army in 1808, he served with rare distinction as a young brigadier general in the War of 1812 at Lundy's Lane, where he was badly wounded. A politician as well as a soldier, President Polk didn't want him to see field service in the Mexican War even though he was the army's chief general, but was finally forced to do so. Scott planned and led a brilliant drive against overwhelming odds inland from Vera Cruz to Mexico City along the National Road. Watching from his office in London, the ageing Duke of Wellington said that Scott was lost when he cut loose from his lines on the coast, but Scott proved the victor of Waterloo wrong.

When the Civil War started, 'Old Fuss and Feathers', as he was called because of his devotion to elaborate dress uniforms, was stout, ill and unable to mount a horse. None the less, he designed a plan, called the 'Anaconda Plan', to destroy the South by blockading Southern ports, clearing

regular rear admiral. After the abortive Red River Campaign, he was given command of the North Atlantic Squadron, where he participated in the capture of Fort Fisher, North Carolina. Receiving the Thanks of Congress during the war, he was promoted vice admiral in 1866 and superintendent of the US Navy Academy. In 1870 he was appointed admiral. He died in Washington, DC on 13 February 1891.

Quick to take laurels for more than he deserved, Porter was also an excellent naval officer who contributed greatly to the Union cause.

References
David D. Porter, *Naval History of the Civil War*, Castle, Secaucus, New Jersey, 1984
James R. Soley, *Admiral Porter*, D

Appleton, New York, 1913
Robert S. West, *The Second Admiral, A Life of David Dixon Porter*, New York, 1937

*William Starke Rosecrans
(1819–98). (Library of
Congress collection)*

*Winfield Scott (1786–1866) in
an elaborately embroidered
uniform of his own design.
(David Scheinmann collection)*

the Mississippi River and driving against Richmond. At the
end, it was Scott's plan implemented by Grant that won the
war. In the meantime, he had been replaced by McClellan
and retired on 1 November 1861. He lived to see the South
returned to the Union, his last battle fought and won, and
died at the home of the US Army, West Point, on 29 May
1866, where America's greatest soldier now lies.

References

James Barnes, *The Giant of Three
    Wars, A Life of General Winfield
    Scott*, D. Appleton, New York,
    1903
Charles W. Elliott, *Winfield Scott,
    The Soldier and the Man*,
    Macmillan, New York, 1937

Winfield Scott, *Memoirs of Lieut.-
    General Scott, LL.D.*, Sheldon &
    Co, New York, 1864
Arthur D. H. Smith, *Old Fuss and
    Feathers; The Life and Exploits of
    Lt.-General Winfield Scott*, The
    Greystone Press, New York,
    1937

Semmes, Raphael (1809–77)

Appointed a midshipman in the US Navy on 1 April 1826,
Semmes served in the Mexican War and was admitted to
the bar in 1834. In April 1861 he was named the
Confederacy's Chief of the Lighthouse Bureau with the rank
of commander. A believer in the power of commerce-
destroyers to influence the war, he fitted out the CSS *Sumter*
in New Orleans. He commanded this ship in the taking of
more than a dozen prizes, but was forced to abandon her in
Gibraltar when she became unseaworthy. He made his way
to England, where he received command of the CSS *Alabama*
in August 1862. This he took against US commerce for
almost two years, even sinking a US man-of-war, the USS
Hatteras. Weary, Semmes accepted the challenge of the USS
Kearsage outside Cherbourg, France, on 19 June 1864. The

Raphael Semmes (1809–77).
(Library of Congress collection)

Philip Henry Sheridan
(1831–88). (Author's collection)

Alabama's shells failed to take effect, while the *Kearsage*'s heavy pivot guns and well-trained crew shot holes in the *Alabama*'s wooden walls. Semmes was picked out of the water by a British yacht. He returned to the South, where he was appointed a rear admiral and given command of the James River Squadron. When Richmond was abandoned he and his sailors were formed into the Naval Brigade and assigned to duty with Lee's army with whom he surrendered at Appomattox.

Arrested for piracy and treason, the charges were later dropped and Semmes held various careers as a college professor, newspaper editor and lawyer before his death in Mobile, Alabama on 30 August 1877.

Reference
Admiral Raphael Semmes,
    Memoirs of Service Afloat, The
    Blue & Gray Press, Secaucus,
    New Jersey, 1987

Sheridan, Philip Henry (1831–88)
Although Sheridan was to graduate from the US Military Academy in 1852, a fight with a cadet officer and a following suspension, delayed his graduation, at close to the bottom of his class, until 1853. On graduation he was assigned to Grant's old regiment, the 4th Infantry. In 1861 he was quartermaster and chief commissary for his regiment and then for Halleck's forces near Corinth, Mississippi. Unhappy with staff work, he managed to get appointed colonel of the 2nd Michigan Cavalry on 25 May 18962. After his victory at Booneville, Mississippi, he was commissioned a brigadier general of volunteers on 13 Setember 1862. Fighting stubbornly at Perryville and Murfreesboro, he was promoted on 16 March 1863. He fought equally stubbornly at Chickamauga and Missionary Ridge when in command of XX Corps, where he attracted the attention of U.S. Grant. When Grant went East, he gave Sheridan command of the cavalry of the Army of the Potomac, some three

divisions strong. He virtually destroyed Stuart's cavalry outside Richmond. Next he was given the job of clearing the Shenandoah Valley, where he saved his forces at Cedar Creek after a desperate ride to rally his broken units. There being virtually no more resistance in the Valley, he returned to Grant in time to cut off Lee's retreat at Appomattox. Thereafter, he commanded along the Mexican Border where he played a part in the downfall of Maximilian. Becoming a lieutenant general after Sherman's promotion to general, he became the army's chief in 1884 and was named a general in 1888. He died in Nosquitt, Massachusetts on 5 August 1888.

Sheridan combined a coolness under fire with a hot temper which he was not afraid to unleash on his superiors.

References

Henry E. Davies, *General Sheridan*, D. Appleton, New York 1895

Richard O'Conner, *Sheridan, The Inevitable*, Prentice-Hall, New York, 1953

Plilip H. Sheridan, *Personal Memoirs of P. H. Sheridan*, Charles Webster, New York, 1888

Sherman, William Tecumseh (1820–91)

Orphaned when his father, an Ohio supreme court justice, died in 1829, Sherman was taken in by US Senator Thomas Ewing. His foster-father had him appointed to the US Military Academy, from where he graduated in 1840, and gave him his daughter in marriage. He saw Mexican War service, resigning his commission in 1853 to go into the banking business in San Francisco. He then held various jobs, being superintendent of the Louisiana State Seminary of Learning and Military Academy when the state left the Union. He left to become president of a St. Louis streetcar company, but quickly accepted command of the 13th US Infantry Regiment on 14 May 1861. Given command of a brigade at the First Bulll Run, he did well enough to be sent to Kentucky to hold that state. Under a great deal of pressure there, he apparently had a mild nervous breakdown and was relieved by Buell.

Returning to duty, his troops were among the first hit at Shiloh, where he had failed to take precautions against surprise. But he managed to hang on until reinforced and on 1 May 1862 was promoted major general. He took part in the assault on Vicksburg as commander of XV Corps. In September 1863 he went to Chattanooga, his corps taking part in Missionary Ridge. In March 1864 Grant went East to assume overall command and Sherman took over command of the Western Theatre. He then led his troops on a neat dance of manoeuvres against the army defending Atlanta until Johnston was replaced and Hood almost destroyed his own army. On 12 August 1864 Sherman was made a regular army major general. Taking Atlanta, he then burned his bridges behind him and cut loose for Savannah, Georgia, on the Atlantic coast. After that city's fall, he headed North to unite with Grant's army, meeting Johnston for the last time at Bentonville. After his final victory in North Carolina, he proposed peace terms that

were more generous then Grant's at Appomattox and which would have had serious political ramifications. These were turned down by the government, and he finally accepted Johnston's army's surrender on terms quite like those of Lee's.

Sherman's troops trusted him but never seemed wholly to love him. For example, years later one recalled, 'Sherman, with all his great talents and acknowledged ability, was affected with the same weakness that was said to have troubled Napoleon – not being able to look with complacency on the great personal popularity of a subordinate.'[1]

In 1866 he was promoted lieutenant general and, in 1869, full general and commander-in-chief of the army. Not happy

William Tecumseh Sherman (1820–91). (David Scheinmann collection)

with the political scene in Washington, he moved his headquarters to St. Louis in 1874. Retiring in 1883, he settled in New York City where he died on 14 February 1891.

Note
1. Julian W. Hinkley, *Service With The Third Wisconsin Infantry*, Wisconsin History Commission, Madison, Wisconsin, 1912, p. 134.

B. H. Liddell-Hart, *Sherman: Soldier–Realist–American*, Frederick A Praeger, New York, 1958
William T. Sherman, *The Memoirs of William T. Sherman*, Indiana University Press, Bloomington, Indiana, 1957

References
Lloyd Lewis, *Sherman, Fighting Prophet*, Harcourt, Brace, New York, 1932

Sibley, Henry Hopkins (1816–86)
A graduate of the US Military Academy in 1838, Sibley participated in the Seminole War (1838–9), the Mexican War and the Utah expedition in 1856. His major contribution during his pre-war service was the invention of the tent which bears his name and saw use in the early years of the Civil War. He was commissioned a major in the 1st US Dragoons on 13 May 1861. On that date, however, he resigned his commission, despite the fact that his wife came from New York, and travelled South to visit his old friend Jefferson Davis and seek a Confederate commission.

Sibley offered a plan to form a brigade in Texas that would drive through New Mexico and Colorado and end up in San Francisco, taking enough gold along the way to pay for the South's war efforts. However, he paid too little attention to logistics, pinning too much hope on capturing US supply depots and buying supplies from Mexico. As it turned out, supply depots were burned and Mexicans refused to accept Confederate currency. He was eventually beaten at the battles of Valverde and Glorieta Canon, returning to El Paso, Texas, in May 1862. During the campaign, he was constantly in pain from a chronic kidney problem which caused him to spend most of the time drunk in an ambulance. Court-martialled for a later command failure under Taylor, he never again held command in the Confederacy.

Sibley's post-war years were spent as the Inspector General of Artillery in the Egyptian Army (1869–73), from which he was discharged for drunkenness. He lived his last years with his daughter in Petersburg, Virginia, where he scraped together a living as an inventor, writer and French teacher.

References
Jerry Thompson, *Henry Hopkins Sibley, Confederate General of the*

West, Northwestern State University Press, Natchituches, Louisiana, 1987

Stuart, James Ewell Brown (1833–64)
The product of a cold mother and a largely absent father, J. E. B. Stuart was graduated from the US Military Academy in 1854. He served in the cavalry against the Indians and

was badly wounded. On the war's outbreak, he was commissioned a Confederate lieutenant colonel. As such he gained great praise for his excellent training and organizational abilities. Within a year he was a major general commanding what amounted to a corps.

According to a fellow Confederate officer, Stuart ' . . . was a remarkable mixture of a green, boyish, undeveloped man, and a shrewd man of business and a strong leader. To hear him talk no one would think that he could ever be anything more than a dashing leader of a very small command, with no dignity, and much boastful vanity. But with all he was a shrewd, gallant commander.'[1]

In many ways he was more lucky than able, leading such efforts as his 'ride around McClellan' in June 1862 against poorly trained and organized Union cavalry. All this created the myth of the 'bold cavalier'. Therefore, when finally a trained and organized Union cavalry struck unprepared cavalry under Stuart at Brandy Station, Virginia, in 1863, he was taken aback by the outcry of criticism he received. His attempt to repeat his ride around the Union Army during Gettysburg to redeem his reputation deprived Lee of his intelligence-gathering source and was one cause of Lee's defeat there.

Stuart continued to attempt to gain promotion to the rank of lieutenant general, submitting official reports on such battles as Brandy Station and Gettysburg that placed blame elsewhere and were, in fact, simply inaccurate. On top of that, Stuart seemed unable to accept that fact that his beloved Virginia was facing defeat in the war's ebb. His death at Yellow Tavern on 11 May 1864 seems almost as if he had arranged it in order to maintain the 'Stuart magic'.

Note
1. John Haskell, *The Haskell Memoirs*, G. P. Putnam's Sons, New York, 1960, p. 19

References
William W. Blackford, *War Years With Jeb Stuart*, Charles

Scribners' Sons, New York, 1945
Emory M. Thomas, *Bold Dragoon, the life of J. E. B. Stuart*, Harper & Row, New York, 1986
John W. Thomason Jnr, *Jeb Stuart*, Charles Scribners' Sons, New York, 1941

Taylor, Richard (1826–79)
Son of the Mexican War hero and US President Zachary Taylor, Richard Taylor was graduated from Yale University in 1845, after which he served as his father's military secretary, Louisiana planter and state senator. Although he had never held a command, he was appointed colonel of the 9th Louisiana Infantry when the state left the Union. Serving well at the First Bull Run, he was promoted brigadier general on 21 October 1861 and major general on 28 July 1862 while serving under the District of West Louisiana where he repulsed Banks's Red River Campaign and was therefore appointed a lieutenant general on 8 April 1864. He was then given command of the Department of Alabama and Mississippi, despite his fight with his superior, Kirby Smith, which led to his offering to give up his command – an offer which was declined. On 4 May 1865 his

James Ewell Brown ('Jeb') Stuart (1833–64). (Library of Congress collection)

was the last force east of the Mississippi River to surrender. Seemingly one of the best all-round Southern generals, he managed never to be tested by the best all-round Northern generals, so history must remain silent on his actual abilities. After the war, he worked for leniency for the South and especially for Jefferson Davis. He died in New York on 12 April 1879.

Reference

Richard Taylor, *Destruction and Reconstruction*, Longmans Green, Toronto, 1955

Thomas, George Henry (1816–70)

A native Virginian, Thomas was graduated from the US Military Academy in 1840. After artillery service in the Seminole and Mexican Wars, he was a major in the 2nd US

Cavalry in 1861 as well as an applicant for the post of commandant of cadets of the Virginia Military Academy. Because of this, although his loyalty was suspect, he was commissioned a US brigadier general on 17 August 1861 and sent to Kentucky where he won the battle of Mill Springs. He was promoted on 25 April 1862, after fighting at Shiloh, and then served at the Siege of Corinth, Perryville and Chickamauga. There, it was his advice to reinforce the Union left that kept the battle from being a total rout, as well as his troops' firm stand. There he earned the nickname 'The Rock of Chickamauga'. Thereafter, his troops further distinguished themselves at Missionary Ridge. He received command of the Army of the Cumberland, which served well in taking Atlanta. When he headed for the sea, Sherman left him behind, as a trusted commander of the defences of Nashville. There his forces virtually destroyed those of Hood, for which he received the Thanks of Congress.

Grant, who did not like his type of soldier, later called him 'slow and deliberate in speech and action; sensible, honest and brave. He possessed valuable soldierly qualities in an eminent degree. He gained the confidence of all who served under him, and almost their love.' But he went on to say that Thomas 'could not be driven from a point he was given to hold. He was not as good, however, in pursuit as he was in action.'[1]

On 16 January 1865 he was promoted major general in the regular US Army, keeping command of the Department of Tennessee until 1867. In 1869 he was named commander of the Department of the Pacific. He died of a stroke in his San Francisco office on 28 March 1870.

Note

1. U.S. Grant, *Personal Memoirs of U.S. Grant*, World Publishing, Cleveland, Ohio, 1952, p. 574

References

Freeman Cleaves, *Rock of Chickamauga, the life of General George Thomas*, University of Oklahoma, Norman, Oklahoma, 1948

Richard Johnson, *Memoir of Major-General George H. Thomas*, J. D. Lippincott, Philadelphia, 1881

F. F. McKinney, *Education in Violence; The Life of George H. Thomas and the History of the Army of the Cumberland*, Wayne State University Press, Detroit, 1961

Richard O'Conner, *Thomas: Rock of Chickamauga*, Prentice-Hall, New York, 1948

Thomas B. Van Horne, *The Life of Major-General George H. Thomas*, Charles Scribners' Sons, New York, 1872

George Henry Thomas (1816–70). (Library of Congress collection)

VIII
SOURCES

SOURCES

PUBLISHED SOURCES

There have been more than 50,000 books and pamphlets published on the Civil War, ranging from serious histories to the apocryphal *Lincoln's Doctor's Dog*. Charles E. Dornbusch has published four volumes of the *Military Bibliography of the Civil War* (New York Public Library, 1990, 1975, 1982, Morningside Bookshop, Dayton, Ohio, 1988).

The newcomer to the scene could do worse than start with one or more of the single-volume histories, several excellent examples of which are available. James M. McPherson won the Pulitzer Prize for *Battle Cry of Freedom* (Oxford University Press, New York, 1988). *None died in Vain* by Robert Leckie (Harper Collins, New York, 1990) is another modern although somewhat uneven single-volume history. Land actions alone are covered in Joseph B. Mitchell's *Decisive Battles of the Civil War* (G. P. Putnam's Sons, New York, 1955). Bruce Catton, one of the deans of Civil War historians, wrote *This Hallowed Ground* (Doubleday & Co, Garden City, New York, 1956) from the Northern point of view, while similar histories from a Southern point of view are Robert S. Henry's *The Story of the Confederacy* (Bobbs-Merrill, Indianapolis, 1931); Clement Eaton's *A History of the Southern Confederacy* (Macmillan, New York, 1954); Clifford Dowdey's *The Land They Fought For* (Doubleday, 1955); E. Merton Coulter's *The Confederate States of America 1861–1865* (Louisiana State University Press ((LSUP)), Baton Rouge, Louisiana, 1950); Emory M. Thomas's *The Confederate Nation: 1861–65* (Harper & Row, New York, 1979); and Frank E. Vandiver's *Their Tattered Flags: The Epic of the Confederacy* (Texas A&M, College Station, Texas, 1987).

There are several valuable references in encyclopedia style with entries arranged by subject matter alphabetically. The first of these is the *Civil War Dictionary* by Mark M. Boatner III (David McKay Co, New York, 1988). This is especially good for campaign descriptions and biographies and has more than 4,000 entries. The *Historical Times Illustrated Encyclopedia of the Civil War*, Patricia L. Faust, editor (Harper & Row, New York, 1986) has more than 2,000 entries which were contributed by a staff of 62 experts, and it includes photographs. *The Civil War Day by Day: An Almanac* by E. B. Long (Doubleday, New York, 1973) describes what happened on a daily basis.

Slightly longer narrative style histories include Allan Nevins's eight volumes which cover American history from 1847 until the end of the war. The excellent four volumes that cover the war itself are *The Improvised War: 1861–1862*; *War Becomes Revolution: 1862–63*; *The Organized War: 1863–1864*; and *The Organized War to Victory: 1864–65* (Scribner's, New York, 1959, 1960, 1971, 1971). Novelist Shelby Foote produced a three-volume history of the war that is a benchmark of excellence in writing as well as research. His books are *The Civil War: Sumpter to Perryville*; *The Civil War: Fredericksburg to Meridian*; *The Civil War, Red River to Appomattox* (Random House, New York, 1958, 1963, 1974).

Going beyond general histories, the questions of how the war was fought and why the result was as it was is one that many question today. Thomas L. Connelly and Archer Jones in *The Politics of Command: Factions and Ideas in Confederate Strategy* (LSUP, 1982) describe the high-level thinking that led to defeat. Frank Vandiver's *Rebel Brass: The Confederate Command System* (LSUP, 1956) is thin but invaluable. *Why The South Lost The Civil War* by Richard E. Beringer, Herman Hattaway, Archer Jones, and William N. Still Jr. (University of Georgia Press, Athens, Georgia, 1987) suggests a variety of reasons for the war's result. *How the North Won: A Military History of the Civil War* by Herman Hattaway and Archer Jones (The University of Illinois Press, Urbana, Illinois, 1983) offers a study of the war's strategy and the personalities that shaped it. Douglas B. Ball believes the war's result was due to a single reason – top-level Confederate ineptitude, especially in the field of economics, and he so says in *Financial Failure and Confederate Defeat* (University of Illinois Press, 1991). Steven E. Woodworth says that the Confederate cause was lost in the Western Theatre and he blames Jefferson Davis' leadership for that loss in *Jefferson Davis And His Generals: The Failure of Confederate Command In The West* (University Press of Kansas, Lawrence, Kansas, 1991).

All these authors, indeed virtually anyone who has written seriously about the war, started with certain basic references. *War of the Rebellion: A Compilation of the Official Records of the Union and Confederate Armies* (Government Printing Office ((GPO)), Washington, DC, 1880–1901) is the most frequently consulted source. Its 70 volumes in 128 books contain as many Union and Confederate messages and official reports as post-war War Department researchers could find.

The *Atlas to Accompany the Official Records of the Union and Confederate Armies* (GPO, 1891–5) contains many maps, often taken from several sources which were merged together and therefore it is not always totally accurate. It also contains photographs and line-drawings of physical items ranging from weapons to engineering equipment. Although less complicated, the maps in Craig L. Symonds' *A Battlefield Atlas of the Civil War* (The Nautical and Aviation Publishing Co, Annapolis, Maryland, 1983) are more accurate. Another excellent source of maps is the *West Point Atlas of American Wars* by Colonel Vincent J. Esposito (Vol. I, Praeger, New York, 1959).

Not to be outdone by the Army, the Navy Department issued the *Official Records of the Union and Confederate Navies in the War of the Rebellion* (GPO, 1894, 1927) in 31 volumes similar to the Army's ORs. All these suffer from inaccuracies caused by immediacy, as well as a desire to make the author look as good as possible. Alan C. Aimone produced a most useful guide on how to use the official records, *Official Records of the American Civil War: A Researcher's Guide* (US Military Academy Library Bulletin No 11A, West Point, 1977). An earlier version of the ORs is Frank Moore's *The Rebellion Record; A Diary of American Events . . .* (GP Putnam, 1861–3; D. Van Nostrand, 1864–8), but Moore's documents are thrown together in no particular order and are largely confined to what was available in the North during the war. *The Annals of the War*, a collection of 56 articles written by participants immediately after the war and published in the *Philadelphia Weekly Times* in 1878, is a valuable source. It was reprinted by Morningside Bookshop, Dayton, Ohio, in 1988. It should be mentioned that students of the war owe Morningside Bookshop a major round of applause since for several decades this company has reprinted hundreds of valuable sources ranging from unit histories to memoirs, and secondary sources long since out of print. Morningside even publishes *The Gettysburg Magazine*, which contains articles strictly about that battle.

Many participants had a chance to rewrite history when the *Century* Magazine published a series of articles about specific events written by those who took part in them. These articles were published in four volumes as *Battles and Leaders of the Civil War* (The Century Co, New York, 1887–8, and often reprinted). The line-drawings in these volumes are also valuable, since many were executed by eyewitnesses.

Southern contemporary accounts are to be found in several magazines. *The Southern Historical Society Papers* fill 52 volumes with their monthly issues over 90 years starting from January 1876. They have been reprinted by Morningside. Confederate veterans wrote many of their accounts for the UCV publications, the *Confederate Veteran*. These magazines have been gathered into 40 volumes by another important reprinter of original works (Broadfoot Publishing, Wilmington, North Carolina, 1987).

Actual statistics are still being debated today. However, some standard sources include William F. Fox's *Regimental Losses in the American Civil War 1861–65* (Albany Publishing Co, Albany, New York, 1889) which covers mostly Union regimental statistics, and Thomas L. Livermore's *Numbers and Losses in the Civil War in America 1861–1865* (Houghton Mifflin and Co, Boston, 1900) which is largely devoted to battles losses and general army strengths. These classic sets of statistics have been challenged recently in such books as *Regimental Strengths at Gettysburg* by John W. Busey and David Martin (Busey and Martin, Centreville, Virginia, 1982). Union army statistics are also published in Frederick H. Dyer's *A Compendium of the War of the Rebellion* . . . (Dyer Publishing, Des Moines, Iowa, 1980). However, Dyer's *Compendium* is most useful for its Union regiment and smaller unit histories. The basic source for data on each Confederate Army regiment and smaller units is Joseph H. Crute, Jr., *Units of the Confederate Army* (Derwent Books, Midlothian, Virginia, 1987) although Crute's book has less specific data on each unit than Dyer's.

Those who became full generals on both sides are briefly described and depicted in two books by Ezra Warner, *Generals in Gray* (LSUP, 1959) and *Generals in Blue* (LSUP, 1964). Roger D. Hunt and Jack R. Brown contributed to these biographies with their *Brevet Brigadier Generals in Blue* (Olde Soldier Books, Gaithersburg, Maryland, 1990). Brief descriptions of the service of lower-ranking officers of the US

Army can be found in Francis Heitman's *Historical Register and Dictionary of the United States Army 1783–1903* (GPO, 1903). This book also contains lists of battles, actions, Confederate general officers, and Union contract surgeons. Robert K. Krick gives short biographies of lower-ranking Confederates in *Lee's Colonels* (Morningside, 1991). *Personnel of the Civil War*, edited by William Amann (Thomas Yoseloff, New York, 1961), is largely useful for its collection of pre-war volunteer militia titles assigned to war-time units, and Confederate armies, corps, and commands.

At an army level, the definitive study of the Army of the Potomac is Bruce Catton's *Mr. Lincoln's Army, Glory Road,* and *A Stillness at Appomattox* (Doubleday, New York, 1952–5). Catton was one of the first to draw heavily on the thousands of Union small unit histories that participants published after the war and the anecdotes drawn from them brings his history to life. A three-volume set, *Lee's Lieutenants*, by Douglas Southall Freeman (Scribner's, 1942–4), covers the Army of Northern Virginia. In the West, there are Stanley F. Horn's *The Army of Tennessee: A Military History* (Bobbs-Merrill, 1941); Thomas L. Connelly's *Army of the Heartland: The Army of Tennessee, 1862–1865* (LSUP, 1967, 1971), and Bromfield Ridley's *Battles and Sketches of the Army of Tennessee* (Missouri Printing and Publishing, Mexico, Missouri, 1906). Thomas Van Horne wrote the *History of the Army of the Cumberland, Its Organization, Campaigns, and Battles* in two volumes (Robert Clarke, Cincinnati, Ohio, 1875). The far western Southern war effort is covered in *Kirby Smith's Confederacy: The Trans-mississippi South* by Robert L. Kerby (Columbia University Press, New York, 1972). Finally, there is Aurora Hunt's *The Army of the Pacific* . . ., Arthur H. Clark Co, Glendale, California, 1951.

THE GRAPHIC ARTS

During the Civil War artists produced drawings in the field which were sent back to their offices to be redrawn on hardwood blocks and printed as line-cuts. Within several weeks of any event, illustrations by artists who were there could be seen throughout the country.

This method predominated in the North with *Harper's Weekly* and *Frank Leslie's Illustrated Newspapers*, both appearing weekly in tabloid size. Southern efforts were largely limited to poor quality line-cuts of leading officers and an occasional map. Of the two leading Northern publications, *Harper's* had the largest circulation and was able to hire many of the better artists. These included two brothers, Alfred and William Waud, of whom Alfred was somewhat the better sketch artist. These two men also drew for the *New York Illustrated News*. Thomas Nast, who became better known as a political cartoonist in New York after the war, also drew for *Harper's*. Nast painted a picture of the 7th New York State Militia marching down Broadway in 1861 which is now in the Seventh Museum Armory, New York. Other

Harper's artists included Theodore R. Davis and Winslow Homer.

Homer tended to create montages and large scenes, which would be expected since he also worked in oils. He was at the First Bull Run, returning to spend time with the Army of the Potomac in October 1861. An eye-witness to the fight between the *Monitor* and the *Virginia*, he stayed with the army throughout the Peninsula Campaign. He then divided his time between the home front and the battlefield throughout 1863, returning to spend all his time with the Army of the Potomac during the siege of Petersburg until Lee's surrender. In 1866 he sailed for France to pursue his painting career. He left behind not only his sketches and line-cuts, but several canvases which tell us much about the look and mood of the army. These include *In Front of Yorktown* (Yale University Art Gallery), *Playing Old Soldier* (Museum of Fine Arts, Boston), *A Rainy Day in Camp* (The Metropolitan Museum of Art, New York), *Pitching Horseshoes* (Fogg Art Gallery, Harvard University), *Prisoners from the*

Front (The Metropolitan), *Officers at Camp Benton* (Boston Public Library), *A Skirmish in the Wilderness* (New Britain, Connecticut, Museum of American Art), and *Defiance: Inviting a Shot Before Petersburg, Virginia* (Detroit Institute of the Arts).

Frank Leslie's, however, also attracted some leading artists. These included Henri Lovie, Frank H. Schell, William T. Crane, and J. F. E. Hillen. One of this publication's most important artist was Edwin Forbes who had been a student of animal art at the National Academy of Design in New York before the war. He was hired in 1862 to cover the Eastern Theatre, sketching action in the Valley Campaign, the Second Bull Run, Antietam, the Mud March, Chancellorsville, Gettysburg, the Wilderness, Petersburg, and Jubal Early's Washington raid. This was his last assignment. In 1876 he produced a series of copperplate etchings, *Life Studies of the Great Army*. He also produced some oil paintings based on his observations.

The only major sketch artist to draw the Confederates was an Englishman, Frank Vizetelly, who was sent to New York by the *Illustrated London News* in May 1861. He drew

A Winslow Homer sketch of himself at work, drawing two 6-foot 7-inch tall privates, E. Farrin and J. J. Handley of the 1st Maine Regiment.
(Harper's Weekly)

First Bull Run and Battle of Memphis scenes while with Union forces, but then, feeling his readers' sympathies lay with the South, went to Richmond. He observed the Battle of Fredericksburg with Generals Lee and Longstreet, and went on to witness the ironclad attack on Charleston's defences, the siege of Vicksburg, the Battle of Chickamauga, and a Union assault on Wilmington, North Carolina. He went back to England in early 1864, but had returned to sketch the Valley Campaign by June of that year. He also sketched the fall of Fort Fisher and accompanied Davis on his escape after the fall of Richmond.

Some artists accompanied the armies to produce paintings rather than news magazine sketches. James Walker, who had produced oil paintings of the Mexican War, did several paintings of the Army of the Potomac at drill in 1861. He also did several Gettysburg paintings, the best known of which is *Gettysburg: The First Day* (West Point Galleries, US Military Academy). He then went west to paint action scenes at Chattanooga, Chickamauga, and Lookout Mountain.

Conrad W. Chapman served as a sergeant in the 59th Virginia Infantry. After the war he painted scenes of his service, at Charleston, in 1862–3, including Fort Sumter and the submarine *Hunley*. These are in the Valentine Museum, Richmond.

Frederick Cavada, a Pennsylvania lieutenant, painted a large picture of the attack at Fredericksburg which is in the Pennsylvania Historical Society, Philadelphia.

Henry W. Walke commanded the USS *Carondelet* as a commander during the war. Afterwards he produced a number of sketches of naval warfare that appeared in *Battles and Leaders of the Civil War* and *Porter's Naval History*.

Allan C. Redwood, a lieutenant in the 55th Virginia Infantry, produced a number of sketches, watercolours, and paintings of various events such as the first day's fighting at Gettysburg, and illustrations for *Battles and Leaders*. Most of his work is in the Museum of the Confederacy, Richmond.

William L. Sheppard, a second lieutenant in the Richmond Howitzers and later in the Confederate Engineers, also produced sketches for the *Battles & Leaders*. After the war he studied art in Paris and produced watercolours. His watercolours of individual Confederate soldiers are in the Museum of the Confederacy.

Gilbert W. Gaul was born in 1855 and so was not an eyewitness to the war. However, his oil paintings are highly accurate. They include *The Skirmish Line* (West Point Galleries), *Exchange of Prisoners* (Democratic Club, New York), *Holding The Line At All Hazards* (Hermitage Hotel, Nashville, Tennessee), and *Between The Lines* (Birmingham Museum of Art, Alabama), among others.

PHOTOGRAPHY

Methods of fixing images of events and people without pencil or paint brush, through the use of a camera, were invented in 1839 by Fox Talbot in England, who produced paper prints, and Louis Daguerre in France, who produced prints on silver-plated sheets of metal. Americans took to this new art form with enthusiasm. Indeed, they produced some of the first war photographs during the Mexican War. By 1861 the camera had become common throughout America. The 1863 Philadelphia city directory has 187 listings for photographers, 'Daguerrotypists' and 'Ambrotypists'. It was a rare man who did not get himself photographed in his brave soldier's outfit for the folks back home; the result is that hundreds of thousands of original photographs survive today and they make up an important historical resource.

The Daguerrotype, a unique print on a sheet of copper plated with silver, was the first type of photograph used. These images tarnished, so were displayed in leather or plastic-type cases which could open and shut, having a plush cloth, often impressed with a design, on one side and the image, within an ornate brass frame and under glass, on the other. They were available as were later hard images, as sixteenth plates ($1\frac{5}{8} \times 2\frac{1}{8}$ inches), eighth plates ($2\frac{1}{8} \times 3\frac{1}{4}$ inches), sixth plates ($2\frac{3}{4} \times 3\frac{1}{4}$ inches), quarter plates ($3\frac{1}{4} \times 4\frac{1}{4}$ inches), half plates ($4\frac{1}{4} \times 6\frac{1}{2}$), and full plates ($6\frac{1}{2} \times 8\frac{1}{2}$ inches). By 1861, however, the Daguerrotype had lost ground to the less expensive Ambrotype, tintype (also called the Melainotype or ferrotype), and paper print.

The Ambrotype, invented in 1854, was simply a negative taken on a chemically coated sheet of glass, backed with black paint or material so that it became a positive. It was displayed in the Daguerrotype case and came in the same sizes as the Daguerrotype.

The tintype, invented in 1856, was even cheaper than the Ambrotype. It consisted of a photograph on a thin sheet of black-coated iron. It was often produced in the same sizes as other hard images and displayed in leather cases. However, tintypes were also mounted in cards to be placed in leather-bound photograph albums or in frames to be hung on walls. Card-mounted tintypes can be dated by the design on the card. Before 1863 these designs were printed; after 1863 the paper holders were usually embossed. Moreover, a revenue-raising law in the North required every photograph taken between 1 September 1864 and 1 August 1866 to have a tax stamp on its back, thus further dating such images. Blue playing-card tax stamps were used in the summer of 1866 when regular revenue stamp supplies ran out. Lacking materials to produce them, extremely few Southern-made Civil War period tintypes are known to exist today.

In 1857 the Duke of Parma had paper prints made of his photograph and placed them on a calling card. The *carte de visite*, as it was known, became all the rage throughout the world thereafter. It had the advantage of being inexpensive, offering multiple copies of the same image, and being easy to mail and store. The *carte de visite* is a thin paper print mounted on a card $4\frac{1}{2} \times 2\frac{1}{2}$ inches in size. The photographer's name usually appears on the back, although it is sometimes on the bottom of the card. The earliest cards often have two parallel lines around the photograph's edge, the inner one being thinner than the outer one. Tax stamps were also required on cartes. Another date identification of cartes can be found in their thickness; prior to 1870 they are 0.4mm thick, later ones are thicker.

Ordinary people had cartes taken of themselves to send home and trade with friends. Manufacturers began producing albums, usually leather bound, to store cartes. Finally, photographers made cartes of famous people, ranging from military figures to circus stars, without charge in exchange for the rights to sell prints to the public. The leading company in this business, E. and H. T. Anthony Co, New York, printed as many as 3,600 celebrity cartes a day during the war.

Some photographers themselves became celebrities. Mathew B. Brady had studios in New York and Washington where his photographers captured the images of most of the day's leading figures. He sold many of these cartes through Anthony. Although cursed with bad eyesight that limited his own picture-taking, he hired some outstanding artists, including Scotsman Alexander Gardner and Timothy Sullivan.

Brady's men also took stereoscopic views, two paper prints mounted on a card which, when seen through a Brewster or Holmes-Bates viewer, appeared in three dimensions.

Brady took it upon himself to make a photographic record of the war; he lost his equipment in the stampede from the First Bull Run. He took both ordinary prints and stereographs. An exhibition in his New York studio of photographs of the field at Antietam after the battle brought the war to the civilian population as no previous work, written or graphic, had done.

The Army hired its own photographers to produce pictures of such things as field fortifications, bridges, and major buildings. Even equipment was photographed for patent purposes. Maps were photographically printed on fabric as well as paper for quick distribution to different headquarters. Hence, between the work of civilian and official photographers, there is a substantial photographic record of the Civil War.

During the war, photographs could only be reproduced as continuous tone, i.e., direct, prints. Shortly after the war several photographer released books with tipped-in prints made from their war-time negatives. Alexander Gardner's *Photographic Sketch Book of the Civil War* was published in two volumes in Washington, DC, in 1866. That same year George N. Bernard published a portfolio of his *Photographic Views of Sherman's Campaign*. And, Andrew J. Russell, an official army photographer, published an album of 136 photographs of the late-war Eastern Theatre. None of these sold well to a war-weary public and most copies have disappeared, but they have all been reprinted by Dover Publications, New York, in paperback format.

It was not until 1911 that a major photographic work appeared when Francis T. Miller produced the 10-volume *The Photographic History of the Civil War*. The many rare images in this work are supplemented by a text that includes articles written by participants in the war, which makes the work even more valuable. A reprint of Miller's work first appeared in 1957 and the volumes have been frequently reproduced since then.

Many of Brady's photographs were purchased by the government for the Library of Congress. The Library's huge collection formed the basis for *Divided We Fought: A Pictorial History of the War, 1861–1865*, by David Donald, Hirst D. Milhollen, Milton Kaplan, and Hulen Stuart (Macmillan, 1952). This book also features a number of the original sketches produced for news magazines which later appeared as line-cuts.

William C. Davis, a prolific Civil War writer and historian, edited a book attempting to correct some caption errors in Miller's work and publishing many newly found images. His six-volume work, *The Image of War: 1861–1865* (Doubleday, New York, 1981–4), includes essays by many of the day's leading Civil War historians. Many images that did not appear in the six volumes appear in *Touched By Fire* (Little Brown, Boston, 1985), which Davis also edited. It is markedly inferior to the original six volumes.

In the 1970s a photo analyst, William A. Frassanito, began studying images compared to actual physical settings today with the idea of correcting previous caption errors and learning more about the battles. He published his findings in three volumes: *Gettysburg, A Journey In Time*; *Antietam*; and *Grant and Lee, The Virginia Campaigns 1864–65* (Scribners, 1975, 1978, 1983). These broke new ground in Civil War photographic research.

Photograph collections of little more than individual portraits help describe uniforms and equipment. William A. Albaugh produced two of the first of these books, *Confederate Faces* (Verde Publishers, Solana Beach, California, ndg) and *More Confederate Faces* (ABS Printers, Washington, DC, ndg). These books were followed by William A. Turner's *Even More Confederate Faces* (William Turner, Clinton, Maryland, 1983) which was largely built around the photograph collection of Southern diarist Mary C. Chestnut which was discovered by the author. *Cavalry*, a paperback by Harris Andrews, Christopher Nelson, Brian Pohanka, and Harry Roach (Guidon Press, Henryville, Pennsylvania, 1988) covers cavalrymen on both sides.

Roach is also the editor of *Military Images* (Henryville, Pennsylvania), the only magazine to deal specifically with Civil War photography. Period photographs also appear in three other popular magazines: *Civil War Times Illustrated* (Harrisburg, Pennsylvania); *America's Civil War* (Leesburg, Virginia); and *Civil War* (Berryville, Virginia).

VIDEOS

One of the revolutions of the late 20th century has been the widespread use of VCRs which allow films to be shown on television sets at the viewer's whim. At first availability was limited, but by the end of the 1980s some videos that were serious historical efforts began to appear.

The major example of these is the 11½-hour series *The*

Civil War produced by Ken Burns for the Public Broadcasting Service (Alexandria, Virginia, 1990). The series mixes music, original images and the spoken word in a spellbinding account of the entire war. *Gettysburg: The Final Fury* (Parade Video, Newark, New Jersey, 1989) was largely filmed on the battlefield, the action being described by actor Stacy Keach.

Echoes of the Blue & Gray (Belle Grove Publishing, Kearny, New Jersey, 1988) appeared in two hour-long volumes. Each contained actual newsreel film interviews and footage of Civil War veterans that enable the viewer to see such things as the manual of arms as it was actually performed and heard the famed 'Rebel yell'.

The vast collection of uniforms in the Smithsonian Institution, Washington, DC, was filmed by Roberts Video Publishing (Washington, 1990) in a series of hour-long videos. The first release covered regulation Union uniforms and both showed exact material, markings and hues in a way that it would be difficult for the print medium to match.

Starting in the late 1950s, Civil War enthusiasts began wearing replica uniforms and equipment of the war, to hold shooting-matches with original weapons, battle re-enactments, and living history demonstrations. At first their level of authenticity was quite low. By the mid-1980s, however, so many people had become involved in the hobby that it became possible to obtain reasonably priced yet good replicas of uniforms and equipment.

These enthusiasts have gathered a great deal of information, and video-makers have been quick to tap it.

American Historical Productions (Gaithersburg, Maryland, ndg) used the enthusiasts to show the daily life of the common soldier, North and South, in the hour-long *The Civil War Soldier: The Infantryman*. *Witness to the Storm* (Historical Videos International, Edgemont, Pennsylvania, 1985) combined some living history vignettes about a fictional period photographer with hand-colored lantern slides made from original photographs.

Most living history enthusiasts like re-enacting battles, and gathered by the thousands for battle re-creations during the 100th and 125th anniversaries of the war. Classic Images (Columbia, Maryland) combined sequences filmed at the 125th anniversaries with maps and graphics for half-hour tapes on the First Bull Run, Shiloh, Chancellorsville, Vicksburg, and Franklin, and hour-long tapes on Antietam, Gettysburg, Spotsylvania, and Atlanta (various dates).

Notes

George Gilbert, *Photography: The Early Years*, Harper & Row, New York, 1980

Alexander McC Graighead, 'Military Art in America, 1750–1914', *Military Collector & Historian*, Vol. XVI, Nos 1–2, pp. 10–13, 42–5, Company of Military Historians, Washington, DC

Julian Grossman, *Echo of a Distant Drum, Winslow Homer and the Civil War*, Harry N. Abrams, New York, ndg

Harold F. Jenkins, *Two Points of View*, E. G. Warman Publishing, Uniontown, Pennsylvania, 1973

Robert Taft, *Photography and the American Scene*, Dover, New York, 1964

Carroll H. Walker, 'Gilbert Gaul Paintings,' *Military Collector & Historian*, Vol. III, No I, pp. 22–3,

George F. Witham, *Catalogue of Civil War Photographers*, no place given, 1988

IX
MISCELLANEA

MISCELLANEA

CONFEDERATE INFLATION

The approximate value of Confederate currency compared with $100 worth of gold.

Date	Currency
1 January 1862	$120
20 December 1862	$300
20 December 1863	$1,700
1 January 1864	$1,800
20 December 1864	$2,800
1 January 1865	$3,400
1 February 1865	$5,000
1 March 1865	$4,700
10 April 1865	$5,500

(Source: Varina H. Davis, *Jefferson Davis*, Belford Co., New York, 1890, Vol. II, p. 535)

CONFEDERATE ARMY PAY, 1863

Grade	Pay per Month	Number of Horses allowed
General (all ranks)	$301	4
Colonel of Engineers, artillery, cavalry, or staff except medical	$210	3
Lieutenant colonel of cavalry	$185	3
Major of cavalry	$162	3
Captain of cavalry	$140	2
First lieutenant of cavalry	$100	2
Second lieutenant of cavalry	$90	2
Additional pay for being an adjutant	$10	
Colonel of artillery	$210	3
Lieutenant colonel of artillery	$185	3
Major of artillery	$150	3
Captain of artillery	$130	0
First lieutenant of artillery	$90	0
Second lieutenant of artillery	$80	0
Colonel of infantry	$195	3
Lieutenant colonel of infantry	$170	3
Major of infantry	$150	3
Captain of infantry	$130	0
First lieutenant of infantry	$90	0
Second lieutenant of infantry	$80	0
Surgeon General	$250*	3
Surgeon (10 years' service)	$162	3
Surgeon (less than 10 years' service)	$150	2
Assistant Surgeon (10 years' service)	$130	2
Assistant Surgeon (less than than 10 years' service)	$110	2
Engineers sergeant, master workman	$34	
Engineers corporal, overseer	$20	

Grade	Pay per Month	Number of Horses allowed
Engineers artificer	$17	
Engineers laborer	$13	
Sergeant Major of cavalry or infantry	$21	
QMS of cavalry or infantry	$21	
Principal musician	$21	
Chief bugler	$21	
First Sergeant of cavalry or infantry	$20	
Sergeant of cavalry or infantry	$13	
Musician of cavalry	$13	
Musician of artillery or infantry	$12	
Private of cavalry	$12	
Private of artillery or infantry	$11	
Ordnance Sergeant	$21	
Hospital Steward at post of more than four companies	$21	
Hospital Steward	$20	
Hospital matron	$6	
Chaplain	$80	

* $3,000 per annum
(Source: Official, *Regulations for the Army of the Confederate States*, Richmond, 1863, pp 175–7)

UNION ARMY PAY, 1863

Grade	Monthly Pay	Monthly Subsistence
General Officers		
Lieutenant General	$270	$360
His *aide de camp*	$80	$45
Major General	$220	$135
Senior aide to general in chief	$80	$36
Brigadier general	$124	$108
Aide de camp (additional pay)	$20	
Staff Departments		
Adjutant General	$124	$108
Colonel, Asst AG	$110	$54
Lieutenant Colonel, Asst AG	$95	$45
Major, Asst AG	$80	$36
Colonel, Judge-Advocate General	$80	$36
Major, Judge-Advocate	$80	$36
Colonel, Inspector General	$110	$54
Major, Asst IG	$80	$36
Major, Signal Officer	$80	$36
Quartermaster General	$124	$108
Colonel, Asst QMG	$110	$54
Lieutenant Colonel, Deputy QMG	$95	$45
Major, Quartermaster	$80	$36
Captain, Asst QM	$70	$36
Commissary General of Subsistence	$110	$54

Grade	Monthly Pay	Monthly Subsistence
Lieutenant Colonel, Asst CGS	$95	$45
Major, Commissary of Subsistence	$80	$36
Captain, Commissary of Subsistence	$70	$36
Additional pay to a lieutenant	$20	
Surgeon General	$124	$108
Surgeons (10 years' service)	$80	$72
Surgeons (less than 10 years' service)	$80	$36
Assistant Surgeons (10 years' service)	$70	$72
Assistant Surgeons (less than 10 years' service)	$53.33	$36
Paymaster General	$228.33*	
Deputy Paymaster General	$95	$45
Paymaster	$80	$36
Chief of Ordnance	$124	$108
Chaplain	$100	$18
Corps of Engineers		
Brigadier general	$124	$108
Colonel	$110	$54
Lieutenant Colonel	$95	$45
Major	$80	$36
Captain	$70	$36
First Lieutenant	$53.33	$36
Second Lieutenant	$53.33	$36
Sergeant	$34	
Corporal	$20	
Private, first class	$17	
Private, second class	$13	
Musician	$12	
Cavalry and Light Artillery		
Colonel	$110	$54
Lieutenant Colonel	$95	$45
Major	$80	$36
Captain	$70	$36
First lieutenant	$53.33	$36
Second lieutenant	$53.33	$36
Cavalry Enlisted Men		
Sergeant major	$21	
Quartermaster sergeant	$21	
Chief bugler	$21	
First sergeant	$20	
Sergeant	$17	
Corporal	$14	
Bugler	$13	
Farrier and blacksmith	$15	
Private	$13	
Artillery and Infantry		
Colonel	$95	$54
Lieutenant Colonel	$80	$45
Major	$70	$36
Captain	$60	$36
First lieutenant	$50	$36

Grade	Monthly Pay	Monthly Subsistence
Second lieutenant	$45	$36
Sergeant major	$21	
Quartermaster sergeant	$17	
First sergeant	$20	
Sergeant	$17	
Corporal	$13	
Artillery artificer	$15	
Private	$13	
Principal musician	$21	
Musician	$12	
Other		
Medical cadets	$30	
Hospital stewards	$30	
Master wagoners	$17	
Wagoners	$14	
Matrons	$36	

* $2,740 per annum.
(Source: *Wells' Illustrated National Hand-book*, John G Wells, Cincinnati, Ohio, 1864, pp. 168–70)

UNION ARMY CLOTHING ISSUES

The regulation issues for a five-year enlistment.

Clothing	Years				
	1st	2nd	3rd	4th	5th
Cap, complete	2	1	2	1	1
Hat, complete	1	1	1	1	1
Fatigue forage cap	1	1	1	1	1
Cap cover	1	1	1	1	1
Coat	2	1	2	1	2
Trousers	3	2	3	2	3
Flannel shirt	3	3	3	3	3
Flannel drawers	3	2	2	2	2
Bootees*, pair	4	4	4	4	4
Stockings, pair	4	4	4	4	4
Leather stock	1	0	1	0	0
Greatcoat	1	0	0	0	0
Stable frock**	1	0	1	0	0
Fatigue overalls***	1	1	1	1	1
Blanket	1	0	1	0	0

* Mounted men may receive one pair of boots and two pairs of bootees instead of four pairs of bootees.
** For mounted men only.
*** For engineers and ordnance only.
(Source: Official, *Revised Regulations for the Army of the United States*, Lippincott, Philadelphia, 1863, p. 170)

THE 10-POUNDER PARROTT GUN

Its ranges and times of flight at different elevations.

Elevation Deg	Time Min	Seconds	Range Yards
0	00	½	300
1		1	450

Elevation	Time		Range
Deg	Min	Seconds	Yards
2		2	900
3		3	1,300
4		4½	1,600
4	30	5	1,760
5		6	1,950
5	30	6½	2,200
6		7	2,300
7		8½	2,600
10		10½	3,000
12		12½	3,600
15		16	4,100
20		19¾	5,000
25		23½	5,600
30		27½	5,900
35		31½	6,200

(Source: ibid., p. 122)

PENETRATION OF SMALL ARMS

The depth to which the regulation bullet with the regulation load would penetrate seasoned white pine, in inches.

	Distance in yards			
Weapon	30	200	600	1,000
.577 rifle-musket	–	11	6.33	3.25
.69 smoothbore musket	–	10.5	6.33	3.5
.58 rifle	–	9.33	5.66	3.0
.58 pistol carbine	–	5.75	3.0*	
.55 Sharps carbine	7.27			
.55 Burnside carbine	6.15			

*At 500 yards.

(Source: Official, *Field Manual for use of Officers on Ordnance Duty*, Richmond, 1862, p. 126)

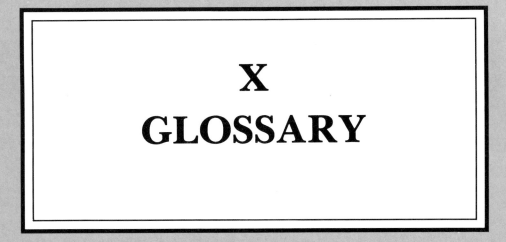

X
GLOSSARY

The purpose of this glossary is to define words commonly found in Civil War reference works but which might not be found in a modern dictionary. The nicknames of some units which were common then, but are not now well known, are also listed.

abatis: trees felled and laid with their branches sharpened and interwoven so as to present a thick row of pointed stakes towards the enemy. They were generally used in front of field works.

aiguillette: the worsted red cord and tassel worn with the US Army's dress light artillery shako.

apron: in gunnery, a piece of leather covering the vent of a cannon.

Armstrong Gun: An English-made breech-loading cannon whose projectile had cast lead bands wound about it; these could kill the gun crew when they flew off.

banquette: a small elevation of earth three or four feet wide and four feet nine inches below the crest of the parapet to enable the shortest man to fire over it easily.

battle flag: a color displaying battle honors carried in battle; in the Confederate Army, a regimental flag that was less formal than the color. On 23 July 1862 battle honors were allowed to be inscribed on Confederate battle flags.

Beardslee telegraph: a telegraph used in the US Army that used a dial for pointing to the appropriate letter rather than a key which required knowledge of Morse code, a lighter cable and a hand-cranked magneto instead of a battery.

berm: a narrow space between the ditch and parapet to keep the parapet from falling into the ditch.

bootee: an ankle-high, laced shoe or boot, termed the 'Jefferson boot' in US Army regulations.

braid: woven colored band, often of worsted cotton or wool and sometimes having metallic thread, used to trim uniforms.

brogans: ankle-high bootees laced in front.

brevet rank: temporary, often

honorary, commissions enabling the owner to wear the uniform and collect the pay of that rank while yet being listed in official lists with a lower rank.

buck and ball: the 0.69in calibre cartridge containing one .069in calibre ball and three buckshot.

buff leather: a heavy but flexible leather of a natural buff color and dyed on one side. It was used for belts in the Union army.

bullseye canteen: the M1858 US canteen as made between 1862 and 1865 with nine concentric rings pressed into each side for added strength.

bummers: foragers with the Army of Tennessee in Sherman's campaign through Georgia.

bummer's cap: a modern term for the US Army's regulation forage cap.

Burnside hat: a regular US Army officer's dress felt hat made with a lower crown.

butternut: a dye used in the South for uniform cloth during the early years of the war; it was made from the oily nut of the white walnut mixed with copperas.

Cadet gray: a gray tending towards blue rather than brown. The regulation Confederate coat color.

California Brigade: in the Army of the Potomac, the 1st California (71st Pennsylvania), 2nd California (72nd Pennsylvania), 3rd California (69th Pennsylvania), and 5th California (106th Pennsylvania) were recruited in Philadelphia under command of Edward D. Baker, but reverted to their Pennsylvania designations after Baker's death at Ball's Bluff and became the Philadelphia Brigade (which see).

California 100: Co A, 2nd Massachusetts Cavalry was recruited in California, travelled East and mustered in 3 January 1863. Its members wore the brass roman letters 'CAL 100' or 'CALIFORNIA 100' on the top of their forage caps.

camouflet: an explosive device placed

in front of works that would explode inward in shafts tunnelled under the works.

camp colors: flags, 18 inches square, used to mark the color line, points of wheeling, etc.; they were also carried by the markers in evolutions. In the Union Army they were white for infantry and red for artillery, with the regimental number on them, mounted on eight-foot poles.

caponniere: in fortifications, a passage from one part of the work to another.

cascabel: that part of a cannon behind the base ring made up of the knob, the neck, the fillet and the base of the breech.

chase: the length of a gun from the trunions to the muzzle.

chevaux-de-frise: logs, some 12 feet long and ten inches thick, pierced at 12-inch intervals throughout their length, by holes at right angles. Sharpened stakes about seven feet long, were thrust through the holes. They were used to present an obstacle to cavalry in front of defensive works.

cheeks: the pieces of timber that form the sides of gun carriages and upon which the trunions rest.

color: the flag carried by a dismounted unit.

columbiad: a siege gun differing from most guns in that it had no chamber, the bore being of equal distance throughout, although it was much thicker at the breech than the bore.

Corcoran Legion: A brigade in the Army of the Potomac's II Corps formed of the 155th, 164th, 170th and 184th New York Volunteer Infantry Regiments.

crows-foot: a trefoil created by stripes of embroidery or lace at the end of a buttonhole.

dalhgren: similar to the columbiad, it was a standard US Navy artillery piece.

duck: a heavy canvas cloth used for tents.

epaulement: an elevation thrown up to

cover troops from enemy fire, usually made of gabions filled with earth or sandbags.

epaulette: a shoulder decoration consisting of a strap that buttoned near the collar, with a crescent at the shoulder from which was hung a fringe.

éprouvette: a small mortar used to test the projectile force of gunpowder.

Excelsior Brigade: In the Army of the Potomac, the 70th to 74th New York Volunteer Infantry Regiments, joined in December 1862 by the 120th New York and in March 1864 by the 11th Massachusetts and 84th Pennsylvania.

Excelsior hat: *see* Whipple hat.

facing: a distinctive colored collar and cuffs.

fascines: long bundles of thin saplings used mostly for the sides of trenches.

fez: a brimless oriental head-dress used by zouaves.

fireman's shirt: a shirt made with a buttoned plastron in front, often bearing an engine company's number. These were often worn in units such as the 11th New York (New York Fire Zouaves).

flying telegraph train: a mobile communications post consisting of two wagons equipped with two Beardslee telegraphs, two hand-cranked magnetos, five miles of wire (the maximum effective range), 150 15-foot poles, 50 18-foot poles and five wire hand reels.

forage cap: the floppy version of the 1851 shako, similar to the French kepi, worn by troops for fatigue.

fougasse: a charge of gunpowder dug into a pit which was exploded when an enemy passed over it.

frog: the attachment of a scabbard to a belt, and the worsted or silk button on a cloak or coat.

gabion: cylindrical basket made without top or bottom, some three feet high and two feet in diameter, weighing 50–60 pounds, used in siege works.

gaiters: lower leg coverings made of cotton or leather.

garrison flag: the national color, 36

feet in fly and 20 feet in hoist.

glacis: a parapet of the covered way in fortifications.

Greek fire: an incendiary composition used in projectiles and bombs on occasions such as the Confederate attempt to burn New York with bombs, and the Union attempt to burn Charleston with artillery projectiles.

guidon: small silk standard for cavalry.

gum blanket: a waterproofed, often by rubberizing, canvas blanket or poncho. The white underside was often inscribed with gaming table markings by troops in the field.

gutta-percha: a hardened rubber used in talmas and often incorrectly referred to when discussing buttons and hard image cases which were actually made of a plastic substance.

Hardee hat: a modern term for the US Army dress felt hat.

havelock: a cotton or linen covering for the forage cap with a flap that covered the neck to protect against heat, widely used in 1861 but quickly abandoned as useless.

haversack: the cloth bag worn on a strap from the right shoulder to the left hip in which rations, personal items and, at times, spare ammunition was carried. Union haversacks were waterproofed; Confederate haversacks were made of plain cotton.

housewife: a sewing kit containing needles and thread, carried by most soldiers.

Irish Brigade: in the Army of the Potomac, the 63rd, 69th, and 88th New York Infantry Regiments, joined in the spring of 1862 by the 29th New York which was replaced by the 28th Massachusetts in October 1862. Its members wore a green hat band with the regimental number in the centre. A Second Irish Brigade, made up of the old regiments plus the 7th New York Heavy Artillery was formed in November 1864.

Iron Brigade: in the Army of the Potomac, the 2nd, 6th, and 7th

Wisconsin and 19th Indiana Infantry Regiments, joined by the 24th Michigan in late 1862. Its members wore a dress frock-coat and hat with white gaiters, even in action.

Jeans: a twilled cotton cloth.

Jeff Davis hat: a modern name for the US Army dress felt hat.

kepi: the French army cap, a low forage cap.

kersey: a heavy wool cloth, often ribbed, used for outer garments and blankets, mostly for enlisted men.

Knights of the Golden Circle: A secret pro-Southern society in the North which performed subversive activities.

lace: woven silk or worsted, usually made of branch-of-service colors, used to decorate uniforms.

Laurel Brigade: In the Eastern Theatre, the 7th, 11th, and 12th Virginia Cavalry Regiments and the 35th Virginia Cavalry Battalion. In February 1864 its members were ordered to wear laurel leaves on their hats.

Lightning Brigade: In the Army of the Tennessee, the 17th, 72nd, and 75th Indiana, and 98th Illinois Infantry Regiments and the 18th Indiana Light Artillery Battery, all mounted although infantry. The 123rd Illinois soon replaced the 75th and saw most service with the Brigade, which also was reinforced by the 92nd Illinois during the Chickamauga campaign. Unit enlisted men wore a cavalry jacket with the lace removed, mostly a black slouch hat, and carried repeating rifles.

lunette: a small field work.

McClellan cap: a low soft, true copy of the French kepi preferred by Union officers to the issue forage cap.

Minié ball: the soft lead conical bullet with a hollow base used in rifle-muskets and designed by the French army's Captain Minié.

New Jersey Brigade: In the Army of the Potomac, the 1st to 4th New Jersey Volunteer Infantry Regiments joined by the 10th New Jersey in October 1861, the 15th New Jersey in August 1862, the 40th New Jersey in February 1865, and, for a short time, by the 1st Delaware Cavalry.

nitre: a compound of nitric acid and potash used in the manufacture of gunpowder.

Orphan Brigade: In the Army of Tennessee, the 2nd, 3rd, 4th, 5th, and 6th Kentucky Infantry Regiments and Byrne's Battery.

Osnaburg: a coarse linen or cotton used mostly for linings and shirts.

palisade: a fence of strong stakes.

panda: a mixture of crumbled hardtack and water or whiskey given to weak patients in hospitals.

Philadelphia Brigade: in the Army of the Potomac, the 69th, 71st, 72nd and 106th Pennsylvania Infantry Regiments. At first the 72nd wore a blue, trimmed with red, zouave uniform jacket with a light-blue kepi trimmed with red, and sky-blue trousers with red cords down each leg and white gaiters; the 69th wore the same uniform trimmed in green. After 1862 both were worn for dress only.

plastron: a piece of cloth, usually shield-shaped, worn on the front of a coat or shirt, often of a facing color.

plume: a feather, horsehair, or worsted, standing decoration worn from the top and front of a hat or cap, sometimes called a pompom.

polka: a form of jacket skirt slit on both sides and around descending some six inches below the waist-line, usually cut with a slight flare.

poncho: a blanket or rubberized blanket made with a slit in the middle so as to be worn as a cape.

prolonge: a stout rope with a hook at one end and a toggle at the other, with two intermediate rings into which the hook and toggle are fastened to shorten the distance between a limber and a cannon carriage, sometimes used to connect the lunette of a carriage with a limber when the piece was fired.

roundabout: a waist-length jacket.

sennit hat: a broad-brimmed hat usually made of woven straw, which could be waterproofed black when worn by seamen in foul weather.

shako: a tall stiff cap, usually worn with a pompom or plume, a visor and a cap badge on the front.

shell: sometimes 'shell jacket', a waist-length jacket.

shoddy: old woollen rags passed through a machine that reduced them to wool, then saturated with oil or milk, mixed with new wool, and then run into large shallow pans, partially dried, and then pressed between cylinders to make new cloth. The result looked good but lasted only a short time in the field. Many 1861 Union uniforms were made of shoddy.

shoulder-straps: rectangular stripes edged in gold embroidery worn on each shoulder over a ground of a facing color with officers' rank badges embroidered inside.

shoulder-tab: a piece of cloth sewn into the shoulder seam and buttoning near the collar. Sometimes called epaulette.

Sicilian cap: a cap without a visor and with a bag ending with a tassel, worn by many Southern volunteers in 1861.

standard: the flag carried by a mounted command.

stock: a tight-fitting strap worn around an enlisted man's neck, usually of leather, which was regulation but rarely worn during the war.

Stonewall Brigade: in the Army of Northern Virginia, the 2nd, 4th, 5th, 27th and 33rd Virginia Infantry Regiments.

sutler: a civilian retailer attached to a specific regiment, who sold goods such as food, tobacco, newspapers, magazines, and even clothing. Some issued their own chits or paper money, while all could keep accounts to be deducted from a soldier's pay. By regulations, prices were to be 'reasonable' and hours were limited to before nine at night and Sundays except during religious services. Sutlers were more common in Union armies than among Confederates.

Texas Brigade: In the Army of Northern Virginia, the 1st, 4th and 5th Texas Infantry Regiments, at first with the 18th Georgia Infantry Regiment (nicknamed 3rd Texas), then with 3rd Arkansas. Rielly's North Carolina Battery served with the Brigade from time to time.

traverse: parapet of earth raised to cover troops from enflilading fire.

uniform jacket: a short jacket cut long in the front and back to fit under a waist-belt.

vedette: sentry on horseback.

Vermont Brigade: In the Army of the Potomac, the 2nd to 6th Vermont Volunteer Infantry Regiments, joined in May 1864 by the 1st Vermont Heavy Artillery Regiment and the 2nd New Jersey Regiment from October 1862 to June 1863.

volley: the simultaneous discharge of a number of firearms.

wellingtons: ankle-high boots made without laces in front.

whipple hat: known as the 'Excelsior hat' by Confederates, it was made from light-blue felt with a brim running two-thirds around the hat's perimeter with a leather visor in front. Made by the 'Seamless Clothing Mfg. Co.' in 1861, it was patented by J. F. Whipple of New York on 16 July 1861 and was worn by troops from New York and New Hampshire as well as by the US Sharpshooters.

Whitworth Gun: An English-made breech-loading cannon that saw Confederate service. Whitworth rifles, using the same boring procedures, were also issued to sharpshooters.

zigzag: defiladed trenches run out from parallels of attack so as to form a covered road by which the attackers could approach the enemy's lines.

INDEX